PENGUIN REFERENCE BOOKS

THE PENGUIN DICTIONARY
OF COMMERCE

MICHAEL GREENER was born in Barry, Glamorgan, in 1931. He was educated, *inter alia*, at Douai School and graduated in economics, law and accountancy at the University of Wales, Cardiff, in 1953. Articled with Deloitte, Plender, Griffiths – Chartered Accountants – he became an Associate Member of the Institute of Chartered Accountants in England and Wales in 1956, and a Fellow in 1966. He was personal assistant to the Secretary of the *Western Mail and Echo*, Cardiff, where he was mostly responsible for the reorganization of accounting systems (1957–60). He was then assistant lecturer, later lecturer, in accounting at the College of Commerce, Wednesbury, Staffordshire, until forced to resign due to ill-health in 1963. After a short period in the family retail business he devoted his energies to writing. He has published two books, *Between the Lines of the Balance Sheet* (1968), and *Problems for Discussion on Mercantile Law* (1968). Articles by him have appeared in professional journals throughout the world.

THE PENGUIN
DICTIONARY OF COMMERCE

Michael Greener

PENGUIN BOOKS

Penguin Books Ltd, Harmondsworth, Middlesex, England
Penguin Books Inc., 7110 Ambassador Road, Baltimore, Maryland 21207, U.S.A.
Penguin Books Australia Ltd, Ringwood, Victoria, Australia
Penguin Books Canada Ltd, 41 Steelcase Road West, Markham, Ontario, Canada
Penguin Books (N.Z.) Ltd, 182–190 Wairau Road, Auckland 10, New Zealand

—

First published 1970
Reprinted with revisions 1971
Reprinted 1973, 1974

—

Copyright © Michael Greener, 1970, 1971

—

Made and printed in Great Britain
by Hazell Watson & Viney Ltd
Aylesbury, Bucks
Set in Monotype Times

for Max

PREFACE

I T is not easy to compile a dictionary. One must, in both senses of the phrase, define one's terms. Many people will find much included that they do not need, or that they consider quite irrelevant; others will find much that they consider necessary omitted. Some will complain of a lack of balance, some will complain of a lack of detail, some will just complain. It is dangerous to state the course charted before the work was begun, for this is to invite complaints that the course was not followed. Nevertheless, perhaps one or two observations may be helpful or relevant.

I have tended to give greater weight to commercial law than practice, and to concentrate on terms which concern the man in the street in his dealings with the business world, rather than on the esoteric language, or should one say, jargon, peculiar to certain professions, and used solely for communication within these professions. The reader will now say that this pattern has not been applied consistently. He will complain that a great deal of space has been given, say, to accounting terms or language used in shipping. The answer is that the common man in his role of investor is, or should be, taking an increasingly serious interest in published accounts in all their complexity. In order to protect his own interest it is as well if he is as familiar as possible with the terminology involved. As for shipping – we are after all a maritime nation and a great part of commerce is directly or indirectly concerned with the sea. A third and final point: some distinction has to be drawn between commerce and economics though the two subjects overlap. It is not intended to give a comprehensive definition of commerce here, for that would be merely provocative. But it might be generally observed that a dictionary of commerce should deal with the paraphernalia of institutions which serve industry by providing finance, improving communications and in any way facilitating the economic distribution of goods and services.

So much for the apologies that are made necessary by the nature of the work, now for the acknowledgements and schedule of creditors. A great deal of help has been given indirectly by writers of various books. Obviously, as these are so numerous and have contributed in such different proportions, any attempt to list them would be ridiculous. Various organizations have given direct assistance by providing free brochures and informative, and advertising, material. I must thank these people. Some of the senior professional associations were particularly helpful. Some of the lesser-known refused to reply to inquiries and were, as a result of this, reluctantly omitted. The State, having perhaps more time and paper available, provided a considerable amount of material particularly through the Board of Trade. It was gratifying to see so much printed and helpful information available to the small businessman, if he knows where to find it.

On a more personal level, I must record my thanks to various individuals. In the first place there were those who propped me up during the process. Secondly there were those who provided information, allowed me to pick their brains or listened while I attempted to clarify my own ideas. To all these, thank you. They know their names, I need not mention them here. Then there were those who did the typing, principally Margaret Beckinsale, Janet Davies and Jean Wishart. To them I am particularly grateful, when I consider my style and the quality of the manuscripts. Finally there were my kinsfolk who suffered in varying degrees, particularly my sister, Angela Tarling, who apart from carrying the greater part of the load, acted both as amanuensis and secretary. These people will never really be aware of the amount that I owe them. Nor, I suppose, will they care.

Barry, Glam., 1969

LIST OF ABBREVIATIONS

A.A.C.C.A.	Associate of the Association of Certified and Corporate Accountants
A.A.I.A.	Associate of the Association of International Accountants
A.C.A.	Associate of the Institute of Chartered Accountants in England and Wales
A.C.C.A.	Association of Certified and Corporate Accountants
A.C.C.S.	Associate of the Corporation of Certified Secretaries
A.C.I.S.	Associate of the Chartered Institute of Secretaries
A.C.W.A.	Associate of the Institute of Cost and Works Accountants
A.G.M.	annual general meeting
A.H.C.	Accepting Houses Committee
A.I.M.T.A.	Associate of the Institute of Municipal Treasurers and Accountants
A.I.Q.S.	Associate of the Institute of Quantity Surveyors
a.m.	before noon (Latin: *ante meridiem*)
A.M.B.I.M.	Associate Member of the British Institute of Management
A.M.I.W.M.	Associate Member of the Institute of Works Management
A.M.Inst.M.	Associate Member of the Institute of Marketing
A.M.Inst.M.S.M.	Associate Member of the Institute of Marketing and Sales Management
A.M.I.W.S.P.	Associate Member of the Institute of Works Study Practitioners
A.R.C.U.K.	Architects Registration Council of the United Kingdom
A.R.I.B.A.	Associate of the Royal Institute of British Architects
A.R.I.C.S.	Associate of the Royal Institution of Chartered Surveyors
A.T.I.I.	Associate of the Institute of Taxation
b/d	brought down
B.E.A.	British European Airways
b/f	brought forward
B.E.H.A.	British Export Houses Association
B.I.M.	British Institute of Management
b.l., B/L.	bill of lading
B.O.A.C.	British Overseas Airways Corporation
B.R.	British Rail

List of abbreviations

B.R.S.	British Road Services
B.S.I.	British Standards Institution
C.A.	Chartered Accountant (Scottish)
C.B.I.	Confederation of British Industries
c/d	carried down
C.D.F.C.	Commonwealth Development Finance Company
C.Eng.	Chartered Engineer
c/f	carried forward
C & F	Cost and Freight
C.I.F.	Cost Insurance and Freight
Co.	company
C.O.D.	cash on delivery
C.O.I.	Central Office of Information
C.P.A.	Critical Path Analysis
Cr.	creditor
D.C.F.	discounted cash flow
Dip.Ed.	Diploma in Education
Dr.	debtor
E.C.G.D.	Export Credit Guarantee Department
E.D.I.T.H.	Estate Duty Investment Trust
E.D.P.	electronic data processing
E.E.C.	European Economic Community
E.F.T.A.	European Free Trade Area
E.I.R.	earned income relief
E.M.I.P.	equivalent mean investment period
encl.	enclosure
E. & O.E.	errors and omissions excepted
f.a.a.	free of all average
F.A.C.C.A.	Fellow of the Association of Certified and Corporate Accountants
F.A.I.A.	Fellow of the Association of International Accountants
f.a.s.	free alongside ship
F.B.I.	Federation of British Industries
F.B.I.M.	Fellow of the British Institute of Management
F.C.A.	Fellow of the Institute of Chartered Accountants in England and Wales
F.C.C.S.	Fellow of the Corporation of Certified Secretaries
F.C.I.S.	Fellow of the Chartered Institute of Secretaries
F.C.W.A.	Fellow of the Institute of Cost and Works Accountants
F.H.A.	Finance Houses Association
F.I.F.O.	first in first out
F.I.M.T.A.	Fellow of the Institute of Municipal Treasurers and Accountants
F.Inst.M.S.M.	Fellow of the Institute of Marketing and Sales Management

10

F.I.Q.S.	Fellow of the Institute of Quantity Surveyors
f.o.b.	free on board
f.p.a.	free of particular average
F.R.I.B.A.	Fellow of the Royal Institute of British Architects
F.R.I.C.S.	Fellow of the Royal Institution of Chartered Surveyors
G.A.T.T.	General Agreement on Tariffs and Trade
H.N.C.B.S.	Higher National Certificate in Business Studies
h.p.	hire purchase
I.C.A.	Institute of Chartered Accountants
I.C.A.B.	International Cargo Advisory Bureau
I.C.F.C.	Industrial and Commercial Finance Corporation
I.H.A.	Issuing Houses Association
I.M.F.	International Monetary Fund
I.O.M.	Institute of Office Management
I.Q.S.	Institute of Quantity Surveyors
I.R.C.	Industrial Reorganisation Corporation
I.W.M.	Institute of Works Management
I.W.S.P.	Institute of Works Study Practitioners
J.Dip.M.A.	Joint Diploma in Management Studies
L.I.F.O.	last in first out
Ltd	limited
M.B.I.M.	Member of the British Institute of Management
M.I.O.M.	Member of the Institute of Office Management
M.I.P.E.	Member of the Institution of Production Engineers
N.P.V.	no par value
P.A.Y.E.	pay as you earn
P/E	price/earnings ratio
P.E.R.T.	project evaluation review techniques
p.m.	afternoon (Latin: *post meridiem*)
P.P.I.	policy proof of interest
R.H.A.	Road Haulage Association
R.I.B.A.	Royal Institute of British Architects
R.P.M.	Resale Price Maintenance
S.E.T.	Selective Employment Tax
T.D.C.	Technical Development Corporation
T.S.B.	Trustee Savings Bank
W.I.P.	work in progress

11

NOTES ON USING THE DICTIONARY

WORDS and phrases printed in small capital letters are themselves the subjects of articles elsewhere in the dictionary. Some of these are preceded by ⋄, which means that they should be followed up, as they will give a clearer understanding of the articles where they occur. Others are preceded by ⋄⋄, which stands for 'see also'.

Alphabetical order follows Telephone Directory practice in that only the first word (excluding 'a' or 'the') counts for alphabetical purposes.

DECIMALIZATION

After D-Day the official currency became £p, as opposed to £s d. During the transitional period either system may be used for settling accounts; though the £p system is mandatory for cheques. After this period the £p system only will be used. Prices have been restated as necessary; but in the absence of agreement a conversion table, provided by the 1969 Decimal Currency Act, is used.

New coins have been introduced. They are 50p, 10p, 5p, 2p, 1p and ½p. The legal tender rules have been slightly changed: silver is legal tender up to £5, copper and bronze up to 20p. The 50p piece is legal tender up to £10.

A

a.a. 'Always afloat'. This term concerns MARINE CHARTERING. The charterer agrees that the ship will remain afloat whether at port or at sea during the time of the charter. This is to avoid damage to the hull.

'A' list of contributaries. ◊ CONTRIBUTARIES.

A1. A term particularly applicable to shipping. When applied to a ship, the letter indicates the condition of the hull and the number, the condition of the trappings. To be A1 is therefore to be in perfect condition.

To be more precise, 100 A1 after a Maltese Cross indicates that the ship was built completely under Lloyds survey. Without the cross, it indicates that it was built to Lloyds specifications.

The term is now also used in a more general sense.

Abacus. An elementary form of calculating machine not often used in the West today, though it may be seen in the British Museum or in the nursery. It normally takes the form of beads strung upon wire. The operator moves the beads along the wire in the process of counting.

Abandonment. A MARINE INSURANCE term for abandoning a ship as dangerous or unseaworthy. This would normally be a total loss and the insurer would have a right to claim the subject matter. Notice of abandonment should be given to the insurer immediately.

Able-bodied seaman. Strictly, one who has served three years before the mast, at least one of them in a trading vessel.

Above par. A STOCK EXCHANGE term: SHARES are said to be above par when their PRICE is above the SHARES' NOMINAL VALUE.

Acceptance. When a CONTRACT is made there must be both ◊ OFFER and acceptance, unless it is a CONTRACT BY DEED. If one person offers to do something for another, the contract is not complete until the offer is accepted. Acceptance must be in the same terms as the offer and must be communicated to the offeror. A conditional acceptance is equivalent to an offer and is not an acceptance.

Acceptance for honour. ◊ ACCEPTANCE SUPRA PROTEST.

Acceptance house. A financial institution whose business is lending money on the SECURITY of BILLS OF EXCHANGE. They are often MERCHANT BANKS but are governed by the ACCEPTING HOUSES COMMITTEE. The acceptance house may itself lend money on a bill, or may add its name to a bill drawn on another party, particularly in foreign trade. The signature of the acceptance house considerably strengthens the bill and it can probably be discounted at a very low rate. Acceptance houses will often lend money to an exporter to cover the gap between the manufacture of GOODS and the receipt of proceeds. The loan is made by way of a bill of exchange and is sometimes called an acceptance credit.

Acceptance supra protest. If a BILL OF EXCHANGE is protested and then accepted by another party to save the name of the drawer, this is known as acceptance supra protest, or acceptance for honour.

Acceptilation. A term used in Scottish law: it means formal release from debt.

Accepting houses committee. Some of the bigger MERCHANT BANKS and ACCEPTANCE HOUSES are affiliated to this committee. This indicates that they are of high standing and that BILLS OF EXCHANGE drawn on them are likely to be discountable at fine rates.

Acceptor. The person drawing a BILL OF EXCHANGE is the drawer and the person on whom the bill is drawn is the drawee. When the drawee has accepted the bill, i.e. has accepted liability, he is known as the acceptor. The normal form of acceptance is by signature on the face of the bill. He cannot deny the existence and capacity of the drawer or payee or the signature of the drawer – he can however question an ENDORSEMENT (he would not be obliged to pay on a forged endorsement). Delivery is necessary for complete acceptance: this means the acceptor willingly parts with possession or gives notice of acceptance. If the bill is in the hands of a HOLDER IN DUE COURSE, delivery is presumed.

It is possible for a bill to be negotiated before acceptance. It is then up to the holder of the bill to present it for acceptance before, or at the time of payment. Presentation for acceptance is not obligatory except where the bill so stipulates or where it is payable after sight, or payable elsewhere than at the residence or place of business of the drawer.

Accommodation bill. A BILL OF EXCHANGE signed by one person to accommodate another. The person signing is a GUARANTOR and receives no CONSIDERATION. Once value has been given for the bill, he is liable should that ACCEPTOR fail to pay at the proper time.

Accord and satisfaction. When one party has completed his obligations in a CONTRACT he may agree to release the other party from that party's obligations. This may be by a document under seal, or by receiving some new CONSIDERATION. Release in return for new consideration is known as accord and satisfaction.

Account, credit. This term has a wide number of meanings, though normally it means the account kept by a business for the benefit of a customer, whereby the customer can obtain GOODS on credit and pay for them at a later date, usually stated at the time of SALE.

Account, current. An account kept by a customer at a BANK, from which he can make payments by CHEQUE. Cheque books are free, but cheques are subject to STAMP DUTY. Customers receive ◊ BANK STATEMENTS periodically or on request. Charges are made for current accounts at the discretion of the bank. Normally they are only applied to small accounts and are related to the number of transactions involved.

Account days. A STOCK EXCHANGE term for the days set aside for the settlement of accounts (bargains between members). They are also called 'settling days'. Transactions in GILT-EDGED SECURITIES are accounted for daily, other transactions are settled fortnightly on alternate Tuesdays. Clients receive statements on preceding Thursdays to give them time to send in the necessary money. Accounts may be carried over from one period of account to another – a payment is made for this privilege, known as contango, or the contango rate. (Strictly speaking, this applies to transactions where the buyer does not wish to take up the SHARES at the particular time, i.e. BULL transactions. Where it is a question of the non-delivery of shares, e.g. where the client has not yet obtained them and does not wish to at prevailing rates, the rate is known as backwardation.)

Account, income and expenditure. This shows the income and expenditure for a stated period and the surplus or deficit resulting. These accounts are usually used by clubs and other non-profit-making organizations.

Account, period of. ◊ ACCOUNT DAYS.

Account, profit and loss. This shows the GROSS PROFIT and net profit made by a manufacturing or trading organization. It normally commences with gross profit on trading, and after adding exceptional items of income and deducting administrative expenses, shows profit before tax, taxation, profit after tax, amounts distributed or put to reserve, amounts brought forward from the previous year, and amounts to be carried forward to the following year. This is the general form. There may be variations where the business is rather specialized.

Account, sales. A term used when GOODS are consigned for sale to an AGENT in another country. The agent submits an account of SALES to the CONSIGNOR of the goods, giving details of the goods sold,

15

together with the SELLING PRICE, COMMISSION, expenses and the net profit. It usually accompanies the amount due.

Account, stated. An account showing a BALANCE agreed on by two parties as due from one to another. It is legally binding unless it can be shown to be untrue.

Account, statement of. A document received from a BANK or business by an individual or organization, detailing the transactions during a stated period and showing the amount due to or from the individual or organization at the date stated. The terms of credit are usually repeated.

Account, trading. This shows income from SALES and deductions from them, together with the cost of buying the GOODS and/or putting them into a condition for sale. The final figure is the GROSS PROFIT on trading which is transferred to the ◊ PROFIT AND LOSS ACCOUNT.

Accountancy. The trade or business of an ◊ ACCOUNTANT.

Accountant. A person who is concerned with the keeping of ACCOUNTS. In a more specialized sense it is used to describe a position in industry: the accountant being the man responsible for producing *inter alia* the ANNUAL ACCOUNTS of the organization, a position of considerable responsibility. The word is often used as the name of a profession, in much the same way as the word 'LAWYER' is used.

Accounting period. An accounting term. The books of a COMPANY or other business are periodically closed for the purpose of making up ACCOUNTS. Each account runs from the end of the preceding period, and the time that it covers is known as the period of account. The periods are normally of equal length: a year unless circumstances are exceptional.

Accounts, annual. Financial statements showing the state of affairs at a particular date and the results of operations during the preceding ACCOUNTING PERIOD. Sometimes required by law in a particular form (◊ ACCOUNTS, GROUP). Profit-making organizations would show a ◊ TRADING ACCOUNT and a ◊ PROFIT AND LOSS ACCOUNT, and a ◊ BALANCE SHEET. Other types of organization would provide an ◊ INCOME AND EXPENDITURE ACCOUNT and a form of balance sheet.

Accounts, consolidated. The accounts which must be submitted by a holding company: these accounts show the results and position of the group as a whole. When the ◊ GROUP ACCOUNTS are shown in one set of accounts, this set is known as a consolidated account.

Accounts, final. The final accounts are a COMPANY'S (or other association's) official accounts for the financial year. (◊ ACCOUNTS, ANNUAL.) 'Final account' can have other meanings, for instance, the account presented by a LIQUIDATOR at the end of a LIQUIDATION, or sometimes a final settlement between parties.

Accounts, group. A holding company must publish what are known as group accounts. These are the accounts of the holding company and its SUBSIDIARIES taken together (the form of accounts is established by the relevant Companies Act). There are exceptions to this rule in certain specified instances, e.g. where the accounts of the holding company and one or more of its subsidiaries cannot be combined because of the basic difference in the form of business. In such a case the information required by law is given in a rather different way. ◊ GROUP ACCOUNTS: OMISSION OF SUBSIDIARIES.

Accounts, interim. Usually, say, half-yearly accounts, probably un-audited, produced by a COMPANY or other association. ◊ ACCOUNTS, FINAL.

Accounts, nominal, real and personal. Terms used in book-keeping. LEDGER accounts are divided into these three broad categories, though the distinction is of no particular value. Personal accounts are those of debtors and CREDITORS, real accounts are those giving details of ASSETS and CAPITAL of the business, nominal accounts deal with expenditure and revenue.

Accounts, variance. ◊ STANDARD COSTING.

Accrued charges. The opposite of PAYMENT IN ADVANCE, these are charges which are known, but not yet due for payment, such as electricity charges for the ACCOUNTING PERIOD, or rent due but not payable until a stated date after the end of the accounting period.

Accrued interest. INTEREST due but not yet received or paid. ◊ ACCRUED CHARGES.

Accumulated depreciation. A term used in published accounts for the total ◊ DEPRECIATION written off to date on a FIXED ASSET, or group of fixed assets.

Acknowledgement of statute-barred debt. ◊ STATUTE-BARRED DEBT.

Acre. An area of land (4,840 square yards). One square mile is 640 acres. Irish and Scottish acres are larger than English ones. 100 Irish acres = 162 English, 48 Scottish = 61 English. The United States acre is equal to the English one.

Act of God. A loss to be caused by an act of God is one arising from a direct, irresistible, unpreventable act of nature. CONTRACTS often exclude liability from damages arising from an act of God.

Actual total loss. A term used in INSURANCE, particularly MARINE INSURANCE, where the subject matter is completely destroyed, or effectively destroyed insofar as the owner can no longer make use of it. If a ship is missing for a long time, an actual total loss can be presumed. No notice of ABANDONMENT need be given to the insurer.

Actuary. A person normally employed in INSURANCE, who is skilled in the complicated task of assessing and calculating risks and premiums.

Ad referendum. When applied to a CONTRACT, this term means that although the contract has been signed, certain matters have been left over for consideration.

Ad Valorem. 'According to the VALUE'. STAMP DUTIES, etc. often vary according to the value of the subject matter.

Adding machine. A machine used to facilitate addition, as the name suggests. It may take any form, from an ABACUS to the most up-to-date comptometer. It is used extensively in business today, very often for work which could be done more quickly without using a machine. In the hands of an experienced operator, the comptometer is a particularly valuable piece of equipment when a great many figures have to be added together, e.g. the INVOICES issued in a day. Although the machine is made for addition, a little ingenuity with the simpler and inexpensive machine, and a number of devices on the more complex, make it usable for subtraction, multiplication, division, etc.

An adding machine should be distinguished from an ⟡ ADD-LISTER.

Add-lister. An adding machine which also records the figures added, on a roll of paper. It fulfils the functions of an ADDING MACHINE and it is often used in retail business, for recording takings or listing goods in, say, a SELF-SERVICE STORE. The more complex machines enable the operator to include a reference alongside each figure, these reference numbers not being added unless required. They may also have two or more registers, enabling figures to be tabulated in more than one column, and give separate totals for each column.

Address commission. A COMMISSION paid to the CHARTERER'S AGENT for arranging the loading of a vessel.

Adjusted selling price. ⟡ STOCK VALUATION.

Adjustment. Settling the due amount by an insurer, particularly by one of a number of insurers involved in, say, a MARINE INSURANCE claim.

Administration expenses. A category of expenses: those incurred in the administration of a business (e.g. in running an accounts department) as opposed to DIRECT EXPENSES, selling expenses, etc. It is often used as a heading in published accounts.

Admiralty measured mile. 6,080 feet. It is distinguished from a nautical mile, which varies from 6,045·93 feet on the equator to almost 6,107·98 feet in latitude 90°. The mean nautical mile is 6,076·91 feet.

Advance freight. FREIGHT paid in advance. A shipper may pay the freight, enabling the ship-owner to endorse the BILL OF LADING with a freight release, and the importer to take immediate delivery. It may be payable even though the ship is lost, provided the voyage was actually commenced.

Advanced notes. Drafts on ship-owners given by captains to their crews before sailing but payable, say, three days after sailing. They help the sailor to provide for his family.

Advances. ◊ BANK ADVANCES.

Advertisements (Hire Purchase) Act 1957. Any advertisement offering GOODS on HIRE PURCHASE, CREDIT SALE, or CONDITIONAL SALE, and stating details of DEPOSITS, INTEREST and hire purchase price, must comply with the provisions of this Act (as amended by the HIRE PURCHASE ACT 1964). This specifies that certain information must be given, in particular and *inter alia*, (1) details of the deposit, (2) the amount and number of instalments, (3) the frequency of the instalments, and whether any are payable before delivery, (4) the cash price and the hire purchase price.

Advertising. The publication of facts or opinions of GOODS or services, to awaken the public's interest and persuade them to purchase. There are various forms: ◊ ADVERTISING, COMPETITIVE, ◊ ADVERTISING, INFORMATIVE, ◊ ADVERTISING, PERSUASIVE.

Advertising agency. An organization concerned with MARKETING. It considers the GOODS and services that clients wish to offer to the public and advises on the best method of advertising them in order to maximize profit or goodwill. The agency is therefore interested in the product itself, in alternative methods of promotion, in presentation, and in effective copywriting. It may wish to study the product, and the persons to whom it is hoped to sell it, and will wish to know the pattern and areas of distribution. It will need to be conversant with all methods of advertising, with appropriate magazines, journals, newspapers, etc.

Advertising agencies are necessarily independent but in order to preserve standards and prevent abuse, an Institute was formed as long ago as 1917, becoming known in 1954 as the INSTITUTE OF INCORPORATED PRACTITIONERS IN ADVERTISING. There is a British Code of Advertising Practice which attempts to establish legal, clean, honest and truthful advertising. The practice and interpretation of this code is supervised by a Code of Advertising

Practice Committee. The Institute helped to form the code of practice and is also represented on the Committee. It also took part in forming the ♢ ADVERTISING STANDARDS AUTHORITY.

Advertising, competitive. ADVERTISING designed to sell one's own products at the expense of those of others. It is sometimes advantageous to advertise against oneself, for instance by bringing out a new product that competes with one already made, provided the amount of business taken from competitors exceeds the loss on SALES of one's own first product. ♢ ADVERTISING, INFORMATIVE ♢ ADVERTISING, PERSUASIVE.

Advertising, informative. ADVERTISING intended to inform the public of the existence or quality of GOODS, and most often found in technical journals. For instance, a new invention might be advertised as useful to a manufacturing industry. ♢ ADVERTISING, COMPETITIVE ♢ ADVERTISING, PERSUASIVE.

Advertising, Institute of Incorporated Practitioners in. An organization founded in 1917 for the benefit of ADVERTISING agents and the public. It assumed its present title in 1954. It is both a trade association and a professional institute representing those employed in ADVERTISING AGENCIES. Its present membership includes 275 agencies: 1,800 indiviudals. It aims to preserve high standards in advertising by means of training and supervision, and has various by-laws aimed at promoting acceptable codes of practice. Members are admitted by either examination or interview. Members may be Fellows (F.I.P.A.), Members (M.I.P.A.), or Associate Members (A.M.I.P.A.). Address: 44 Belgrave Square, London SW1.

Advertising, persuasive. ADVERTISING which aims solely at persuading to buy, irrespective of need, and which uses any suitable means to further this objective. ♢ ADVERTISING, COMPETITIVE, ♢ ADVERTISING, INFORMATIVE.

Advertising standards authority. An independent organization composed of five persons connected with ADVERTISING, five with no connexion and an independent chairman. The objects are 'to promote and enforce throughout the United Kingdom the highest standards of advertising in all media and to ensure in cooperation with all concerned that no advertising contravenes or offends against these standards.'

Advice note. A document sent by a supplier to the customer prior to the INVOICE. Sometimes it precedes the GOODS, and sometimes accompanies them; it states nature and quantity of the goods but not their PRICE. Essentially just an indication that the goods are on the way, it is sometimes confused with a DELIVERY NOTE.

Advice on production for export. Various government departments offer free advice. The principal departments are: the Board of Trade; the Ministries of Technology; Agriculture, Fisheries and Food; Power; Defence; Public Building and Works; and Health.

Advocate. A term used in Scotland to describe a person admitted to plead at the Bar (corresponding to the English BARRISTER).

Affidavit. A declaration in writing made on oath before a person entitled to administer oaths (a commissioner for oaths, normally a SOLICITOR). It is a criminal offence deliberately to make a false statement in an affidavit.

Affirmation of contract. A person induced to enter a CONTRACT by a MISREPRESENTATION may be bound by the contract, and lose his right to rescission and/or damages, if he expressly or implicitly affirms the contract with full knowledge of the facts. This he may do by verbal affirmation or simply by failing to take action within a reasonable time.

Affreightment, contracts of. These are CONTRACTS for the carriage of GOODS by sea. They may be part of a CHARTER PARTY, or the terms may be set out in a BILL OF LADING. ⟡ FREIGHT.

After date. A term used with reference to BILLS OF EXCHANGE, indicating that they are payable at a certain time after the date of the bill.

After sight. A BILL OF EXCHANGE drawn after sight is payable when it has been accepted and the ACCEPTOR has written a date of acceptance on the bill.

Against all risks (a.a.r.). A MARINE INSURANCE term, which legally means 'insured against all generally accepted risks'.

Age, misrepresentation of by infants. If a MINOR misrepresents his age to bring about a CONTRACT he will still not be bound by the contract but EQUITY will not normally allow him to take full advantage of his fraud and may force him to restore any gains he has made and release the other party from any obligation. It will not, however, enforce the contract.

Agency, appointment of. A CONTRACT of agency may be express or implied (for instance a wife has implied authority to pledge her husband's credit when buying NECESSARIES). The agency could also be created by ratification (for instance where an AGENT has apparent but not real authority but the principal ratifies his acts), or AGENCY OF NECESSITY, or by ESTOPPEL (for instance where an agent ceases to be an agent but the fact is not made known).

Ratification relates back to the time when the agent made the contract but if the contract is made subject to ratification it is not binding until ratified. Also, the principal must personally have been able to make the contract at the time. The contract must have been made expressly on behalf of the principal, i.e. the third party must have known he was dealing with an agent.

Agency bills. BILLS OF EXCHANGE drawn on, and accepted by, the London branches of foreign BANKS.

Agency, determination of. An agency may be determined by express agreement. A SPECIAL AGENT will cease to be an AGENT when he has completed the task for which he was employed. A UNIVERSAL AGENCY will be terminated by agreement. The principal must remember that if a person has acted for him for some time or has been looked upon as his agent, then it may be necessary to give express notice to persons with whom the agent has dealt and perhaps general notice to the public, before the agency can be considered terminated (◊ ESTOPPEL). The principal may otherwise continue to be responsible for debts incurred by the agent. Agency is automatically terminated by the death or bankruptcy of the principal or the agent (except that if the agent is bankrupt the agency may continue where he is still capable of acting as agent).

Agency, fiduciary nature of. A CONTRACT of agency is a contract that creates a special relationship between the parties. The agent must act in good faith, and even though there is no express agreement he must not make any private or secret profit out of the agency. He must always act in his principal's interest, and if he professes any skill he must use this to the best of his ability.

Agency of necessity. This occurs where one person acts on behalf of another without that other's express permission, in order to safeguard the interests of the other party. The other party will be bound by the agency. Agency of necessity cannot arise, and there would be no legal agency unless: (1) it is impossible to communicate with the principal, (2) a CONTRACT of agency already exists, and (3) immediate action is necessary.

Agency: undisclosed principal. Where an AGENT contracts without disclosing that he is an agent, many problems arise. Generally the principal or the agent may sue or be sued. However, if the third party had reason to believe that he was dealing with the agent as principal and that this was a relevant fact, only the agent may sue on the contract: if A will not contract with B, B cannot evade this by contracting through C, an undisclosed agent. Where the third party may sue principal or agent, he must make a decision and cannot sue both.

Agency: un-named principal. A term used in a CONTRACT of agency where the agent discloses that he is contracting as AGENT but does not give the name of his principal. There is little difference from a normal contract made by an agent, though it must not be used to persuade third parties to contract where they would not had they known the identity of the principal.

If the agent subsequently refuses to disclose the name of the principal he becomes personally liable.

Agenda. A list of business to be done at a MEETING, made in a form that facilitates smooth-running. An agenda paper is often sent in advance to those who are to attend.

Agenda paper. ◊ AGENDA.

Agent. A person with express or implied authority to act for another person (the principal), the object being to establish a contractual relationship between the agent and third parties. ◊ AGENCY, APPOINTMENT OF ◊ AGENCY, FIDUCIARY NATURE OF ◊ AGENCY, DETERMINATION OF ◊ AGENT: DUTIES TO PRINCIPAL ◊ AGENT, UNIVERSAL ◊ AGENT, GENERAL ◊ AGENT, SPECIAL.

Agent de change. The French equivalent of a STOCKBROKER. ◊ BOURSE.

Agent: Duties to principal. These are generally a matter of common sense, but in particular an AGENT must: (1) observe the agency agreement, (2) follow his principal's instructions when not illegal, (3) always act in the interest of his principal, (4) use the skill that he is supposed to have, (5) not in any way compete with his principal or take on any other work which competes with his duties to his principal, (6) respect the confidence of his principal, even after the end of the agency, (7) not make any secret profit or take a bribe, (8) compensate his principal for any loss arising from breach of duty, (9) account properly to his principal.

Agent, general. An AGENT with authority to act for his principal in all matters concerning a particular trade or profession, or in some specified field. A travelling representative is one example.

Agent: misrepresentation. MISREPRESENTATION by an AGENT is equal to misrepresentation by his principal, whether fraudulent or innocent. However, if an agent makes an innocent misrepresentation it does not become fraudulent by reason of the principal's knowledge of the true facts. e.g. A contracts with B through agent C. B is aware of faults in goods being sold to A. C is not. A relies on C's representation. A cannot then claim damages for fraudulent misrepresentation.

Agent, special. An AGENT with authority to do one particular act, or to represent his principal in one specific transaction.

Agent, universal. One with unrestricted authority to CONTRACT on behalf of his principal, e.g. a person holding ◊ POWER OF ATTORNEY.

Agent's lien. If an AGENT legally possesses GOODS owned by the principal, he may have a PARTICULAR LIEN or GENERAL LIEN for monies due from the principal on those goods. There are many exceptions to this rule.

Agent's torts. The principal is jointly and severally liable for his agent's torts if the AGENT is acting in the normal course of his agency or on the instruction of his principal. The agent must indemnify the principal where the principal has not expressly or implicitly condoned the tort.

Agricultural Mortgage Corporation Ltd. This was established in 1928. SHARE CAPITAL was subscribed by the BANK OF ENGLAND and other BANKS; the bulk of the funds, however, comes from DEBEN-TURES (over £100,000,000 outstanding) plus grants and loans from the Ministry of Agriculture, Fisheries and Food. Its primary purpose is to grant long-term loans against first MORTGAGES of agricultural land and buildings. It has power to grant sixty-year loans, but forty-year loans are more common. Its secondary purpose is to make loans to land-owners, to help carry out improvements to agricultural land and buildings.

Borrowers apply through bankers or directly to the Corporation. Advances are limited to two-thirds of the estimated value of the property. Rates of INTEREST vary from loan to loan, depending on market conditions. Repayments are made by half-yearly instalments. Loans for improvements depend on the annual VALUE of the land being increased by at least the annual amount of the loan charges.

The Corporation confines its activities to England and Wales. There is, however, a Scottish Agricultural Securities Corporation Ltd, subscribed by three Scottish banks.

Agricultural Research Council. This was established by royal charter in 1931. There are eighteen members including representatives of the Agricultural Departments of the Government, distinguished scientists, and men with practical farming experience. The Council may be directed by the Secretary of State for Education and Science, but is otherwise autonomous. It takes advice from the Ministry of Agriculture and Fisheries, and the Department of Agriculture and Fish for Scotland. It is responsible for fourteen independent state-aided Agricultural Research Institutes, controls ten others and has established fifteen more (this is in addition to the eight in Scotland). It also makes grants to further university research, whose purpose is to help farmers increase efficiency and produce better and cheaper food and agricultural products. This involves the study of soils, plants, animals and food. It publishes annual reports, an Index of Agricultural Research and a booklet, *The Agricultural Research Service* (published by Her Majesty's Stationery Office). Specialized reports are published on particular research. Address: Cunard Building, Regent Street, SW1.

Air transport. Air transport in this country is partly a private and partly a nationalized industry. Both parts are concerned with the carriage of both passengers and goods. The nationalized part consists of the ◊ BRITISH OVERSEAS AIRWAYS CORPORATION (BOAC) and also the British European Airways (BEA). PRIVATE CARRIERS are governed by the Air Transport Licensing Board and the Civil Aviation Licensing Act 1960, which forbids any person without a licence either to fly a U.K.-registered aircraft for money or in connexion with trade, or to fly an aircraft, wherever registered, to or from the United Kingdom.

Compensation is available to persons whose property is damaged during take-off or landing or in flight. This is payable by the owner of the aircraft, irrespective of negligence. Third party insurance is compulsory.

Air transport's principal advantage is speed, which perhaps compensates for its increased cost. Time can mean money: goods purchased are idle while being transported, and a great deal of money can be saved by air- rather than land-travel. Consideration should be given though to the problems involved in travelling, or consigning goods, to or from the nearest terminal.

For passengers, long distance travel is obviously quickest by air, though short journeys inland may be most quickly undertaken by land. Some airlines, particularly the larger ones, offer transport for passengers and goods to and from air terminals, and also additional aids.

Other relevant Acts of Parliament are the Carriage by Air Act 1932, and the Carriage by Air Act 1961. The 1932 Act made air companies common carriers, and also gave effect to the International Convention 1929. If the carrier complies with the conditions imposed by the convention, he can claim limitation of liability. For physical injury, this is fixed at 125,000 gold francs per passenger and for luggage 250 francs per kilo. The amount can be increased but not reduced. The 1961 Act increased the first amount to 250,000 gold francs. The Acts should be read together with the Carriage by Air (Supplementary Provisions) Act 1962. Liability for cargo is a matter for agreement between the consignee and the company.

Air way bill. An air-transport term for the document made out on behalf of the shipper as evidence of the CONTRACT of carriage. It is also called an air consignment note.

Aliens, contracts with. Distinguish between alien friends and alien enemies. Alien enemies are those who reside in a hostile country or in a country occupied by a hostile power (the nationality of the alien is not relevant). The subject of a foreign power would also be enemy if resident here at the outbreak of hostilities with his country. Alien friends may normally CONTRACT in the ordinary manner. Resident enemies cannot enter into contracts during hostilities; nor can non-resident enemies without permission from the proper authorities. Contracts in force at the time of hostilities are not cancelled unless this would be in the public interest, but they are unenforceable until the cessation of hostilities, when rights are reinstated. Sovereign and official representatives of foreign states are immune from liability on contracts unless they choose otherwise. However they may bring an action themselves. The protection extends to diplomatic staff and certain other foreign nationals but normally only while they are acting in an official capacity.

Allocatur. When costs are ordered to be taxed by a taxing master, i.e. when costs incurred in an action, LIQUIDATION, etc., must be approved, the certificate given by the taxing master is known as an allocatur.

Allonge. A slip attached to a BILL OF EXCHANGE to allow for extra ENDORSEMENTS. It does not need a stamp.

Allotment note. A note signed by a sailor authorizing the master of his ship to pay part, or all, of his wages while at sea to his wife, family, or BANK.

Allotment of shares. When a company receives an ◇ APPLICATION FOR SHARES issued by means of a PROSPECTUS, it proceeds to allot the ◇ SHARES on a predetermined basis (which is set out in the prospectus). Where applications exceed the shares available, allotment is made proportionately, though often applications for shares up to a stated number are accepted in full. The allotment of shares is made by means of a letter of allotment. This entitles the recipient to a certificate for the number of shares stated in the letter. His title may however depend on his paying the sum previously stated as due on allotment. The same procedure would apply to shares issued through an ISSUING HOUSE.

Allowance, additional personal. This usually means the additional allowance accruing to a married man with a working wife. It could also mean the husband's allowance for an incapacitated wife (an alternative to the HOUSEKEEPER ALLOWANCE); or a widowed or single person's child allowance (£100 in this instance) though if the person is a single woman she must be fully employed or totally incapacitated.

Allowance, age. Some of those over sixty-five may claim total exemption from tax. These are: single people whose incomes do not exceed £504, and married people (they must cohabit, and one party must be over sixty-five) with an income not exceeding £786. Marginal relief is given where incomes slightly exceed these amounts. ⟡ RELIEF, AGE.

Allowance, blind person's. This is available to single blind persons and married couples where one is a registered blind person. The allowances vary: they are greater when both persons are blind but are restricted by other tax-free payments. The blind person's allowance cannot be claimed as well as a DAUGHTER'S SERVICES ALLOWANCE.

Allowance, children. Allowances are available for children, both one's own and others in one's custody. No two persons can have relief in respect of the same child. The child must be less than sixteen or receiving full-time education. The allowances are (for 1971–72): (1) up to eleven years, £155, (2) eleven to fifteen inclusive, £180, (3) sixteen and over, £205. The child must not earn more than £115 per annum. Children's investment income is not aggregated with the parent's income for tax purposes.

The children allowances were slightly reduced by the Finance Act 1968. This gave additional family allowances but stated that persons receiving them should deduct a certain amount from the child allowance. The intention was to confine the benefit to persons not paying standard rate.

Allowance, daughter's services. This is available to an aged or infirm taxpayer who finds it necessary to rely on the services of a resident daughter whom he or she maintains. The allowance 1971–72 is £40. Where the taxpayer is widowed, he or she will normally claim HOUSEKEEPER ALLOWANCE as this is at present more advantageous.

Allowance, dependent relative. An allowance for persons who maintain relatives totally dependent on them. The dependent person should also be incapacitated by age or infirmity and should not receive an income of more than £260. The allowance can also be claimed for widowed, divorced or separated mothers or mothers-in-law, whether incapacitated or not. The allowance 1971–72 is £75. For incomes between £210 and £260 the allowance is reduced. The

27

allowance is £110 where the claimant is a single woman, or a married woman not living with her husband.

Allowance, housekeeper. This is available to a single or widowed person employing a housekeeper for the purpose of caring for himself or herself or for any children in respect of whom he or she receives CHILDREN ALLOWANCE. The allowance for 1971–72 is £100.

Allowance, Income Tax. ♢ INCOME TAX ALLOWANCE: NATIONAL INSURANCE CONTRIBUTIONS ♢ INCOME TAX ALLOWANCE: PURCHASED LIFE ANNUITIES ♢ INCOME TAX ALLOWANCE: RETIREMENT ANNUITIES ♢ INCOME TAX ALLOWANCE: SUPER-ANNUATION.

Allowance, life assurance. Available to those holding policies on their own lives or their wives'. The policies may be ENDOWMENT policies. Certain conditions apply: (1) relief must not exceed total income after deduction of charges; (2) the relevant premium must not be more than 7 per cent of the sum assured excluding bonuses; (3) the allowance must not exceed tax at the relevant rate on £100 on policies which are purely endowment policies There is a distinction between policies taken out before 22 June 1916 and those taken out after that date. For the latter the relief is two-ninths of the premium where it is over £25; where it is less, the relief is £10 or the amount of the premium, whichever is the less. For the former, the system of relief is quite different. Relief is given on premiums at 17½p for incomes not exceeding £1,000; 26p for incomes not exceeding £2,000; and 35p for incomes exceeding £2,000. Special provisions apply to sums payable by Act of Parliament or in a CONTRACT of employment to secure a deferred ANNUITY for the widow. Since the 1968 Finance Act certain other conditions must be fulfilled before premiums are allowed against income. Basically, for an endowment policy, the period must be for more than ten years and the premiums fairly equally spaced, and for a life policy the premiums must again be fairly evenly spaced; it must be a genuine long-term life policy and not the payment of an initial large sum of money to obtain long- or short-term life cover.

Allowance, personal. A proportion of a person's income is tax free. How much depends on the status of the person: an unmarried or widowed person is at present entitled to £325, a married man to £465, with an additional personal allowance if his wife is working. ♢ RELIEF, WIFE'S EARNED INCOME ♢ TAXATION: RELIEF, SEPARATE ASSESSMENT.

Alternate director. A DIRECTOR who acts in the absence of another named director. The appointment must be authorized by the COMPANY at a general MEETING.

Amalgamation. The joining together of businesses for their mutual advantage. ◊ MERGER.

Amalgamation of companies. ◊ COMPANIES: RECONSTRUCTION, REORGANIZATION AND AMALGAMATION.

Amounts paid in advance. ◊ PAYMENTS IN ADVANCE.

Amstel club. A Swiss company, its official title is Amstel Finance International A.G. Representative FINANCE HOUSES of fifteen different European countries have made reciprocal agreements to help finance trade. They are: Austria, Belgium, Denmark, Finland, France, West Germany, Holland, Italy, Norway, Portugal, Spain, Sweden, Switzerland, the United States and United Kingdom. The U.K. member is United Dominion Trust. This company arranges the finance of exports from the United Kingdom; the credit risk is taken by the overseas finance company although the exporter is liable *re* the quality, etc. of the GOODS.

The scheme is designed to benefit the smaller exporter. It is simple, but charges are probably higher than when finance is obtained by more traditional means. Enquiries should be sent to the Manager, European Division, United Dominion Trust Limited, Eastcheap, London, EC3.

Anchorage. Dues paid for anchoring in certain ports or harbours.

And reduced. Words appended to the name of a COMPANY where, after reorganization, the CAPITAL is reduced, with court approval. The court may order these words to be added to the name.

Annual allowances. ◊ CAPITAL ALLOWANCES.

Annual general meeting. ◊ MEETING, ANNUAL GENERAL.

Annual report. A report sent out each year by a COMPANY to its members. It normally contains those documents which must legally be published and filed at Bush House: the BALANCE SHEET, the PROFIT AND LOSS ACCOUNT, the AUDITOR'S REPORT and the DIRECTORS' REPORT. It also contains what is known as the CHAIRMAN'S REPORT. Other information may also be supplied if the company is of the opinion that such information is helpful to a proper appreciation of the state of affairs at a particular date. Where the company is part of a group the report must also contain a consolidated balance sheet and consolidated profit and loss account ◊ ACCOUNTS, CONSOLIDATED. The latter, provided certain conditions are satisfied, may supplant the holding company's profit and loss account.

Annual return. A return which must be made annually to the REGIS-

TRAR OF COMPANIES. It must be completed within forty-two days of the ANNUAL GENERAL MEETING and must contain particulars set out in the Sixth Schedule to the Companies Act 1948, e.g. details of SHARES and DEBENTURES issued and changes in ownership of those shares. Also particulars of DIRECTORS and SECRETARY. With the return must be copies of any BALANCE SHEETS, and documents to be attached, laid before the company during the period to which the return relates. There are penalties for default.

Annuitant. ◊ ANNUITY.

Annuity. A fixed sum payable each year for a number of years, either following a certain event or else for a definite period of time. Annuities may be purchased, e.g. an ASSURANCE company might be approached and asked how much it would be necessary to pay now to guarantee the payment of £1,000 per year, either for the next, say, twenty years or for life, starting at a given age. A person receiving an annuity is known as an annuitant.

Ante-date. To ante-date a document is to put a date on it earlier than that on which it was issued.

Anti-trust laws. A system of laws in the U.S.A. aimed at preventing the formation of large CARTELS, ◊ MONOPOLIES, etc., and similar in purpose to the Monopolies and Mergers Act of this country.

Application and allotment account. In book-keeping, the account to which moneys paid on APPLICATION FOR SHARES and ALLOTMENT OF SHARES are credited before they are transferred to SHARE CAPITAL account.

Application for shares. When a person wishes to purchase ◊ SHARES on a new issue, he sends in a formal letter of application stating the number of shares he requires, and enclosing the sum of money payable on application. The form of application is usually published with the PROSPECTUS. The company will then proceed to allot the shares, though not necessarily the number applied for. ◊ ALLOTMENT OF SHARES.

Appreciation. The opposite of DEPRECIATION. Certain ASSETS (e.g. land) become more valuable as times goes on. They are said to appreciate. ◊ REVALUATION.

Where the ◊ MARKET VALUE of FIXED ASSETS shown in a company's BALANCE SHEET is greater than the book value and the difference is significant, attention should be drawn to this in the DIRECTORS' REPORT. Problems of valuation arise and the Companies Act is at present not clear as to which method of valuation should be adopted. There is a difference between value in present use and value in alternative use. ◊ VALUE.

Apprentice. One who signs a CONTRACT or indenture, agreeing to serve for a definite period with one employer or master. The apprentice's object is to learn a trade; he generally receives only a low wage, but should gain considerable experience. The master agrees to teach his trade to the apprentice.

Appropriation of payments. This concerns the manner in which a CREDITOR will treat payments made to him by a debtor. If a debtor owes two separate amounts and does not specify which debt he is paying (the amount paid does not correspond to one debt only), then the creditor can choose to which debt he will appropriate it. This can be important, e.g. the payment may be appropriated to a STATUTE-BARRED DEBT, allowing the creditor to sue on the second debt, where this is not statute-barred. Again, it has been held that payment to a BANK in repayment of loans can be appropriated to unsecured loans, allowing the bank to use the security on the remainder of the debt in a LIQUIDATION.

The creditor's right to appropriation does not apply where the debtor specifies the debt he is paying, or if there is a current account, when it is presumed that payment is made in date order. A creditor cannot appropriate to an illegal debt.

Arbitrage. Buying and selling currency, BILLS OF EXCHANGE, etc. in different markets, taking advantage of different rates to make a profit. Persons engaged in arbitrage can be providing a useful service in making money or bills available where they are wanted.

Arbitrageur. A person conducting an ARBITRAGE business.

Arbitration. The reference for settlement of a dispute normally arising out of CONTRACT, to one or more independent persons, rather than to a court of law. The arbitration must be agreed initially, it cannot be imposed afterwards. Some advantages are: simplicity, speed, economy, and the avoidance of publicity. There is, of course, no guarantee of justice or impartiality on the part of the arbitrator. Contracts of arbitration may be oral or may be in writing in accordance with the Arbitration Act 1950. This Act rules that: the arbitrator need not be named but the parties must sign, though signatures may be dispensed with where the contract is obvious from the behaviour of the parties. An agreement to refer a matter to arbitration does not prevent either party taking legal proceedings instead. This right to take proceedings cannot be denied by the contract. A court may, however, insist on the arbitration. Costs of arbitration will be apportioned by the arbitrator. Where there is more than one arbitrator, an umpire is appointed. His decision is final if the arbitrators fail to agree (known as umpirage). The decision of the arbitrator is called the award. In order to be binding, it must be final, certain, possible and consistent. It must also take all matters submitted into account. The arbitrator must not act outside his jurisdiction. He may, and if required to do so must, state a case for a court to decide where a point of law is at stake. The award may be set aside, referred back, or enforced, by the court, depending on circumstances. Certain awards made in foreign countries may be enforced in England.

Arbitration of exchange. ◊ ARBITRAGE.

Arbitrator. ◊ ARBITRATION.

Architect. A person qualified to design buildings and to supervise their erection. In Britain the title is restricted to those on the register of the ARCHITECTS' REGISTRATION COUNCIL OF THE UNITED KINGDOM.

Architects' Registration Council of the United Kingdom. This was formed in 1938 and has three main duties: (1) the maintenance and annual publication of the Register of Architects, (2) the maintenance of correct standards of professional conduct and (3) the award of scholarships and grants to needy students. The Council has disciplinary powers over members who have committed criminal offences or been guilty of disgraceful conduct in a professional respect. Public complaints are referred to the disciplinary committee, less serious complaints are dealt with by the professional services committee. There is a code of professional conduct, similar to that of the ROYAL INSTITUTE OF BRITISH ARCHITECTS. Architects are, for instance, not allowed to advertise, or take part in a building or decorating company.

Architects, Royal Institute of British. This was formed in 1834, received a royal charter in 1837 and now has over 21,000 members. It controls a Board of Architectural Education to supervise the teaching of architecture in schools and colleges and to help with educational guidance. The Architects' Registration Acts 1931 and 1938 restricted the use of the name 'architect' to persons who had passed the necessary examinations. There are various bodies of architects, the R.I.B.A. being the most important. All members of these bodies must have their names entered in the Register of the ◊ ARCHITECTS' REGISTRATION COUNCIL OF THE UNITED KINGDOM. The R.I.B.A. has a comprehensive library, and various publications including the *Architect and his Office*, and a monthly journal. Address: 66 Portland Place, London W1.

Arrears. Monies due but unpaid.

Arrears of dividends. Where DIVIDENDS are in ARREARS and are payable, the amount due should be shown in the ANNUAL ACCOUNTS, or in a note to the accounts. The amount shown should be the gross amount, distinguishing between classes of SHARES.

Arrestment. Scottish equivalent of ◊ ATTACHMENT.

Arrived ship. A vessel that has arrived at the agreed port of discharge or loading, proper notice having been given that it is ready to start discharging or loading.

Articled clerk. A sophisticated name for an ◊ APPRENTICE, usually applied to a person apprenticed in a professional firm, e.g. of ACCOUNTANTS or SOLICITORS.

Articles of association. These are the internal regulations on the running of a COMPANY. They must be registered when the company is formed. They bind the company and the members as if each member had signed them, but do not bind the company or the members to outside persons. The articles are subject to the MEMORANDUM OF ASSOCIATION and must not contain anything illegal or ULTRA VIRES. They can be altered by the company by SPECIAL RESOLUTION at a general meeting. The effect of registration is to give general notice to the public – any person may inspect the memorandum or articles of any company at Bush House, Aldwych, London WC1, on payment of a fee. A specimen form of articles, ◊ TABLE A, appears as an appendix to the Companies Act 1948. This may be adopted in part or in whole.

Articles of association, alteration of. The articles may be altered by a SPECIAL RESOLUTION at a general meeting. The alteration must be within the powers given by the MEMORANDUM OF ASSOCIATION. It must concern legal acts and must not be a fraud on a minority of shareholders: that is, it must be for the good of the COMPANY and must not be an attempt by the majority to take advantage of their position. Where alteration of the rights of any class of shareholders is concerned, the articles often provide that special class meetings must be held and that the consent of the class must be obtained. Where the rights are fixed by the memorandum, then if the method of alteration is not specified it may be necessary to appeal to the court.

Articles of partnership. Strictly, the clauses in a ◊ PARTNERSHIP AGREEMENT.

As per advice. If these words are written on a BILL OF EXCHANGE it is an indication that the drawee has been notified that the bill has been drawn on him.

Assay. The trying of metals (particularly those used for coin or bullion) to determine their content.

Assay master. An official responsible for ◊ ASSAY.

Asset. A general term used to describe property owned: it may be real property, or personal property including CHOSES-IN-ACTION. ◊ FIXED ASSETS ◊ CURRENT ASSETS.

Assignment. The transfer of rights and/or obligations by one person to another particularly with reference to a CONTRACT, so that under certain strictly defined conditions the second person takes over those rights and obligations and can enforce them, or have them enforced against him. For certain types of assignment the permission of a third party must be obtained. A building contractor can assign work to a subcontractor without the permission of his employer but an artist employed to paint a portrait cannot assign the work to another artist without permission. Generally speaking, a person cannot assign a duty to another when it is of a personal nature. The owner of a business who sells cannot assign to the purchaser the various contracts of employment which he has made. Assignment falls into three categories: where there is an agreement that A shall do something for B, A may wish to assign his obligation to C; similarly B may wish to assign the benefit to D: (1) Basically A may assign with the permission of B. This then becomes in effect a new agreement between B and C, and A is no longer concerned. ◊ CONTRACT OF NOVATION. (2) A may assign to C by custom of trade, e.g. subcontracting. B cannot complain but has a remedy both against A and against C. (3) A may assign without consulting B and without having any implied right by trade to do so. B may ignore the assignment and treat A as wholly responsible and as having breached the original agreement.

Where B is assigning the benefit much the same rules apply.

◊ ASSIGNMENT, LEGAL ◊ ASSIGNMENT, EQUITABLE.

Assignment, equitable. Most ASSIGNMENTS which are not proper LEGAL ASSIGNMENTS. The assignee takes the assignor's rights subject to equities. CONSIDERATION is not necessary provided the assignment is complete and is not conditional. The assignment is valid between assignor and assignee, even if notice is not given to the debtor. If the debtor does not receive notice, he may pay the assignor, leaving the assignee no right. If he has received notice, he should pay the assignee. Assignees rank, not according to date of assignment, but according to the date of notice to the debtor.

The disadvantage of an equitable assignment is that the assignee must sue in the name of the assignor. This only applies to the assignment of legal rights. If the rights are equitable he can sue in his own name.

Assignment, legal. It is possible legally to assign a debt or other legal

Assurance

CHOSE-IN-ACTION so that the assignee acquires all rights and remedies, legal and equitable, provided that the assignment is absolute, in writing, and signed by the assignor. Notice in writing must also be given to the party to be charged, usually the debtor. If these conditions are not fulfilled the assignment may still be enforceable as an EQUITABLE ASSIGNMENT. Legal assignments are governed by the Law of Property Act 1925.

Assignment of leases. Where a lease is wholly assigned, the original lessee remains liable to the lessor but may have redress against the sub-lessee. The lessor may also sue the sub-lessee directly. Where only part of the term of a lease is assigned, the lessor's rights are only against the original lessee.

Assurance. Distinguished from INSURANCE in that assurance does not depend upon a possibility. It is a payment of premium at regular intervals in return for a fixed sum which will become payable at a stated time. The obvious examples are life and endowment assurance. With life assurance, payment becomes due on the death of the life assured. With endowment assurance, payment becomes due at a stated date. It is common to combine both in a life and endowment policy. Certain companies deal only with life assurance. As an assurance contract is one of the category known as UBERRIMAE FIDEI, all facts relevant to the risk taken by the COMPANY must be stated. Some companies often insist on a medical examination. If not, this does not always prevent them disclaiming liability if the claimant was suffering from some serious complaint (unknown to them) at the time the policy was taken out. Policies often contain long and complex clauses limiting liability. Care should be taken to read these before the CONTRACT is signed.

Assurance policies may be with or without profits. A policy with profits entitles the holder to a share in the profits of the company during the term of the policy. This can amount to a considerable sum. Premiums on these policies are of course higher. In comparing one company with another it should be remembered that those who offer the higher profits possibly charge the higher premium. It is usually a question of whether one wishes to pay more now for a higher sum in the future.

There is an increasing tendency for assurance companies to offer what are known as equity linked policies. The premiums are then invested in what is equivalent to a UNIT TRUST. The idea is to compete with unit trusts that are offering assurance policies.

Assurance policies are often used in connexion with house purchase. As with most contracts of assurance, the assured must have an 'assurable interest', e.g. it is not possible for A to take out a policy on the life of B unless A stands to suffer loss. His claim will be restricted to the amount of the loss. The interest need only exist at the time the policy is taken out. A CREDITOR can insure his debtor and a wife has an interest in the life of her husband and *vice versa*, but a parent has not normally an interest in the life of a child nor a child in the parent (save where a parent is supporting a child).

If a man takes out a policy for the benefit of his dependants the money will be treated as a separate estate for duty purposes. This could be a considerable advantage. The advantage however has been modified considerably by the Finance Act 1968. In order now to avoid aggregation, the policy must have been irrevocably taken out in the name of another and the premium should have been part of normal expenditure. The gifts *inter vivos* rule may also apply.

Assurance companies offer variously-named policies of an endowment nature for, for example, educational purposes.

Profits of assurance companies are determined by quinquennial valuations. The profit is the difference between the value of the ASSETS and an estimate of the probable liability to the policy holders.

At and from. A MARINE INSURANCE term for policies covering a ship in port as well as at sea.

At call. ◊ MONEY AT CALL.

At par. ◊ PAR VALUE.

At sight. A term used for BILLS OF EXCHANGE payable on presentation, as opposed to on a particular date.

Attachment. Prevention of a debtor from disposing of specific money or GOODS in the hands of third parties, until the debt has been settled. ◊ CHARGING ORDER ◊ GARNISHEE ORDER ◊ NOTICE IN LIEU OF DISTRINGAS.

Attorney. In England, a person practising at the bar. It may also mean someone who holds a POWER OF ATTORNEY.

Attorney, power of. ◊ POWER OF ATTORNEY.

Auction. This occurs when GOODS are offered for SALE in public by an AUCTIONEER. The conduct of an auction varies according to custom. Normally goods are sold to the highest bidder. The auctioneer acts as AGENT for the seller. SALE OF GOODS at an auction may be subject to a RESERVE PRICE stated by the seller (this should be known to those persons attending the auction though the price need not be stated). If the hammer is brought down before the price is reached the sale can be avoided. This does not apply if the auctioneer signs a memorandum, when the CONTRACT is one to be evidenced in writing.

It is illegal for a dealer to offer a person a reward not to bid at the sale: penalties can be levied on both parties. A dealer is a person who buys for resale.

Auctioneer. A person authorized to sell GOODS or land at a public AUCTION or sale. Initially the AGENT of the seller, he becomes also the agent of the buyer after the item has been knocked down; he can therefore bind both parties where writing is necessary. Sale is normally only for cash where the custom is not otherwise; the auctioneer has a LIEN on goods for his charges provided he has the goods; he has no implied authority to warrant the goods sold, nor the owner's right to sell; he must act in good faith.

Advertisement of an auction does not bind the auctioneer as it is not an OFFER but an invitation.

Audit. Inspection of a set of books and/or accounts by a person other than the one who prepared them (with the object of ascertaining whether or not the books are properly kept and/or the accounts show a TRUE AND FAIR view of the state of affairs of the organization at the date stated) followed by a report to the persons by whom the ◊ AUDITORS were appointed.

In certain circumstances an audit is ordered by law, and the qualification of the auditor may be specified. For example, the ANNUAL ACCOUNTS of limited COMPANIES must be audited by a person approved by the BOARD OF TRADE.

Auditor. One whose job it is to examine the records of a business in order to be able to give an opinion on the accuracy of the profit or loss shown and to report on the state of affairs of the business at a particular time. He may also examine the records of non trading organizations, clubs, etc. for the same purpose. He may also perform specialized investigation work when asked to do so by the proprietor of a business or by the court.

The ACCOUNTS of a COMPANY must be audited by law: the auditor is independent and is employed by and responsible to the shareholders. A company auditor must belong to one of certain recognized accountancy bodies or must be specially approved by the BOARD OF TRADE. The recognized accountancy bodies for this purpose are: the Institute of Chartered Accountants in England and Wales, the Institute of Chartered Accountants of Scotland, the Institute of Chartered Accountants in Ireland, the Society of Incorporated Accountants (in voluntary LIQUIDATION), and the Association of Certified and Corporate Accountants.

Auditor, appointment of. The AUDITOR of a COMPANY is appointed at each ANNUAL GENERAL MEETING and holds office from the end of one meeting to the end of the next. Reappointment is automatic unless he is in any way disqualified from acting, is unwilling to act, or a RESOLUTION has been passed removing him. Where no auditor is appointed, the Board of Trade may appoint one. The company must inform the Board of Trade that no auditor has been appointed. The first auditor may be appointed by the DIRECTORS at any time before the first annual general meeting; they may also fill vacancies, but such appointments are subject to the company's approval at a general meeting. The AUDITOR'S REMUNERATION is usually fixed by the company at a general meeting.

Auditor, removal of. An AUDITOR can be removed at any time. If he is auditor of a COMPANY there are certain formalities to be observed: he must be removed by a RESOLUTION of a general MEETING; notice of the resolution must be given to the company twenty-eight days prior to the meeting; the company must then give members twenty-one days' notice and must also notify the auditor. The auditor may then speak at the meeting, or may make a written statement, and request that this be notified to members and/or be read at the meeting. (This need not be done if the statement is judged in court to be in any way defamatory.)

Auditors and third parties. AUDITORS have no duty normally to persons relying on accounts audited by them. The CONTRACT is between the COMPANY or other organization and the auditor. The auditor has a duty to the organization and can be sued in the normal way for negligence. He is not generally liable to persons who might rely on the accounts in, say, lending money. However, there is a tendency for the law to take the attitude that where the auditor knows the purpose for which the accounts are wanted (i.e. to persuade someone to lend money) then if he is negligent he may incur liability.

Auditor's remuneration. In a COMPANY this is fixed either by the DIRECTORS of the company, or by the company in general MEETING. In other instances it would be a matter of CONTRACT. The remuneration of auditors is shown in accounts. It must be shown in the accounts of limited companies. The remuneration will include expenses. Auditors' remuneration should be distinguished from amounts paid to the auditors for other work, e.g. for accountancy work and taxation. These items are often treated as general expenses.

Auditor's report. The report made by an AUDITOR asked to examine

the records of an institution. The term is normally used for the
report which must by law be attached to every BALANCE SHEET
issued by a COMPANY.

A qualified report is one which includes certain reservations, e.g.
the auditor's opinion that he has not been given all the information
he needs.

Authority to negotiate. A term used with reference to BILLS OF
EXCHANGE, and the finance of overseas trade, particularly with the
Far East. The London branch of a foreign BANK discounts bills
drawn on overseas buyers, which are then sent to the other country
for collection. The bills are not popular in the London money
market – collection must be made in the other country. If payment
is not forthcoming the exporter himself will be liable as drawer.
These bills are therefore not easy to negotiate.

Authorized capital. The amount of CAPITAL stated in the MEMORAN-
DUM OF ASSOCIATION of a COMPANY. A company cannot issue
more unless the amount is first increased by the methods prescribed
in the Companies Act 1948. The authorized capital is usually stated in
the company's BALANCE SHEET and is distinguished from ISSUED
CAPITAL. Authorized capital as stated in the memorandum must
be divided into SHARES of a certain amount. It does not necessarily
have to be divided into ORDINARY SHARES, PREFERENCE SHARES,
etc. This can be done at a later date. ◊ CAPITAL CLAUSE.

Authorized depository. The Exchange Control Act 1947 disallowed the
circulation of BEARER SECURITIES, e.g. bearer bonds. It ordered
that all such SECURITIES should be deposited with specified institutions, which would then be responsible for collecting and paying the
dividend. These were known as authorized depositories and were
BANKS, members of recognized stock exchanges, SOLICITORS and
certain specialized financial institutions. The issue of bearer securities
was also prohibited in 1947, but the ban on the issue was removed
in 1963.

Average. ◊ MEAN.

Average adjustor. A person responsible for preparing average claims in
INSURANCE contracts, particularly MARINE INSURANCE. ◊
GENERAL AVERAGE ◊ PARTICULAR AVERAGE.

Average bond. A bond given by a person receiving cargo, stating that
he will contribute to any GENERAL AVERAGE claim. ◊ AVERAGE
ADJUSTOR.

Average clause. A clause in an INSURANCE policy whereby should the
insurer not insure the property for its full VALUE, then in the event
of any loss, the amount paid will be a proportion only of the loss,

the proportion being that of the value of the policy to the value of the property. For example: a building worth £1,000 is insured for £500; loss by fire amounts to £500; amount paid out is £250.

Average cost. ◊ STOCK VALUATION.

Average due date. The average date on which a number of payments due at different times, may be paid.

Averaging. A term used in speculation on the STOCK EXCHANGE, for making further purchases or sales at a time when price movements are disadvantageous, with the intention of minimizing losses.

Avoir dupois. The system of weights used in England and America consisting of, *inter alia*, ounces, pounds, quarters, hundredweights and tons. An ounce contains 437½ grains, and the value of the grain was defined by Act of Parliament in the reign of George IV.

Award. The decision of an arbitrator. ◊ ARBITRATION.

B

'B' list of contributaries. ⟡ CONTRIBUTARIES.

Back freight. FREIGHT payable when delivery is not taken within a reasonable time at the port of discharge and the master, who has implied power to do so, deals with the GOODS at the owner's expense, perhaps by transferring them to another port.

Back to back credit. A term used in finance. It is a credit given by a British FINANCE HOUSE acting as go-between between a foreign buyer and a foreign seller. The foreign seller delivers the relevant documents to the finance house, the finance house then issues its own documents in place of them, and the seller's name is not mentioned.

Backed note. A receiving note endorsed by a ship-broker and authorizing the master of a ship to take on board water-borne GOODS. It is evidence that FREIGHT has been or will be paid.

Backfreight. FREIGHT payable by a CONSIGNOR for the return journey when the cargo could not be delivered through the consignor's fault, or when the consignee refuses to take the GOODS.

Backwardation. ⟡ ACCOUNT DAYS.

Bad debts. An accounting term specifically for debts known to be irrecoverable and therefore treated as losses.

Bailee. A person who has possession of the GOODS of another (known as bailor) with the consent of that other. Common examples of bailees are shoe repairers, dry cleaners, and garages. There are various categories, depending on whether the bailee is being paid or is paying, and also on whether he is voluntarily or involuntarily a bailee. Generally speaking, if one has possession of another person's goods, one is expected to take care of them, but the standard of care depends on the circumstances. A bailee for reward, or a voluntary bailee, must take particular care of the goods; an involuntary bailee is bound to take reasonable care, but no more than he would of his own goods.

Special laws apply to people who accept goods for repair – particularly where those goods are not collected at the time stated. ⟡ BAILMENT.

Bailment. Possession of the GOODS of another without ownership. This may be voluntary, e.g. borrowing an article, or involuntary, e.g. having an item left on one's premises by accident. A ⟡ BAILEE is, if voluntary, expected to take care of the goods. The degree of care depends on circumstances. Problems appear frequently in CON-TRACTS for repair. Generally speaking the repairer is a voluntary bailee until time for collection. After this he is an involuntary bailee. As involuntary bailee he is not bound to take particular care but in most instances is nevertheless bound by statute law. This insists that he retain the goods for a period at the bailee's expense. He may then, after advertising sale in open market, sell, and after deducting costs he must retain the net proceeds for a specified period. ◊ UNCOL-LECTED GOODS, DISPOSAL OF. Another common form of involuntary bailment occurs when goods are sent to a third party in the hope that he may purchase them. In such a case the recipient need take no care of the goods provided he does not indicate acceptance of the OFFER. It is sufficient that he redirects the goods to the sender at the latter's expense, or notifies him that the goods are not required and are to be removed forthwith. If they were perishable the bailee may be forced to dispose of them. He would then retain the net proceeds until the bailor collected them.

Balance. In accounting, the balance of an account is the difference between the total of the credit entries and the total of the DEBIT entries. It is ascertained at certain intervals, monthly or weekly for debtors or CREDITORS, and perhaps annually for the ANNUAL ACCOUNTS.

Balance sheet. A statement produced periodically, normally at the end of a financial year, showing an organization's ASSETS and liabilities. Balance sheets were originally in two-sided form, the left hand side showing liabilities and the right showing assets, with equal totals. Sometimes they are now in vertical form showing FIXED ASSETS and net CURRENT ASSETS and describing this as CAPITAL EMPLOYED, then showing the details of the CAPITAL itself from the point of view of ownership. The balance sheets of limited COMPANIES must conform to the regulations of the Companies Act 1948 as amended by the Companies Act 1967 particularly to those of the ◊ EIGHTH SCHEDULE.

Balance ticket. ◊ CERTIFICATION OF TRANSFER.

Ballast. Material used in lieu of, or in addition to, cargo to stabilize a ship.

Baltic Mercantile and Shipping Exchange. One of the biggest FREIGHT markets in the world. It deals with both shipping and air freight and the chartering of ships and aircraft. It is also the centre of one of the largest grain markets in Europe: it deals with imported grain and has a very flourishing FUTURES market in barley. MARGINS must be settled daily. The exchange is situated at St Mary Axe, London EC3. Its title is often abbreviated to the Baltic Exchange.

Bank. Institutions whose business is handling other people's money. ◊ BANK, JOINT STOCK.

Bank account, deposit. An account kept by a customer at a BANK. It differs from a CURRENT ACCOUNT inasmuch as the money is intended to remain for a longer period. Withdrawals are made subject to notice (often waived); payments out cannot be made by CHEQUE (though this again is a rule not always enforced provided the cheques are infrequent). Depositors have a pass book recording the BALANCE – INTEREST is at deposit rate (normally 2 per cent below BANK RATE).

Bank advance. A loan made by a BANK against SECURITY. Usually the amount is fixed and INTEREST is payable at an agreed rate on the total amount – contrast with BANK OVERDRAFTS where interest is only paid on the amount outstanding. Security for the loan must usually be at least twice the VALUE of the LOAN. The availability of bank advances may be restricted by government interference. The State may restrict credit available by, for instance, directives to the banks, perhaps through the BANK OF ENGLAND, or by insisting on ◊ SPECIAL DEPOSITS.

Bank bill. A BILL OF EXCHANGE issued or accepted by a BANK. A bank bill is more acceptable than a normal trade bill, as the risk is less; DISCOUNTS therefore tend to be less also.

Bank: credit information. The major BANKS normally obtain confidential advice on the financial positions of COMPANIES or individuals at home or abroad, for trading purposes.

Bank for International Settlements. This was set up after the First World War, and is situated in Basle. Its purpose is to speed up settlements between international BANKS, particularly European and American ones. It has monthly board meetings where representatives of the various central banks can meet for discussion.

Bank giro. A giro system operated by a number of JOINT STOCK BANKS collectively. It differs from the ◊ NATIONAL GIRO insofar as accounts are not held at one centre but at the branches of the various banks. Services offered are similar to those offered by the National Giro.

Bank holidays. Public holidays on which BANKS are traditionally closed, and commerce generally comes to a halt. In England and Wales, bank holidays are: Good Friday, Easter Monday, Boxing Day, the spring bank holiday (at present the first Monday in June) and the August bank holiday (the Monday following the last weekend in August). In Scotland, New Year's Day is also a bank holiday, in Ireland, St Patrick's Day.

Bank, joint stock. A COMPANY whose business is banking. These are more particularly those institutions dealing directly with the general public, as opposed to the MERCHANT BANKS and other institutions more concerned with trade and industry. The main joint stock banks in this country were those known as the big five: the National Provincial, Lloyds, the Midland, Barclays and the Westminster. (There are now only four, since the Westminster has merged with the National Provincial.)

Bank loan. A loan made by a BANK. This may be of a stated sum repayable at a fixed rate of ◊ INTEREST at a stated time, or it may be a loan, such as a PERSONAL LOAN, where the interest rate is fixed but the loan is repayable in instalments over a stated period (in this instance the interest rate is in effect higher than that stated). The former type of loan is usually made for business purposes and the latter to individuals for private purposes. Some type of SECURITY is normally required and banks will rarely lend more than half the value of the security. ◊ BANK ADVANCE.

Bank loans and overdrafts, disclosure of. Bank loans and overdrafts must be disclosed in the BALANCE SHEETS of limited COMPANIES. Only one figure need be given.

Bank notes. These are pieces of paper on which the BANK OF ENGLAND states it owes the holder £1 or 10s., as the case may be. At one time, not so very long ago, it was possible to demand gold in exchange for a note at the Bank of England. Since 1925 this has no longer been practicably possible. The currency of this country is now a non-convertible paper currency controlled by the government. Since 1931 the gold standard has been abolished and the 'promise to pay' has no significance. The Bank of England is the only note-issuing BANK in Great Britain apart from certain BANKS in Scotland, Ireland and the Isle of Man whose right to issue notes is limited. At one time all banks could issue notes – originally all bank notes were backed entirely by gold. Subsequently notes were legally issued in excess of 'cash' held. The Bank of England note has been LEGAL TENDER since 1833. The number of notes in circulation is controlled by government policy. ◊ NOTE CIRCULATION

Bank of England. The central bank of the country – nationalized in 1946 by the Labour Government. It was originally a FINANCE COMPANY founded by a Whig government. The goldsmiths of the City of London deposited their gold by tradition with the treasury. Charles II, being rather hard up, shut the treasury and confiscated the gold. The credit of the government was ruined from then on. The depositors devised a new scheme for banking their gold: they formed a 'COM-

PANY'. To induce subscriptions, the subscribers were to be known as the Governor and Company of the Bank of England. £1,200,000 was raised at 8 per cent. The Bank came to work hand in hand with the government, lending it money and helping it to raise a NATIONAL DEBT. In return, it received from the government three important privileges: (1) it was the government's banker; (2) for some time it had monopoly of LIMITED LIABILITY; (3) it was the sole JOINT-STOCK COMPANY allowed to issue bank notes in England. Previously private bankers could issue notes, but today the bank has a complete monopoly. ◊ BANK OF ENGLAND, FUNCTIONS OF ◊ NOTE ISSUE.

Bank of England, functions of.

(1) It acts as a BANK in the normal sense of the word, though its customers are for the most part the government, the commercial banks, overseas central banks, and international organizations. There are some private accounts: these are kept for sentimental reasons and also to keep the Bank in touch with everyday banking problems.

(2) The government keeps all its main accounts at the Bank, though subsidiary accounts are kept at commercial banks outside London. Monies paid into these accounts, however, would normally find their way to the Exchequer Account at the Bank of England. The Bank does not make short-term loans to the government on a large scale – these needs are satisfied by borrowing in the Market by means of TREASURY BILLS etc. The Bank however, may act as the government's AGENT in these matters.

(3) The Bank is also known as the bankers' bank. It is banker to the commercial banks and also to DISCOUNT HOUSES and ACCEPT-ANCE HOUSES. It acts thus as lender of last resort to these institutions. The most important accounts are those of the London clearing banks, and because of this the Bank can, by market operations and calls for ◊ SPECIAL DEPOSITS, control the amount of money in circulation in accordance with government policy (the ability of the clearing banks to lend being geared to their balances at the Bank of England).

(4) The Bank acts as banker to other central banks and has about ninety accounts for overseas central banks and organizations such as the INTERNATIONAL MONETARY FUND, the INTERNATIONAL BANK FOR RECONSTRUCTION AND DEVELOPMENT. Many central banks, particularly those in the STERLING AREA, hold the bulk of their external reserves in London – others keep large working balances in STERLING.

(5) The Bank is a central note-issuing authority (◊ NOTE CIRCULA-TION).

(6) The Bank acts as registrar of government STOCKS, stocks issued by nationalized industries, and stocks of some local authorities, public boards and commonwealth governments. This involves over 5,000,000 DIVIDEND payments annually.

(7) The Bank is the Government's agent in administrating ◊ EX-CHANGE CONTROL. It also supervises limitation of investment in developed countries of the sterling area, and manages on behalf of the Treasury the EXCHANGE EQUALISATION FUND. Some of the Bank's principal duties are concerned with the foreign exchange and gold markets, the bank acting for the EUROPEAN ECONOMIC COMMUNITY and other customers.

Bank overdrafts. Basically an amount due to a BANK by a customer on his account. The bank will give overdraft facilities in place of a BANK LOAN to a person or organization, with or without SECURITY. A charge is made by the bank and is calculated on the amount over-drawn on a day to day basis. A limit is usually placed on the amount a customer may draw in this way, i.e. in excess of the amount which he has deposited. An overdraft should be distinguished from a BANK LOAN: the overdraft varies from day to day, the loan is a stated amount, and INTEREST is paid on the total, or on the BALANCE outstanding at certain times. Bank overdrafts, like BANK ADVANCES, are sometimes indirectly State controlled.

Bank rate. The official rate of INTEREST charged by the BANK OF ENGLAND as lender in the last resort. Also the rate at which the Bank of England DISCOUNTS BILLS OF EXCHANGE. It is normally higher than interest rates generally. Movements in the bank rate influence these in as much as DISCOUNT HOUSES, etc. must guard against being forced into the Bank (i.e. borrowing from the Bank of England) and will therefore increase their rates accordingly. Again, it is accepted practice that clearing banks follow the Bank of England, and therefore anyone relending money borrowed from them will need to raise his rate also. The bank rate also determines the amount paid by the Bank of England to foreigners depositing money with it. ◊ STERLING BALANCES.

In theory the bank rate is determined by the Bank of England alone, but in practice it is done in consultation with the government. Changes in the bank rate are by tradition announced initially in the STOCK EXCHANGE. A messenger from the Bank of England arrives each Thursday and anxious eyes watch the board on which the rate is written in anticipation of changes.

Bank reconciliation. As at any particular time CHEQUES etc., issued or received, may not be banked, the BALANCE shown on a BANK STATEMENT at a particular date will not necessarily agree with the balance shown at that date in the CASH BOOK. It is therefore necessary, in order to prove that the records have been properly kept, to prepare a bank reconciliation. This begins with the balance in the cash book and then details the cheques issued but not banked, and the monies received but not banked. The former will be added and the latter deducted. After any other necessary adjustment, the resultant balance should be the same as that on the bank statement.

Bank: savings account. Savings accounts are designed for small savings. INTEREST is $4\frac{1}{2}$ per cent up to £250 and over £250 at deposit rate ⟡ BANK ACCOUNT: DEPOSIT.

Bank statement. A statement issued in debit and credit form to the customers of a BANK, detailing the transactions and showing the BALANCE outstanding on their accounts at the date stated. Statements are issued to individuals whenever a page is complete, or else on demand. The frequency with which they are issued to businesses depends on the size of the business: some businesses receive statements daily.

Banker, disclosure of information by. A banker must not normally disclose information on a customer's account. He may do so: (1) if the court orders him to do so, (2) if it is a matter of public duty, (3) if it is to protect his own interests, (4) if the customer has given express or implied authority to do so (this could be by giving the BANK as a referee).

Banker's cheque. A cheque drawn by one BANK on another either for clearing purposes or for transferring customers' money.

Banker's draft. A BILL OF EXCHANGE drawn by a banker on himself. It is often used in international trade. A foreign exporter receiving a banker's draft may cash it at the local branch of that BANK.

Banker's guarantee. A 90 per cent GUARANTEE given directly by the EXPORT CREDITS GUARANTEE DEPARTMENT to an exporter's BANK against the non-repayment of advances or discount facilities given by the bank to the exporter, against goods shipped and accepted by the buyer. These guarantees are given as an alternative to direct credit INSURANCE with the Department, where the exporter wishes to obtain immediate finance from his bank. This finance takes the form of say 10 per cent on shipment and 80 per cent spread over the credit period. The guarantees only apply to amounts over £100,000, or for credit periods of over three years. In other circumstances, the Department's cover against credit risks is limited to 85 per cent, and finance provided would probably not be guaranteed. For this reason, exporters may, in these instances, find difficulty in obtaining funds. The gap has been filled by institutions such as Exports Re-finance Corporation. The Department's cover is still required, but the institution assumes financial responsibility. It hands over down payments received from the buyer, and may make advances to the exporter, within fifteen days of shipment, of 85 per cent of the balance due. Obviously it makes a charge in addition to the Department's charge.

Bankers, Institute of. This was founded in 1879 to afford opportunities to acquire knowledge of banking theory, and to facilitate consideration and discussion of matters of interest to bankers. It is also intended 'to help our members to educate themselves not only for banking but also for responsible citizenship' (Sir E. A. Carpenter). The Institute has a series of examinations leading to a Banking Diploma. Holders of a Diploma may use the letters A.I.B. (Associate of the Institute of Bankers). They may also be elected Fellows (F.I.B.). Syllabuses may be obtained from the Institute without charge. Exemption from certain papers is given to persons with other recognized professional qualifications. There is a journal available to members published in alternate months. Address: 10 Lombard St, London EC3.

Banker's order. ⟡ STANDING ORDER.

Banker's revocation of authority to pay cheques. A banker may refuse to pay a CHEQUE when: (1) payment is countermanded by the customer, (2) he receives notice that the customer is drawing CHEQUES unlawfully or for unlawful purposes (e.g. in breach of trust), (3) he receives notice that the customer is dead, insane, or an undischarged bankrupt, (4) he receives a GARNISHEE ORDER attaching to the customer's balance, or (5) he receives an instruction or court order restraining him from making any payment.

Bankrupt, disabilities of. No undischarged bankrupt may: (1) act as a DIRECTOR or take part in the management of a COMPANY, (2) sit or vote in the House of Lords or any committee of it, (3) be elected as a peer of Scotland or Ireland to sit and vote in the House of Lords, (4) be elected to sit and vote in the House of Commons or any committee of it, (5) be appointed or act as a justice of the peace, (6) be elected to or hold the office of mayor, alderman, councillor or county councillor.

Bankrupt shareholder. If a shareholder is bankrupt, the TRUSTEE in BANKRUPTCY may sell or DISCLAIM his SHARES.

Bankruptcy. A person is bankrupt when declared so by the court, which may happen at his own request or as a result of action taken by his CREDITORS. A RECEIVER will be appointed of the bankrupt's property, which will be realized (insofar as this is in the interest of the creditors) and distributed amongst the creditors according to law. A bankrupt remains so until discharged. While bankrupt he has certain disabilities (♢ BANKRUPT, DISABILITIES OF) but he can carry on in business. He may be discharged by the court completely or conditionally. Discharge does not depend on debts being paid in full. When he is discharged, any balance still owing is effectively cancelled.

Bankruptcy, act of. BANKRUPTCY proceedings may be begun only when there is proof that the debtor has committed an act of bankruptcy. These are: (1) a conveyance or ASSIGNMENT of one's property to a TRUSTEE for the benefit of CREDITORS generally, (2) a FRAUDULENT CONVEYANCE, GIFT, etc., of any part of one's property, with intent to defraud any creditor, (3) a conveyance or transfer that would be a FRAUDULENT PREFERENCE if one were adjudged bankrupt, (4) intent to defeat or delay creditors by departure from the country, remaining out of the country if already there, absenting oneself from one's dwelling house, or beginning to keep house, (5) seizure and sale of GOODS, or holding for twenty-one days by the sheriff after execution has been levied against the debtor, (6) the debtor's filing in court of a declaration of inability to pay his debts, (7) presentation of a BANKRUPTCY PETITION by the debtor, (8) final judgment for a creditor against a debtor for any amount and the serving of a bankruptcy notice, which is not complied with for any good reason (e.g. a counter claim), (9) notice by the debtor to any creditor that he has suspended payment of debts.

Bankruptcy: adjudication. After the RECEIVING ORDER a debtor must be made bankrupt if the CREDITORS resolve so, or if no meeting is held or no resolution passed, or a composition or scheme is not approved within fourteen days of the public examination. The debtor may (he does not *have* to) be adjudicated bankrupt where (1) the debtor applies, (2) insufficient creditors attend the first meeting to form a QUORUM, (3) the court believes the debtor has absconded, (4) a composition or scheme is not accepted at the first creditors' meeting, (5) the public examination is adjourned *sine die*, (6) the debtor defaults in moneys due, where a composition or scheme has been accepted or where the latter was obtained by fraud, (7) the debtor, without good reason, does not submit a statement of affairs. Notice of adjudication is published in the LONDON GAZETTE and a local paper. On adjudication, the debtor becomes a bankrupt and his property vests in a TRUSTEE for the benefit of his creditors.

Adjudication may be annulled where (1) the court is of the opinion the debtor ought not to have been made bankrupt or, (2) it is proved the debts have been paid in full or, (3) a composition or scheme is accepted.

Bankruptcy: application for discharge. A debtor may apply at any time after being made bankrupt. The court will appoint a date for the hearing, normally in open court. Twenty-eight days' notice must be given to the OFFICIAL RECEIVER and the TRUSTEE. The Official Receiver gives fourteen days' notice to creditors and files a report on the bankrupt seven days before the hearing. The hearing is also published in the LONDON GAZETTE. The court listens to the Official Receiver, trustee and any CREDITOR, it also considers the report submitted by the Official Receiver, and may question the debtor. If a creditor intends to oppose the discharge he must give two days' notice to the Official Receiver. The court may: (1) grant an absolute discharge, (2) suspend discharge for a particular time, (3) make it conditional on the payment of some money out of future income or, (4) refuse it.

The position is slightly different when the debtor has committed a felony or misdemeanour, has performed certain acts, or where certain conditions obtain, *inter alia*: where less than 50p in the £1 has been paid to SECURED CREDITORS, the debtor has traded knowing he was INSOLVENT, brought forward frivolous defences, made undue preferences within three months before the RECEIVING ORDER, been previously bankrupt, or made composition, etc., with creditors, been guilty of FRAUD, failed to account for any particular losses, failed within the previous three years to keep proper books of account, speculated rashly, etc. In these instances the court must either refuse the discharge, or suspend it either *sine die* until 50p in the £1 has been paid or until judgement has been entered for a certain sum.

Bankruptcy: arrest of debtor. Where a debtor shows signs of absconding, or appears to be making efforts to prolong or delay the BANKRUPTCY proceedings, or hides his books and papers, the court has power to issue a warrant for his arrest. This also is so where after the RECEIVING ORDER, or presentation of the petition, he removes GOODS of more than £5 in VALUE without the leave of the OFFICIAL RECEIVER or TRUSTEE.

Bankruptcy, commencement of. ◊ BANKRUPTCY, DEBTOR'S PROPERTY.

Bankruptcy: committee of inspection. A committee appointed by a meeting of the CREDITORS to supervise the administration of the BANKRUPTCY. Members must be creditors or persons holding general PROXIES or POWERS OF ATTORNEY. Membership must be not more than five nor less than three. The committee must meet monthly. It acts by majority resolution. No member of the committee may receive payment or profit, nor deal with the debtor's property (e.g. purchase any part of it). The committee may give directions to the TRUSTEE and must inspect and AUDIT his books at least once every three months.

Bankruptcy: composition and arrangements. These apply to schemes agreed to by the CREDITORS after a RECEIVING ORDER. Schemes before a receiving order are deeds of arrangement. There are two forms of Composition and Arrangement – one before adjudication (Section 16 of the Act), one after adjudication (Section 21).

(1) Section 16. This scheme must be lodged by the debtor within four days of his STATEMENT OF AFFAIRS. It is sent to the creditors. To be accepted it must be passed by a majority in number and three-quarters in value of all CREDITORS who have proved. Once accepted it binds dissenting creditors. The scheme must be approved by the court. The court hearing is after the public examination of the debtor. The court will not pass the scheme if it does not consider it beneficial to the creditors generally, or does not provide for prior payment of preferential debts. The scheme does not in any event release the debtor from liability for damages for seduction or under an affiliation order or against him as co-respondent in a divorce case.

(2) Section 21. The procedure is similar to that under Section 16 but the consequences of court approval are not identical as the debtor is already bankrupt. Whether the adjudication is annulled depends on the court.

Bankruptcy: creditors' first meeting. This is held within fourteen days of the receiving order. It is summoned with six clear days' notice by the OFFICIAL RECEIVER by publication in the LONDON GAZETTE and a local paper, and by post to all CREDITORS named in the STATE-MENT OF AFFAIRS. A summary of the statement should accompany the notice to the creditors. The debtor must receive three days' notice. The purpose of the meeting is to discuss whether a composition or scheme of arrangement should be accepted or whether the debtor should be adjudged bankrupt. For proceedings at creditors' meeting, ⟡ First Schedule to Bankruptcy Act 1914.

Bankruptcy: debtor's property. There is some difficulty in deciding what property is available to CREDITORS in a BANKRUPTCY. Certain property is not available – this includes trust property where the bankrupt is a trustee, tools of trade, clothing, etc., for debtor and wife up to £20, certain personal rights of action, property settled on protective trusts, GOODS subject to a LIEN, State benefits. Certain property is available only where the court orders it to be so. This includes: (1) Army, Navy, Air Force and Civil-Service pay, (2) the salary and income of the bankrupt (the court will normally allow the debtor to keep enough of his salary to maintain himself, his wife and his family), (3) property situated abroad, where the law of the foreign country does not allow the TRUSTEE to take possession.

Apart from these two categories all property in the possession of the debtor at the commencement of the bankruptcy will be available to creditors. The trustee's title relates back to the commencement of the bankruptcy – this is known as the doctrine of relation back. The bankruptcy commences with the first ◊ ACT OF BANKRUPTCY within three months of the presentation of the petition. To avoid the hardships that could be caused by the application of the doctrine of relation back, certain transactions are protected. Which types of transaction are protected is normally just a matter of common sense: they include payments to creditors, transfers to the debtor, CONTRACTS etc. by the bankrupt for valuable CONSIDERATION. The last only applies where the transaction took place before the receiving order and the other party had no notice of an available act of bankruptcy. This is something of an over-simplification and the reader is advised to consult the Bankruptcy Act 1914. The purpose is to protect innocent transactions in the normal course of business.

Property acquired by the bankrupt after adjudication vests in the trustee. Property in the possession of the debtor with the consent of the true owner may also be vested in the trustees for the benefit of creditors where the true owner has allowed the debtor to give the impression of ownership. The property must have been acquired for the purposes of trade or business. The property vests in the trustee by virtue of what is known as the Order and Disposition Clause of the Bankruptcy Act 1914. It applies only to goods and not to debts. The trustee may also obtain property by avoiding fraudulent preferences, fraudulent conveyances (◊ BANKRUPTCY, ACT OF) and certain voluntary settlements. The trustee is given protection where without negligence he seizes and disposes of property that does not really belong to the debtor.

Bankruptcy, disclaimer in. By becoming the owner of the debtor's GOODS, a TRUSTEE may be saddled with onerous liabilities and CONTRACTS *re* property in the debtor's possession. He is therefore given power to disclaim, i.e. wash his hands of, these items. The items include land where there are onerous covenants, unprofitable contracts, STOCKS and SHARES, etc. Disclaimer is by notice to the other party normally within twelve months of the trustee becoming aware of the property. The permission of the court is not generally necessary, but may be so where a lease is to be disclaimed. Where property is disclaimed the trustee loses the benefits as well as the obligations. The CREDITOR, if any, may of course prove his debts in the BANKRUPTCY.

Bankruptcy: doctrine of relation back. ⟡ BANKRUPTCY: DEBTOR'S PROPERTY.

Bankruptcy: duties of debtor. It is the duty of the debtor to cooperate in every possible way with the court, and the TRUSTEE. Failure to do so could be contempt of court. He must: (1) give a full list of his property and CREDITORS, (2) attend meetings when required to do so, (3) submit to an examination (either a public examination or an examination by the creditors), (4) generally, when adjudicated bankrupt, go to more than ordinary trouble to help realize his property and distribute it among his creditors.

Bankruptcy: effect of discharge. Discharge releases the bankrupt from all provable debts in the BANKRUPTCY. The debts he is not released from, apart from non-provable debts, are certain debts due to the revenue authorities, debts incurred by fraud, and debts incurred by seduction, matrimonial offences and the COMMON LAW liability to support a wife. Where the discharge is conditional the debtor, after two years, may apply to have the terms modified, but such a discharge may also be rescinded if the debtor fails to observe the conditions. An order of discharge may be accompanied by what is known as a certificate of misfortune. This states, more or less, that it was not the debtor's fault he became bankrupt.

Bankruptcy offences. Where a bankrupt does certain things after an adjudication he may be guilty of a misdemeanour. These things are listed in the Bankruptcy Act 1914 (amended by the Act of 1926). The offences are generally speaking deeds by the bankrupt which hinder the realization of his property and payment of his CREDITORS.

Bankruptcy: partners. Many difficult problems arise when a PARTNER is responsible for the debts of his firm. Distinction must be made between joint CREDITORS and separate creditors: joint creditors are creditors of the partnership firm, separate creditors are creditors of the individual partners. The firm may be made bankrupt, or partners made bankrupt separately. Where the firm is made bankrupt on the petition of a joint creditor, a receiving order *re* the firm applies to all partners, but each partner must be adjudicated separately. Generally speaking the BANKRUPTCY of a firm does not necessarily involve the INSOLVENCY of all partners. However, if a firm is made bankrupt, all partners are fully liable for all debts and as this is so, the separate creditors may also wish to prove lest one partner be called upon to pay the debts of the others. In fact, the bankruptcy of a firm will normally involve the bankruptcy of all partners though the bankruptcy of a partner would not necessarily involve the bankruptcy of the firm. Where the firm is made bankrupt problems arise with reference to the priority to be given to joint or separate creditors. There will be a number of separate bankruptcies, separately administered: the bankruptcy of the firm and the separate bankruptcy of each partner. Generally speaking the Bankruptcy Act 1914 provides that in these circumstances the TRUSTEE should apply the joint estate first to satisfy joint creditors, and that separate estates shall be applied primarily to the settlement of claims of separate creditors. This means that the joint creditors have first pick of the ASSETS of the firm but that separate creditors have first pick of the assets of each separate partner. There are certain exceptions: (1) where joint creditors pay off all separate creditors, (2) where a breach of trust is involved on the part of a partner (in this case the creditor may prove his debts in either joint or separate estate but not both), (3) where there is no joint estate and no SOLVENT partner, (where the creditor petitioning against a separate partner is also a joint creditor he can prove in the separate bankruptcy for both debts). Joint and separate DIVIDENDS are usually declared simultaneously. There will be one trustee for all bankruptcies but various COMMITTEES OF INSPECTION. Where the bankruptcy is a separate bankruptcy and not a joint one, the creditors of the firm may prove for their debts but only after separate creditors have been paid in full. These bankruptcies normally dissolve the partnership and the trustee.

Bankruptcy: payment of dividends. DIVIDENDS are payable by the TRUSTEE. The first dividend is payable four months after the first meeting of the CREDITORS, subsequent dividends at six monthly intervals. The COMMITTEE OF INSPECTION can authorize postponement. When a dividend is to be paid, the trustee must notify the BOARD OF TRADE and every creditor in the STATEMENT OF AFFAIRS who has not yet proved his debts. The notice must give the last day for receiving proofs. The trustee must reject proofs within fourteen days if he intends to reject them at all. When the dividend is paid the trustee must notify the Board of Trade, also submitting a list of proofs filed with the registrar. The Board of Trade will publish the dividend in the LONDON GAZETTE. Each creditor who has proved must receive notice together with a statement of the condition of the estate. A final dividend is paid when the trustee has got in all the property he can without needlessly protracting the bankruptcy. Before declaring the dividend he must notify all creditors whose proofs have not been admitted.

Bankruptcy petition. This is a petition presented to the High Court or county court by a CREDITOR. The creditor must prove: (1) that he is owed £50 or more (creditors may plead jointly to make up this amount), (2) that the debt is a liquidated amount though it need not be immediately payable, (3) that an ACT OF BANKRUPTCY has been committed and that the debt was in existence at that time, (4) that the act of bankruptcy was committed within the previous three months, (5) that the debtor is domiciled in England or has had a dwelling house or place of business in England, either personally or by means of an AGENT or parties, within the twelve months preceding the petition. The creditor must act in good faith.

The consequences of such a petition are that the court, if it is satisfied, will make a RECEIVING ORDER, and: (1) the OFFICIAL RECEIVER will become a receiver of the debtor's property (the court may appoint an INTERIM RECEIVER if it thinks fit, pending the receiving order), (2) he will take possession of the debtor's property but not ownership – he does not take ownership until after adjudication, (3) ordinary creditors will lose all rights except that of pleading in the BANKRUPTCY, though SECURED CREDITORS may rely on their SECURITY with certain reservations, (4) all actions and proceedings against the property and estate of the debtor are stayed unless the court says otherwise, (5) a sealed copy of the receiving order is sent to the Official Receiver who serves a similar copy on the debtor. Notice is given to the BOARD OF TRADE, to the LONDON GAZETTE, to a local paper, and to the Chief Land Registrar.

Bankruptcy: proof of debts. A CREDITOR wishing to share in the proceeds of a bankrupt estate must prove his debt. He does this by submitting to the OFFICIAL RECEIVER or TRUSTEE an AFFIDAVIT giving a statement of account. This statement must be detailed and give means of verification. If the creditor has any SECURITY he must say so; if he does not he may be deemed to have surrendered it. Trade discounts are deducted and also agreed cash discounts but not exceeding 5 per cent. (Special rules apply to MONEYLENDERS.) The cost of the proof must be borne by the creditor. Double proof is not allowed, i.e. two creditors cannot prove for the same debt (both GUARANTOR and creditor cannot prove, for instance). However, one creditor could prove in two bankruptcies. Proofs must be stamped and be dealt with within a specified period. Proofs may be admitted, rejected or held over for consideration. It is not necessary for each employee to prove separately for wages.

Bankruptcy: protected transaction. ⟡ BANKRUPTCY: DEBTOR'S PROPERTY.

Bankruptcy: provable debts. These include debts or liabilities, certain or CONTINGENT, present or future, that exist either at the time of the RECEIVING ORDER or are likely to be incurred thereafter because of circumstances that arose before the receiving order. In particular: (1) a wife may prove for ARREARS of maintenance and the capitalized value of future payments, (2) where the liability is contingent the debt may be proved, for where the court is not of the opinion that they are not capable of being estimated, (3) there are special rules with reference to rates and taxes, (4) a GUARANTOR can prove where he has paid the debt but no two persons can prove *re* the same debt (therefore the CREDITOR and the guarantor cannot both prove *re* the same debt); (5) with reference to a FRAUDULENT CONVEYANCE that has been avoided, the injured party may claim for the amounts paid, (6) STATUTE-BARRED DEBTS are not provable, (7) calls on SHARES may be proved for even before they are made, (8) the capitalized value of ANNUITIES may be proved for, (9) with reference to BILLS OF EXCHANGE, the holder can prove even though the bill is not matured; so might an endorsee where the liability is contingent, (10) liquidated damages can be claimed, (11) unliquidated damages may be estimated and proved for when they arise from CONTRACT or breach of trust but not when they arise from tort. Certain debts are not provable, *inter alia* illegal debts, e.g. gaming debts, and also debts incurred when the creditor had express or implied notice of an available ACT OF BANKRUPTCY.

Bankruptcy: public examination. After issuing a receiving order and receiving a STATEMENT OF AFFAIRS, the court must hold a public examination of the debtor's conduct, dealings, and property. Notice of the examination is given to creditors, advertised and published in the LONDON GAZETTE. CREDITORS who have proved debts may question the debtor. The debtor is examined on oath and must answer even incriminating questions. However, if criminal proceedings are likely, the examination may be postponed to prevent the debtor incriminating himself.

The court can also order a private examination.

Bankruptcy: set-off. A CREDITOR can set off a debt owed to him by the bankrupt against a debt owed by him to the bankrupt. This right only arises with references to mutual credits, mutual debts and other mutual dealings between the bankrupt and the creditor, and where the creditor had no notice of an available ACT OF BANKRUPTCY when he gave credit. The creditor cannot set off a debt owed to him in one capacity against a debt owed by him in another.

Bankruptcy: special manager. ◊ SPECIAL MANAGER.

Bankruptcy: statement of affairs. After a receiving order, a debtor must submit a STATEMENT OF AFFAIRS in a prescribed form and verified by AFFIDAVIT. It must show: (1) particulars of ASSETS, debts and liabilities, (2) names, residences and occupations of CREDITORS, (3) SECURITIES held by creditors and dates when they were given, (4) other information that may be required by law or by the OFFICIAL RECEIVER. The statement must be submitted within seven days of the PETITION (or three days of a debtor's petition). The statement may be inspected and copied by persons stating themselves in writing to be creditors or AGENTS of creditors. If the debtor fails to comply with the regulations, the court may declare him bankrupt. The Official Receiver may permit professional assistance in compiling the statement.

Bankruptcy: summary administration. There are special regulations relating to what are known as small BANKRUPTCIES. These are when the total ASSETS are not likely to exceed £300. Some of the differences are: (1) advertising is reduced, (2) notices are only sent to CREDITORS whose debts are over £2, (3) there is no COMMITTEE OF INSPECTION, (4) ADJUDICATION is made forthwith if no composition is proposed or approved, (5) the OFFICIAL RECEIVER acts as TRUSTEE unless the creditors object (if they do object, the bankruptcy ceases to be a small bankruptcy), (6) the estate is normally distributed in one dividend after six months. There are provisions for even smaller insolvencies where the estate is less than £50. These are settled by the county courts on application by a creditor.

Bankruptcy: trustee. An official appointed by the CREDITORS either at their first meeting, if they intend that the debtor be adjudged bankrupt, or otherwise after ADJUDICATION. The trustee must give SECURITY and the appointment must be confirmed by the BOARD OF TRADE. The appointment may be made by a COMMITTEE OF INSPECTION. If no appointment is made within four weeks the Board of Trade will appoint the trustee. The trustee's remuneration is fixed by the creditors. His job finishes when he is dismissed by a resolution of the creditors or when, having done all he can, having been removed, or resigned, he applies to the Board of Trade for his release. Where no trustee is appointed the OFFICIAL RECEIVER will act as such.

Bankruptcy: unclaimed funds and dividends. These are paid into the Bankruptcy Estates Account at the BANK OF ENGLAND. Applications must then be made to the BOARD OF TRADE.

Banks: open credit facilities. Facilities enabling customers to cash CHEQUES at other branches or branches of other specified BANKS. Alternatively, circular letters of credit or TRAVELLERS' CHEQUES may be used. These are issued in various denominations, e.g. £2, £5, £10, £20, £50, and may be cashed at any bank. They are also accepted by British Rail, big shipping companies and certain hotels. They do not only apply to foreign travel.

Banks: shipping. BANKS frequently deal with problems involved in shipping GOODS, and financial problems attached to owning ships; for example they will see to registering vessels, placing INSURANCES and handling claims. They will also receive FREIGHT, and make remittances to captains.

Bareboat charter. The charter of a ship where the charterer pays all expenses during the time of hire.

Barge. A flat-bottomed FREIGHT boat commonly used on canals. ◊ INLAND WATERWAYS.

Barratry. This refers to improper acts of the master or seamen of a ship which, apart from being wilful, cause damage to the ship or cargo.

Barrel. A container, and also a measure of liquids: in the U.K., 36 gallons; in the U.S.A., 42 gallons. The word is also used for solids, e.g. a barrel of butter = 224 lb.

Barrister. One who acts for a client in court, pleading or defending a case. He does not deal directly with the client but through the client's SOLICITOR. By custom a barrister cannot sue for debts incurred in his profession. One becomes a barrister by being called to the bar, which involves sitting various examinations, serving an apprenticeship, and eating a number of meals at what are known as Inns of Court.

Base stock. ◊ STOCK VALUATION.

Bear. A STOCK EXCHANGE term for an individual who sells SHARES in the belief that PRICES will fall, when he will replace them. The very act of selling can affect the confidence of the public and cause the price to fall. ◊ BULL.

Bearer securities. A document of TITLE, to STOCKS, SHARES, DEBENTURES etc. transferable by hand, being made out to bearer and not to a named person. ◊ SHARE WARRANTS. These should now be deposited with ◊ AUTHORIZED DEPOSITORIES but are nevertheless dealt with on the STOCK EXCHANGE.

Bells. A complicated system of announcing time on board ship. Starting at midnight, a bell is sounded at each half hour, the number of strokes increasing by one every thirty minutes up to eight bells, after which the whole process begins again. Therefore eight bells is sounded at 4 a.m., 8 a.m., 12 noon, 4 p.m., 8 p.m. and twelve midnight. A bell is also sounded fifteen minutes before each watch. Watches are of four hours' duration, coinciding with eight bells. The one difference is that the period 4 to 8 p.m. is divided into two dog watches, 4 to 6 p.m., and 6 to 8 p.m.

Beneficial interest. Where a person is not the official holder of property, i.e. does not have legal TITLE to it, but by reason of a trust or private agreement enjoys all or part of the benefits of it, he is said to have a beneficial interest. ⟡ NOMINEE SHAREHOLDER ⟡ TRUSTEE.

Beneficial owner. The person who, although not having the TITLE documents or being registered as the owner of property, is entitled to all benefits accruing from ownership by reason of the fact that the person holding the title has it on trust only, e.g. is a beneficiary under a trust, or is the true shareholder as opposed to the NOMINEE SHAREHOLDER.

Benefit in kind. Benefits other than money received by employees, by reason of their employment. Generally speaking, employers cannot force employees to take wages in kind. ⟡ TOMMY SHOPS; ⟡ TRUCK. However, benefits (e.g. use of car, cost-price purchase, etc.) may be given in addition to wages and used as incentives. Benefits in kind may be taxable, particularly those received by DIRECTORS, and also where the receiver has a right to forego the benefit and receive additional income. Certain minor benefits, sometimes appropriated rather than given, are known as 'perks' or 'perquisites'.

Betterment levy.* This was a new form of taxation introduced by the Land Commission Act 1967. It is a charge on the development VALUE of land when this is realized. It is not concerned with minor alterations to property provided the use of the property is not changed. It is however concerned with major developments. When land is sold or let for development purposes, or when the owner develops the land himself, a charge, at present of 40 per cent, is made on the person receiving the benefit. The charge is based on the difference between the disposal value and what is known as the base value (this has some relation to the original cost of the land). The provisions of the Act are particularly complicated and it is not possible to give a comprehensive precis. It should be noted however that the charge is payable when the land is developed. It does not matter whether the owner has actually sold the land. There is limited

* Abolished as from 22 July 1970.

relief, *inter alia*, (1) for the building of single houses to be owner-occupied, and (2) where the disposal value does not exceed £1,500 in any one year. See the Finance Act, 1969,

Bidding rings. It is a criminal offence for a dealer to give or receive CONSIDERATION (i.e. a bribe) with the aim of preventing a person, or himself, from bidding. A third party, i.e. a seller of GOODS, can avoid the CONTRACT unless the sale is to a BONA FIDE person, even then he can claim damages from the guilty parties.

Bill broker. This is similar to a DISCOUNT HOUSE except that whereas both buy and sell BILLS OF EXCHANGE the broker *may* merely act as an intermediary.

Bill of entry. ⇨ CUSTOMS: FINAL CLEARANCE INWARDS AND ENTRY OUTWARDS.

Bill of exchange. This is defined officially as 'an unconditional order in writing, addressed by one person to another, signed by the person giving it, requiring the person to whom it is addressed to pay on demand, or at a fixed or determinable future time, a sum certain in money, to, or to the order of, a specified person, or to the bearer'. Bills of exchange involve the payment of money only. The time of payment must be definite in the sense that it is bound to occur, even though the actual date may not be known. One payable x days after an event which may never happen will be invalid. If the words and figures do not agree the words take precedence (though if it is a CHEQUE the bank will probably send it back). The sum stated on the bill may be subject to INTEREST. The payee must be specified, e.g. a cheque 'pay cash' would not be a bill of exchange and therefore would not be negotiable. The person drawing the bill is called the drawer, the person to whom the bill is addressed is called the drawee, the person to whom it is payable is called the payee and anyone signing the bill on the reverse is called the endorser. If the endorser endorses the bill to a specified person that person is known as the endorsee. The drawee becomes the ACCEPTOR when he has accepted the bill. A bill is not invalid because it is ante-dated, post-dated, or dated on a Sunday, nor is it invalid if it is not dated at all, nor need it state the place where it is drawn or that where payment is to be made. If a bill is not dated the holder could date it himself. Bills are either 'inland' or 'foreign': an inland bill is defined by statute as 'both drawn and payable within the British Islands or drawn within the British Islands upon some person resident therein'. Any other bills are foreign. Inland bills must be stamped – STAMP DUTY is at the moment twopence. Generally speaking, inchoate bills, i.e. bills in any way incomplete, can be completed by the holder –

this does not of course give him authority to forge another's signature.

Bill of exchange: dishonour. Bills are dishonoured by: (1) non-acceptance, i.e. having been presented for acceptance and not accepted (allowing for the normal time lag, e.g. twenty-four hours), (2) non-payment, e.g. when payment is refused and the payer cannot be traced, or when presentation is not necessary and no payment has been made, (3) where a receiving order in BANKRUPTCY has been made against the ACCEPTOR before payment is due.

Notice of dishonour must be given to all parties whom it is intended to charge: drawer, acceptor, and all endorsers. Notice need not be in writing but it is advisable to make it so. Notice should be given promptly but unavoidable delay will be excused. It need not be given where the relevant party cannot be found or is a fictitious person, or where it has been waived expressly or by implication.

Bill of exchange: stamping. BILLS OF EXCHANGE are not stamped on an AD VALOREM basis. All bills negotiated in this country pay a STAMP DUTY of 2d. The stamp may be an adhesive stamp or the bill itself may be stamped. The stamp is cancelled by the person stamping the bill. If FOREIGN BILLS are drawn and payable abroad, stamp duty is not payable: the liability arises when the bill is negotiated in this country.

Bill of lading. A document used in foreign trade similar in some respects to a DELIVERY NOTE. It sets out the name and address of the customer, the nature of the GOODS, etc. In carriage by sea there are three copies: one retained by the seller, one given to the master of the ship, one forwarded to the buyer or his AGENT. The buyer obtains the goods by presenting his copy to the master of the ship. The bill is usually accompanied by a BILL OF EXCHANGE drawn upon the purchaser. Though not legally a document of ◊ TITLE it is effective as such inasmuch as a person who has possession of it with the consent of the true owner of the goods can give a good title to an innocent purchaser for value. ◊ TITLE ◊ MARINE INSURANCE ◊ STOPPAGE IN TRANSITU.

Bill of quantities. ◊ QUANTITY SURVEYOR.

Bill of sale. A document transferring TITLE to GOODS (other than real property) absolutely or conditionally to another person, possession remaining with the person making the transfer. It is often used to raise money – the borrower retakes the title when he repays the money. Bills of sale must be registered and are subject to the Bills of Sale Acts 1878 and 1882. ◊ BILL OF SALE, ABSOLUTE ◊ BILL OF SALE, CONDITIONAL.

Bill of sale, absolute. This occurs when the TITLE to the GOODS is transferred absolutely: the transferor cannot retake the title and the transferee may take possession at a specified time. An absolute bill of sale must be witnessed by a SOLICITOR.

Bill of sale, conditional. This is a bill where the transferor reserves the right to retake the TITLE. It must be witnessed but not necessarily by a SOLICITOR. It must be in the form stated in the Bills of Sale (1878) Amendment Act 1882 and must show the CONSIDERATION, rate of INTEREST, date of repayment and any conditions. The VALUE must be more than £30, a list of the GOODS must be attached, the transferee can only take possession if (1) the conditions are not observed, (2) the transferor becomes bankrupt or allows the goods to become distrained for RENT, rates or taxes, (3) the transferor attempts to dispose of the GOODS, (4) the transferor allows the law to take possession of his goods. After taking possession, the transferor cannot move or sell the goods for five days.

Bill of sight. A shipping term used where an importer is not able to give full details of his cargo. He completes a bill of sight. The cargo is then inspected by customs authorities. The importer then completes the entry, and the completion is known as perfecting the sight.

Bill of sufferance. A shipping term for a bill giving coastal vessels authority to trade from port to port with dutiable GOODS on board. The goods must be placed in a bonded WAREHOUSE when landed.

Bills in a set. One BILL OF EXCHANGE issued in duplicate or triplicate. Payment of one discharges the whole. The same reference number appears on each bill – only one must be accepted. If the drawee accepts more than one, he will be liable on more than one.

Bills payable. An accounting term for BILLS OF EXCHANGE held and due for payment by the holder at some time in the future. They will be included with CURRENT LIABILITIES.

Bills receivable. An accounting term for BILLS OF EXCHANGE held and due to be paid to the holder at some time in the future. They will be included with CURRENT ASSETS.

Bin card. A card kept in a storehouse recording the actual quantity of material in a bin or other receptacle. The card is marked each time items are purchased or requisitioned.

Blank bill. A BILL OF EXCHANGE where the name of the payee is not stated.

Blank cheque. A CHEQUE where no sum of money is stated. The holder can fill in the amount himself. Blank cheques are often used in letter transactions where the amount of the GOODS to be purchased is not known. The buyer may send a blank cheque but write e.g. 'Not to exceed £2' on it. The bank will usually respect this instruction.

Blank credit. Letter of credit where the amount of credit is not recorded.

Blank endorsement. ◊ ENDORSEMENT.

Blank transfer. A blank transfer of SHARES. Shares are transferred by completion of a transfer form. Where the name of the transferee is left blank, this is known as a blank transfer. It may be used when shares are MORTGAGED, the mortgagee having a right to fill in his own name if the money is not repaid by a certain date. It is also used when persons hold shares as nominees for others, the registered owner giving the BENEFICIAL OWNER a blank transfer.

Blanket policy. An INSURANCE term for a policy which covers many different types of risk. For instance property may be insured against fire, theft, etc.

Blue chip investment. A colourful term for that type of investment which, though not GILT-EDGED, is considered to be safe, so that there is little likelihood of losing CAPITAL or income. They are usually the SHARES of particularly well known and sound companies.

Board meetings. ◊ MEETINGS OF DIRECTORS.

Board of Trade. Founded in 1786, the Board is a committee of the Privy Council; the last recorded full meeting of the Committee took place on 23 December 1850. The functions of the Committee have been taken over by the President of the Board of Trade – a political appointment, with a parliamentary secretary responsible for the textile industry, and three ministers of state, one for home industry and commerce, one for overseas trade and the third for shipping, the shipbuilding industry, and tourism. Permanent staff number about 9,300. The main functions of the Board concern: (1) commercial relations with other countries including the promotion of exports and dealing with the EUROPEAN FREE TRADE AREA and the GENERAL AGREEMENT ON TARIFFS AND TRADE, (2) providing a link between home industry and the government and supervising regional development and redistribution of employment, (3) supervising all aspects of the shipping industry, (4) collecting, evaluating and publishing statistics relating to trade and industry regarding the United Kingdom and the Commonwealth, and also preparing censuses of production and distribution, (5) administrating long-term legislation on, for instance, PATENTS, TRADE MARKS, copyright, INSURANCE companies, BANKRUPTCY, and weights and measures, (6) various other activities with reference to new or temporary legislation concerning the country's commerce. Address: 1 Victoria Street, London SW1.

Board of Trade: British National Export Council. Formed by government and industry, to help industry in export drives. It has many organizations in various continents. Its aims are: (1) to bring trade opportunities to the notice of exporters, (2) to find new openings for British GOODS, (3) to support organizations able to help British exports. It also gives aid for trade missions, translations, collective MARKET RESEARCH, and publication of good trade directories and buyers' guides. Associations may obtain 50 per cent of the cost of translation, type setting, and postage or FREIGHT, for journals sent abroad free. Apply for details to 6–14 Dean Farrar Street, London SW1.

Board of Trade: Commercial Relations and Exports Department. This gives advice on overseas commercial regulations or restrictions, and also on relationships with the GENERAL AGREEMENT ON TARIFFS AND TRADE, the Organization for Economic Co-operation and Development (O.E.C.D.), specialized agencies of the United Nations, and on international law.

Board of Trade: Export Marketing Partnerships. An enterprise set up in 1966 by Marketing Ltd, a subsidiary of the INSTITUTE OF MARKETING. It gives advice and organizes meetings between firms interested in operating jointly overseas.

Board of Trade: Export Services Branch. The Branch gives up-to-date information on TARIFFS, import licensing regulations, quota restrictions, etc., and also information regarding particular problems connected with exporting certain products (e.g. animals) or to certain countries. It will also obtain SAMPLES of GOODS manufactured overseas, at a price. It will find AGENTS overseas, but it will not necessarily take responsibility for them. It will give reports on the commercial standing of overseas organizations, and help with business visits abroad, giving information and introductions. It will also put a firm in touch with a larger firm so that the latter may handle the former's goods. Aid is also given in helping to find facilities for manufacture under licence abroad, and also in any dispute which might arise between British firms and overseas buyers. ⟡ BOARD OF TRADE: MARKET ASSESSMENT ⟡ BOARD OF TRADE: EXPORT SERVICE BULLETIN.

Board of Trade: Export Service Bulletin. The daily publication of the Export Services Branch. It gives details of CONTRACTS put out to TENDER by overseas governments, etc. and general information about overseas demand. It gives prospects for specific GOODS in individual countries, and for background information. It also gives details of export opportunities arising from activities of international organizations, e.g. the INTERNATIONAL BANK FOR RECONSTRUCTION AND DEVELOPMENT.

Board of Trade: Information Division (Overseas Section). This helps to find effective ways of publicizing products overseas, and gives details of free facilities offered by the Central Office of Information, the B.B.C., the overseas journalists in London, etc. It also helps to obtain specialist advice from people on the spot, and translations of brochures.

Free booklets published are: Overseas Press Correspondents in London (Board of Trade), Agency Legislation Abroad (Board of Trade), How to Export (Board of Trade), A Guide for the Newcomer (Board of Trade), The World at Your Doorstep (B.B.C.), World-wide Export Publicity Service (Central Office of Information). Address: 66 Victoria Street, SW1.

Board of Trade Journal. A weekly paper which includes most of the information given in the *Export Services Bulletin*, and also market surveys, changes in TARIFFS, Customs, import regulations etc., details of recent export orders, fact-finding missions, lists of trade fairs and overseas promotional activities. It also gives general information regarding the state of the economy, by publishing statistics concerned with production, consumption, employment, etc., and general information on the state of trade in this country. Annual subscription: £5·34, or obtainable from Her Majesty's Stationery Office.

Board of Trade: market assessments. The BOARD OF TRADE EXPORT SERVICES BRANCH offers advice on overseas markets regarding business conditions, local conditions, tastes, etc.

Board of Trade: Statistics and Market Intelligence Library. There are three sections, dealing with: (1) trade production and economic data on overseas countries, (2) foreign trade and telephone directories, (3) catalogues published by overseas firms. Inquiries (by telephone, telex or post) on addresses and other details to: The Library, Hillgate House, 35 Old Bailey, London EC4. A ten-page descriptive brochure of services and stock was provided free by the library in 1965.

Board of Trade: Statistics Division. This gives statistical information regarding foreign trade by extracting figures from overseas publications on payment. It also gives advice on market STATISTICS. The information is obtained from the BOARD OF TRADE STATISTICS AND MARKET INTELLIGENCE LIBRARY at Hillgate House, which gives details of trade, production, and sundry economic data concerning many countries. It has market survey material. There are trade and telephone directories dealing with relevant AGENTS, importers, manufacturers, etc., and also many catalogues (these are available for loan). Anyone may use the library either in person or by telephone and there is a staff waiting to advise. United Kingdom import and export statistics are available in the monthly *Overseas Trade Account of the United Kingdom* or in greater detail, on payment of a small fee, from: Statistical Officer (Bill of Entry Section), Her Majesty's Customs and Excise, 27 Victoria Avenue, Southend-on-Sea. The address of the Statistics Division is: Hillgate House, 35 Old Bailey, London EC4.

Board of Trade: trade promotions overseas. A programme of overseas promotions supported by the BOARD OF TRADE and lists of trade fairs throughout the world are published in the BOARD OF TRADE JOURNAL, March, July and November (with amendments sometimes published in other months). Advice about prospects is obtainable from the BOARD OF TRADE EXPORT SERVICES BRANCH. Detailed information regarding the events is obtainable from Overseas Trade Fairs Directorate, Board of Trade, 54 Broadway, London SW1, and also from the British Weeks and Store Promotions Directorate, Board of Trade, 66 Victoria Street, London SW1. (British Weeks are organized in conjunction with the ⋈ BRITISH NATIONAL EXPORTS COUNCIL.) Information is given on joint ventures, joint ADVERTISING, etc.

Board wages. A term for payment made to hotel staff etc. for buying their own meals.

Boarding Preventative Officer. The person responsible for boarding an incoming ship to check against infectious diseases.

Bona fide. 'In good faith'. The phrase is used frequently in the law of CONTRACT, e.g. 'a *bona fide* purchaser for value'. To gain the full protection of the law, persons are expected to contract in good faith, i.e. they must not feign ignorance of facts which are material to the contract. *Mala fide* means 'in bad faith'.

Bona vacantia. This refers to property where there is no apparent owner and no claimant. This could be property remaining in the hands of a LIQUIDATOR when a COMPANY has been dissolved. Such property passes automatically to the Crown or the Royal Duchies of Lancaster or Cornwall. They could also disclaim it, and then its ultimate destination would depend on the nature of the property: SHARES would be surrendered to the company; land would probably be compulsorily acquired by a local authority. A liquidator may need to apply to a court for direction.

Bond and disposition in security. ⋈ SCOTLAND: COMPANY LAW.

Bond note. A term used in shipping with reference to BONDED GOODS. Dutiable goods must be put in bond. A bond note is issued indicating that the necessary formalities have been observed. The note acts as authority for recovering the goods from the WAREHOUSE and exporting them.

Bonded carmen. ◊ BONDED LIGHTERMEN.

Bonded goods. Imported GOODS on which duty, either Customs or excise, has not been paid. They are put in a bonded WAREHOUSE pending either payment of the duty or re-export. The owner of the warehouse GUARANTEES that duty will be paid if the goods are released. If he does otherwise he is subject to stringent penalties, stated in the bond itself. Bonded goods may be moved from one bonded warehouse to another. Goods may be released in any quantity in the presence of a customs official. The document authorizing removal is called a warehouse warrant. This describes the goods and the duty and is also a delivery order. If goods are re-exported the Customs authorities issue a bond note on one side of which is an order authorizing release of the goods and on the other a statement that the warehouse owner will pay twice the duty if any irregularities occur.

Bonded lighterman. A person responsible, with bonded carmen, for moving GOODS from one bonded WAREHOUSE to another.

Bonded stores. Similar to BONDED GOODS, these are stores to be used on board ship and so placed in bond, duty not being payable.

Bonded vaults. These are bonded WAREHOUSES for wines and spirits.

Bonds. Another name for SECURITIES, particularly those issued by the government. The security offered is the government's GUARANTEE of repayment.

Bonds, long. Bonds with a life of more than twenty years.

Bonds, medium. Bonds with a life of between ten and twenty years.

Bonds, short. Government bonds which mature within a period of five years.

Bonus issue. ◊ SCRIP ISSUE.

Boodle. Money obtained by corrupt dealing in public affairs, and also counterfeit money.

Book debts. A book-keeping term meaning amounts due to the trader.

Book-keeping. Keeping an organization's accounts. ◊ DOUBLE ENTRY BOOK-KEEPING.

Boom. The point in the trade cycle where the upward movement is complete, PRICES and employment being at their maximum. A boom tends to break suddenly, when government action is not sufficiently strong. This can result in a sudden depression and quite severe economic hardships. ⋄ SLUMP ⋄ TRADE CYCLE. The term 'boom' is also applied generally to periods when business is particularly good from the proprietor's point of view.

Bottom. In mercantile language, another name for a ship – hence BOTTOMRY BOND.

Bottomry bond. A master of a ship may need money quickly during a voyage. He may then borrow it on the SECURITY of the ship and cargo by means of a bottomry bond. He only does so when money is necessary to complete the voyage and when communication with the owner is impossible. If money can be obtained on the shipowner's credit, this must be done. A bottomry bond holder loses all his money if the ship is lost. If there are several bond holders, the last is paid first. The ship cannot be disposed of until the bond is paid.

Bought notes. ⋄ CONTRACT NOTES.

Bourse. The French equivalent of the London STOCK EXCHANGE. A member of the Bourse is known as an agent de change. He must put up a very large sum of money to obtain membership, and is usually the head of a group of sleeping partners. It is almost unheard of for a member to fail: if he did so his brother members would be liable for his debts.

Bradburys. A slang term for £1 and 10s. notes, issued by the Treasury in place of gold coin in 1914. The name derives from the then Secretary of the Treasury, John Bradbury. In 1928 the BANK OF ENGLAND took over the issue of notes from the Treasury.

Branded goods. GOODS marked as proprietary brands, pre-packed by manufacturers, with the name of the product displayed. In law a RETAILER has some additional protection when selling branded goods. The Sale of Goods Act 1893 states that when goods are sold under a PATENT or trade name, there is no implied condition as to their fitness for any particular purpose. Most branded goods were once subject to ⋄ RESALE PRICE MAINTENANCE.

Breach of warranty of authority. Where an ⋄ AGENT acts outside his actual and apparent authority, the principal is not liable and a third party can sue the agent for breach of warranty of authority.

Break-even chart. This usually takes the form of a graph showing what level sales revenue must reach before fixed and variable OVERHEAD EXPENSES and VARIABLE COSTS are fully recovered. Sometimes it also shows the rate at which profit increases with sales, after break-even point is reached.

Bretton Woods agreement. ⋄ INTERNATIONAL MONETARY FUND

◊ INTERNATIONAL BANK FOR RECONSTRUCTION AND DEVELOPMENT.

Bribe. A bribe is a payment by which the payer obtains some right, benefit, or preference to which he has no legal entitlement and which he would not have obtained but for the payment of the money. It is a criminal offence to accept a bribe. Any bribe taken by an AGENT must be handed over to the principal. It is an offence, punishable by two years imprisonment and/or a fine of £200 for an agent to accept a bribe, or for a person to offer a bribe to an agent.

British Association for Commercial and Industrial Education. A voluntary organization specializing in all aspects of commercial and industrial education and training in the United Kingdom. Membership includes industrial and commercial firms, nationalized industries, government departments, industrial training boards, local educational authorities, universities, technical and commercial colleges, trade associations, trade unions, etc. It offers to members *inter alia* (1) a bibliography of publications in the field of education and training in industry, (2) a quarterly journal, (3) courses for education and training officers, (4) conferences, exhibitions, publications, handbooks, etc., (5) general advice. Subscriptions vary according to the size of member organizations. Address: 16 Park Crescent, London W1.

British European Airways. ◊ BRITISH OVERSEAS AIRWAYS CORPORATION.

British Export Houses Association. The Association formed by British ◊ EXPORT HOUSES to give free advice to exporters on finding an Export House and/or ◊ CONFIRMING HOUSE suitable to their needs. Address: 69 Cannon Street, London EC4.

British Insurance Association. Founded in 1917, this acts as a central association of British INSURANCE companies, tariff and non-tariff, MUTUAL and PROPRIETARY, transacting any class of insurance or re-insurance business. As a condition of membership, a company's head office must be in the British Commonwealth or the Republic of Ireland. Membership is voluntary. The Association claims to represent 95 per cent of the British company market in premium income. With over 250 members, it works alongside the Corporation of LLOYDS. It defines its objects as 'the protection, promotion and advancement of the common interest of all classes of insurance business'. In particular it attempts to act as single voice for members in dealing with the government and the public, including the promotion of public relations. It publishes a quarterly review, and provides speakers. It does not concern itself with the premium rates or staff matters. It welcomes inquiries from the public, at Aldermary House, Queen Street, London EC4.

British National Exports Council. ⟡ BOARD OF TRADE: BRITISH NATIONAL EXPORTS COUNCIL.

British Overseas Airways Corporation. In 1938 a bill was introduced merging Imperial Airways with British Airways to produce the state-owned British Overseas Airways Corporation, formally established in 1939. It claims to be the world's second largest international airline. Based at London Airport (Heathrow), its route network covers about 175,800 miles, and it carries over 1,000,000 passengers a year. It has a large cargo unit at London Airport, with buildings totalling over 90,000 square feet. Mail business brings in more money than cargo business. There is a training centre for staff.

Among the many services offered, there is a trucking service between Manchester and Birmingham airports to provide a direct link between Midland FREIGHT agents and B.O.A.C. jet airliners. There are also special types of container available for special types of cargo. The European traffic is handled by B.E.A. – the two organizations working closely together. B.E.A. have set up an International Cargo Advisory Bureau to help exporters with their problems. The I.C.A.B. provides customers with air versus surface total cost comparisons and will also conduct limited investigations without obligation or cost. Address: I.C.A.B., B.E.A., West London Air Terminal, London SW7.

British Overseas Engineering Services Bureau. This was set up with government help in order to promote overseas work by British consulting engineers, ARCHITECTS, MANAGEMENT CONSULTANTS, etc. It helps by collecting and passing on information, sends missions overseas, and may help meet the cost of feasibility studies. It also helps to form organized consortia. Part of the cost is met by the government and part by members' subscriptions. Address: 237–40 Abbey House, 2 Victoria Street, London SW1.

British Productivity Council. This was formed in 1952. Its members are normally nominated by sponsoring bodies, i.e. the Confederation of British Industry, the Trade Union Congress, the Association of British Chambers of Commerce, and the nationalized industries. Its statement of policy runs 'the British Productivity Council represents management and workers in every type of industrial sector. It is non-political, free of government control and concerned only to stimulate the improvement of productivity in every section of the national economy by every possible means'. The chairmanship alternates between employers and trade unionists. It publishes

Target, taken over from the Central Office of Information. It encourages inter-firm relationships and cooperation, and team visits abroad. It has local committees, holds study groups, seminars and work-study groups. It services the National Association for Quality and Reliability. It releases many publications. Inquiries should be sent to: Vintry House, Queen Street Place, London EC4.

British Rail. British Rail run two basic services: passenger and FREIGHT. Attempts are being made to speed travel between major centres. There are advantages in travelling at off-peak periods, and special day-tickets are available for passengers travelling after a certain time. It is difficult to give detailed information on freight transport: much depends on the nature of the GOODS and the speed with which they must be delivered. The railways have tried to speed up delivery by means of, e.g. ◊ FREIGHT LINERS, and the ◊ TOTE SYSTEM. There are facilities for carrying various sorts of freight and many different types of wagons are available. For details one should consult the local divisional manager. British Rail also, of course, have Channel ferries, with drive-on facilities for both trains and cars. The situation has been modified by the establishment of the ◊ NATIONAL FREIGHT CORPORATION and various subsidiary bodies set up by the Transport Act 1968.

British Road Services. This was once an independent organization controlled by the Transport Holding Company, and is now part of the NATIONAL FREIGHT CORPORATION. It is concerned with general haulage, and operates about 7,000 vehicles of all types: most types of loads can be carried. Some 200 branches are linked by teleprinter; there are regular overnight services between main industrial centres, as well as nationwide warehousing and distribution services. There are direct services to the continent, Northern Ireland and Eire. Vehicles include bolster vehicles, bulk carriers, cable carriers, coiled steel carriers, insulated containers, livestock containers, low loaders, pole carriers, etc. There is also a specialized car-carrying service, and British Road Services Parcels Ltd. specializes in collecting, conveying and delivering pacels and small consignments.

British Standards Institution. This originated in 1901, received a royal charter in 1929 and became the British Standards Institution in 1931. An independent body, government assisted but not government controlled, its objects include: (1) the cooperation of producers and users in the improvement, standardization and simplification of engineering and industrial materials in order to avoid production of an unnecessary variety of patterns and sizes for one purpose, (2) the setting of standards of quality and dimensions and promoting adoption of British Standards specification, (3) registering in the name of the institution marks of all descriptions and licensing the affixing of these marks. Some products must be marked with British Standard numbers. It is also possible, if the standard is sufficiently comprehensive, to apply to have compliance with British Standards Institution's standards certified by use of the Kite Mark. This is used under licence from the British Standards Institution on terms requiring regular inspection and testing and the observance of an agreed scheme of supervision and control. The use of this mark can be very valuable to a manufacturer. Attempts are made to promote the adoption of international standards, particularly within the Commonwealth. The British Standards Institution plays an active part in the International Electrotechnical Commission. Publications available include *The British Standards Year Book* (free to members), and the monthly *British Standards Institution News*. The institution's head office is at 2 Park Street, London W1.

British Transport Docks Board. A publicly-owned and profit-making authority responsible for nineteen active ports in England, Scotland, and Wales. It was formed by the Transport Act 1962 with the intention of increasing the number of ports in the United Kingdom, and gradually taking most of them over. Profits have exceeded £1,000,000 *per annum*. The ports were at one time controlled by the Docks and Inland Waterways Executive, which was abolished in 1953, when separate boards of management were set up for docks and waterways. The boards are appointed by the British Transport Commission. The 1962 Act made British Transport Docks Board an independent authority, directly responsible to the Ministry of Transport, which appoints the members. There is also a South Wales Local Board (established in 1966) and Local Boards in the Humber and Southampton areas. The various ports and docks are in the charge of local managers 'with the maximum atonomous powers consistent with efficient group control'. The Board is responsible for the following ports: (1) England: Silloth, Barrow, Fleetwood, Garston, Hull, Goole, Immingham, Grimsby, Kings Lynn, Lowestoft, Plymouth, and Southampton, (2) Scotland: Troon, Ayr, (3) Wales: Swansea, Port Talbot, Barry, Cardiff, and Newport. These ports handle approximately one-third of Britain's dry cargo trade. There are ore terminals, oil berths, container berths, and roll-on and roll-off berths at certain ports. The Board owns tugs, dredgers, floating cranes, floating grain elevators, and launches. The capacities of the ports vary: the larger ports can deal with most types of cargo: Southampton for instance has a floating crane of 150 tons capacity. Handbooks and folders on individual ports may be obtained from docks managers. There are various staff training schemes. The Board's headquarters are at Melbury House, Melbury Terrace, London NW1.

British Waterways Board. ◊ INLAND WATERWAYS.

Broken stowage. A shipping term for cargo space lost due to packages of uneven shape.

Broker. A mercantile AGENT who, in the nature of his business, makes CONTRACTS *re* GOODS or property, where he has neither the goods nor the documents of TITLE. There are specialized brokers, e.g. INSURANCE BROKERS, dealing in services rather than goods. A broker is not bound by the Factor's Act. If acting as broker he does not have any personal liability unless custom dictates. He has implied authority to sell on normal credit terms, receive payment, and do other things consonant with his trade.

Brokerage. COMMISSION charged by ◊ BROKERS.

Bubble company. A COMPANY that has never had any real business or intended to trade honestly, or a company formed with the intention of defrauding the public. It probably takes its name from the SOUTH SEA BUBBLE.

Bucket shop. Slang expression used to describe unlawful institutions for doubtful dealing or GAMBLING in commodities, or STOCKS and SHARES, etc.

Budget controller. The head of the committee responsible for ◊ BUDGETARY CONTROL in an organization.

Budgetary control. A system of controlling expenditure and income used by the management of a business. Each department in the business forecasts its probable expenditure or income for the coming financial period. These forecasts or budgets are scrutinized and approved at top management level, so that a provisional PROFIT AND LOSS ACCOUNT for the coming year can be drawn up and if necessary, expenses pruned or sales policies revised. The system varies from firm to firm. Generally speaking budgets must be adhered to and any deviations during the relevant period are reported so that action can be taken if necessary.

Building, Institute of. Founded in 1834, this is a professional institution for people involved in building practice in a managerial, technical, commercial or administrative capacity, or engaged in teaching building or building research. The object is to establish and maintain standards of competence and professional conduct. Membership is personal and open to all nationalities. Various publications are issued, and there are also conferences, seminars, etc. Disciplinary powers are the responsibility of a Professional Conduct Committee.

It collaborates with the ◊ ROYAL INSTITUTE OF BRITISH ARCHI-
TECTS and the ◊ ROYAL INSTITUTION OF CHARTERED SURVEY-
ORS. It has its own examinations, leading to four grades of membership: Fellow, Associate, Licentiate and Technician. A Technician
must be twenty-one, hold the Construction Technicians Certificate
of the City and Guilds of London Institute or a similar qualification
and have had two years' practical experience; a Licentiate must be
twenty-one, have had two years' experience and have passed one of
various examinations, e.g. G.C.E. O level in four subjects; an
Associate, similar to the former, but must be twenty-three and have
slightly higher educational qualifications, e.g. G.C.E. O level in six
subjects plus one at A level. Members are expected to comply with
the Rules of Professional Conduct. Address: 48 Bedford Square,
London WC1.

Building Societies. Organizations that obtain money from the public by
issuing SHARES and taking deposits, with the object of advancing
money for house purchase. Money is lent on the SECURITY of
freehold or leasehold property by the way of MORTGAGE. Building
Societies are governed by various statutes particularly the Building
Societies Act 1962.

The Building Society makes its profit on the difference between
INTEREST charged on money lent and interest paid on money borrowed. There are various rules and regulations governing the
calculation of deposit interest and mortgage payments, the transferability of mortgages, etc., and the work of Building Societies in
general. Information can be obtained from an individual Society or
from the Building Societies Institute. This was formed in 1934 and
is a professional organization designed to promote the education,
efficiency, progress and general development of men and women
engaged in Building Societies' work. It publishes a quarterly journal
The Building Societies Institute Quarterly. Address: 6 Cavendish
Place, London W1.

Building society interest. Where INTEREST is paid to BUILDING
SOCIETIES approved by the Inland Revenue, it may in certain circumstances defined by the Finance Act 1969, be deducted from
taxable income. Tax is not deducted at source.

Bulk cargo. A shipping term meaning cargo which is all of one commodity.

Bull. A STOCK EXCHANGE term applied to an individual who buys on
a short term in the hope that the SHARES will rise quickly in PRICE
enabling him to make a profit. Occasionally by buying in sufficient
quantities he can force the price to rise. This is because, by creating

an artificial demand, he leads others to believe that the shares are worth purchasing. Demand then exceeds supply and the price rises, though probably only for a short period. ⟡ BEAR.

Bullion. Gold and silver of a recognized degree of purity. It may be in various forms, normally gold or silver bars.

Bunkering. A shipping term for taking on coal as fuel for the voyage.

Buoy dues. Dues claimed by TRINITY HOUSE from ships using ports where there are buoys.

Burden. The carrying capacity of a ship. This is not the same as the TONNAGE.

Burglary insurance. A specialized form of INSURANCE. Claims will normally be made for damage done by genuine burglars – uninvited persons breaking into a premises between the hours of 6 p.m. and 6 a.m. This type of insurance does not normally cover loss through pilfering by members of staff or persons invited onto the premises.

Business reply service. ⟡ POST OFFICE BUSINESS REPLY SERVICE.

Business travel (British Rail). British Rail attempts to afford special help to businessmen by providing fast trains between important centres at convenient times, providing food, de luxe cuisine or light meals, sleeping accommodation if necessary, wash-rooms and facilities for shaving. There are also facilities for carrying on business on the train: a private compartment with office equipment. Businessmen using British Rail regularly can often obtain reduced rates. British Rail also runs a good hotel service.

Buyers over. A STOCK EXCHANGE term for a situation where there are more buyers than there are sellers.

Buying in. On the STOCK EXCHANGE, when a seller fails to hand over SECURITIES or SHARES, which he has promised to sell, at the due time, the buyer buys in wherever he can obtain shares, and the seller is responsible for all additional expenses.

C

Calculating machine. A machine used for mathematical calculations, particularly calculations other than straightforward addition and subtraction, e.g. percentages.

Calendar. The old style Julian Calendar was arranged by Julius Caesar in 47 BC. The year was to be 365¼ days, to provide for which the ordinary year was to be 365 days and every fourth or leap year 366 days. The old style was still used in Russia until 1918.

Because the solar year is less than the lunar year by over eleven minutes, the old style involved a surplus of about three days in four Centuries. For this reason, Pope Gregory XIII altered the Calendar in 1582, omitting ten days in that year and making each fourth centurial year a leap year: 1600 was a leap year, 2000 will be a leap year, but not 1700, 1800 or 1900. The new style was adopted in England in 1792, when eleven days had to be cancelled. The difference between the old style and new style is now thirteen days.

Call money. ⟡ MONEY AT CALL AND AT SHORT NOTICE.

Call of more. A STOCK EXCHANGE term concerning OPTIONS. It is the right to call again for the same amount of GOODS as have been purchased previously.

Called-up capital. When SHARES are issued the total nominal value may not be immediately payable. For instance when £1 shares are issued: 25p may be payable on application, 25p on allotment, and 50p on call. The 50p may not be called up for some time. Until then the called-up CAPITAL is only 50p for each share, though members are always liable for the additional 50p in the event of a WINDING-UP. ⟡ PAID-UP CAPITAL.

Calls. A term used in COMPANY law for demands made by a company that MEMBERS should pay certain sums due on the SHARES they hold. ⟡ CALLED-UP CAPITAL. In a LIQUIDATION, the LIQUIDATOR may make a call immediately irrespective of any agreement the company has made with the shareholder.

Calls in arrears. ⟡ PAID-UP CAPITAL.

Canals. ⟡ INLAND WATERWAYS.

Capacity to contract. ⟡ CONTRACT: MARRIED WOMEN ⟡ CONTRACT INFANT'S ⟡ CONTRACT, DRUNKARD'S ⟡ CONTRACT, TRADE' UNION.

Capital. The total resources of a person or organization (though normally only tangible items are taken into account). The term is very vague and is usually qualified in some way. ◊ SHARE CAPITAL.

Capital clause. The clause in the MEMORANDUM OF ASSOCIATION of a COMPANY dealing with its CAPITAL. It states the amount of the company's nominal capital, and the number and amount of the SHARES it is permitted to have. It need not classify the shares though sometimes does. This makes it more difficult for rights to be altered. ◊ AUTHORIZED CAPITAL.

Capital commitments. CAPITAL expenditure contracted for by COMPANIES or other organizations, of which nothing has been paid by BALANCE SHEET date. The Companies Act 1967 provides that these commitments should be shown in the accounts of limited companies, as a note or otherwise, and that a distinction should be made between items contracted for, and those agreed by the DIRECTORS but not yet contracted for.

Capital employed. An accounting term difficult to define but frequently used in published accounts. As there is no agreement as to how it should be calculated, the method of arriving at the figure varies considerably. It is generally taken to be the NET ASSETS.

Capital employed from the point of view of the analyst is the total capital used in a business for the acquisition of profits. It may be thought of as the ORDINARY SHARE capital or on the other hand as total ASSETS, depending on a point of view.

◊ RETURN ON CAPITAL ◊ YIELD.

Capital expenditure. Expenditure on FIXED ASSETS rather than ASSETS purchased for resale.

Capital gains tax, long-term. A tax levied on all gains made after 7 April 1965 which are not subject to SHORT-TERM CAPITAL GAINS TAX. The tax is not retrospective, so only that part of the gain applicable to the period after 6 April 1965 is taxable. The apportionment of the actual profit on SALE is made on a time basis but for most ASSETS acquired before this date, the tax-payer can choose to pay on the actual surplus, i.e. the difference between SELLING PRICE and VALUE at 6 April 1965. The tax can never exceed the gain, and losses can be set against profits or carried forward against future capital gains. Both individuals and COMPANIES are liable. The profit is calculated after selling expenses. For individuals the present maximum rate of tax is 30 per cent. The actual rate is slightly lower due to a somewhat complicated way of calculating the proper charge defined as 30 per cent or a sum representing the income tax and surtax which would be due if one half of the gains were treated as ordinary investment income. A different basis is used where the

gains exceed £5,000. Companies pay at CORPORATION TAX rate.
Gains arising from the sale of certain properties are not taxable.
These include: principal private residences, owner-occupied and not
bought for resale, NATIONAL SAVINGS CERTIFICATES, PREMIUM
SAVINGS BONDS, DEFENCE BONDS, NATIONAL DEVELOPMENT
BONDS, life ASSURANCE policies, certain government securities,
taxable movable property sold for less than £1,000, most chattels
whose predictable life is less than fifty years, gifts of £100 or less,
private cars, and gambling and pools winnings. 'Sale' means disposed
of, whether for cash or otherwise; tax is payable when property is
given away.

Capital gains tax, short-term.* A tax levied on gains from ASSETS held
and disposed of within twelve months. These gains are taxed as
income. Losses may be set against profits and carried forward. The
tax applies to all tangible movable property and to land, but not to
motor cars. Where the CONSIDERATION is less than £1,000, no
tax is payable. If the consideration is greater than £1,000, the tax is
limited to half the difference.

Capital gearing. The relation between the various types of CAPITAL
within a business (usually a COMPANY), e.g. the relationship between
ORDINARY SHARE capital and RESERVES, PREFERENCE SHARE
capital and fixed-INTEREST loan capital. A company relying principally on equity (i.e. ordinary share) capital for its funds is said to be
low geared. The greater the number of different types of capital
employed, the higher the gearing becomes.

Capital issues. The issue of SHARES in a COMPANY, by means of
introductions, PLACINGS, OFFERS for sale, TENDERS, and more
commonly by PROSPECTUS. ◊ RIGHTS ISSUES. ◊ SCRIP ISSUES.

Capital loss. The opposite of ◊ CAPITAL PROFIT. It is sometimes
important to distinguish between a real loss and a nominal loss
resulting from a change in the VALUE of money. Inflation can often
hide real capital losses. ASSETS may appear to have increased in value
by 50 per cent, but if the price level has increased by more than this,
there may in fact have been a real loss.

Capital profit. Profits made by the sale of ASSETS not bought for resale.
At one time these sales were not taxable but now they are subject to
◊ CAPITAL GAINS TAX. The capital profits of a COMPANY could
at one time be distributed, if certain conditions were fulfilled. These
conditions seem no longer to apply, though the company's ARTICLES
OF ASSOCIATION would still need to permit (or at least not to
prohibit) the distribution.

* Ceased to apply April 1971. All gains now as long term.

Capital redemption reserve fund. When a COMPANY redeems PREFER-
ENCE SHARES, a sum equal to the SHARES' NOMINAL VALUE
redeemed is transferred to this fund. The fund is treated as part of
the PAID-UP CAPITAL of the company and cannot be used for
DIVIDENDS. The fund can, however, be used to pay up BONUS
SHARES.

Capitalization of profit. Profits when earned are put normally to a
revenue reserve account. CAPITAL PROFITS may be put to a
RESERVES, CAPITAL account, though frequently COMPANIES
capitalize them. This is normally effected by ◊ SCRIP ISSUE. Strictly
speaking scrip issues cannot be made gratis, so a DIVIDEND is
declared and used to pay up the amounts due on shares. ◊ CALLED-
UP CAPITAL.

Captain's entry. Details of cargo given by the master of a ship when he
wishes to unload at a port.

Captain's protest. This is made by a captain on any damage suffered
by his ship or cargo. It takes the form of an official declaration.

Car hire. There are three kinds of car hire business: (1) the ◊ TAXI
business, (2) the businesses which hire cars for specified periods at an
agreed rate, normally based on time and mileage, (3) a variation of
(2), the organizations which put cars at the disposal of customers at
particular places and for specified purposes. These customers may
then leave the cars at agreed places at the end of their journeys, for
example: a businessman arrives at London airport, takes a self-drive
car for the remainder of his journey to Glasgow, as planes are
grounded. The car is then collected at Glasgow by the owners.
Car hiring in this third sense should be distinguished from car rental
where a person, rather than purchase a car, rents one on a permanent
basis. He does not own the car but enjoys all the privileges of ownership. The charges and responsibilities will depend on individual
CONTRACTS. The car is usually replaced at specified intervals.

Carat. A unit in measurements of gold refinement. Pure gold is twenty-
four carat. Gold is theoretically divided into twenty-four parts, so
that eighteen carat gold would be eighteen parts gold and six parts
alloy. ◊ HALLMARK.

Carnet. An international Customs document allowing temporary duty-
free import of certain GOODS into certain countries. There are two
types, E.C.S. (*echantillons commerciaux* – commercial samples) for
SAMPLES, A.T.A. (*admission temporaire* – temporary admission) for
exhibition. Carnets are obtainable from the London Chamber of
Commerce and some provincial chambers.

Carriage by rail. ◊ BRITISH RAIL ◊ PRIVATE CARRIER ◊ COMMON

CARRIER ◊ TOTE SYSTEM ◊ FREIGHT LINER ◊ PASSENGER'S LUGGAGE.

Carriage by road. ◊ COMMON CARRIER ◊ PRIVATE CARRIER ◊ ROAD HAULAGE ◊ BRITISH ROAD SERVICES.

Carry-over day. A STOCK EXCHANGE term. Accounts are made up at stated intervals, normally of two weeks. The first day of each new account is known as the carry-over day, because those who have not the money, when the time comes for settlement, to take the shares they have asked a STOCKBROKER to buy, often wish to carry over payment into the following accounting period. ◊ ACCOUNT DAYS.

Cartel. The carving up of markets by various COMPANIES in one industry in order to avoid competition. ◊ TRUSTS ◊ MERGERS. The word 'cartel' is used particularly of German companies. The word is also applied where companies in one field agree amongst themselves to divide export orders on an agreed basis.

Case of need. When a BILL OF EXCHANGE is endorsed 'case of need', a name is given of someone to whom the holder may apply if the bill is not paid.

Cash book. In book-keeping, the basic book of account, where all receipts and payments are recorded. Receipts are shown as DEBITS, payments as credits. Each side normally has two columns, one dealing with transactions in cash, the other with BANK transactions.

Cash discount. The reduction given by a CREDITOR on an account paid before a certain date, to encourage quick payment. It is usually stated as a percentage. Cash discounts may sometimes be quite high – very often the higher PRICE is a penalty for late payment.

Cash flow statement. ◊ SOURCE AND DISPOSITION OF FUNDS.

Cash-on-delivery. ◊ POST OFFICE: CASH-ON-DELIVERY.

Cash price. The PRICE at which a VENDOR is prepared to part with GOODS: that is, the money to be tendered at the time when they are required. This is opposed to the HIRE PURCHASE price, which includes INTEREST over the period of payment.

Cashier. A person responsible for keeping a ◊ CASH BOOK.

Casting vote. The chairman of a meeting's vote, used if the votes cast for and against a particular resolution are the same. The casting vote is not a legal right – the chairman must be given it by, for example, the ARTICLES OF ASSOCIATION.

Causa causans. The true cause, or the sum of all incidents bringing about a particular situation, as opposed to the *causa proxima*, the final cause or last straw, or the *causa remota*, the most remote cause. The *causa proxima* is normally taken to be the actual cause in legal proceedings.

Caveat emptor. Legal expression meaning 'let the buyer beware'. Generally speaking the law presumes that a man uses common sense when buying GOODS, and if he suffers loss through his own fault he will not find the law sympathetic.

Caveat subscriptor. A legal maxim meaning 'let the signer beware'. Anyone who signs a CONTRACT is bound by the terms even though he has not read them or is unaware of their precise legal effect.

Central Office of Information. A government department acting as the central government agency for preparation and supply of publicity material required by other government departments. Some of its products are made available to the public, but its main function is not to answer independent inquiries from members of the public.

It runs a Central Film Library (Government Building, Bromyard Avenue, Acton, London W3) which supplies a large variety of short films dealing with *inter alia* education, farming, other countries, health, industry, safety, etc. There are affiliated film libraries in Scotland and Wales, and catalogues of films are available. The Office also maintains a library of black and white photographs and colour transparencies illustrating the British way of life at home and in U.K. dependencies. These pictures are available for publication, research, teaching, or publicity, and are obtainable at the library (Hercules Road, Westminster Bridge Road, London SE1). Selections are sent by post but not on approval.

A third function of the Office is the publication of books and pamphlets of interest to the public; these are available from Her Majesty's Stationery Office, and a list is available. There are three subscription publications: the quarterly *Commonwealth Today*, the fortnightly *Survey of British and Commonwealth Affairs*, the quarterly *Anglia* – in Russian. There is also a catalogue of reference documents and a quarterly diary of coming events. Central Office of Information also provides social survey reports. Lists of reports and prices are available on application. Address: Hercules Road, Westminster Bridge Road, London SE1.

Centre for inter-firm comparison. This was established by the British Institute of Management and the British Productivity Council in 1959. Membership is voluntary, and information supplied confidential. The object is to advise businesses whether or not they are above the average and suggest reasons for any apparent inefficiencies.

Certificate of damage. A document issued by a dock company when it receives damaged GOODS. The damage is inspected by the docks surveyor who states the nature and cause of the damage.

Certificate of origin. A certificate which states the country of origin of imported GOODS. It has become more important with the growth of the EUROPEAN ECONOMIC COMMUNITY and the EUROPEAN FREE TRADE AREA, which give privileges to goods of member countries.

Certification of transfer. A shareholder transferring part of his holding hands his SHARE CERTIFICATE plus a transfer form to the COMPANY. Before the transfer form is handed to the purchaser the company marks on it that a certificate for X SHARES has been lodged at the company's office. This is signed by the SECRETARY and is said to be certification of transfer. It is accepted by the STOCK EXCHANGE as a good delivery of shares. The company then proceeds to make out two new certificates.

Certified and Corporate Accountants, Association of. This comprises the Corporation of Accountants, founded in 1891, the Institute of Certified Public Accountants (1903) and the London Association of Certified Accountants (1904). It has more than 11,000 members, and is recognized by the BOARD OF TRADE for the AUDIT of accounts of PUBLIC COMPANIES. A professional organization for persons practising as accountants, it aims to set standards of efficiency and behaviour, and increase knowledge and experience within the profession. Membership is obtained by passing examinations and satisfying conditions as to experience and character. Members may be Fellows (F.C.C.A.) or Associates (A.C.C.A.). There are rules of professional conduct and a disciplinary committee. A library is available to members. There are many publications, including a monthly *The Certified Accountants Journal*. Address: 22 Bedford Square, London WC1.

Certified transfer. When a shareholder wants to sell only part of his holding, he sends the SHARE CERTIFICATE with the transfer form to the SECRETARY of the COMPANY. The transfer form is then certified, i.e. endorsed by the secretary showing that the certificate has been deposited. ⬦ CERTIFICATION OF TRANSFER.

Cesser of action. This applies in a LIQUIDATION where after a winding-up petition, the court may stay proceedings pending against the COMPANY. When a winding-up order is made actions must be stayed. This also applies in BANKRUPTCY after a petition has been presented.

Cesser clause. A clause in charter agreements meaning that a charterer's responsibility ends when the cargo is loaded. The ship-owner may, however, have a LIEN on the cargo for FREIGHT charges.

Chain store. A shop which is part of a large organization with branches in many towns. This may specialize in one item, like shoes, or it may be a multiple store, like Woolworths.

Chairman of a Company. Normally the senior person in a COMPANY, and often merely a figurehead who takes no active part but presides as chairman at meetings of DIRECTORS (a chairman is necessary by law on such occasions). An active Chairman is often both Chairman and MANAGING DIRECTOR. ◊ CHAIRMAN'S REPORT.

Chairman's report. A report, generally made annually on the activities of a COMPANY, and signed by the ◊ CHAIRMAN. It is normally given at the ANNUAL GENERAL MEETING and included in the annual report, often accompanied by a photograph of the chairman radiating benevolence. It may contain tributes to staff, and generally discusses the results of the year and the prospects for the future. The tendency is to draw attention to success and away from failure, thus painting a picture of an organization emanating from El Dorado. It is not one of the documents that have, by law, to be issued by the company each year.

Chamber of commerce. ◊ NATIONAL CHAMBER OF TRADE.

Chamber of shipping. An organization of ship-owners and others interested in shipping trade, performing functions similar to those of a chamber of commerce, i.e. looking after the interests of shippers and ship-owners, and making representations on their behalf.

Chamber of trade. ◊ NATIONAL CHAMBER OF TRADE.

Champerty. This occurs when a person pays for a court action in which he is not sufficiently personally involved, in return for a share of any damages received. It is illegal, and any CONTRACT concerning champerty is also illegal.

Chandler. Originally one who made and sold candles, now any person selling groceries, provisions, etc.

Charges forward. The buyer pays for the GOODS and the cost of sending them, only when he receives them.

Charging order. A court order attaching to a debtor's GOODS for the benefit of a CREDITOR. If the debt is not paid within a specified time the creditor may have the right to sell the goods for his own benefit.

Charter by demise. A charter agreement which gives the charterer complete control of the ship. It is navigated by his own men. Such CONTRACTS are not very common today.

Charter party. ◊ CHARTERING, MARINE.

Chartered accountant. A member of the ◊ INSTITUTE OF CHARTERED ACCOUNTANTS in England and Wales (or in Scotland or Ireland). The Institute, being the governing body, establishes certain rules of

conduct to which the chartered accountant must conform at his peril.
◊ AUDITOR.

Chartered Accountants, Institute of. This comprises the Institute of
Chartered Accountants in England and Wales, the Institute of
Chartered Accountants in Scotland and the Institute of Chartered
Accountants in Ireland. Its total membership is around 60,000. The
English Institute was incorporated by royal charter in 1880, the Irish
was established in 1888. The Scottish was the earliest in fact though
not in name – it originated in 1854 but did not become known as the
Institute till 1951. While there is no generally accepted and written
code of conduct, each Institute exerts strong disciplinary control over
its members. It is looked on as the senior accounting body in the
country.

Members are selected by examination, taken after a period of time
articled to a member of the profession. Industrial experience before
qualification is not necessary. The examinations cover a wide field
including, apart from all aspects of accounting, mercantile and
company law, executive law, auditing, management techniques, and
taxation.

Members of the Institutes are recognized by the Board of Trade for
the purpose of auditing the accounts of public companies. The
Society of Incorporated Accountants amalgamated with the English
Institute in 1957 but certain members continue to use the designatory
letters applicable to the Society (F.S.I.A. or A.S.I.A.). This qualification ranks equally with that of a chartered accountant. Members
of the English or Irish Institutes may be Fellows (F.C.A.) or Associate
Members (A.C.A.). In Scotland only the letters C.A. are used.

Chartered Auctioneers' and Estate Agents' Institute. Originally the
Institute of Estate and House Agents, founded in 1872, this was
renamed the Estate Agents' Institute in 1904. It became nationwide,
rather than concerned with London only. In 1886 the Institute of
Auctioneers and Surveyors of the United Kingdom was founded. In
1889 it became the Auctioneers' Institute of the United Kingdom.
In 1912 it amalgamated with the Estate Agents' Institute to become
the Auctioneers' and Estate Agents' Institute of the United Kingdom.
In 1947 it received a royal charter. There are over 13,000 members,
20 per cent of them in public service. In 1920 rules of conduct were
formulated and the conduct of members is closely supervised. There
are four types of membership, Fellows (F.A.I.), Associates (A.A.I.),
Licentiates, and Students. There is a library and an appointments
bureau. There is also a monthly journal. Address: 29 Lincolns Inn
Fields, London WC2. Membership of this organization is not com_

pulsory. Auctioneers and Estate Agents may set up privately without qualifications. In this case the public does not receive the protection the Institute affords. From June 1970 the Institute is to merge with the Royal Institution of Chartered Surveyors and entrance requirements and rules of this latter Institution will then apply.

Chartered company. A COMPANY created by royal charter. These were once more common than they are today – they were used for developing international trade. One well-known company still in existence is the Hudson's Bay Company, or more properly the Governor and Company of Adventurers of England trading into Hudson's Bay. This was formed in 1670. Other famous companies include the East India Company and the South Sea Company.

Today charters tend to be reserved for special organizations, such as the governing bodies of certain professions. These companies must observe the rules of their charter. Members have no personal liability unless this is stated in the charter. There is, however, another type of chartered company known as a patented company, formed by letters patent. Here the liability is unlimited unless the terms of the letters patent state otherwise.

Chartered Secretaries (Institute of). This was founded in 1891, and given a royal charter in 1902. Its present membership is approximately 30,000. Members are not only COMPANY SECRETARIES. The Institute's objectives are: (1) to provide examinations to test the capacity of potential administrators in the fields of commerce, industry and the public service, (2) to hold conferences and meetings and publish papers, documents and lists of members, (3) to represent members' interests in dealings with government departments and the public, (4) to provide professional supervision over membership through a disciplinary committee. Members may be Associates (A.C.I.S.) or Fellows (F.C.I.S.). An Associate must be twenty-one or over, have passed the necessary examinations and have had appropriate experience (which might be as much as six years). Publications include a monthly: *The Chartered Secretary*. Address: 16 Park Crescent, London W1.

Chartered Surveyor. ⟡ CHARTERED SURVEYORS, ROYAL INSTITUTION OF.

Chartered Surveyors, Royal Institution of. Formed in 1868, and given a royal charter in 1881, this is the oldest and largest professional body of chartered surveyors in the world. It deals with all sections of the surveying profession. Most senior posts are open only to members of the Institution. It has a code of professional conduct. A member is accepted as an authority on building costs, practice, and CON-

TRACT procedure. Education is carried on by professional experience and official examinations. To become a Corporate Member a person must pass the final examination and have had five years' experience. Various exemptions are available to candidates with degrees or similar qualifications. Members may use the letters F.R.I.C.S., or A.R.I.C.S. depending on whether they are Fellows or Associates. The members specialize in their examinations in either general surveying, agriculture and land agency, quantity surveying, land surveying, or mining surveying. The Institution publishes a monthly: *Chartered Surveyor*. Address: 12 Great George Street, London SW1.

Chartering agent. A BROKER responsible for finding space for cargo on board ship.

Chartering, marine. A vessel is chartered when it is, as it were, hired in part or whole for a particular time or a particular purpose. The CONTRACT is known as a charter party. Where the contract does not otherwise specify it is covered by the Carriage of Goods by Sea Act. There are various forms of charter. ◊ VOYAGE CHARTER ◊ TIME CHARTER ◊ CHARTER BY DEMISE.

The sum paid by the charterer is known as FREIGHT. Charter conditions vary considerably: the ship may be taken over completely, or with the ship-owner's crew.

Chattels. Movable as opposed to real property.

Cheap jack. A person who specializes in selling GOODS quickly by somewhat unorthodox means. He normally obtains a quantity of goods cheaply (bankrupt stock perhaps) and sells in the manner of an AUCTIONEER either in the open air or in empty shop premises. He appears to sell items of value at ridiculously low prices initially in the expectation that this will enable him to sell the remainder of his stock without difficulty. He relies upon the gullibility of his customers, and moves from place to place depending on circumstances and the police. ◊ MOCK AUCTIONS.

Cheap money. Money is said to be cheap when credit is easily obtainable and interest rates are reasonably low.

Chemist. Amongst other things, a dealer in medicinal drugs.

Cheque. A BILL OF EXCHANGE drawn on a banker payable on demand: a common way of settling debts. Cheques may be open or crossed. An open cheque is payable over the counter provided it is in order. A crossed cheque can only be paid into a bank account. There are various CROSSINGS, e.g. NOT NEGOTIABLE, ACCOUNT PAYEE ONLY. These have no real legal force, except that where a cheque is marked 'not negotiable' the holder has no better TITLE than the person from whom he obtained it: for example, if X steals such a cheque and cashes it at Y's shop, Y has no better title to it than X. A BANK would also not normally cash or accept a cheque marked 'account payee only' except for the payee.

There are special forms of cheques, e.g. PERSONAL CHEQUES, GIFT CHEQUES. A cheque is not LEGAL TENDER.

Cheques, alteration of. Bankers are wary of altered CHEQUES. Alterations should be initialled by the drawer or customer. When a crossed cheque is opened, the full signature of the drawer should appear. Bankers will even then refuse to pay over the counter unless they know the customer.

Cheques: endorsement. CHEQUES being BILLS OF EXCHANGE are transferable by ENDORSEMENT. No endorsement however is necessary where they are paid into the account of the payee. A BANK will however still require an endorsement where the payment is over the counter or to a person other than the payee.

Cheques: protection of banker. Where a banker in good faith and in the normal course of business pays a CHEQUE drawn on himself and the ENDORSEMENT does not appear to be irregular, he will not normally incur any liability if the cheque is irregularly endorsed. The BANK is not expected to know the signatures of his customers' CREDITORS. This protection does not apply if the cheque is paid outside hours or if CROSSINGS or other instructions are not observed. So far as the collecting banker is concerned, if he collects the cheque for a person and that person has in fact no right to the money, he will not be liable to the true owner when he has acted in good faith and without negligence. The person from whom he collects must be a customer, that is a person with an account at the bank. The banker could be liable if he opened an account for a person not known to him and without good references. Negligence is a matter of interpretation: a banker would be negligent in collecting a cheque for an employee when the cheque is made out to the firm, even where it appears to be endorsed.

Choses-in-action. Strictly speaking a chose-in-action is a right to, but not possession of, property or a sum of money; taking possession may be contingent on some event. The right can be enforced in a court of law. Examples of choses-in-action are debts, NEGOTIABLE INSTRUMENTS, MORTGAGES, INSURANCE policies, WARRANTS. A particular quality of a chose-in-action is that it can be assigned to another person, though this may be conditional upon permission being obtained from some other party. ⇨ CHOSES-IN-POSSESSION.

Choses-in-possession. GOODS or other rights which a person has in his possession and for his enjoyment. ⟡ CHOSES-IN-ACTION.

Circuity of action. If a BILL OF EXCHANGE comes back to a person who has already signed it, he may re-negotiate it, but has no right of action against persons signing the bill between the time he first signed it and the time it came back to him.

Circular notes. Similar to ⟡ TRAVELLERS' CHEQUES.

Circulating capital. ⟡ WORKING CAPITAL.

City Code on take-overs and mergers. A code of conduct concerning TAKE-OVER BIDS and MERGER agreements. It originated on the initiative of the government of the BANK OF ENGLAND as far back as 1959. In its present form it was compiled in 1968. Those compiling it were the City Working Party, that is, the Association of INVESTMENT TRUSTS COMPANIES, the BRITISH INSURANCE ASSOCIATION, the ISSUING HOUSES ASSOCIATION, the ACCEPTING HOUSES COMMITTEE, the London Clearing Bankers, the STOCK EXCHANGE, the CONFEDERATION OF BRITISH INDUSTRY, the National Association of Pension Funds. As the code is not legally enforceable, a panel was appointed to supervise its implementation. This Panel was made up from members of the City Working Party. There has been some discussion recently as to the desirability of introducing legally enforceable rules as it appears that, however good the Panel's intentions, without any ultimate sanction they have no real power, and if there is a serious revolt against the rules there is very little that they can do except express regret. The Stock Exchange can theoretically withdraw permission to deal in the SHARES of a COMPANY breaking the rules but where big names are involved there may naturally be some reluctance to act.

The Panel is always available to give advice to parties involved, that is, to the offeror COMPANY or the offeree company, but not to individual shareholders as to whether they should sell their SHARES. The principles involved and the specific rules on the conduct of take-overs or mergers are contained in a booklet, *City Code on Take-Overs and Mergers* available from the Secretary, The Issuing Houses Association, St Albans House, Goldsmith Street, London EC2. It is not possible to give these principles or rules in detail here but one or two points of general interest are:

(1) A bid should be fair to all the shareholders of the offeree company. Minorities should be protected and no particular category of shareholders should obtain an advantage. For this reason DIRECTORS are asked to put their personal interests aside, and if private dealings in shares are made after the announcement of a bid at terms

more advantageous than the bid price, similar terms should be offered to all the other shareholders.

(2) When a bid is made it should be made to the board of the offeree company. This company should then communicate immediately with shareholders, initially by press advertisement, and secondly by a written communication. Where no definite bid has been made but rumours are leading to speculation in shares, the board should make a statement so that the shareholders of the offeree company and possibly also of the offeror company should be fully aware of what is going on.

(3) There is a fairly general insistence that clandestine dealings in shares prior to a merger and even after the announcement of a prospective bid should be prevented.

(4) The importance of keeping shareholders informed is stressed. At the earliest possible opportunity after a bid a full statement, preferably a joint statement by both companies concerned, should be sent to the shareholders. Where this statement is followed by a further statement giving figures or reasons for accepting or rejecting the bid, the provisions of the Fourth Schedule of the 1948 Companies Act concerning PROSPECTUSES should be observed.

(5) When an offer has been made any dealings in the shares of either company by the companies themselves or any other interested parties should be reported to the Stock Exchange.

(6) It is very important to prevent a false market arising in the shares of either offeror or offeree company and both parties should take all possible steps to avoid this.

(7) It is most important that the directors, particularly of the offeree company, should act honestly and in the interests of all shareholders. They should therefore: (a) take competent advice if necessary, (b) refrain from any action aimed at frustrating the bid without consulting the shareholders, (c) make no material changes in the business of the company while the bid is being considered, (d) make all necessary information available to shareholders without giving any one group a particular advantage, (e) where they themselves have a controlling interest, tread carefully, and if possible seek the advice of the Panel.

(8) After a bid is made the true identity of the bidder must be disclosed and also the number of shares already held.

(9) Bids for less than 100 per cent of the shares of a company are not considered desirable.

City terminal service. An air transport term for the surface carriage of consignments between the carrier's city handling station and the relevant airport.

Civil engineer. A person concerned with the design and construction of engineering works. Members of the INSTITUTION OF CIVIL ENGINEERS are known as chartered civil engineers.

Civil Engineers, Institution of. This was established in 1828, and is the governing body for CIVIL ENGINEERS. To become a member a candidate must obtain an engineering degree or some similar qualification, have had a number of years' practical experience, and pass an oral examination. There are rules of professional conduct and a disciplinary committee. There are various publications, including a monthly: *Proceedings of the Institution of Civil Engineers*. Address: Great George Street, Westminster, London SW1.

Classified telephone directory. ⟡ POST OFFICE TELEPHONES: DIRECTORIES.

Claused bill. A BILL OF LADING containing ENDORSEMENTS. ⟡ CLEAN BILL OF LADING.

Clean bill of lading. At one time this was a BILL OF LADING free from any ENDORSEMENT, now it is one which bears no superimposed clauses expressly declaring a defective condition of the GOODS or packaging. Bills with endorsements are known as CLAUSED BILLS. ⟡ FOUL BILL OF LADING ⟡ RECEIVED FOR SHIPMENT.

Clear days. When reckoning days in a CONTRACT, clear days do not include the days when the contract commences or terminates.

Clearance outwards. ⟡ EXPORTERS' DECLARATIONS.

Clearing house, bankers'. Each day a great number of CHEQUES are drawn on various BANKS and their branches. The clearing house exists to set off the amounts owing between banks so that only one sum need be paid by one bank to another. That is, rather than that Lloyds should have to hand over to Barclays the amount due on each cheque drawn by its customers and banked at Barclays bank, and *vice versa*, cheques are effectively set one against the other at the clearing house, and the total balance owing to or by each bank is calculated.

Clearing, town and general. A term used in banking with reference to clearing CHEQUES. There are two town clearings, a morning and an afternoon one. The first deals with cheques of less than £500 received the previous day. The other deals with cheques of more than £500 received the same day. The morning clearing is carried forward to the afternoon clearing.

'Town clearing' refers to London. 'General clearing' refers to the rest of the country where there is one clearing a day dealing with cheques received the previous day. ⟡ CLEARING HOUSE, BANKERS'.

Clerk. A person concerned with keeping records.

Clock cards. Cards used in a factory to record the time worked by employees paid on a time basis. Times are stamped automatically by a clock in an office or entrance to the works.

Close company. A COMPANY controlled by the DIRECTORS or by five or less participants (for this purpose a director could be a person who is not specifically appointed). It suffers from various disadvantages, the principal one being that it may be liable to a SURTAX direction; that is, if the tax inspector is of the opinion (and there are certain tests) that insufficient profits are being distributed in order to avoid surtax, he may make a direction that a certain proportion of the undistributed profits are to be treated as distributed for the purposes of collecting surtax (they are theoretically apportioned among the persons who would have received them). There were also serious restrictions on directors' fees and directors' emoluments, but these have for the most part been removed by the Finance Act 1969.

It is often difficult to decide whether a company is a close company or not. This is because 'director' and 'participant' are such vague terms. The word participant does not necessarily mean one person: it includes all the persons associated with him – his lineal descendants and antecedents, his brothers and sisters, his wife. It also includes the TRUSTEES of any settlement made by one of his associates, fellow beneficiaries in a trust founded by an associate, and also associated companies. Directors are not only those people named as such, but also persons receiving money for work done for the business, and owning 20 per cent or more of the ORDINARY SHARES. On the other hand, where the public are beneficially interested in 35 per cent or more of the voting capital, this is *prima facie* evidence that the company is not a close company. The public of course does not include directors, associates, etc.

Closed indent. ◊ OPEN INDENT.

Closing price. The PRICE at which shares are quoted at the close of any day's STOCK EXCHANGE dealings. The prices can be found in the OFFICIAL LIST, published daily by the Stock Exchange. Two prices are given for any share. This is because STOCK JOBBERS always quote two prices: one for buying and one for selling.

When shares are being valued the mean price is usually taken (this is known as the MIDDLE MARKET VALUE). The closing prices are also given in certain daily newspapers. The list is not necessarily complete as the option of publication lies with the COMPANY. The price given in the newspaper may be in double form, or may be the middle market price.

Coast guards. An organization originally formed to prevent smuggling, but now a general coast police force in the employment of the Admiralty.

Coasters. Vessels trading along the coast, dealing only with home trade.

Coasting trade. ◊ COASTERS.

Coemption. Buying up the whole supply of any commodity. ◊ COR-NERING THE MARKET.

Cohabitation. Under the law of CONTRACT, where a man and a woman are living together the woman has an implied right to pledge the man's credit for NECESSARIES, irrespective of whether they are married.

Collateral. A slang term for SECURITY put up by a borrower in addition to his own promise to repay – it may take the form of a GUARANTEE from a third party or deposit of documents of TITLE.

Collateral agreement. An agreement or CONTRACT running alongside an existing agreement or contract. If the initial contract is void the collateral agreement is not necessarily void: much depends on whether the second contract restates the void agreement. However, if the initial contract is illegal, the collateral agreement will also be illegal.

Collateral security. SECURITY given for a loan. It is often additional security given over and above ASSETS on which the loan is charged.

Collision clause. ◊ RUNNING-DOWN CLAUSE.

Colporteur. A HAWKER or PEDLAR of books or newspapers, particularly religious ones.

Commencement of business. ◊ TRADING CERTIFICATE.

Commercial Accountants, Society of. This was founded in 1942 as a professional organization for ACCOUNTANTS employed in commerce and industry. Membership is open to all employed in AC-COUNTANCY work and is obtained by examination and experience. Members may be Fellows (F.Comm.A.) or Associates (A.Comm.A.). There is a quarterly publication, *The Commercial Accountant*. Address: 40 Tyndalls Park Road, Clifton, Bristol 8.

Commercial credit. ◊ ACCEPTANCE CREDIT ◊ OPEN CREDIT FACILITIES.

Commission. Payment to a middleman for services rendered, often based on the VALUE of the GOODS handled. For instance, the commission paid to an ESTATE AGENT varies with the PRICE of the house.

Commission agent. An ◊ AGENT acting on a COMMISSION basis.

Committee of inspection. A committee appointed by CREDITORS in a WINDING-UP to supervise the LIQUIDATION of a COMPANY. The company may appoint up to five persons to be members of the committee but the creditors must approve the choice. A committee of inspection is only necessary in a creditors' VOLUNTARY WINDING-UP or a winding-up by the court. ⟡ BANKRUPTCY: COMMITTEE OF INSPECTION.

Commodity exchanges. Markets where dealings in commodities are made on a national and international scale. London is a very important centre for these exchanges. Many organizations specialize in one particular commodity. The London commodity exchange is situated in Plantation House, Mincing Lane, London EC3. There are also important exchanges in Liverpool and Manchester. ⟡ RUBBER EXCHANGE ⟡ CORN EXCHANGE ⟡ LIVERPOOL COTTON EXCHANGE ⟡ TEA AUCTIONS ⟡ WOOL AUCTIONS ⟡ FUR AUCTIONS ⟡ LONDON METAL EXCHANGE.

Common carrier. A person offering to transport GOODS for anyone who will employ him. He may specify the type or size of goods, or his area of work, but provided he implies that he is willing to carry goods for anyone he is a common carrier. He is bound to carry goods when requested to do so, subject to any limitations he has previously made known. This does not apply if his vehicle is already full or there is an extraordinary risk attaching to the goods. He must carry them without unnecessary delay and by his normal route (unless another is agreed on) and for a reasonable PRICE. The price need not be uniform. He has a LIEN at COMMON LAW on the goods. This is usually a ⟡ PARTICULAR LIEN, i.e. it only attaches to the charge for the particular jobs and not to debts previously incurred. At COMMON LAW he is an insurer of the goods, i.e. he warrants to carry and deliver them safely and securely and is liable irrespective of negligence. He is not, however, liable for damage from an act of God or the queen's enemies, or damage due to the negligence of the CONSIGNOR (e.g. bad packaging) or the INHERENT VICE of the goods. These limitations do not apply at a time when he was not fulfilling his contract, or when the loss could have been foreseen and was not avoided. He must provide a proper carriage. Where bad packing is concerned, the loss will always be attributed to the consignor. He is not liable for loss due to delay if delay would not normally have damaged the goods, special circumstances should be made known to him. A contract of carriage is not a contract UBERRIMAE FIDEI, therefore the consignor is not expected to make known all facts relating to the goods. He must, however, state if they are of a dangerous character. For details of carrier's liability, it is advisable to consult a standard work on the subject. Generally speaking, he may limit his liability by private notice to the consignor. This might take the form of a printed notice at the depot. If he has been negligent, however, only fraudulent concealment of VALUE would limit his liability.

Common law. This is the common law of the land, which has accumulated since time immemorial. It is based almost entirely on what is known as the rule of precedent, whereby decisions are made on the basis of previous decisions: judges are bound to follow rulings made in previous cases, unless they can find some means of distinguishing the case before them, so as to give a new ruling and thus create a new precedent. One commentator, perhaps unkindly, spoke of precedent thus: 'It is a maxim ... that whatever hath been done before may legally be done again, and therefore they take special care to record all the decisions formerly made against common justice and the general reason of mankind. These, under the name of precedents, they produce as authorities, to justify the most iniquitous opinions and the judges never fail of directing accordingly.'

Common market. ◊ EUROPEAN ECONOMIC COMMUNITY.

Commonwealth Development Finance Co., Ltd. This was formed in 1953 with a CAPITAL of £15,000,000, later increased to £30,000,000. Fifty per cent is held by 172 industrial, commercial, mining, shipping concerns and FINANCE COMPANIES, and 45 per cent by the BANK OF ENGLAND and other Commonwealth BANKS. It has also borrowed from banks and has issued £12,500,000 DEBENTURES to the public. Loans are made to U.K. COMPANIES operating in the COMMONWEALTH, particularly for projects designed to increase resources and strengthen the balance of payments in the STERLING AREA.

Companies: Board of Trade investigations. The Companies Act 1948 gave the BOARD OF TRADE certain powers to inspect COMPANIES' books and accounts, to discover whether any are being carried on for unlawful purposes or in a manner calculated to defraud CREDITORS, and to discover whether DIRECTORS or OFFICERS OF A COMPANY are guilty of MISFEASANCE, etc. If so, the Board of Trade may present a petition for the COMPANY'S WINDING-UP. The 1967 Act has altered the position in the favour of authority by making it possible for the Board of Trade to present a petition whenever it seems 'just and equitable' that the company shall be wound up. It need not have specific reasons for appointing inspectors as previously, but may act on suspicion.

The 1948 Act also provided that a MEMBER OF A COMPANY could petition the court and complain that the affairs of the company were being conducted in a manner oppressive to some members, including himself. The new Act allows the Board of Trade to petition on these grounds also. It also gives additional powers to the Board of Trade to appoint inspectors not only where they think that fraud *is* being perpetrated but also where they think it *has been* perpetrated in the past. There are sections in both Acts making it necessary for AGENTS and OFFICERS OF COMPANIES to assist the inspectors, to produce all books and documents, and also to appear before them. Refusal to do so can be contempt of court.

The Board of Trade can bring civil proceedings in the name of the company against officers, etc., when it appears from the inspector's report that they have been guilty of fraud. The inspectors must report to the Board of Trade when they find ground for such actions during the inspection.

Companies: reconstructions, reorganizations and amalgamations. Generally speaking the easiest way to make a major reconstruction is to wind up one COMPANY and form another. There are, however, special methods of doing this which take less time and avoid additional STAMP DUTIES, etc. The three principal methods, two of them contained in the Companies Act 1948, are:

(1) Sale of the old company to the new, if the new company does not need additional CAPITAL. Here the SHARES in the new company are exchanged for shares in the old. There is usually no difficulty though if the new company is also an amalgamation of several old companies then the provisions of the Monopolies and Mergers Act 1965 need to be consulted (this applies to the other methods also). The company must make provision for the shares of dissenting members to be purchased at a reasonable PRICE. The resolution for transferring the company must be a SPECIAL RESOLUTION, and dissenting shareholders are those who did not vote for the resolution. If the company is wound up within one year of the special resolution Section 287 will apply (see (2) below).

(2) A scheme provided by Section 287 of the Companies Act 1948. There are many similarities with (1). The essential point of this method is that it applies when a company has already gone into LIQUIDATION. The scheme can be put forward then either by the company or by the LIQUIDATOR, or if necessary by the CREDITORS. If a creditors' VOLUNTARY WINDING-UP is in process, the sanction of the court and/or COMMITTEE OF INSPECTION is necessary. The Act provides for various other matters and insists that the rights of dissenting shareholders should be respected as in (1).

In both these methods there are provisions for stamp duty whereby duty is not necessarily payable on the total nominal capital of the new company but on, say, the difference between the new and old.

(3) On a reconstruction, whether or not it involves a liquidation where the rights of creditors are affected, or the rights of MEMBERS, or the rights of certain classes of members, the procedure to be followed is rather more complex. Basically a scheme in accordance with Section 206 of the 1948 Act is appropriate. This scheme is controlled by the court and arrangements are made for calling meetings of all classes of creditors, DEBENTURE holders, and members affected by the scheme. In any of these meetings it is sufficient for the scheme to be approved by a majority of three-quarters (in share value) of those present and voting either in person or by PROXY. If the scheme is so approved it will be presented to the court and the court may or may not give its approval according to whether it thinks the scheme reasonable and fair to all parties concerned. It is sometimes an advantage for the company to go into LIQUIDATION, for actions against the company may then be stayed, and the liquidation need not be final. Although a majority of members may bind the others there are special provisions to protect minorities. The court will not allow a company to use Section 206 to avoid giving the protection to dissenting minorities given by Section 287 and provision must usually be made for the purchase of the shares of such minorities. In any event, where the shares of company A are transferred to company B in accordance with the scheme, and the scheme is approved by the holders of nine-tenths (in value) of the shares transferred, not including shares held by the transferee company, the latter can, on certain condition, insist on purchasing the shares of the minority on certain terms. Similarly the minority can insist that their shares are purchased. This is important in the case of ▷ TAKE-OVER BIDS.

Take-over bids are perhaps the easiest method of amalgamating one company with another. Where a company buys the shares of another in the OPEN MARKET, no reconstruction is necessary and therefore no particular scheme applies, though there are of course special rules applying to take-over bids.

▷ DISSENTIENT: PURCHASE OF INTEREST.

Companies: reduction of capital. A company can only reduce CAPITAL if its ARTICLES OF ASSOCIATION and MEMORANDUM OF ASSOCIATION permit. A SPECIAL RESOLUTION is required and the leave of the court must be obtained. Much depends on the reason for the reduction – it may be because the COMPANY is over-capitalized, or it may be because the company has lost capital (that is to say, it is necessary to eliminate a very large trading loss). This is more of a REORGANIZATION (▷ COMPANIES: RECONSTRUCTIONS,

REORGANIZATIONS, AND AMALGAMATIONS). Where reduction of capital involves a return to shareholders, or a reduction in UNCALLED CAPITAL, the court will insist on an inquiry into the debts and liabilities of the company. It will settle a list of CREDITORS – all these must consent or be paid off.

Where there is no return to shareholders or no reduction in liability, there will be no inquiry. This type of situation arises when capital is lost irretrievably: the shares may be nominally of £100 each but represented by ASSETS of only £10 each. It may be possible to make a profit on these assets and the company may wish to write off the lost capital by reducing capital from £100 to £10. Creditors may not be affected but the rights of members *inter se* may be altered. The court must approve the scheme but the creditors need not.

Where capital is diminished by writing off uncalled capital an ORDINARY RESOLUTION is sufficient provided the articles do not require some other type of resolution.

A forfeiture of shares is, strictly, a reduction of capital and is in fact the only type for which court sanction is not required.

Company. A body corporate, whose regulation is governed by one of the various Companies Acts, reduced effectively to the Companies Acts 1948 and 1967. In popular usage it is a company with a share capital. COMPANIES may be created by royal charter, by a specific act of parliament, or may be registered with the Registrar of Companies under one of the various Companies Acts, particularly the Act of 1948. ◊ CHARTERED COMPANIES ◊ STATUTORY COMPANIES.

Certain organizations must be registered under the Building Society Acts 1874, 1894, and 1939, the Industrial and Provident Society Acts 1893–5 and 1913. These are not strictly companies but are often called such. There are also ◊ COST BOOK MINING COMPANIES, and there used to be ◊ UNINCORPORATED COMPANIES.

In the case of companies dealt with under the 1948 Act, the liability of members may be limited by shares, or by guarantee, or may be unlimited. ◊ COMPANY LIMITED BY SHARES ◊ UNLIMITED COMPANY.

Companies may also be ◊ PUBLIC COMPANIES or ◊ PRIVATE COMPANIES.

In partnerships the word company is often used to describe the firm, e.g. Bloggs & Company. Where the word 'Limited' does not appear, the organization is not a company in the legal sense. The phrase 'one man company' is often used to describe a private company, where control is effectively in the hands of one person. In fact there must be more than one member.

Company Accountants, Institute of. This was founded in 1928, incorporated in 1929, and is a company LIMITED by GUARANTEE. Its object is to advance the interests of ACCOUNTANTS engaged in industry, commerce, banking and trade. There are over 5,000 members, admitted by examination, or at present sometimes by experience. A member is either an Associate (A.I.A.C.) or a Fellow (F.I.A.C.). Company accountants are not qualified at the moment to AUDIT the accounts of PUBLIC COMPANIES by reason of their membership of the Institute. Publications include the bi-monthly *The Company Accountant*. Address: 11 Portland Road, Edgbaston, Birmingham.

Company, borrowing powers of. These are set out in the MEMORANDUM OF ASSOCIATION of each COMPANY. If they are exceeded the loan is ULTRA VIRES and any SECURITIES given are void. The lenders' remedies are: (1) to have the money returned if the company has not spent it, (2) to sue the DIRECTORS for BREACH OF WARRANTY OF AUTHORITY, (3) to claim SUBROGATION where the money has been used to pay off debts enforceable against the company.

All trading companies have implied power to borrow and to pledge the property of the company. TABLE A provides that a company cannot borrow more than its issued NOMINAL CAPITAL.

Company: change of name. This may take place *inter alia*: (1) by SPECIAL RESOLUTION with Board of Trade consent, (2) at the Board of Trade's direction, (3) where the name is considered undesirable. The change does not affect proceedings pending in the old name.

Company, exempt private. A form of PRIVATE COMPANY abolished by the Companies Act 1967. It observed the following conditions: (1) no COMPANY or other body corporate could be the holder of any SHARES or DEBENTURES, (2) no person other than the holder could have any interest in any of the company's shares or debentures, (3) the number of persons holding debentures had to be fifty or less, (4) no company or other body corporate could be a DIRECTOR of the company, and there could be no agreement, whereby the policy of the company could be determined by persons other than directors, MEMBERS, and debenture holders or TRUSTEES for debenture holders.

Condition (1) did not apply where the holder was an exempt private company and the total membership of both companies did not exceed fifty, excluding employees, nor did it apply to shares, for example, registered in the name of, say, a BANK as a nominee. An exempt private company had certain privileges, apart from those of a private company. *Inter alia* (1) it was exempt from filing an annual BALANCE SHEET and PROFIT AND LOSS ACCOUNT, (2) it could make loans to directors, (3) the books might be audited by a partner or employee of a servant or OFFICER OF THE COMPANY, or by unqualified persons, (4) it was exempt from filing *printed* copies of certain resolutions or agreements.

Company, formation of. Anyone wishing to form a new COMPANY must file certain specified documents with the Registrar of Companies: (1) the MEMORANDUM OF ASSOCIATION, (2) the ARTICLES OF ASSOCIATION, (3) a list of the persons who have consented to become DIRECTORS, (4) written consent of the directors to act, (5) a statutory declaration that the requirements of the Companies Act have been complied with, (6) notice of the situation of the REGISTERED OFFICE, (7) particulars of directors and SECRETARY. [(3) and (4) not required for PRIVATE COMPANIES.] Certain fees and duties must be paid before the Registrar will issue a certificate. If the company is a PUBLIC COMPANY certain other conditions must be fulfilled before it can commence business.

Company limited by shares. This is the commonest type of company in existence in this country. They have a ◊ SHARE CAPITAL stated in the MEMORANDUM OF ASSOCIATION – not all of this may have been issued. For the formation of these companies ◊ COMPANY, FORMATION OF. Most large trading organizations are companies limited by shares. They may be ◊ PUBLIC or ◊ PRIVATE COMPANIES (there used also to be ◊ EXEMPT PRIVATE COMPANIES).

The principal characteristics of a company limited by shares are (1) that each is a separate 'legal *persona*' (i.e. can CONTRACT as a person separate from its members), and (2) that the liability of the members is limited to the nominal value of the SHARES they have taken up.

Company, name of. A COMPANY may have any name provided that the BOARD OF TRADE does not think it undesirable. The last word must be 'Limited' except in the case of certain non-profit-making companies formed to promote the arts, science, etc. The name must be fixed or painted outside every office or place of business and must be conspicuous and easily legible. It must also appear on all business letters, notices, CHEQUES, advertisements, bills, etc. If the word 'Limited' is omitted the consequences could be serious. The Registration of Business Names Act 1916 applies to any company carrying on business under a name not its corporate name. The names of DIRECTORS must also appear on catalogues, circulars, etc.

Undesirable names are those too much like those of other companies. At one time words like 'royal' and 'imperial' were prohibited. They may still be disallowed by the Board of Trade.

⟡ COMPANY: CHANGE OF NAME.

Company, objects of. The objects of a COMPANY must be stated in its MEMORANDUM OF ASSOCIATION. Anything inconsistent with these objects would be ULTRA VIRES. For this reason the powers or objects of the company tend to be stated in very broad terms.

If the main object of the company disappears, the company may be wound up. Objects must not be illegal. Objects or powers may be changed by altering the memorandum by SPECIAL RESOLUTION. This alteration must be to enable the company to achieve its objects more effectively, to carry on some other business that can be conveniently combined with its own, to restrict or abandon some of its objects, to sell the business, or to amalgamate with another company. Application to the court to have the alteration cancelled may be made by holders of at least 15 per cent of issued SHARE CAPITAL, or DEBENTURES, or any class of these. The application must be made within twenty-one days of the resolution. The court may confirm or cancel the alteration or may order the interests of the objectors to be purchased. Whatever the alteration, the court can do nothing if application is not made within the specified time. No alteration can be made which increases the liability of any member.

Company, private. About 97 per cent of the limited COMPANIES registered in Great Britain are private companies. A private company is one which restricts the right to transfer its SHARES, limits its members to fifty (but has a minimum of two), and cannot invite the public to subscribe for shares. It has certain legal privileges, but these are not of great consequence and the tendency today is towards removing them. There used to be ⟡ EXEMPT PRIVATE COMPANIES, with further privileges, but these have been abolished.

Company, public. All COMPANIES registered as companies under the Companies Act 1948 are public companies, unless they satisfy the conditions necessary to constitute them. ⟡ PRIVATE COMPANIES.

Company: purchase of own shares. A COMPANY cannot be a member of itself, neither can a SUBSIDIARY COMPANY hold SHARES in a holding company. Difficulties arise when shares are held by a company which is acquired. They may continue to be held but have no votings rights. A company cannot lend money to finance the purchase of its own shares, though a person may hold shares as TRUSTEE for the company provided none of the company's funds are used in acquiring them.

Company seal. Every limited COMPANY must have a common seal, which must be affixed to certain documents. The company must keep a seal book recording details of all these documents.

Company secretary. The person concerned with keeping the COMPANY's statutory books and generally supervising the administration of its affairs. *Inter alia* he keeps the minute books for board and company meetings, maintains the SHARE REGISTER, sees to payment of DIVIDENDS, INTEREST, etc. It is a position of particular responsibility and perhaps one of the senior positions in a company. The company must keep details of the Secretary in the REGISTER OF DIRECTORS. In some companies the legal duties of the Secretary are performed by an outside organization specializing in this form of work (that is of course keeping the books and not administrating the business).

Company, statutory. These were COMPANIES needing specific powers (for instance to purchase land). They were intended to develop communications such as railways, roads, or canals, or to provide services such as gas, water, or electricity. They were set up and governed by special act of parliament. SHARES were normally only transferable by DEED.

Most of these companies have now been nationalized.

Company, unincorporated. These can no longer be formed. They took the form of large PARTNERSHIPS with transferable SHARES. They were governed by Deed of Settlement between shareholders and TRUSTEES. They had UNLIMITED LIABILITY. A COMPANY formed in such a way can register under the Companies Act as an UNLIMITED COMPANY, substituting a MEMORANDUM OF ASSOCIATION and ARTICLES OF ASSOCIATION for the Deed of Settlement.

Company: winding-up. A COMPANY may be wound up but cannot be made bankrupt. Winding-up may be (1) voluntary, (2) by the court, (3) voluntary but under supervision of the court.

Company: winding-up by a court. A company may be wound up by a court where (1) it passes a SPECIAL RESOLUTION, (2) it has not carried on business for a year and there is no indication that it is to continue, (3) it does not commence business within a year of incorporation, (4) there is a default in delivering the STATUTORY REPORT or in holding the STATUTORY MEETING, (5) the number of MEMBERS falls below the minimum, (6) the company is unable to pay its debts (a company cannot pay its debts when (a) a CREDITOR for £50 or more has served on the company a demand for payment and the debt is not paid in three weeks, (b) an execution or judgment

101

remains unsatisfied, (c) the court is satisfied the company cannot pay its debts, (7) the court considers it just and equitable that the company be wound up because, for instance, the sub-stratum has gone, or the company is a bubble or the members are reduced to two who cannot agree and are unable to carry on business amicably.

Company's liquidation account. When a COMPANY is dissolved and monies are left with the LIQUIDATOR (because DIVIDENDS have been unclaimed, etc., for more than six months) these monies must be paid into the company's liquidation account at the BANK OF ENGLAND.

Compensating errors. A book-keeping term for two separate errors, one on the DEBIT side and one on the credit side, which happen to cancel each other out.

Compensation for loss of office. A sum of money given to a DIRECTOR on his leaving a COMPANY. It is often given in addition to, or in lieu of, a retirement pension, but more frequently is in effect a REDUNDANCY PAYMENT following a change of ownership, when a new board of directors is being substituted for the old. These amounts must be shown separately in the accounts of limited companies. They are often very high, particularly if the director was also an important shareholder and is retiring. Because the size of the figure very often seems to bear no relation to the actual loss suffered or work done, these payments have become known as 'golden handshakes'.

Compound interest. INTEREST calculated on an accumulating CAPITAL (original capital plus interest already credited).

Compounding with creditors. ◊ DEEDS OF ARRANGEMENT.

Comptometer. ◊ ADDING MACHINE.

Compulsory winding-up. ◊ WINDING-UP, COMPULSORY.

Condition. A term in a CONTRACT, failure to fulfil which allows the other party to repudiate. It must be a statement of fact. Conditions should be distinguished from ◊ WARRANTIES. ◊ CONDITION SUBSEQUENT ◊ CONDITION PRECEDENT.

Condition precedent. A condition which must be fulfilled before an obligation shall arise.

Condition subsequent. A condition which if not fulfilled cancels an obligation or liability.

Conditional order. An order given to a banker to pay a certain amount provided a RECEIPT is completed.

Conditional sale agreement. Defined in law as 'an agreement for the SALE OF GOODS under which the purchase price or part of it is payable by instalments, and the property in the goods is to remain in the seller (notwithstanding that the buyer is to be in possession of the goods) until such conditions as to the payment of instalments or otherwise as may be specified in the agreement, are fulfilled'. These agreements are governed by the ◊ HIRE PURCHASE ACT 1965 where the purchase price does not exceed £2,000. ◊ HIRE PURCHASE ◊ HIRE PURCHASE: CONDITIONS AND WARRANTIES.

Confederation of British Industry. This was formed in August 1965 by a MERGER of the National Association of British Manufacturers with the British Employers Confederation and the Federation of British Industry. The aim was to present one face to the public on questions of labour relations, taxation, technical legislation, industrial training, management, education, public purchasing, overseas trade policy, etc. It has regional and local councils, headed by the Confederation of British Industry Council, which has monthly meetings. It is politically neutral, but represents industry in dealings with the government and attempts both to respond to and to stimulate government action, often advising on policy and legislation. It is sometimes called the employers' Trades Union Congress. In its own words it is 'not a sinister pressure group dominated by top tycoons who meet clandestinely to manipulate the reins of power, essentially a democratic organization – draws its strength from the grass roots of industry, from firms of all shapes and sizes, in all kinds of manufacturing enterprise, in consultation with them and with their trade associations, puts forward views and policies not only in their interest, but also in what it feels to be the national interest'. Membership includes manufacturing firms, trade associations, employer organizations and commercial associations – not only large COMPANIES. Regional councils deal with local industrial problems. Experts are employed to give free advice to members on all matters connected with industry, including taxation, rating and valuation, company and mercantile law, town and country planning, fuel economy, clean air and noise abatement and trade effluent disposal. Also, in the export field, advice on markets, distribution, AGENTS, customers, TARIFFS, etc.

Membership is open to all companies engaged in productive or manufacturing industy in Great Britain, or in construction and transport, and to national employers' federations, national trade associations, etc. Associate membership is open to nationalized industries and commercial associations. Subscriptions vary according to the number of persons employed in the member firm: e.g. £12 for up to twenty-five people, £4,400 for 100,000 people. Publications are: the fortnightly *British Industry* and *C.B.I. Overseas Trade Bulletin*, the quarterly *C.B.I. Education and Training Bulletin*, the half-yearly *Fanfare for Britain*, and the annual *Fuel Economy*. Address: 21 Tothill Street, London SW1.

Conference lines. Ship-owning lines in the same trade working together to offer a standard charge to shippers.

Confidence trick. ◊ CON-MAN.

Confirmed credit. ◊ CONFIRMING HOUSE.

Confirming house. A form of EXPORT HOUSE acting for overseas buyers. The buyer uses the confirming house as a U.K. office. The house places an order with a U.K. exporter and to all intents and purposes becomes the buyer from the point of view of the exporter. The advantages to the exporter are: (1) that he has a CONTRACT enforceable in his own country, (2) that he is paid promptly in his own currency, (3) that the confirming house GUARANTEES payment and often finances the buyer, (4) that dispatch and documentation is facilitated, (5) that advice is obtainable on conditions in overseas markets, and (6) that help is given in finding overseas AGENTS, etc. Advantages to the buyer are: (1) that credit is made available on a flexible basis, (2) that the confirming house will negotiate best prices, (3) that information is supplied on local trade conditions, (4) that the confirming house ensures that GOODS are supplied promptly, (5) that shipment, INSURANCE, etc., of goods is supervised, (6) that the best rates of FREIGHT are obtained.

◊ BRITISH EXPORT HOUSES ASSOCIATION.

Conflict of law. In CONTRACT, difficulties sometimes arise as to which particular law applies, where more than one country is concerned. As a general rule, the law of the country where the contract is to be performed will apply, though the intentions of the parties as expressed in the contract are relevant. There are various supplementary provisions. For instance, one country may not enforce a contract valid according to its own law but illegal in the place where it is to be carried out.

Conjunction ticket. A term used in transport for two tickets issued simultaneously and constituting one CONTRACT of carriage.

Con-man. Short for 'confidence-trick man', this is a slang expression for a person whose ambition is to sell as little as possible for as much as he can get. He does this by creating quite unreasonable confidence in his honesty and integrity. This happens at all levels of business.

Consideration. If a CONTRACT other than a CONTRACT BY DEED is to be binding, the promise of the one party must be supported by the agreement of the other party to do or not do some act, or to pay some money. The agreement by the other party is known as the consideration.

This consideration, to be effective, must have some VALUE, i.e. it must be capable of being valued in monetary terms. Valuable consideration has been defined as 'some right, interest, profit or benefit accruing to one party, or some forebearance, detriment, loss or responsibility given, suffered or undertaken by the other'. Two examples: (1) A agrees to sell X to B in return for £10. Both A and B receive something. (Whether X is worth £10 is not always relevant provided both parties act in good faith.) This can be a good contract. (2) A owes B £10. A is a slow payer. B says that if A will pay him the £10 now he will agree to a discount of 5 per cent. This is not a good contract for A already owes the money and has done nothing extra in return for B's promise. A discount offered for payment before the agreed date might create a new contract.

Consignee. ◊ CONSIGNOR.

Consignment note. A shipping term for a note accompanying a consignment of GOODS. This is sometimes an alternative to a ◊ BILL OF LADING.

Consignor. A term used to indicate a person who consigns GOODS to another in a CONTRACT of SALE. The recipient is known as the consignee. In a restricted sense it can mean the person who consigns goods to an AGENT with a view to his selling the goods. The consignor retains the property in the goods until those goods are sold.

Consolidation of capital. This applies to a limited COMPANY. SHARES are consolidated when the SHARE'S NOMINAL VALUE is raised by stating that e.g. thereafter every twenty 1s. shares shall be one £1 share. This may be done by an ORDINARY RESOLUTION at a general MEETING, unless the MEMORANDUM OF ASSOCIATION requires some other form of resolution. SHARE CAPITAL may also be subdivided – the reverse procedure.

Consols. Government consolidated STOCK. This stock is irredeemable. It is issued at various times at various rates of INTEREST. The PRICE varies according to the rate of interest prevailing at the time. In fact, the price of consols is a good indication of current GILT-EDGE interest rates because there is no question of capital repayment to be taken into account. Consols are quoted per £100. That is, if $2\frac{1}{2}$ per cent consols are quoted at fifty, this means that to obtain £100 worth at $2\frac{1}{2}$ per cent it is necessary to pay £50, and the gilt-edged interest rate is therefore 5 per cent, i.e. $2\frac{1}{2}$ over 50.

Constructive industry. That branch of industry concerned with the building and construction of factories, houses, roads, etc.

Constructive total loss. A term used in INSURANCE, particularly

MARINE INSURANCE, where a ship is not completely lost but has been abandoned because the cost of saving it would exceed its VALUE when saved. The insured may treat it as a total loss, or partial loss. In the latter instance he claims for damage done, in the former instance he gives notice of ABANDONMENT and the insurer takes over all rights. ◊ SUBROGATION.

Consulage. ◊ CONSULAR INVOICE.

Consular invoice. When GOODS are exported the importing country may insist that they are accompanied by an INVOICE certified by their own consul in the exporting country. This enables import duties to be correctly charged. The consul will charge a fee known as consulage.

Consumer Association. An independent, non-profit-making organization established in 1956 to help shoppers, by testing GOODS that are on SALE to the public. The goods are obtained anonymously from RETAILERS. It is a COMPANY limited by GUARANTEE and publishes a monthly magazine *Which?* which gives the results of the tests. It also publishes a *Motoring Which?* and various paperbacks including *The Law for Consumers, The Legal Side of Buying a House* and *Buying Secondhand*. It makes recommendations to the government and provides information for use in schools. It is also prepared to send speakers. Address: 14 Buckingham Street, London WC2.

Consumer Council.* A council of twelve people set up by the government in 1963 as a result of the *Moloney Report*, and supported by the BOARD OF TRADE. Its object is to afford greater protection for the public as consumers by informing itself about consumer problems and matters affecting consumer interest, considering action necessary to deal with these problems, promoting this action, providing advice to the consumer, and publishing an annual report. The Council does not test products, nor does it deal with complaints, or institute proceedings. It claims that it keeps in touch with problems of consumers through information from many sources including local consumer groups, citizens' advice bureaux, trade associations, manufacturers, RETAILERS, the press, and also the public (the last through letters or field surveys). Contacts are maintained with organizations such as the BRITISH STANDARDS INSTITUTION, ADVERTISING STANDARDS AUTHORITY, the NATIONAL COUNCIL FOR QUALITY AND RELIABILITY. It promotes legislation where necessary and will make direct approaches to suppliers. It makes its views known to the press, broadcasting services, television and radio, through films which it lets out, exhibitions, and various publications

* To be disbanded.

including a monthly magazine, *Focus*, available at bookshops. Other publications available from Her Majesty's Stationery Office are the booklets: *About Shopping, About Buying Furniture, About Buying Toys, About Buying Food and Drink, About Credit, About Buying School Uniform.* Address: 3 Cornwall Terrace, London NW1.

Contango rate. ◊ ACCOUNT DAYS.

Contingent liabilities. An accounting term for liabilities that may or may not arise, i.e. a debt contingent on an uncertain event.

Continuation clause. A MARINE INSURANCE clause covering situations where a ship is still at sea when its INSURANCE runs out. The insurer agrees to cover risks at a PRO RATA rate of premium.

Continuous stock-taking. ◊ PERPETUAL INVENTORY.

Contract. An agreement between two or more persons which is legally enforceable provided certain conditions are observed. It normally takes the form of one person's promise to do something in ◊ CONSIDERATION of the other's agreeing to do or suffer something else in return. There are also certain special forms of contract known as ◊ CONTRACTS OF RECORD.

Contract, ambiguity in. Where a CONTRACT is in writing, or needs to be evidenced in writing, and there is ambiguity, the court may allow oral evidence to determine the intentions of the parties. So far as oral contracts are concerned, ambiguity is more likely to arise from MISTAKE or MISREPRESENTATION.

Contract, anticipatory breach of. This happens when one party to a CONTRACT announces in advance that he does not intend to perform his part. The other party may then sue immediately for anticipatory breach or he may refrain from taking action and wait until the contract date. If he does this he may fail to recover anything if, by that time, the contract has become impossible through the fault of neither party, i.e. has been frustrated.

Contract, breach of. The failure by one party to a CONTRACT to perform his part. Breach may be: (1) by renunciation: one party may state that he has no intention of doing what he said he would do, (2) by making performance impossible, (3) by a mere failure to perform the agreed part. Whatever form the breach takes, the aggrieved party has various rights of action. He may sue for ◊ DAMAGES, or may apply to the court for ◊ SPECIFIC PERFORMANCE. Where a contract is only partially performed then if the plaintiff has accepted the part performance he must pay for it though he may be able to claim on any balance due. He cannot be made to accept part performance only. Similarly, when the contract is only partly performed and the part-performance is expressly or

Contract by deed

implicitly accepted, the part-performer may sue for work done ◊ QUANTUM MERUIT.

Contract by deed. Certain contracts are not binding unless made by deed. These are: (1) gratuitous promises, (2) transfers of SHARES in statutory COMPANIES (3) transfers of British ships or shares in them, (4) conditional BILLS OF SALE, (5) legal MORTGAGES of land or an interest therein, (6) certain leases of lands, tenements or hereditaments for more than three years.

Contract, continuous. A CONTRACT where agreement is not restricted to one transaction, but applies to a number of contracts during a period of time, as in a contract of PARTNERSHIP.

Contract, drunkard's. A drunkard can avoid CONTRACTS if the other party knew of his condition. He must, however, pay for NECESSARIES supplied to him.

Contract evidenced in writing. Certain CONTRACTS although valid are unenforceable unless evidenced in writing. These are (1) contracts of GUARANTEE, and (2) contracts for the SALE or other disposition of land or interest in land. The memorandum in writing must usually state the names of the parties and the subject matter of the contract. It must be signed by the party to be charged. The terms of the contract should be stated. The CONSIDERATION should be shown when the contract is in category (2). Various documents can be put together, e.g. letters and envelopes to provide the necessary writing in bringing the action and parole evidence may be admitted to connect them.

Contract for differences. STOCK EXCHANGE transactions are controlled by the normal rules of CONTRACT. Contracts for differences on the Stock Exchange come into a slightly different category. There is no deliberate intention to take or sell STOCKS and SHARES – the investor buys and sells on the same account, receiving or paying the difference. These are known as dealings in differences and are, strictly speaking, wagers, so are governed by the rules relating to ◊ WAGERING CONTRACTS.

Contract, gaming. A CONTRACT where two persons stand to win or lose as the result of a game. These contracts are void, some were even illegal. However, certain forms of gaming have now been made legal by the Betting, Gaming and Lotteries Act 1963. Gaming is not illegal providing the provisions of this Act are followed, though gaming contracts are still void.

Contract, illegal. A CONTRACT formed for an illegal purpose, or one declared illegal by statute, such as (1) a GAMING CONTRACT which does not fulfil the conditions of the Betting, Gaming, and Lotteries Act 1963 (all gaming contracts are void if not illegal), (2) agreements to commit an indictable offence or civil wrong. (3) agreements against the national interest, (4) agreements to defraud the Inland Revenue, (5) agreements to pervert the cause of justice, (6) agreements involving MAINTENANCE or CHAMPERTY, (7) agreements of an immoral character. Illegal contracts are void *ab initio*. If both parties are equally at fault, neither can sue the other. Money or property can be recovered however (1) by an innocent party from a guilty party, (2) before performance or FRUSTRATION, (3) if the illegality is not revealed.

Contract in writing. Certain CONTRACTS must be in writing if they are to be valid. These are: (1) BILLS OF EXCHANGE and PROMISSORY NOTES, (2) ASSIGNMENTS of copyrights, (3) contracts of MARINE INSURANCE, (4) transfers of company SHARES, (5) HIRE PURCHASE, CREDIT SALE AGREEMENTS, and CONDITIONAL SALE AGREEMENTS under the Hire Purchase Act 1965. In the last instance the contract is valid but normally unenforceable.

Contract, infant's. Generally speaking an infant, that is, a person under twenty-one, cannot make CONTRACTS enforceable against him, except contracts for necessaries ('GOODS suitable to the infant's condition in life and to his actual requirements at the time of sale or delivery'), or beneficial contracts of service (e.g. contracts for apprenticeship). In addition, the Infant's Relief Act 1874 provides that all contracts made by an infant (1) for repayment of money lent or to be lent, (2) for goods, other than necessaries supplied or to be supplied, (3) for ACCOUNTS STATED, are absolutely void. Although an infant cannot be sued on contracts generally, he will find it difficult to bring an action himself where he has obtained some benefit. Generally speaking an infant cannot ratify on coming of age a contract made in infancy; there must be a new contract. There may be an exception where the contract is a continuing business contract (e.g. a PARTNERSHIP) which the infant does not repudiate within a reasonable time of coming of age. If he continues to act as a party to the contract he may be held liable on it, but only for the period since his coming of age.

A person legally comes of age on the day before his twenty-first birthday.

Contract note. A note issued by a STOCKBROKER as evidence of a transaction to buy or sell SHARES. It is a legal document setting out details of: (1) the number of SHARES or amount of STOCK bought or sold, (2) the COMPANY involved, (3) the PRICE, (4) the CONSIDERATION, (5) the broker's COMMISSION (about 3d. in the pound). The note must be stamped – 1 per cent of the consideration.

This is the transfer stamp. There is also a CONTRACT stamp at an AD VALOREM rate. The note must also show the amount payable to or from the broker and the date of settlement. It should be retained for CAPITAL GAINS TAX purposes. Contract notes are often referred to as bought notes or sold notes.

Contract of affreightment. A CONTRACT made by a shipper with a ship-owner for the carriage of GOODS by sea.

Contract: of married women. A married woman may now CONTRACT quite freely, as though she were single. At one time in COMMON LAW the husband and wife were one person, the husband being that person. The wife was not allowed to contract on her own account. This was true until the late nineteenth century. ⟡ NECESSARIES.

Contract of novation. Rights and liabilities in CONTRACT may be transferred by the substitution of a new contract for the old (with the consent of all the parties affected). This contract is known as a contract of novation. It is common in PARTNERSHIPS where one partner is introduced in place of another.

Contract of personal service. Certain types of CONTRACT of employment are of a personal nature: they can only be performed by the person's agreeing to do so. If the person is unable to act the contract becomes impossible and DAMAGES may accrue depending on whether or not the responsibility was or was not the fault of the person concerned. Distinguish from contracts where delegation is possible. A builder may subcontract work but an artist generally cannot.

Contract of record. This is not a CONTRACT in the normal sense of the word, but takes the form of, e.g. a court order where one person is obliged to perform some act such as payment of maintenance. The obligation is entered in the records of a superior court and is binding for this reason – it does not depend on the consent of the parties.

Contract, parole. A simple CONTRACT which is not in writing, though of course the absence of writing may make it difficult to enforce, because absence of writing may mean absence of evidence.

Contract, privity of. Rights and obligations generally attach only to parties to the CONTRACT. An outsider has no right to claim unless he is, for example, a beneficiary under a trust, a third party in a motor INSURANCE policy, or a supplier of GOODS who may enforce prices subject to the Resale Prices Act 1964.
⟡ NEGLIGENCE OF AUDITOR.

Contract, speciality. A CONTRACT IN WRITING in the form of a DEED, signed, sealed and delivered. Delivery has a particular meaning – at present the promissor has to touch the seal saying 'I deliver this as my act and deed.' No CONSIDERATION is necessary and the ESTOPPEL rule applies. Nevertheless, EQUITY will not allow SPECIFIC PERFORMANCE where there has been no consideration.

Contract: substantial performance. Where a CONTRACT is breached because one party has not completed his part, the court will not allow the plaintiff to consider himself completely discharged from his obligations. Where there is substantial performance, the other party must pay up and sue for damages for the amount by which the work is badly done. For example if A asks B to build him a house and B builds the house but paints one or two walls a colour not in the contract, A cannot say that B has not performed the contract and that therefore he need not pay for the house. The court would say the contract was substantially performed and A can only sue for any damage on the additional cost of changing the colour scheme. There may also be a question of a QUANTUM MERUIT claim where a contract is frustrated. ⟡ FRUSTRATION OF CONTRACT.

Contract, trade union. The position is somewhat anomalous. Where the union is registered under the Trade Union Acts 1871–6, it is governed by certain rules applicable to corporate bodies. It can sue and be sued in its own name. However, it has not yet been decided whether a union is a legal *persona* distinct from its members or an association of individuals who can appear in a collective name. It may be sued for BREACH OF CONTRACT both by persons outside the union and by its own members.

Contract, void. A CONTRACT which in fact never existed, for example where there is a fundamental mistake on both sides as to the subject matter or the identity of the parties. No action can be taken on a void contract.

Contract, voidable. A CONTRACT voidable at the action of one of the parties to it. For example, if A is persuaded to contract with B on the basis of a misrepresentation made by B, then A may avoid the contract.

Contributory. A person liable to contribute towards the debts of a COMPANY on WINDING-UP. This might be a MEMBER OF A COMPANY holding fully-paid SHARES, though strictly speaking these cannot be called on to pay anything further.

Lists of contributories distinguish between those liable personally and those liable through representing some other person. There are A and B lists. The A list shows present members; the B list, past members. A past member is not liable: (1) if he ceased to be a member a year or more before the commencement of the winding-up, (2) for debts incurred after he has ceased to be a member. Otherwise he is liable for debts incurred while he was still a member, when the other members fail to pay.

Contribution. A term used in INSURANCE when one insurance company claims contribution from another in settling a claim. This frequently happens in MARINE INSURANCE, and may also happen in other policies where the insured is dealing with two separate companies for the same property. A person cannot obtain more than the VALUE of the property by insuring twice: each company will pay a proportion of the claim. ⟫ OVER-INSURANCE.

Control accounts. An accounting term for accounts showing total trade debtors and total TRADE CREDITORS. When INVOICES or cash receipts are posted to individual accounts, the total for the day is entered in the control account. The balance on the control account should therefore always equal the total of the individual balances on the personal accounts.

Controller. Usually the person financially in charge of a business.

Convertible loan stock. Occasionally COMPANIES issue loan stock, with a right to convert this stock into ORDINARY SHARES or PREFERENCE SHARES at some stated time in the future. This is known as convertible loan stock. The term is also applied to stock issued by the government, which the holder has the right to convert into new stock instead of, or rather than, obtaining repayment.

Copyright: assignment of. A CONTRACT that must be in writing. ◊ CONTRACTS IN WRITING.

Copy typist. A person trained to use a typewriter, and typing from manuscripts or printed matter but not from SHORTHAND.

Corn Exchange. The London Corn Exchange is situated in Mark Lane, London EC3. It has been there for over 200 years. It is the most important cereal market in the United Kingdom, and is open daily, but the most important market day is Monday. Business is mainly done by SAMPLES. Members include millers, merchants, manufacturers, brewers, etc. There is also a well known corn exchange at Liverpool where dealings in FUTURES take place (these are made possible by the storage facilities available in the area).

Cornering the market. A person corners a market when he obtains a virtual MONOPOLY over particular GOODS or services. He is then able to name his own PRICE. In the past this sometimes happened to the market in raw materials. Markets may be cornered for a short term: a person may make a fortune by controlling the supply of a particular raw material for a particular period. The possibilities are now somewhat restricted by state intervention. ◊ MONOPOLIES COMMISSION ◊ ANTI-TRUST LAWS.

Corporation. An association of persons recognized by the law as having a collective personality. The corporation can act as if it were distinct from its members: it has 'perpetual succession' and a common seal. It can therefore CONTRACT quite freely – it can also be fined, but it obviously cannot be sent to prison or incur penalties which can only be applied to individuals. Corporations are either ◊ CORPORATIONS SOLE or ◊ CORPORATIONS AGGREGATE.

Corporation aggregate. A corporation consisting of a number of individuals: the opposite of a ◊ CORPORATION SOLE. The most common forms of corporation aggregate are local councils and limited COMPANIES.

Corporation sole. A CORPORATION of which there is only one member. It is a public office, such as a bishop's, the reigning monarch's. When these persons CONTRACT in their official capacity they incur no personal liability, and successive holders of the office will be bound.

Corporation tax. A straight percentage levy on profits of all COMPANIES in place of income and profits tax. It applies to all bodies corporate or unincorporated associations, but not to PARTNERSHIPS. INCOME TAX remains payable on DIVIDENDS distributed. Assessments for accounting periods, e.g. the accounting year ending 31 December, are taxed at one rate till 5 April and at another from 5 April to 31 December. Losses may be carried forward, including previous income tax losses. The tax was introduced in 1965; its present rate is 40 per cent.

Cost accountant. Often called management accountant, this is a person employed in industry to provide and maintain a continuous and up-to-the-minute check and control over every form of expenditure. He ascertains the cost of the products, processes, and various operations of a business, and provides information for the guidance of the management, particularly on cost control and SELLING PRICES. There are also consulting cost accountants who work privately and are employed for specific purposes.

Cost and freight (C.F.). A kind of foreign trade contract, which is similar to a COST, INSURANCE, AND FREIGHT contract, except that the importer looks after the INSURANCE. The seller must give the buyer sufficient notice to enable him to do this.

Cost and Works Accountants, Institute of. This was set up with the objects of (1) promoting scientific methods in cost and works accounting, (2) providing a professional organization, establishing certain minimum standards of skill and knowledge in members and issuing the relevant certificates, (3) assisting with education, (4) exercising professional supervision over members, (5) holding

113

conferences and meetings for discussion and (6) collecting and publishing information helpful to members. Members may be Associates or Fellows. Associates must be twenty-one with three years' practical experience and must have passed, or been exempted from, various examinations. Fellows must be twenty-six years of age with five years' practical experience at a high level. Associates may use the letters A.C.W.A., and Fellows, F.C.W.A. The institute's publications include the monthly: *Management Accounting*. Address: 63 Portland place, London W1.

Cost book mining companies. COMPANIES formed for working metalliferous mines, or tinstreaming in Devon and Cornwall. These were originally governed by local custom and subject to jurisdiction of the Stanaries Court. Jurisdiction is now vested in the county court of Cornwall at Bodmin. The rules governing them are found in the Stanaries Acts 1869 and 1887.

Cost, insurance and freight (C.I.F.). A term used in foreign trade CONTRACTS where the exporter, in addition to the ⋄ FREE ON BOARD charges, pays the cost of the INSURANCE and the FREIGHT. His price therefore includes all charges up to the port of delivery. He must supply the buyer with the documents necessary to take delivery of the GOODS on arrival. These documents are normally: a BILL OF LADING, an INSURANCE policy (not a cover note), and an INVOICE. The seller may not actually pay the freight but is responsible for it and if the buyer is to pay for any part of it this will be shown as a credit on the invoice. The goods are usually at the buyer's RISK after shipment. He must pay when the documents are tendered whether or not, (1) the goods actually arrive, (2) they have been lost en route, (3) he has had any opportunity of examining them. Property will pass when the documents are accepted by the buyer. Payment is often made by accepting a BILL OF EXCHANGE. The buyer can always reject the goods if they are not as described in the CONTRACT.

Cost, insurance, freight, and interest (C.I.F.I.). A type of foreign trade CONTRACT. It is similar to ⋄ COST, INSURANCE AND FREIGHT except that the exporter also pays INTEREST on the VALUE of the GOODS. This may be for the benefit of some middle man acting for the importer.

Cost price. A vague term normally used for the amount paid by a middle man or manufacturer for the GOODS he proposes to sell.

Costing. ⋄ COST ACCOUNTANT.

Council for Small Industries in Rural Areas. Previously the Rural Industries Loan Fund, it makes treasury loans available in specified rural areas of Great Britain or towns with a population of less than 10,000, to manufacturing and service industries (agriculture, horticulture, and retail trades excluded). The industries must employ less than twenty skilled workers. The loans will be up to 80 per cent of cost, and up to £20,000. Repayment terms vary. For conditions apply to: Victoria House, London Road, North Cheam, Surrey. The Council has also taken over the functions of the RURAL INDUSTRIES BUREAU.

Council of Industrial Design. This was set up in 1944 by the coalition government to draw industry's attention to the importance of good design for Britain's export trade 'and to promote by all practical means, the improvement of design in the products of British Industry'. An advisory and promotional organization, it does no designing itself nor has it power to ban bad design. It deals with all aspects of industrial design: durable consumer GOODS, capital goods, street furniture, prefabricated farm buildings, graphic design, etc. It encourages the manufacturer to make well-designed goods, distributors to stock them, and consumers to buy them. It is government aided, and also earns money from services given to industry, etc., and from the sale of publications. Members of the Council are not paid and are appointed by the BOARD OF TRADE. A record of designers is kept for the benefit of manufacturers wishing to be put in touch with reputable designers. The Council's monthly magazine *Design* is read in more than eighty countries. The Council runs the ⟡ DESIGN CENTRE and organizes Design Centre exhibitions in provincial centres and keeps a Design Index, which is a sample record of well-designed modern British consumer goods. Products accepted for the Design Index are eligible to carry a black and white triangular label. The Council co-operates with the CONSUMER COUNCIL, the CONSUMERS ASSOCIATION and Local consumer groups. Address: 28 Haymarket, London SW1. There is a Scottish Committee, with its own Design Centre, at 46 West George Street, Glasgow C2. Various publications and film strips are available on application.

Counterclaim. The claim by a defendant against a plaintiff whereby he hopes to reduce or wipe out the DAMAGES he may have to pay, the claim being one which could give right to a cause of action as opposed to ⟡ SET-OFF.

Coupon. A slip often attached to transferable BONDS, the surrender of which gives right to a DIVIDEND at a particular date. There are normally a number of coupons. A coupon is torn off the coupon sheet each year, or other period.

Courts of arbitration: international trade. These are run by chambers of commerce in London, Manchester and Bradford. They advise on ARBITRATION clauses suitable to particular CONTRACTS and also provide arbitrators when disputes are referred to them.

Cover note. A provisional document issued by an INSURANCE company to bide over the time between the acceptance of a risk and the issuing of a policy.

Credit. ⟡ DEBIT.

Credit cards. There are many forms of credit cards, but they are all meant to obtain credit for the holder in certain circumstances although the party with whom he is dealing is a stranger to him. They are sometimes issued by shops for use in various branches. The customer can obtain credit up to a stated amount. The commonest form is that issued by a BANK. Bank credit cards fall into two basic categories. Firstly, there is the card which states that the bank will honour the CHEQUES of the holder up to the amount stated on the card. The holder's signature and number appears on the card with the name of the bank. The person taking the cheque should see that the signature and number on the cheque agrees with the signature and number on the card. If he does not do so this would be negligence and might relieve the bank from responsibility. The second type of bank credit card is the card which is put into a machine with the INVOICE: the machine imprints details on the invoice, which is then sent to the bank by the CREDITOR. The bank pays, provided the amount is within the limit stated on the card, and either periodically presents the invoices to the customer for payment or debits them to his account. There is a third type of credit card issued by an institution or company which specializes in this type of business. By becoming a member of a particular 'club' one obtains a credit card, similar to those described above and issued by banks, which GUARANTEES payment of a cheque up to a certain amount or payment of an invoice properly signed by the customer, a specimen signature being shown on the card. Two particular advantages of a credit card issued by a bank or recognized credit card company are (1) the holder can rely on his cheque book rather than carry cash about with him as the bank or organization will guarantee payment of the cheque even if the holder is not actually in funds, and (2) a person can obtain cash by presenting his card at almost any well-known bank and making out a cheque within the limit. Naturally credit cards are not issued indiscriminately, but it is not necessary to have an account at the issuing bank provided one can prove one's creditworthiness in some other way. Credit cards are becoming increasingly popular, though are still in their infancy.

Credit insurance. A system operated by INSURANCE companies to help exporters with reference to the risks incidental to foreign trade due to lack of knowledge of the credit-worthiness of customers. The insurance is against commercial risks, but not those concerned with political and exchange transfer risks. These are the province of the ◊ EXPORT CREDITS GUARANTEE DEPARTMENT.

Credit note. A document issued by a VENDOR giving credit to the debtor for, say, GOODS returned, or over-charges made on an INVOICE.

Credit sale agreement. Defined by law as 'an agreement for the SALE OF GOODS under which the PURCHASE PRICE is payable by five or more instalments not being a conditional sale agreement'. These agreements are governed by the ◊ HIRE PURCHASE ACT 1965 when the purchase price is between £30 and £2,000. ◊ HIRE PURCHASE ◊ HIRE PURCHASE: CONDITIONS AND WARRANTIES.

Credit transfer. A method of settling a debt. It is often used by persons or businesses with a great many debts to settle at any one time. A list of the CREDITORS is given to the BANK, together with the amounts due, and the name and address of each creditor's bank. The bank then transfers the amounts due. The debtor then notifies each creditor that the transfer has been made. The obvious advantage of this method is that it saves writing out and signing a great number of CHEQUES.

Creditor. A person to whom money is owed.

Creditors' voluntary winding-up. ◊ WINDING-UP, VOLUNTARY.

Critical path analysis. An OPERATIONAL RESEARCH technique used in management. The idea is to examine a project in detail with the objective of (1) breaking it down into component parts, and (2) examining each part both in isolation and in its relationship to the other parts. By this means it may be seen how the project can be completed in the best possible way in the shortest possible time.

Crofting counties agricultural grant. This is a specialized grant applicable to certain counties in Scotland. Information is obtainable from Department of Agriculture and Fish for Scotland, 53 Church Street, Inverness.
Loans can be obtained to purchase livestock; application should be made to the Secretary, Crofters' Commission, 9 Ardross Terrace, Inverness.

Cross offer. Where two parties make an OFFER simultaneously in a manner that, had one followed as an acceptance, would have comprised a CONTRACT. As an example: A writes to B offering to sell a certain horse for £1,000. B writes to A offering to buy the same horse at the same price. The letters cross in the post. There is no contract.

Crossed cheque. ◊ CROSSING.

Crossing. There are various ways in which a CHEQUE may be crossed: it may have a GENERAL CROSSING, a SPECIAL CROSSING, be crossed 'account payee only', or 'account payee'.

An uncrossed cheque may be crossed by the holder and a general crossing may be made a special crossing. The words 'not negotiable' may be added. Otherwise the crossing should not be interfered with as it is part of the cheque itself. The holder could not uncross a crossed cheque, though the drawer could by writing 'pay cash'. ◊ Other crossing headings.

Crossing: account payee. 'Account payee' is often written across a crossed CHEQUE indicating the cheque should be paid only into the account of the payee. It has no legal force but the collecting banker would probably be adjudged guilty of negligence were he to pay the cheque into any other account. In fact a BANK would normally observe such a crossing.

Crossing, general. Two parallel transverse lines drawn across the CHEQUE. These prevent payment over the counter at the BANK: the holder would have to pay the cheque into an account. It is common to include the words 'and Co.' between the lines but this is quite unnecessary.

Crossing: not negotiable. If a CHEQUE is crossed 'not negotiable' the holder cannot give a better TITLE than that which he possesses. This does not stop the holder from transferring the cheque to another party but that other party cannot get a better title than that possessed by the holder himself. The negotiability of the cheque has in fact ceased – it is no longer a NEGOTIABLE INSTRUMENT. As an example: A draws a cheque. If it is not crossed 'not negotiable' B may steal it and cash it or pass it on to C – A would have no redress. If it was crossed 'not negotiable' B having no title could not give one to the banker or to C and therefore A could recover the money. A cheque is the only type of BILL OF EXCHANGE which can be crossed not negotiable. An ordinary bill, if it is to be not negotiable, must state this on the face of the bill.

Crossing: special. A CHEQUE with a special crossing has the name of a banker stated between the lines, or the name of an account and a bank, such as Blogg's Charities Account, Dimland Bank. The instructions must be followed by the holder and the banker.

'Cum' dividend and 'ex' dividend. When the price of a SHARE is quoted it is quoted 'cum div' or 'ex div'. This indicates that the price includes or does not include, the right to receive the next DIVIDEND.

Quotations are normally 'cum div', i.e. the buyer receives the next dividend. 'Ex div' prices are generally given only for the period (e.g. one month) immediately before the payment of the dividend. When a share goes 'ex div', the price naturally drops rather suddenly.

Cum new. A STOCK EXCHANGE term applied to SHARES when they are offered for sale with the right to any SCRIP ISSUE or RIGHTS ISSUE.

Currency of a bill. A term used with reference to BILLS OF EXCHANGE. It relates to the time between the drawing of a bill and the date it becomes payable. If the bill is payable AFTER SIGHT then the time only runs from the date of acceptance.

Current account. ♢ ACCOUNTS: CURRENT. The term is also used in book-keeping with reference to proprietors' personal accounts which are not their CAPITAL accounts.

Current assets. An accounting term for ASSETS continually turned over in the course of business. They should be distinguished from FIXED ASSETS and other assets bought for permanent use. Examples of current assets are debtors, STOCK, WORK IN PROGRESS, cash and also perhaps investments which are not TRADE INVESTMENTS. The phrase 'net current assets' is often used and refers to the total of current assets less the total of CURRENT LIABILITIES. Another name for this difference is WORKING CAPITAL.

Current liabilities. An accounting term for those monies owed in the near future, usually within the next accounting period. These will include TRADE CREDITORS, current taxation, and DIVIDENDS declared and due. They should be distinguished from long-term liabilities and SHARE CAPITAL or LOAN CAPITAL.

Current ratio. The ratio of CURRENT ASSETS to CURRENT LIABILITIES. This should normally be greater than one. Movements in the ratio are often useful indicators of SOLVENCY, OVER-TRADING, etc., as also is the ♢ LIQUID RATIO.

Current taxation. An accounting term used to describe amounts due to the Inland Revenue in respect of taxation and payable in the near future.

Custom of trade. This phrase generally refers to implied terms in a CONTRACT – terms may be implied by usage or custom in particular trades. Words take on different meanings in different trades. Usage of trade will also be relevant to the interpretation of written CONTRACTS. ♢ ORAL EVIDENCE.

Customs: Airports. Regulations at airports are similar to those at sea-ports, particularly in the case of stores. Commanders of aircraft arriving from or leaving for abroad must use, except in emergency,

Customs airports, and declare cargo carried inwards and outwards. There are facilities for clearing goods from the airports before the entry of the goods is passed and the duty paid. A 'provisional' entry is made and the importer leaves a sizeable cash deposit with the Customs authorities. Airports often have a duty-free shop for the convenience of departing passengers. Goods are sold here free of duty and are controlled by Customs officials.

Customs and Excise. ⟡ HER MAJESTY'S CUSTOMS AND EXCISE.

Customs bills of entry. Daily lists published by the Customs and Excise Authorities, which deal with British shipping leaving and entering the country, and give details of cargo and ports. *Bill A* deals with ships generally, *Bill B* with the Port of London.

Customs: crews' effects. The Preventive Officer checks all GOODS obtained abroad or during the voyage: forbidden imports are confiscated. A limited amount of duty-free goods is allowed in, and the remainder are either taxed or put in BOND until the ship leaves again.

Customs debenture. ⟡ ENTREPÔT TRADE.

Customs entry. ⟡ CUSTOMS: FINAL CLEARANCE INWARDS AND ENTRY OUTWARDS.

Customs: final clearance inwards and entry outwards. ⟡ RUMMAGING continues during the landing of a ship's cargo and again when all cargo is landed. The captain then receives a clearance inward certificate. He will need to present this before his next voyage. If the next voyage is outwards he must enter his ship 'outwards' at the Customs House.

Customs: land boundary. There are special regulations relating to persons bringing GOODS across the Irish land boundary. A carrier must make a report of goods carried. Before exporting goods to the Republic of Ireland it is necessary to present a 'carrier's MANIFEST'.

Customs: landing cargo. The landing of cargo is supervised. A Customs officer insures that all cargo landed is declared and that nothing declared has not been landed. Cargo is also examined: this is done on a selective basis. The importer or AGENT opens the cargo on the direction of the Customs officer. Customs officers do not open, unpack or repack any goods.

Customs: ships' stores. An incoming ship is boarded by a preventive officer who takes account of all dutiable GOODS in store on board – all such goods are put under Customs seal. There are heavy penalties for breaking such a seal – the goods may not be used while the ship is in port.

Customs tariff. The list of GOODS, etc., on which duty is payable. Details can be obtained from Her Majesty's Stationery Office.

D

Damages, contemptuous. Where the court is of the opinion that a case has been mischievously or unnecessarily brought, it may award what are known as contemptuous damages, such as one farthing.

Damages, exemplary. These apply in tort but not in CONTRACT. They are punitive damages as opposed to damages for actual loss suffered.

Damages, liquidated. Damages stated in a CONTRACT to be payable on BREACH. They must be a fair estimate of the damage likely to be suffered. Round sums which do not appear to be related in any way to possible damage are known as penalties and are not enforceable. Where damages are difficult to assess, what might appear to be a penalty may be adjudged to be liquidated damages, if the court considers that the sum was an attempt to evaluate the possible loss. ⇨ DEMURRAGE.

Damages, nominal. Damages awarded by the court as an acknowledgement of a BREACH OF CONTRACT even though no loss has been incurred.

Damages, remoteness of. ⇨ RULE IN HADLEY V. BAXENDALE.

Damages, substantial. Damages awarded when loss has actually been incurred.

Damages, unliquidated. Damages not stated in the CONTRACT but awarded by the court.

Dandy note. A document used for obtaining GOODS from a WAREHOUSE OFFICER which are required for exportation, etc. It is issued on the authority of the Customs House.

Day book. A book-keeping term. Day books are books of PRIME ENTRY. They record the details of purchases and SALES as these take place, or rather make lists of INVOICES in and invoices out. The LEDGER is then written up from these books.

Day to day loans. ⇨ OVERNIGHT LOANS.

Days of grace. The additional time allowed by custom for payment of a BILL OF EXCHANGE or INSURANCE premium after the actual date on which the amount was due. In the law merchant, customs can set precedents. With bills of exchange, three days of grace are usually allowed (not including Sundays and BANK HOLIDAYS).

Dead freight. Payable where the charterer fails to load a complete cargo and the ship-owner then charges FREIGHT for the space that he otherwise could have sold.

Dead rent. A term often found in mining leases, for the RENT payable whether or not the mine is worked.

Dear money. Money is said to be dear when loans are difficult to obtain and INTEREST rates are very high. ◊ CHEAP MONEY.

Debenture. Strictly speaking a document setting out the terms of a loan. In the case of a single loan it will be held by the lender. Where the loan is in the form of an issue of debentures, that is to say where many people lend money to a business rather than buy SHARES in it, the debenture deed will be held by TRUSTEES for those people. The deed will state the terms of the loan, when it becomes repayable, and the powers of the debenture holders. If it is charged on specific property, this will be a fixed charge, if on property of the business generally it will be a ◊ FLOATING CHARGE. Where it is a fixed charge on land or INTEREST in land, it should be registered as a land charge. Debentures secured on property may be referred to as ◊ MORTGAGE debentures. Consequently in accounts one finds, for instance, first- and second-mortgage debentures.

They receive a fixed interest annually – this must be paid before any DIVIDENDS are paid. The interest is deductable for CORPORATION TAX purposes. When a business is wound up, debenture holders have a first claim on ASSETS charged.

Debentures at a discount. DEBENTURES may be issued at a discount without any restrictions. The amount of the discount must be shown separately in the BALANCE SHEET.

Debentures, re-issue of. DEBENTURES that have been redeemed by a COMPANY may be re-issued provided the ARTICLES OF ASSOCIATION do not forbid it, and that the company has not contracted to redeem them or shown any intention to cancel them. When re-issued they rank PARI PASSU with other debentures. Details of debentures available for re-issue must be shown in the BALANCE SHEET.

Debit. A term used in DOUBLE-ENTRY BOOK-KEEPING for an entry made on the left-hand side of an account. A credit is an entry made on the right-hand side.

Debit note. A term used in accounting. A debit note is sent to a customer when it is intended to debit his account, normally in an unusual situation – say when a person has been insufficiently charged for GOODS.

Debtor. A person indebted to another. The debt usually takes the form of money.

Deck cargo. Cargo on deck rather than in the hold of the ship. The Carriage of Goods by Sea Act 1924 does not apply to this type of cargo.

Declaration of solvency. ◊ WINDING-UP, VOLUNTARY.

Deed. ◊ CONTRACTS BY DEED.

Deed of arrangement. An alternative to BANKRUPTCY. This is a composition or arrangement with CREDITORS made by the debtor in an attempt to avoid bankruptcy. It may be made before a BANKRUPTCY PETITION is presented, or after the petition where the court does not object. There are certain differences: if the arrangement is made before the receiving order it only binds assenting creditors; if it is made after the receiving order and the court approves, all creditors are bound. There are various forms of arrangement: (1) a ◊ LETTER OF LICENCE, (2) a ◊ DEED OF INSPECTORSHIP, (3) ASSIGNMENT of property (the debtor assigns property to the TRUSTEE on trust for his creditors, the creditors agreeing to accept this as a discharge from liability), (4) deed of composition (where the debtor agrees to pay so much in the pound to each creditor. This may be accompanied by a ◊ DEED OF ASSIGNMENT to a trustee. There may also be GUARANTEES, BILLS OF EXCHANGE, etc.)

When the arrangement is made before the bankruptcy petition, it is a CONTRACT between the debtor, the assenting creditors, and the trustee. Where a contract under any of the previous four headings is made for the benefit of creditors generally, or where the debtor was insolvent and it was made for the benefit of three or more creditors, it is governed by the Deed of Arrangement Act 1914. These sorts of agreement must be registered (this does not apply to limited COMPANIES) within seven days, and the agreement must be in writing, otherwise it is not a deed of arrangement. It must mention the residence and occupation of the debtor and his place of business, the total estimated ASSETS and liabilities included in the deed, the amount of the composition, and the names and addresses of creditors. Where a trustee has been appointed the deed must also be signed by the trustee. STAMP DUTY is payable on registration on an AD VALOREM basis. A register of deeds of arrangement is kept by the Registrar and is open for inspection by any person at any time.

The deed will be void where: (1) it is not registered within seven days, (2) it is for benefit of creditors generally, but has not received the assent in number and value of creditors, within twenty-one days.

There are various provisions in the Act regarding the duties of the trustee as to accounts and AUDIT.

Assenting creditors are bound by the deed. Dissenting creditors are free to bring a petition for the debtor to be made bankrupt. When a bankruptcy happens within three months, the trustee must hand over all property to the trustee in bankruptcy, by the doctrine of relation back – this is only if the trustee in bankruptcy insists, for he may ratify actions made in compliance with the deed. If the deed is void, the trustee is protected where he acted innocently.

Deeds of Arrangement generally are governed by the BOARD OF TRADE.

Deed of assignment. A term used in BANKRUPTCY, when rather than become bankrupt a debtor assigns all his property for the benefit of his CREDITORS generally. As it is an alternative to bankruptcy, agreement with his creditors would be necessary for it to be legally enforceable.

Deed of covenant. An agreement drawn up in a proper manner whereby a person drawing the deed agrees to pay a fixed sum to a named person or organization for a fixed time. The payer deducts tax at the standard rate. If the payment is to a charity the charity may recover the tax paid if the covenant is for more than seven years. The payer must account for the tax to the Inland Revenue but provided he is paying tax on his income at the standard rate, the payment is treated as an annual charge and he will not pay any additional tax.

Deed of inspectorship. When a businessman is INSOLVENT and it is possible that he may become BANKRUPT, he may hand over his business to the charge of his CREDITORS by a deed of inspectorship. The creditors will appoint inspectors to manage the business either as a going concern or with a view to its being wound up.

Defence bonds. Government SECURITIES introduced in November 1939, and on sale until May 1964. Bonds were issued in units of £5 and there was a maximum holding. At maturity certain issues had a tax free bonus, free of CAPITAL GAINS TAX. Holders could always convert into a new issue. These were similar to ◊ NATIONAL DEVELOPMENT BONDS.

Deferred annuity. An ◊ ANNUITY that becomes payable at a stated time in the future.

Deferred charges. ◊ PRE-PAYMENTS.

Deferred credit. Monies received in one ACCOUNTING PERIOD but actually applicable to a following period.

Deferred taxation. A term used in company accounts. It may refer to amounts set aside for tax deferred by CAPITAL ALLOWANCES. This may also be called a tax ◊ EQUALIZATION ACCOUNT, etc. Profits of a business are calculated after DEPRECIATION. Depreciation allowed for tax purposes may differ from depreciation used in accounts, though the total over a number of years will be the same. As tax will not therefore be related to the actual profits shown in the accounts, adjustments are made by adding to, and subtracting from, a reserve set aside for the equalization of taxation with reference to the profits. CORPORATION TAX payable more than a year hence but based on the profits for the relevant year is sometimes also shown as a deferred liability. The difference is, that whereas this amount is a known liability not payable for some time, the first amount is more like a reserve.

Defunct company. ◊ REGISTER OF COMPANIES.

Del credere agent. An AGENT who GUARANTEES that the persons to whom he sells GOODS on behalf of his principal, will pay for them. He normally receives an additional COMMISSION for this.

Delegatus non potest delegare. A legal maxim that states effectively that when an AGENT has contracted to do a work for a principal, he has no implied right to delegate the work to a third party. In practice this does not always apply. Subcontracting is customary in many trades. The maxim applies mostly where the personality of the agent is important.

Delivered docks. A term used in foreign trade where the responsibility of the seller ceases when the GOODS are delivered at the docks and unloaded.

Delivery. ◊ CONTRACTS BY DEED.

Delivery note. A note similar to an advice note accompanying GOODS sent by a VENDOR, often in duplicate, the recipient returning one copy and signing the other. The signed copy is then taken by the person delivering the goods to the vendor and is evidence of proper delivery.

Demise charter. ◊ CHARTER BY DEMISE.

Demurrage. Liquidated DAMAGES included in a CONTRACT, usually a building or shipping contract. Normally takes the form of a payment for each day completion is delayed or ships are kept waiting. The fact that the loss is less than the demurrage is not relevant.

Department store. A large retail shop where there are various departments each dealing in a separate type of GOODS. ◊ MULTIPLE STORE.

Deposit. An amount of money paid to a VENDOR as part of the purchase money and to secure the SALE. The depositor is entitled then to buy the property if he pays the balance within a stated period. Normally, if the balance is not paid, he will lose the deposit, assuming good faith on both sides.

Depreciation. An accounting term for the amount by which the usefulness of a FIXED ASSET has diminished. In fact the methods of calculating the amounts to be shown are somewhat arbitrary. ◊

WRITTEN DOWN VALUE ◊ STRAIGHT LINE METHOD ◊ DIMINISH-
ING BALANCE METHOD.

Design Centre. This is run by the ◊ COUNCIL FOR INDUSTRIAL
DESIGN. It provides a shop window to display examples of well-
designed modern British GOODS, and bring the achievements of
British manufacturers and designers to the attention of industry,
commerce, and the general public. It keeps a Design Index and issues
special black and white triangular labels for fixing on goods in the
Index. It is open daily, from 9.30 a.m. to 5.30 p.m.; on Wednesday
and Thursday from 9.30 a.m. to 9 p.m. There is no admission fee.
General and special exhibitions are held. The Centre also wishes to
be satisfied with technical efficiency of products, but has no testing
facilities; instead it employs other organizations, e.g. the British
Electrical Approval Board for Domestic Appliances, the Coal
Utilization Council, Gas Council and the BRITISH STANDARDS
INSTITUTION. Products cannot be purchased at the Centre, but
information is given as to manufacturer and probable price. It
publishes a monthly, *Design*. Address: 28 Haymarket, London SW1.

Design Index. ◊ COUNCIL FOR INDUSTRIAL DESIGN.

Detinue. An action in tort for the recovery of property.

Devaluation. The alteration of the value of the currency of one country
in relation to the currency of another. This happens when RATES OF
EXCHANGE generally are controlled. At present most currencies are
stated in terms of the dollar or gold. When a country devalues its
currency it restates that currency in terms of the dollar or gold. The
rate of exchange alters and the currency becomes cheaper from the
point of view of other countries where they do not devalue to the
same or a greater extent. In fact devaluation by one country is often
followed by a similar devaluation by other countries particularly
those closely related to the first country. This was noticeable when
the United Kingdom devalued in November 1967: many other
STERLING AREA countries followed suit.

Because all currencies are tied to the dollar or gold, devaluation in
fact involves not only devaluation in terms of the dollar but also in
terms of all other currencies. The principal effect from the point of
view of the devaluing country is to encourage exports and discourage
imports. This is obviously not popular with other countries as it has
an adverse effect on their trade balances. To stop frequent devalua-
tions it was internationally agreed that permission of the INTER-
NATIONAL MONETARY FUND should be obtained before devaluing.
This is not, in practice, always obtained because devaluation is often

made spontaneous to avoid any possibility of SPECULATION. The United Kingdom did not obtain permission when it devalued in 1948.

Development area. An area scheduled (in the Local Employment Acts 1960–66) as in need of more employment. The BOARD OF TRADE provides help for persons or COMPANIES setting up factories in these areas. It does this by providing land or premises for RENT or SALE, or by making grants, not repayable, towards the cost of buildings, plant, machinery, etc. This help is not conditional on the absence of other financial resources. The building grant is 25 per cent including adapting of existing buildings; it may be raised to 35 per cent if good reason for this can be given. There is also a plant and machinery grant better known as an operational grant, which is 10 per cent a year for three years. It only applies to new projects and is not always given. Grants are not obtainable for unnecessary expenditure, or for expenditure on items which could be removed easily from the area. To obtain assistance, an applicant must show that he is providing employment in the area. The MANUFACTURING INDUSTRY is favoured. SERVICE INDUSTRIES must show that they can provide at least fifty additional jobs.

Other benefits include: (1) facilities for obtaining loans on good INTEREST terms, (2) refund of SELECTIVE EMPLOYMENT TAX (S.E.T.) and also regional payments on the basis of numbers employed. This is known as the Regional Employment Premium (R.E.P.) and applies only to manufacturing industries. These are also entitled to claim the balance of the S.E.T. premium, (3) assistance for training employees and housing key workers, (4) preferential treatment for firms in development areas when government CONTRACTS are being awarded, if they tender at a PRICE equal to those from firms outside development areas (they are also given an opportunity of revising their estimates).

There are also special development areas, these being principally colliery areas where additional assistance is given including rent free factories for five years. Special rules apply to Northern Ireland.

There is an additional benefit in Great Britain and Northern Ireland known as free DEPRECIATION, and development areas can write off the cost of certain FIXED ASSETS at whatever rate they prefer for tax purposes.

At present development areas consist of almost the whole of Scotland and Wales, a large part of Northern Ireland, the North of England, Merseyside, and the extreme South-west of England.

Development expenditure. The cost of development in a business that does not necessarily result in visible ASSETS but is aimed at promoting SALES by ADVERTISING and various other devices. This expenditure is sometimes capitalized, i.e. it is shown as an INTANGIBLE ASSET in a BALANCE SHEET, or sometimes as a FIXED ASSET, and then written off over a period. The period will depend upon the estimate of the time sales are expected to benefit.

Deviation. A MARINE INSURANCE term for the circumstances in which a ship may deviate from its course without prejudice to the policy. These are: (1) where the policy authorizes deviation, (2) where deviation is necessary for the safety of the ship or cargo, provided both are insured, (3) to save human life or help a ship in distress, (4) where necessary to get medical help for someone on board, (5) where necessary to comply with an express or implied WARRANTY, (6) when it cannot be helped, e.g. through the mutinous conduct of crew.

Dies non. A Latin tag for a day on which no business can be transacted.

Differences. A STOCK EXCHANGE term concerning the buying and selling of STOCKS where the operator has no intention of personally taking up stocks before ACCOUNT DAY but hopes to make a profit by buying and selling within the one ACCOUNTING PERIOD. He is speculating in differences.

Diminishing balance method. A method of calculating DEPRECIATION. The cost or agreed VALUE of the ASSET is written off over its expected life by the application of a percentage to the WRITTEN-DOWN VALUE. The percentage is calculated so that the asset will be written down to scrap value after a stated number of years. The annual depreciation is charged against profit. This method means that much higher charges are made in the initial years, thus reducing profit artificially. It may also tend to show the value of assets at an artificially low figure, thus making it difficult to estimate the ⬦ CAPITAL EMPLOYED for the purpose of calculating certain ratios.

Direct expenses. Expenses which can be directly associated with the cost of producing a particular article or service, as opposed to ⬦ OVERHEAD EXPENSES.

Direct labour. Labour which can be directly associated with manufacturing a product or receiving a service. ⬦ INDIRECT LABOUR.

Direct taxation. Taxation levied directly on the members of a community and paid directly by them to the revenue authorities either personally or through an employer. This is unlike INDIRECT TAXATION that is not dependent on a person's wealth, but on the goods that he buys (e.g. PURCHASE TAX, Customs and Excise duty, etc.). Direct taxation has taken many forms other than the present INCOME TAX, introduced during the Napoleonic Wars. There have been poll taxes (i.e. taxes per head), window taxes (on the number of windows), chimney taxes, and taxes on servants etc.; these applied mostly to the rich and were known as iniquitous. They were abolished and replaced by LICENCES, levies, duties, etc., which applied to everybody.

Director. Many people who are not normally called directors are considered directors for many purposes of the law. Any person according to whose instructions directors are accustomed to act is to all intents and purposes a director when it comes to directors' shareholdings, CLOSE COMPANIES, etc.

Strictly speaking directors are persons concerned with managing a COMPANY on behalf of the shareholders. They are in one sense AGENTS of the company. They are not liable personally on CONTRACTS made in the name of the company even when acting ULTRA VIRES (though then they might be liable for BREACH OF WARRANTY OF AUTHORITY). If they contract *intra vires* but outside their own powers, the company may be bound (◊ RULE IN ROYAL BRITISH BANK V. TURQUAND).

The first directors are often named in the ARTICLES OF ASSOCIATION and often also in the PROSPECTUS. Mention in the articles does not constitute a valid appointment until each director has: (1) signed and sent to the Registrar of Companies his consent to act, and (2) either signed the memorandum for his QUALIFICATION SHARES, or taken up and paid for them, or contracted for them, or declared that they are already registered in his name.

If there is no appointment in the articles, the first directors are appointed by the subscribers. The manner of subsequent appointments is normally specified in the articles. It is usually done by the company in general meeting, but directors often have powers to fill vacancies on the board subject to confirmation by general MEETING. Only one director can be appointed by one resolution unless all MEMBERS OF THE COMPANY previously agree otherwise. This does not apply to PRIVATE COMPANIES. Private companies may have one director (but he must not also be the SECRETARY). PUBLIC COMPANIES must have two. (◊ REGISTER OF DIRECTORS ◊ REGISTER OF DIRECTORS' SHAREHOLDINGS). Directors act by resolutions made at directors' meetings. Meetings must be properly convened, and notice given to each director. A QUORUM must be present (the number constituting a quorum is usually stated in the articles). Directors must not make contracts with the company, they must declare any interest in contracts made for the company, they must also hand over secret profits – the Articles normally state that in this instance they have no vote. Infringement of these rules will probably make the contract void. Generally, ▷ LOANS TO DIRECTORS are prohibited.

Directors have many responsibilities including: (1) keeping proper books of account and presenting ANNUAL ACCOUNTS and a DIRECTORS' REPORT, (2) calling ANNUAL GENERAL MEETINGS, (3) keeping REGISTERS OF DIRECTORS and secretaries, REGISTERS OF DIRECTORS' SHAREHOLDINGS, SHARE REGISTERS, etc., (4) sending the Registrar all documents he is entitled to receive, (5) submitting a STATEMENT OF AFFAIRS on WINDING-UP.

Remuneration of directors is a matter of agreement between themselves and the company. If it is stated in the articles it can only be altered by SPECIAL RESOLUTION at a general meeting. For rules on disclosure ▷ DIRECTORS' EMOLUMENTS ▷ COMPENSATION FOR LOSS OF OFFICE.

A director may be disqualified if he goes against the articles or loses his qualification. If he becomes bankrupt he can only become a director by leave of the court. The powers of directors cease on a winding-up.

Directors' emoluments. Sums of money and BENEFITS IN KIND received by DIRECTORS. These may include fees, salaries for acting as director (or some other capacity) for the COMPANY, the use of company property, and certain expense allowances. The Companies Acts require that the ACCOUNTS of a company shall distinguish *inter alia* between amounts received in respect of services as director of the company or any of its subsidiaries, and remuneration received for management of the company's affairs or the affairs of any subsidiary. They also require that directors' emoluments should be distinguished from directors' pensions or COMPENSATION FOR LOSS OF OFFICE. The 1967 Act requires that details be given of the number of directors receiving salaries within certain ranges, for instance £0–£2,500, £2,500–£5,000, etc. This also applies to highly paid persons who are not directors. The 1967 Act does not apply to independent companies where the total emoluments are less than £7,500. ▷ CLOSE COMPANY.

Directors' fees. Payments made to DIRECTORS by reason only of their position as directors. Directors' fees tend to be fairly nominal, the greater part of payment being by way of salary and other benefits. ▷ DIRECTORS' EMOLUMENTS.

Directors (Institute of). This was founded in 1903, and given a royal charter in 1908. It began to be more active in 1948: membership was raised from 420 in 1948 to over 42,000 today, probably due to the 1948 Companies Act. Members are elected: applicants are nominated by existing members. The subscription is £8 per year. It is not a trade organization. It aims to provide information valuable to DIRECTORS of all COMPANIES. It describes itself as a fighting organization which hopes to create a climate of opinion more favourable to directors. It is non-political but supports free enterprise, makes representations to the government and has an education committee. It has endowed a Fellowship at Balliol College, Oxford, and a Chair at Warwick University. It publishes, among other things, a monthly, *The Director*. The Institute has over 250 members in Parliament. It offers individual advice, holds branch discussion groups, and has a London Club. Membership is not restricted to nationals of this country and women may also become members. Address: 10 Belgrave Square, London SW1.

Directors: over age. Generally speaking a person who is over seventy cannot be appointed DIRECTOR of a PUBLIC COMPANY or of a PRIVATE COMPANY that is a SUBSIDIARY of a public company. This does not apply where the appointment is made by the company in a general MEETING, after special notice has been given of intention to do so.

Directors, removal of. A DIRECTOR may be removed at any time by the COMPANY; an ORDINARY RESOLUTION will suffice. This does not apply to the director of a PRIVATE COMPANY holding office for life from 18 July 1945. Special notice is necessary. The director may make representations both in advance and at the meeting, and may ask for these representations to be circulated to MEMBERS OF THE COMPANY. Whether he is entitled to compensation or DAMAGES depends on circumstances and on the ARTICLES OF ASSOCIATION. A director may resign at any time in the manner specified in the articles. If nothing is specified then reasonable notice will suffice. A resignation properly given cannot be withdrawn.

Directors' report. A document which must be submitted by every limited COMPANY with its ANNUAL ACCOUNTS. It must contain certain information detailed in the 1948 and 1967 Companies Acts. It must report on the state of the companies' affairs and give details of: (1) DIVIDENDS recommended, (2) the names of DIRECTORS, (3) the principal activities of the company and its SUBSIDIARIES, (4) any substantial difference between the MARKET VALUE and the book value of land, or interest in land held by the company, (5) significant alterations in FIXED ASSETS, (6) any proposed transfers to RESERVES, (7) details of SHARES and DEBENTURES issued during the year, (8) any interest that a director has in a CONTRACT with the company, (9) the directors' interests in shares and debentures as shown in the register the company keeps, with comparative figures for the beginning of the year, (10) an analysis of turnover (◊ TURN-OVER, DISCLOSURE OF), (11) an analysis of profit or loss before tax, distinguishing between the various types of business carried on by the company and its subsidiaries, (items 10 and 11 do not apply to independent companies where the turnover is less than £50,000), (12) the average number of employees per week, ignoring persons working outside the United Kingdon, (13) any other matters necessary to a proper appreciation of the company's affairs and not harmful to the business of the company or its subsidiaries, (14) details of POLITICAL AND CHARITABLE CONTRIBUTIONS, (15) details of exports where their VALUE exceeds £50,000, (16) total remuneration paid to employees for the year, where there are more than 100 excluding those employed outside the United Kingdom, (17) any rights of directors to acquire shares and debentures. Where details are given in the report rather than in the accounts themselves, the report must be annexed to the accounts and it then becomes part of them. This only applies to information that must appear in the accounts or the report.

Corresponding figures for previous years must also be given.

Directors' resignation. ◊ DIRECTORS, REMOVAL OF.

Directors' retirement. ◊ ROTATION OF DIRECTORS ◊ DIRECTORS: OVER-AGE.

Directors' service contracts. COMPANIES must keep (in an appropriate place) details of service CONTRACTS with DIRECTORS. If the contract was in writing, a copy of it must be kept. If not, a memorandum will suffice. The appropriate place is the REGISTERED OFFICE, the place where the REGISTER OF MEMBERS is kept, or the principal place of business. The place where it is kept must be notified to the Registrar of Companies, it must be open to inspection on every business day for at least two hours, free of charge to all MEMBERS OF THE COMPANY. There are certain limited exceptions in the cases of directors working wholly outside the United Kingdom, and of contracts for very short periods.

Directors' shareholdings. ◊ REGISTER OF DIRECTORS' SHARE-HOLDINGS.

Director's valuation. Sometimes ASSETS in a COMPANY'S accounts may be stated to be 'at DIRECTOR'S valuation' or alternatively 'as certified by MANAGING DIRECTOR'. The relevance of this description or the VALUE, will depend on the circumstances. Generally speaking the directors are responsible for all the figures shown in the BALANCE SHEET. Where they are not shown at cost but at valuation, the directors must believe the valuation correct. Where the words 'at valuation' are used, there should be an explanatory note stating the method of valuation and whether it was an expert valuation or not. The directors are not necessarily the best persons to value assets. However, the AUDITORS will be expected to verify the valuation and to state whether they consider it to be a fair estimate. Auditors cannot avoid their liability to shareholders by relying on directors' certificates.

Dirty bill of lading. ♢ FOUL BILL OF LADING.

Discharge of contract. This means the fulfilment of the obligations imposed by a CONTRACT, or else an agreement to negate the contract or put one in its place. It can also mean a situation where a party may be released from his obligations by impossibility of performance or by OPERATION OF LAW. For example, alteration of a written instrument without the consent of the other party will preclude the party altering the instrument from taking action on it and release the other party from all obligations. ♢ WAIVER ♢ ACCORD AND SATISFACTION ♢ CONTRACT, BREACH OF ♢ CONTRACT, PERFORMANCE OF.

Discount (bills of exchange). A BILL OF EXCHANGE may be discounted. This means that it is purchased by a third party for a sum lower than that party will receive when the bill matures. The person discounting the bill gains by receiving money at an earlier date. The amount of discount will vary according to the risk the purchaser takes. A good bill is one which is backed or countersigned by a well known FINANCE HOUSE or BANK. Bills are normally discounted with banks or on a larger scale with institutions known as ♢ DISCOUNT HOUSES.

Discount broker. A BROKER who neither buys nor sells BILLS OF EXCHANGE but acts as intermediary between those who wish to sell and those who wish to buy. If a broker deals on his own account he becomes a DISCOUNT HOUSE. The question to be asked is, 'Do they run their own book?'

Discount houses. These are organizations situated in the City of London whose business is DISCOUNTING BILLS OF EXCHANGE – TRADE BILLS, BANK BILLS and TREASURY BILLS. Business is done on a large scale and funds are obtained principally from the Clearing BANKS. To keep the INTEREST rate as low as possible and be able to vary the amount borrowed at short intervals, a great deal of money is borrowed OVERNIGHT. This suits both bank and discount house: to the bank it is MONEY AT SHORT NOTICE, also earning interest. It is lent on the SECURITY of bills of exchange that have not yet matured.

Discounted cash flow (D.C.F.). ◊ NET PRESENT VALUE.

Discounting back. A process of assessing the present VALUE of an anticipated future sum, e.g. what is the value today of £100 in twenty years' time? The solution is found by establishing a sum of money that, if accumulated at X per cent COMPOUND INTEREST for twenty years, would produce £100 at the end of that time. The rate of INTEREST will depend on the rate of interest ruling at the time the calculation is made. Tables are available for giving the answers to such problems.

Disgorging. The removal of sediment from wine. The bottles are stood on end, the sediment settles in the neck of the bottle, the cork is removed and the sediment disposed of.

Dissentient: purchase of interest. Where a company is being reorganized or sold to another company by a LIQUIDATOR, and shareholders are to receive SHARES in the second company, a MEMBER who has not voted for the SPECIAL RESOLUTION may demand that the liquidator purchases his interest at a PRICE to be determined either by agreement or by ARBITRATION. The dissentor must decide within seven days.

Dissolution. ◊ WINDING-UP: CONDUCT OF.

Distraint. A remedy open to a CREDITOR in certain circumstances (normally a landlord for RENT due). The creditor can enter the debtor's premises and seize property, holding this property until the debt is paid.

Distributor. A MARKETING term for a RETAILER who deals in the wares of certain specified manufacturers, having perhaps the sole agency for an area. He buys and sells on his own account and is not therefore an AGENT for the manufacturer.

Dividend. A share of profits taken by a shareholder of a COMPANY. Dividends may be preference or ordinary. Preference dividends have precedence as to payment. A company need not pay dividends. Payment depends on monies available and the policy of the company. A dividend is not payable until declared (normally at an ANNUAL GENERAL MEETING) and the amount is agreed by the DIRECTORS. The normal practice is to pay one dividend per year shared as a percentage of nominal CAPITAL. Part of this dividend may be paid during the year as an INTERIM DIVIDEND. Dividends are paid by DIVIDEND WARRANTS and after deduction of tax.

Dividend mandate. An authority given by a shareholder to a COM-PANY stating that DIVIDENDS are to be paid directly into his BANK account.

Dividend restraint. Deliberate or enforced restriction of payment of DIVIDENDS to the holders of SHARES without fixed dividend rights. This is often a matter of government policy. Dividend restraint has been encouraged in the past by relief from PROFITS TAX on profits retained and at present by an additional tax on dividends paid.

Dividend stripping. When a COMPANY has accumulated considerable reserves either of CAPITAL or of a general nature, a FINANCIER or a person with sufficient resources may buy a controlling interest in this company, to sell its ASSETS, particularly its property (this may be rented back) and obtain sufficient funds to distribute the RESERVES by way of DIVIDENDS (being mostly to himself). The stripper may then sell his SHARES and go. It is a practice rather frowned upon by those who do not have the resources to do the same, by the STOCK EXCHANGE and by the Chancellor. A serious objection is that it could leave the company in a difficult position, or even facing INSOLVENCY.

Dividend tax. A tax introduced in 1965 at the same time as the COR-PORATION TAX. It is in the form of an INCOME TAX payable on DIVIDENDS paid by limited COMPANIES. The tax is paid in addition to corporation tax and is deducted from the dividend before payment and accounted for by the company to the Inland Revenue. There are certain complicated provisions with reference to dividends received by a company and then paid over to its MEMBERS. The aim of these is to prevent double taxation.

Dividend warrant. A document entitling the recipient to a sum of money which can be obtained from the BANK. It is similar to a CHEQUE. It states gross amount, tax deducted and net amount paid. The shareholder who is not liable to TAXATION AT STANDARD RATE will be able to claim a return (in part or whole) of the tax paid by sending the tax voucher, attached to the warrant, to the appropriate authorities.

Dividend yield. ⟡ EARNINGS YIELD.

Dock dues. A toll on all vessels entering or leaving a dock.

Dock warrant. This is given to the owner of GOODS stored at a dock WAREHOUSE as a recognition of his TITLE to those goods. It is in fact a document of TITLE.

Documents against acceptance. A term used with reference to foreign trade, where documents of TITLE to GOODS exported are handed over by the master of the ship or some other person when the

135

importer signs a BILL OF EXCHANGE. (The bill would be a PERIOD BILL.)

Document against payment. Similar to a ◊ DOCUMENT AGAINST ACCEPTANCE but the bill is a sight bill and the importer must pay immediately before receiving the documents of TITLE.

Documentary credit. BANKS give facilities to customers who are importers, enabling them to open credits in favour of persons overseas, so that these persons can obtain credit more promptly and on the tender of certain documents. ◊ LONDON ACCEPTANCE CREDIT.

Dominion register. Part of the general REGISTER OF MEMBERS of a COMPANY, kept by companies which transact business in any of the colonies or dominions. The register records details of MEMBERS OF THE COMPANY registered in the colonies or dominions. The company must notify the Registrar of Companies of the situation of the register. If the register is not kept at the REGISTERED OFFICE, a duplicate must be kept there.

Donee. The recipient of a GIFT.

Donor. A person who gives property, or a TITLE to property, to another person. This word is usually applied to GIFTS, i.e. where no payment is made.

Double-entry book-keeping. A form of book-keeping devised centuries ago, whereby each transaction is entered twice, a transaction being by its nature two-sided. The purchase of an ASSET necessitates the recording of the asset and also, separately, of the debt incurred or the money paid. The book in which all the accounts are kept is known as the LEDGER, though the cash account is normally kept in a separate book, known as the CASH BOOK. At any time the total debit balances in the ledger should equal the total credit balances. If this is so, it is an indication that (in the absence of compensating errors) double entries have been properly made. This is because, of the two entries made, one is always a debit and one a credit entry.

Double insurance. This occurs where a risk is insured against twice. Generally speaking it is impossible to obtain more than the loss suffered and if a risk is insured against twice, one company will claim CONTRIBUTION from the other. Double insurance should be distinguished from RE-INSURANCE.

Double option. ◊ OPTION.

Double taxation relief. This is a very complex subject. It deals with the relief afforded a COMPANY or other business earning profits abroad, this profit being taxable in the other country. The two principal forms of relief are the following: (1) The tax payable in the United Kingdom will only be enough to make the total tax payable equivalent to the U.K. rate. This applies where there is a double tax agreement with the other country. (2) The tax payable abroad is allowed as a deduction when calculating taxable profits.

When the full United Kingdom tax rate is not paid on profits earned overseas, only the United Kingdom proportion, known as the net United Kingdom rate, can be reclaimed by persons receiving these profits and entitled to make repayment claims. Most companies state 'net United Kingdom rate' when this applies to tax deducted from dividends.

Doubtful debts, provision for. An amount set aside out of profits to provide against the possibility of debts being irrecoverable. These may be specific debts and/or a percentage of total debtors (the percentage is learnt by experience).

Douceur. An eighteenth-century term for a bribe or GRATUITY.

Dozen. A set of twelve items. In the newspaper trade a dozen is by custom thirteen, with reference to supply to RETAILERS. 'Baker's dozen' is slang for thirteen.

Draper. A dealer in cloth.

Drawback. A rebate which may be obtained for duty paid on imported materials used in the manufacture of exported GOODS. Drawback is avoided if goods are kept in a bonded WAREHOUSE for re-export. GOODS for repair may be imported free of duty. For details of drawback, apply to HER MAJESTY'S CUSTOM AND EXCISE, King's Beam House, Mark Lane, London EC3.

Drawee. The person on whom a ◊ BILL OF EXCHANGE is drawn.

Drawer. The person who draws a ◊ BILL OF EXCHANGE.

Drysalter. A dealer in drugs, gums, etc., and sometimes also in oils, pickles, sauces, etc.

Dumping. A term used in international trade for the unloading of large quantities of a particular product in another country at a low PRICE. This may be done where the first country is over-producing and wishes to sell at a low profit rather than at none at all (or even to sell at a loss, so that it may get a foothold in the other market). Again, it can be a rather ruthless way of maximizing the profit of a particular industry: where there is a MONOPOLY at home output is restricted and a high price charged. The bulk of the output is pushed into another country and sold at PRICES which producers in that country cannot afford. Dumping is therefore frowned upon by governments, and steps are often taken to prevent it happening. These may be direct, e.g. by duties, or indirect, e.g. by retaliatory action.

Duplication. In commerce it is often necessary to produce information in duplicate, triplicate or more. Where only one or two copies are required, carbon paper will normally suffice; it is available in various colours. If N.C.R. (no carbon required) paper is used for copies no carbon is necessary. This paper tends to be more expensive and produces about the same number of copies as if carbon had been used. When many copies are required some form of duplicating machine is necessary. There are many machines available, working on different principles. Three of the main ways are: (1) by using a type of carbon process whereby the original is typed with a carbon backing and this, by being kept moist, will reproduce the information on some patent duplicating paper. There is a limit to the number of copies that this process will produce. (2) by producing a stencil as a master copy. In this case the number of copies is unlimited. (3) by various photographic processes. These are obviously more suitable where illustrations are concerned or where it is necessary to reproduce an original document.

Durable goods. GOODS purchased for use over a period, such as washing machines or refrigerators. The consumer's equivalent of a FIXED ASSET.

Duress. The use of force to procure a CONTRACT. The force need not be physical but may result from the relationship existing between parties: father and son, for instance.

Dutch auction. An unusual form of AUCTION, often used with reference to charities, where the AUCTIONEER starts the bidding at a very high price and then reduces the price until he receives a bid.

Duty and tax reliefs (exports). Certain reliefs are available – for details apply to HER MAJESTY'S CUSTOMS AND EXCISE, King's Beam House, Mark Lane, London EC3. Forms, such as shipping bills, may be also provided free. ◊ EXPORT REBATE SCHEME ◊ PURCHASE TAX RELIEF ◊ TEMPORARY EXPORTS.

Duty free shop. ◊ CUSTOMS: AIRPORTS.

Duty paid contracts. EX SHIP contracts where the seller also pays import duty, and may also pay the warehousing charges.

E

Earnings yield. The relationship between profits and CAPITAL. It is used frequently with reference to STOCK EXCHANGE investments and generally means the ratio of annual profit (after tax and fixed INTEREST or fixed DIVIDEND payments) to total EQUITY CAPITAL (at the current market value, the value per the OFFICIAL LIST). It should be distinguished from the 'dividend yield', this being dividend over Stock Exchange price. 'Dividend yield' would apply of course to fixed-dividend SHARES as well as to equity shares. This dividend yield as a percentage will differ from the rate of dividend stated by the company, insofar as the latter is based upon nominal value and the former on MARKET VALUE.

Easement. This is defined as 'the right of using another's land in a defined and specific way without taking any substance from the land' (*Stephen's Commentaries*, nineteenth edition). A right of way is a typical easement. Easements may be positive and negative. The right of way is a positive easement, the right not to be deprived of light is a negative one. Easements are normally created by DEED and may be express or implied. An implied easement may arise when a man sells part only of his property, an implication being that he has a right of way over the part sold to reach the part which is still his.

Edinburgh Gazette. An official Scottish publication similar to the ◊ LONDON GAZETTE, and containing notices which would in England be required to be in the *London Gazette*.

Eighth schedule. The schedule or supplement to the Companies Act 1948 which deals with information which must be given in every BALANCE SHEET and PROFIT AND LOSS ACCOUNT presented to a COMPANY at its ANNUAL GENERAL MEETING. The provisions of this schedule have been amended by the Companies Act 1967.

Ejusdem generis rule. A rule of law (the words mean 'of the same kind'). The rule might be applied in, say, INSURANCE: the court might decide that although a policy may cover losses not expressly mentioned in the policy, they must be of the same kind as those which are mentioned, and not of a completely different kind.

Elasticity of demand. A term used in economics to refer to the reaction of demand to changes in PRICE. Demand for a product is said to be elastic or inelastic according to its sensitivity to marginal price changes (marginal because obviously all demand for any product is

139

ultimately determined by price). In this country, the demand for salt is relatively inelastic. The quantity of salt used is not determined by price, though obviously there would come a point where the public would stop buying and look for an alternative. The demand for a competitive soap powder, on the other hand, is elastic, as there are many substitutes available, and a small price change could have a marked effect on demand.

Embargo. When it is forbidden to export GOODS to certain countries, then goods are said to be subject to embargo. There is now an embargo on the export of certain goods to the U.S.S.R. and China. The embargo may be imposed by either side, and prevents the unloading or loading of certain goods, or else prevents ships entering or leaving certain ports. Goods subject to embargo are listed in the BOARD OF TRADE JOURNAL.

Employees, information regarding. The Companies Act 1967 makes it necessary to give details of amounts earned by employees earning more than £10,000 *per annum* and the number whose emoluments fall in each salary bracket (in multiples of £2,500) starting at £10,000. Details of ◊ LOANS TO EMPLOYEES must be given and also certain other information *re* number and aggregate remuneration. ◊ DIRECTORS' REPORT.

Emporium. A central market for trading. The word is now hardly ever used in this sense, but is reserved for rather ostentatious retail premises.

Endorsement. A term used with particular reference to BILLS OF EXCHANGE. When a bill is negotiated the person negotiating will write his name on the reverse of the bill. This transfers the property in the bill. A valid endorsement must be written on the bill itself or on an ALLONGE. It must be of the entire bill and must be by all parties to whom the bill is made out unless one has authority to act for the others. If the bill is payable to order and the payee's name is wrongly spelt, the endorser may sign it in the incorrect way and add his correct name if he wishes. Where there are a number of endorsements on a bill, they are presumed to have been made in the order in which they appear. Unless the contrary is stated, a bill is presumed to have been negotiated before it is overdue. Any person endorsing a bill becomes liable on the bill to all subsequent endorsees or holders. He cannot deny the drawer's signature or the signatures of persons endorsing the bill if asked to pay by a holder in due course.

Endorsements may be of various types: (1) a bill may be endorsed in blank, no endorsee being named; the bill then becomes payable to bearer, (2) there may be a special endorsement when the name of the endorsee is specified; the bill then becomes a bill payable to order, (3) there may be a restrictive endorsement, where the bill is endorsed 'Pay A only'; the bill then ceases to be a negotiable instrument, (4) the endorsement may be limited, e.g. WITHOUT RECOURSE.

If an endorsement is forged, the position is more difficult. Generally speaking TITLE cannot pass through a forgery and a holder of the bill can only claim from persons signing the bill subsequent to the forgery.

Sometimes bills are endorsed conditionally, e.g. 'To A provided he cashes the bill in X days'. The payer can please himself whether or not he observes the condition.

Endowment. A term used with reference to ASSURANCE policies. An endowment assurance is one where the holder of the policy, by paying a certain annual premium, is entitled to a fixed sum at a stated date. ⟡ ASSURANCE.

Entrepôt trade. This concerns the re-exporting of imported GOODS. The goods may be sold directly from bonded WAREHOUSES. If they are not, and duty has been paid, the re-exporter may be entitled to a refund of the duty. This is known as ⟡ DRAWBACK. Drawback may also be payable where the re-exports contain imported goods only in part. Entitlement to claim is given by a Customs' debenture.

Entry outwards. ⟡ EXPORTERS' DECLARATIONS.

Equipment leasing. There are many opportunities for hiring capital equipment. It has been common practice for many years to rent very expensive equipment to save a large and immediate cash outlay. The rental agreement is usually accompanied by a maintenance agreement.

This principle is now being developed by FINANCE COMPANIES, to encourage more widespread leasing of industrial equipment as an alternative to purchase. There are normally three parties: the manufacturer of the equipment, the finance company or lessor, and the customer. The customer agrees with the lessor a minimum period of lease, probably not more than half the life of the ASSET. (The user then has an option to renew at a lower rental.) When this agreement is signed, the customer orders the equipment from the manufacturer. The equipment is delivered to the customer but invoiced to the lessor. The customer notifies the lessor that the delivery is satisfactory, and the lessor pays the manufacturer. The customer from then on pays a rental to the lessor.

Equity. That part of the law which deals with matters not within the province of the COMMON LAW of the land, or of statute law. It operates where a special remedy is sought (e.g. the SPECIFIC PERFORMANCE of a CONTRACT) or where someone has suffered loss, for which the COMMON LAW or statute law does not provide (e.g. breach of trust). It takes precedence over COMMON LAW or statute law. It originated in the courts of chancery, i.e. with the Lord Chancellor, to whom appeal was made by persons unable to obtain redress in the courts. If the Chancellor, as 'Keeper of the King's conscience', considered that compensation of some sort was right and proper, then he would act accordingly. Because of the nature of the court, it is essential that any applicant must himself be generally beyond reproach. 'He who comes to Equity must come with clean hands.'

Equity capital. ⟡ SHARES, ORDINARY.

Equity of redemption. The right of a mortgagor to redeem his property on the repayment of money borrowed. The law does not approve of clogs on the equity of redemption by way of onerous conditions imposed on the mortgagor, or of conditions aimed at making it difficult for him to redeem his property. ⟡ MORTGAGE.

Errors and omissions excepted (E. & O.E.). These initials were often included at the end of an INVOICE. The legal effect is somewhat doubtful. The idea was to absolve the person issuing the invoice from clerical errors.

Escheat. An old legal term for the right of the lord or the grantor of land or interest in land, to retake the land when the tenant died leaving no heir. This was abolished by the Law of Property Act 1925.

Escrow. A CONTRACT BY DEED delivered subject to a condition, i.e. not becoming operative until the condition is fulfilled.

Establishment charges. A book-keeping term for INDIRECT EXPENSES generally, or sometimes more particularly for administrative expenses.

Estate agent. An AGENT or BROKER is a person who is concerned with the SALE, letting, management and valuation of real and leasehold property. The work is often combined with that of an AUCTIONEER. The agent works on an AD VALOREM COMMISSION. He is a GENERAL AGENT. He is not legally bound to belong to any organization or to have any special educational qualifications in order that he may call himself an estate agent. There is, however, a senior professional body known as the CHARTERED AUCTIONEERS AND ESTATE AGENTS INSTITUTE, and movements are afoot to provide for the registration of estate agents for the better protection of the public.

Estate Duties Investment Trust Ltd (E.D.I.T.H.). An organization founded in 1952 by a number of INSURANCE companies and INVESTMENT TRUSTS. Managed by the INDUSTRIAL AND COMMERCIAL FINANCE CORPORATION LTD which was established by the ◊ JOINT STOCK BANKS to provide long-term CAPITAL to small and medium-sized businesses. Its object is to help soundly-managed businesses with ◊ ESTATE DUTY problems by acquiring SHARES in them without interfering with the running of their business. It deals almost entirely with PRIVATE COMPANIES. In 1969 the ISSUED CAPITAL and reserves was £7,000,000. Total investments amounted to over £7,500,000.

Estoppel. A rule of law, whereby a person is prevented (or estopped) from denying a statement he has made either orally or in writing (or possibly implied by conduct). It applies particularly to statements made in a CONTRACT BY DEED. It also prevents a principal from denying the authority of his AGENT, or a person denying the existence of a PARTNERSHIP, where the conduct of the parties has implied that this exists.

European Economic Community. Otherwise known as the Common Market, this was formed in 1957 by the Treaty of Rome, member countries being at present France, West Germany, Italy, Belgium, Holland and Luxembourg. The objects were mainly economic but there were political implications, the intention being to found a fairly solid European *bloc*. Customs barriers are to be abolished among the member countries and a common tariff offered to the outside world. Certain advantages were given to overseas dependencies of member countries, and protection was given temporarily to certain industries. The organization seems to be flourishing and the United Kingdom has for some time been trying to find an entry, but on terms that do not seem acceptable to member countries, particularly to France.

European Free Trade Association. Formed in 1959 as an alternative to the EUROPEAN ECONOMIC COMMUNITY. It was intended as a much diluted form of Common Market. The objects were to reduce progressively TARIFF BARRIERS and other trade restrictions between the member countries, and thus to foster trade between them. It was looked on as an aid to economic development. There was to be no common tariff barrier against the rest of the world. Members are: Austria, Denmark, Norway, Portugal, Sweden, Switzerland, and the United Kingdom. Finland became an associate member in 1964.

Ex gratia. 'As a matter of favour.' Often used for payments made where, though not legally bound, the payer feels some moral obligation.

Exceptional items. An accounting term used for items of expenditure or income which do not normally arise in the type of business being considered. If material, the amount should be shown perhaps separately in the accounts.

Exchange control. The protection and conservation of gold and foreign exchange RESERVES. Its legal basis is the Exchange Control Act 1947. Control is not applied to dealings within the STERLING AREA, but permission is necessary for transfers to residents outside the Sterling Area. Except for travel, payments *re* current transactions are allowed freely.

Exchange equalisation fund. A fund established by the government and the BANK OF ENGLAND to enable the bank to stabilize RATES OF EXCHANGE by buying and selling in the OPEN MARKET. It was established in 1931 after the abolition of the gold standard.

Excise duty. A tax levied on certain GOODS and services produced in this country (principally beer, wine, spirits, and tobacco, but also matches, mechanical lighters, etc.) together with fees for LICENCES necessary to produce these things. The duty is collected by HER MAJESTY'S CUSTOMS AND EXCISE. There are some instances when goods, such as alcohol, are not subject to duty, for instance when used for medicinal purposes.

Excise duties and PURCHASE TAX bring in about 40 per cent of Customs and Excise revenue. The revenue for 1965–6 was £3,400,000,000.

Exemption clause. A clause put into a CONTRACT, particularly a contract for the SALE OF GOODS, excluding the VENDOR from liability for breach of CONDITION, or WARRANTY, or both. The law is not sympathetic towards exemption clauses, and if they are to be effective they must be carefully worded; e.g. a clause exempting implied conditions will not exempt express conditions; a clause exempting conditions will not apply to warranties.

Ex-new. A STOCK EXCHANGE term. SHARES are quoted ex-new when their PRICE does not include the right to take new shares being offered.

Export assistance register. An aid to exporting. The register gives details of a great many experienced exporting firms which are prepared to help beginners in the field. In doing so they obviously give away some of their own secrets but normally only to non-competing firms. The founders were the FEDERATION OF BRITISH INDUSTRIES, the NATIONAL ASSOCIATION OF BRITISH MANU-FACTURERS, and the INSTITUTE OF DIRECTORS.

Export clubs. Informal associations formed on a regional basis, their members including, apart from local manufacturers, representatives of local SHIPPING AGENTS and FORWARDING AGENTS, BANKS, and INSURANCE companies. For information consult the BOARD OF TRADE, 1 Victoria Street, London SW1.

Export credit insurance. INSURANCE against the risks involved in the export of goods. CREDIT INSURANCE companies insure the commercial risks, e.g. bad debts. The only organization insuring against political and exchange transfer risks is the ◊ EXPORT CREDITS GUARANTEE DEPARTMENT.

Export Credits Guarantee Department. A department of the BOARD OF TRADE whose object is to help exporters by indemnifying them against loss through the default of customers abroad. Premiums are payable – the amount depending on the risks involved. (Information can be obtained from the department at 59–67 Gresham Street, London EC2.) The advantage of the department's cover INSURANCE is that it deals with political and exchange transfer risks in addition to commercial risks.

In addition to insurance the Department helps the exporter in various ways to borrow money. There are three principal methods: (1) By assignment of insurance policies: BANKS accept Export Credits Guarantee Department policies as COLLATERAL SECURITIES. (2) By comprehensive BILL OF EXCHANGE guarantees. These apply to exports and re-exports but not to external trade generally. They are GUARANTEES given to the exporter's bank by the Department. The exporter can obtain money by presenting a bill drawn on the buyer together with evidence of shipment. The bank will normally give 100 per cent without recourse to the exporter though there is an INTEREST rate equal to BANK RATE. (3) By comprehensive open account guarantees similar to (2). They enable the exporter to obtain money from the bank on shipment of GOODS. There may be no bill of exchange. The bank will advance 90 per cent at BANK RATE. The loan is guaranteed by the Department and in this instance the bank has recourse to the exporter. ◊ BANKER'S GUARANTEE.

These facilities do not normally apply to bigger CONTRACTS. Where the loans are needed for periods varying from two to five years, special guarantees are made available by the Department to enable the exporter to obtain funds from his bank.

Export Credits Guarantee Department: comprehensive policy. ◊ EXPORT CREDITS GUARANTEE DEPARTMENT. Continuous or repetitive trade can be insured on a time basis. Rates are set in advance by the E.C.G.D. and vary according to country, and other factors.

Export declarations. Declarations must be completed, for all goods

145

sent abroad, within six days of shipment. The information is used mainly for statistical purposes.

Exporters' declarations. These are made by exporters for Customs purposes. There are various forms available. The Customs check that the necessary LICENCES are available. There are no export duties but export control is necessary for various reasons, for example, some exports are prohibited. Duty-paid goods may be eligible for refund when re-exported. It is also necessary to check that goods which are dutiable if for home use but not if for export, are not re-landed. A Customs officer may attend the loading of a ship to see that no goods are loaded without the necessary licence. Dutiable BONDED GOODS are examined to see that they are properly shipped and not re-landed. The taking on of ships' stores is also supervised. If dutiable they are put in a sealed store and cannot be used till outside British waters. ◊ RUMMAGING continues during the loading of a ship. When loading is complete the captain applies for a clearance outward certificate. This will be given provided all regulations have been observed. The ship may then sail. Within six days the captain or shipping company must also deliver an 'outward MANIFEST' giving details of export cargo. Exporters of goods not controlled must give 'specifications' to the Customs authorities for statistical purposes.

Export house. An experienced organization specializing in selling other people's goods abroad. These set themselves up as market experts regarding language and local conditions abroad. They deal with packing, shipping, INSURANCE, import regulations, TARIFFS, quotas, LICENCES, exchange, and payment terms. Export Houses sell on COMMISSION or on behalf of foreign importers. They also help to finance exporters, e.g. by buying direct and GUARANTEEING payment. When acting for the overseas buyer they will do so as ◊ CONFIRMING HOUSES and receive a commission from the buyer.

Export licensing and restrictions. Most goods can be exported without any restrictions, but there are certain exceptions, such as arms and military equipment, aircraft, strategic goods, some metals (including scrap), live horses, cattle, sheep and pigs, eggs, antiques and diamonds. Application should be made to the Board of Trade Export Licensing Branch, 1 Victoria Street, London SW1.

Export quotation. Export PRICES are quoted in various ways, e.g. COST, INSURANCE AND FREIGHT; FREE ON BOARD; and FREE ALONGSIDE SHIP.

Export rebate scheme. Up until March 1968, certain exported GOODS were relieved from direct taxation (e.g. hydrocarbon oil duty, motor vehicle duty and some elements of PURCHASE TAX). Reliefs varied from $1\frac{1}{4}$ to $3\frac{1}{2}$ per cent of the export PRICE. To be eligible, goods had to be at least 20 per cent U.K. manufactured. Where E.F.T.A. (EUROPEAN FREE TRADE ASSOCIATION) benefits were available, export rebates did not apply. No export rebates were available after March 1968 except on CONTRACTS entered into before 19 November 1967.

Express delivery. ⟡ POST OFFICE: EXPRESS DELIVERY.

Ex ship. Ex ship CONTRACTS are similar to FREE ON BOARD ones, except that the seller is responsible for FREIGHT and INSURANCE and does not pay them on behalf of the buyer. The GOODS are at the seller's RISK until they reach the port of delivery. The seller's responsibility ceases as soon as the goods have left the slings of the ship – if barges are necessary the buyer must provide them. Such contracts are also known as 'free overside'.

Extended protest. A CAPTAIN'S PROTEST made before a NOTARY PUBLIC when there is damage to goods which may result in INSURANCE claims.

Extractive industry. Industry concerned with the extraction of raw materials from the soil or sea, such as mining, agriculture, fishing.

F

Face value. The VALUE stated on the face of an item as opposed to its MARKET VALUE. A SHARE CERTIFICATE may state that it is for 'Shares of £100 being 100 shares of £1 each' but the market price may be very different. The face value of a stamp may be 3d. or 6d. but to a collector this may be irrelevant.

Factor. A general mercantile AGENT dealing with a specified category or categories of GOODS. He is distinguished by the fact that, provided he has possession of the goods coming into these categories with the consent of the owner, he can sell and give a good TITLE to an innocent purchaser for value, whether or not the true owner has given his permission to sell. An art dealer, for instance, could sell pictures lent to him for display, provided the buyer was not aware of this fact.

Factoring. A factor in the financial world is different from a factor in the law of contract. Factoring is similar to ◊ INVOICE DISCOUNTING except that a factor will normally accept responsibility for credit control, debt collection, and credit risk, and of course will charge more correspondingly. There are two principal types of factoring (1) with service, and (2) with service plus finance. The service is the collection of debts and the assumption of credit risk (INVOICES are handed to the factor, who pays monies to the customer at stated intervals). When finance is offered as well, the customer receives up to 90 per cent of the invoice VALUE at once from the factor, rather than 100 per cent, as it were in ARREARS, from the debtor. The debts are in fact purchased for cash; there is no question of repayment (provided of course that the goods are delivered and up to standard). The charge for this financing service might be 1½ per cent over BANK RATE. Naturally, the factor chooses his debtors and customers carefully, and normally only deals with customers whose annual TURNOVER is well over £100,000.

Facultative endorsement. A special form of ENDORSEMENT OF BILLS OF EXCHANGE, which waives certain duties towards the endorser; for instance it may say that no notice of dishonour is necessary.

Farm improvement scheme. The Agriculture Act 1957 allows for payment of grants of one third of the cost of long-term improvements to agricultural land and its fixed equipment. Grants are not made for amounts less than £100. Details of improvements included in the scheme can be obtained from the Ministry of Agriculture.

Farming grants. Various grants are available to farmers and horti-culturalists on application to the Ministry of Agriculture. ⊳ FARM IMPROVEMENT SCHEME ⊳ SMALL FARMERS SCHEME ⊳ CROFTING COUNTIES AGRICULTURAL GRANT ⊳ FARMING: MISCEL-LANEOUS GRANTS AND SUBSIDIES ⊳ HORTICULTURE IM-PROVEMENT SCHEME ⊳ RURAL INDUSTRIES LOAN FUND LIMITED.

Farming: miscellaneous grants and subsidies. Grants and subsidies are available for, *inter alia*, eradicating bracken (50 per cent); building houses for farm-workers; purchasing bulls or boars to be let out on hire; calf rearing and vaccination; ditching and drainage (maximum 50 per cent); purchasing fertilizers; renovating grassland; main-taining bulls, cows and sheep; purchasing lime; grubbing up orchards; ploughing; vaccinating poultry; constructing silos; win-ter keeping; dedicating woodland and planting small woodlands; also for machinery syndicates; market research and development; CAPITAL for small-holdings; water supply; and pest destruction.

Federation of British Industries. ⊳ CONFEDERATION OF BRITISH INDUSTRIES.

Fellow subsidiaries. SUBSIDIARY COMPANIES of the same holding company are known as fellow subsidiaries. Amounts due to and from fellow subsidiaries are normally shown as a separate item in the ANNUAL ACCOUNTS.

Feme covert. A legal term for a married woman.

Feme sole. A legal term for a spinster or widow.

Fictitious assets. An accounting term for ASSETS which appear on a BALANCE SHEET not because they have any particular value, but because the DOUBLE-ENTRY BOOK-KEEPING system demands that they should. An obvious example is a DEBIT balance on a PROFIT AND LOSS ACCOUNT. They should be distinguished from IN-TANGIBLE ASSETS.

Fidelity guarantee. One person may GUARANTEE the integrity or fidelity of another, e.g. in a CONTRACT of employment. INSURANCE companies also offer fidelity policies, agreeing to make good mis-appropriations of employees.

Fiduciary issue. That part of the note issue of the BANK OF ENGLAND that is backed not by gold but by government and other SECURITIES. The total is controlled by Parliament. Any profits on sale of these securities go to the government, being paid into the EXCHANGE EQUALISATION FUND.

Finance company. Those COMPANIES whose business is speculative lending, generally ♢ HIRE PURCHASE FINANCE COMPANIES. The term could also be applied in a limited sense to some of the MERCHANT BANKS, etc.

Finance Corporation for Industry Ltd. Formed in 1945 by the BANK OF ENGLAND, London and Scottish clearing BANKS and many large INSURANCE companies and INVESTMENT TRUSTS. Its AUTHORIZED CAPITAL and ISSUED CAPITAL was £25,000,000. The Corporation may borrow up to four times the nominal value of its issued capital. Most of its finance is by borrowed funds and these are obtained almost entirely from the banks. The object is to supplement other forms of finance with a view to rehabilitating industry. The minimum loan is £250,000. The borrower must show that he cannot obtain funds elsewhere and that the loan is in the national interest. Loans tend to be large, and few. Rates of INTEREST vary but generally are low.

Finance house. A more sophisticated name for a ♢ FINANCE COMPANY. ♢ FINANCE HOUSES ASSOCIATION.

Finance Houses Association. Formed in 1945 by six large FINANCE COMPANIES with the idea of presenting a united front in HIRE-PURCHASE FINANCE, *re* INTEREST rates, DEPOSITS, etc. Membership is now much greater, it represents members' interests in discussions with the government, also acts as an information pool for members and the public. ♢ INDUSTRIAL BANKERS ASSOCIATION.

Financial year. A fairly general term normally meaning the year of account, or ACCOUNTING PERIOD. The 1948 Companies Act defines the term as any period in respect of which any PROFIT AND LOSS ACCOUNT is made up, whether that period is a year or not.

Financier. A fairly meaningless term for those earning their living by financing other people's businesses. They take the place of what were known as usurers.

Fine bill. A BILL OF EXCHANGE discountable at the finest rate, i.e., where there is little or no risk.

Fine trade bill. A TRADE BILL with the backing of an established BANK or FINANCE HOUSE.

Fire insurance. Insurance against losses due to fire. These CONTRACTS usually last for one year, with an option on renewal. Premiums may be changed from year to year. The policy holder should inform the insurance company of any change in the value of the property. He will never obtain more than the VALUE of the actual loss, so it is pointless to over-insure, or to insure for the full amount with more than one company. If the property is under-insured, the policy holder will probably only receive a proportion of the actual loss. ◊ AVERAGE CLAUSE.

The insured must have an ◊ INSURABLE INTEREST. This must exist at the time of loss, and with buildings, also when the policy is made. TRUSTEES may insure trust property, and mortgagees mortgaged property. A COMPANY'S shareholders and UNSECURED CREDITORS have no insurable interest in its property.

A policy may be assigned only with the consent of the insurance company. For this purpose a MORTGAGE is not an ASSIGNMENT.

In the case of buildings, any interested party (i.e. the insurance company, a mortgagee, etc.) may insist that the policy money is used to reinstate the building (under the Fires Prevention (Metropolis) Act 1774). This is to prevent people from letting their houses burn down and taking the money.

The insurer is entitled to take over the property (the wreckage) of the insured, when paying on a total loss. This is known as SUBROGATION.

Firm. Strictly the name given to a PARTNERSHIP business though often used more generally. In Scotland a 'partnership firm' is a separate legal person, though it does not have all the attributes of a corporate body. In England a partnership firm cannot CONTRACT in its own name.

First class paper. When BILLS OF EXCHANGE, GOVERNMENT BILLS, CONSOLS, etc., carry the signature of a well-known BANK, FINANCE COMPANY or DISCOUNT HOUSE, they are called first class papers.

First in first out (F.I.F.O.). ◊ STOCK VALUATION.

Fiscal year. The official government year of account ending on 5 April.

Fishing industry: grants and subsidies. Under the Sea Fish Industry Act 1962 (which applies until 1972), subsidies are payable at rate per day for large vessels, and at rate per stone of fish for small ones. They are available to owners or charterers catching white fish or herring to be landed in the United Kingdom from U.K. registered ships. Details are available from the Fishery Department, Ministry of Agriculture, Fisheries and Food.

Loans are available from the White Fish Authority for improvements to old vessels, or the purchase of new vessels, processing plant, nets, etc. These loans (of up to 60 per cent of requirement) are secured either on the purchased ASSETS or on others, and are repayable half-yearly over twenty years; there is no fixed rate of INTEREST. Grants are also available from the White Fish Authority and the Herring Industry Board for the purchase of new vessels or the acquisition and installation of new engines in vessels less than eighty feet in length. Advances are limited to 30 per cent, and there are certain other maximums (for instance 25 per cent if the vessel is over eighty feet in length). Grants are also available for the purchase of freezer trawlers, and, since 1964, for improvements to white fish vessels.

Fishmonger. A dealer in fish.

Fixed assets. Those business ASSETS which are purchased for continued use in manufacture (e.g. land, machinery, etc.). They are written off against profits over their anticipated life by charging an annual amount calculated so as to eliminate the original cost, less scrap value, over that period. ⟐ DEPRECIATION ⟐ CURRENT ASSETS.

Fixed capital. Another term for ⟐ FIXED ASSETS.

Fixed charges. A book-keeping term for business expenses which are not related to the level of operations.

Fixed costs. ⟐ OVERHEAD EXPENSES.

Fixed interest securities. SHARES or SECURITIES which carry a fixed rate of INTEREST.

Fixtures, fittings, etc. An accounting term for immovable ASSETS affixed to a building in some way though not strictly part of that building itself.

Fletcher. A maker of or dealer in bows and arrows. Not in common use.

Flight coupon. The portion of a passenger's air ticket which indicates particular places between which the coupon is good for carriage.

Floating assets. Another term for ⟐ CURRENT ASSETS.

Floating charge. When a loan to a business is secured on ASSETS generally rather than on a particular item, there is said to be a floating charge. The lender has priority of repayment from the fund of assets that exist when, say, a RECEIVING ORDER is made against the business. At this time the charge is said to be frozen. ⟐ DEBENTURE.

Floating debt. ⟐ UNFUNDED DEBT.

Floating policy. An INSURANCE policy covering goods not all in the same place and not of constant VALUE.

Flotsam. Goods or parts of a shipwrecked vessel found floating on the surface of the sea. If not claimed within a year and a day they belong to the Crown.

Foolscap. A piece of paper measuring seventeen by thirteen and a half inches. The name originates from the water mark – once a fool's cap and bells. (It is suggested that this mark dates from Cromwellian times and replaced the royal arms.)

For the account. A STOCK EXCHANGE term for dealings to be settled on the next half monthly ACCOUNT DAY.

Forbearance. Forbearance to sue can be good CONSIDERATION for an OFFER so as to constitute a CONTRACT. There must be a right to sue: if the claim is invalid then it is no consideration, provided the party knows it to be invalid. The claim must be based upon an enforceable contract and not on an ILLEGAL CONTRACT.

Foreclosure. ◊ MORTGAGEE, RIGHTS OF.

Foreign bills. ◊ BILLS OF EXCHANGE drawn in one country and payable in another.

Foreign judgments. Where a judgment is made in a foreign court and the JUDGMENT CREDITOR wants to enforce it in this country, he must appeal to the High Court within six years to have the judgment registered. If registered, it is equal to a judgment in this country. If it is to be registered, it must be final and conclusive and must not involve payment of taxes, fines, penalties, etc.

Forged transfer of shares. Where a transfer is forged, registered, and a SHARE CERTIFICATE given to a transferee, the true owner is entitled to be reinstated on the register (◊ RECTIFICATION OF REGISTER). The COMPANY cannot deny validity of the certificate issued and may be liable to pay damages to any innocent person who suffers loss by relying on it. Consequently a company will generally notify the transferor when it receives a transfer. The transferor can ensure this by issuing a NOTICE IN LIEU OF DISTRINGAS.

Forward dating. The practice of dating commercial documents in advance. INVOICES may be dated forward, perhaps to give the customer additional time to pay, or where delivery has been delayed. CHEQUES may be forward dated where the drawer has no present funds but expects to be able to meet the cheque at the date specified. The BANK will not cash the cheque before that date.

Forward dealing. ◊ FUTURES, DEALING IN.

Forward purchases. GOODS, STOCKS, or SHARES are often purchased forward where large quantities are involved. This means that the supplier agrees to provide a stated quantity at a certain future date for a stated PRICE. Such transactions are also known as FUTURES.

Forward sales. Agreements to supply GOODS, STOCKS, or SHARES, on a certain future date at a stated price. ◊ FUTURES.

Forwarding agent. A GENERAL AGENT specializing in the transport of GOODS to or from a port.

Foul bill of lading. A BILL OF LADING which states that the GOODS have been put on board in a defective condition. The bill is usually endorsed to this effect by the master of the ship. It is also known as a dirty bill of lading.

Founders' shares. SHARES issued to the founders of a COMPANY.

These shares usually have partial DIVIDEND rights, etc. ◊ DE-FERRED SHARES.

Franchise. A clause in a MARINE INSURANCE policy which disallows claims of less than a certain amount unless the insured ship is stranded or sunk. If the damage is over the minimum, all is re-coverable, if less, then none is recoverable unless the ship is stranded or sunk. The purpose of this clause is to prevent petty claims, and also to restrict liability on perhaps very risky cargo.

Franco, rendu, or free contracts. A variation of EX SHIP contracts where the exporter pays all expenses of delivery to the importer's ware-house. These contracts are unusual because the seller is not usually familiar with conditions in other countries. They are very convenient for the importer, however.

Franked investment income. INVESTMENT INCOME received by a COMPANY which has already been taxed at source. Provided certain conditions are fulfilled this income is not taxed again in the hands of this company.

Franking machine. ◊ POST OFFICE: FRANKING MACHINES.

Fraud. If a CONTRACT is made as a result of fraud on the part of one party, i.e., a fraudulent MISREPRESENTATION, the injured party may rescind the contract and also obtain damages. To be fraudulent, the misrepresentation must be made either with an attempt to deceive, or without caring whether the statement was true or false. It should be a statement of fact (though in *Derry v. Peek* the judge commented that a man's opinion was as much a fact as the state of his digestion). Fraud is an offence in tort as well as in contract. Remedies of the injured party are: (1) to affirm the contract and sue for damages in tort for deceit, (2) to rescind with or without seeking damages in tort.

He may still be able to sue for damages if he has lost his right to rescind.

Fraud, agreements to commit. Agreements to commit a FRAUD are illegal and not enforceable at law. ◊ ILLEGAL CONTRACTS.

Fraudulent conveyance. An act of BANKRUPTCY. The debtor de-liberately signs away part of his property with an intent to defeat CREDITORS.

Fraudulent preference. An act of BANKRUPTCY. A deliberate (it must be deliberate) preference of one CREDITOR or SURETY by an INSOLVENT debtor.

Fraudulent preference: companies. Rules similar to BANKRUPTCY rules apply. If the COMPANY has preferred a CREDITOR or a SURETY within six months of the commencement of the WINDING-UP, the transfer or charge is void as against the liquidator, who can recover the property.

Fraudulent trading. Where DIRECTORS are considered responsible for fraudulent trading (i.e. carrying on business with an attempt to defraud CREDITORS) they may become personally liable without limit for the debts of the COMPANY. The question of fraudulent trading will arise in a WINDING-UP.

Free alongside ship (F.A.S.). When an exporter delivers goods 'free alongside ship', he pays all charges involved up to that point. ◊ FREE ON BOARD.

Free depreciation. An additional aid to industry, particularly in DEVELOPMENT AREAS. COMPANIES or FIRMS are allowed to depreciate at whatever rate they wish, for tax purposes. The normal capital allowances do not apply. This applies to expenditure after 26 October 1970.

Free from particular average. A MARINE INSURANCE term meaning that the insurers are not responsible for anything other than total loss and ◊ GENERAL AVERAGE LOSS. The clause may be qualified in various ways, i.e., the insurer may take responsibility for certain specified items of cargo.

Free of all average. A MARINE INSURANCE term for policies where the insurer takes no responsibility for ◊ GENERAL or ◊ PARTICULAR AVERAGE LOSSES, and will only pay on a total loss.

Free of capture, etc. A MARINE INSURANCE term for policies which exclude liability arising from capture, seizure, detention by foreign powers, or mutiny. It does not normally apply to a blockade.

Free of capture or seizure. In time of hostilities, MARINE INSURANCE policies may contain a 'free of capture or seizure' clause, disclaiming responsibility for those losses.

Free on board (F.O.B.). When an exporter delivers GOODS 'free on board', he pays all charges involved in getting them actually onto the ship. His responsibilities include putting the goods in a condition for shipping, taking them to the ship and loading them (◊ FREE ON BOARD AND TRIMMED). The buyer must provide the ship, and the seller's responsibility ends when the goods are on board. The seller must notify the buyer to enable him to insure the goods; otherwise he may himself be liable for damage at sea. Property in the goods normally passes with risk, though the buyer may reserve the right to reject the goods if he has had no previous opportunity to examine them and they are not up to specification or quality when he receives them.

Free on board and trimmed. A FREE ON BOARD CONTRACT peculiar to the coal trade. The seller, in addition to loading the coal, must see that it is properly stored.

Free overside. ⟡ EX SHIP.

Free port. A port where no duties are paid on imports or exports.

Free trade. Trade (usually international) with no imposed restrictions such as Customs duties etc.

Freeboard. The distance between the main deck and the waterline of a ship.

Freehold land. If a person has the freehold to land, he has the best possible TITLE, being its absolute owner. There may however be encumbrances such as EASEMENTS, etc. The term 'freehold land and buildings' is frequently used in accounts, and indicates freehold land owned by the business, and buildings on it. The freehold land is sometimes bracketed in company accounts with ⟡ LEASEHOLD LAND.

Freight. The money paid by a charterer to a ship-owner in CONSIDERATION of the latter letting the ship, or space within the ship. The money is not payable until the GOODS are delivered. ⟡ ADVANCE FREIGHT ⟡ FREIGHT NOTES ⟡ LUMP SUM FREIGHT ⟡ FREIGHT FORWARD ⟡ PRO RATA FREIGHT ⟡ DEAD FREIGHT ⟡ BACK FREIGHT ⟡ SHIP-OWNER'S LIEN.

Freight forward. A shipping term meaning FREIGHT is payable at port of destination.

Freight Integration Council. A council set up by the Transport Act 1968 to settle differences arising from the coordination of the transport authorities (the NATIONAL FREIGHT CORPORATION, the Railways Board, the Docks Board, the Waterways Board, the Scottish Group, the BRITISH OVERSEAS AIRWAYS CORPORATION, the British Airports Authority, and the Postmaster General).

Freight liner. A door-to-door container service offered by British Rail. The emphasis is on speed and efficiency. Loaded containers are taken by road to a freight liner terminal then transported speedily to another terminal. Space can be reserved in advance. The containers are delivered by road from the terminal. The containers (of a fixed size) are owned by the railway but packed by the user at his own premises. They conform with international standards. There are freight liner lines between most major industrial centres. The containers are loaded onto British Railways vehicles free, but there is a charge for any delay over a stated limit, e.g. fifteen minutes per capacity ton. Containers must be returned within a specified time after use.

Freight notes. Notes from ship-owner to shipper, showing the amount of FREIGHT due.

Freight release. ◊ ADVANCE FREIGHT.

French gold francs. An air transport term for francs consisting of 65·5 milligrams of gold with a fineness of nine-hundred thousandths, i.e. 90 per cent pure.

Frozen assets. ASSETS tied up so that transactions in them are restricted or impossible. Where a COMPANY has floating DEBENTURES and they become repayable, the assets of the company are frozen from the point of view of the debenture holders.

Frustration clause. A MARINE INSURANCE clause. The insurer takes no responsibility if the enterprise is completely frustrated.

Frustration of contract. A CONTRACT is frustrated when it cannot be carried out, though neither party is to blame. Before the Fibrosa case (1942) the law took the view that the loss should lie where it fell; afterwards, that money paid could be recovered where the CONSIDERATION had failed. The position was clarified by the Law Reform (Frustrated Contracts) Act 1943, which stated that monies paid could be recovered, but that the party from whom they were recovered might be allowed to deduct expenses, and charge for the VALUE of work done where the other party had received a benefit. (The Act does not apply to contracts for carriage of goods by sea, certain CHARTER PARTIES, INSURANCE contracts, contracts for the sale of specific goods where the frustration arises from the perishing of the goods.)

Full-time directors. ◊ CLOSE COMPANY.

Fundamental terms. Under the law of CONTRACT, these are terms in a contract which are so fundamental that breach of them would be considered to be complete non-performance, as opposed to breach of CONDITIONS or WARRANTIES. The distinction is important, for EXEMPTION CLAUSES that apply to conditions or warranties do not apply to fundamental terms.

Funded debt. That part of the NATIONAL DEBT which the government is not obliged to repay at any particular time, e.g., CONSOLS.

Fur auctions. These take place at Beaver House, Garlick Hill, London EC4, which is also the head office of the Hudson Bay Company. Sales of individual furs are held throughout the year, and more general sales about four times a year. Buyers inspect the furs at the BROKER'S warehouse (anyone may attend the sales). By tradition the wares of the Hudson Bay Company are sold first. SETTLING DAY, or prompt day, is usually thirty days after the first day of the sale. Brokers may refuse bids from undesirable buyers.

Future goods, sale of. A CONTRACT for the sale of future goods is one where the GOODS contracted for are still to be manufactured. These contracts are governed by the Sale of Goods Act 1893. TITLE passes when the goods are ascertained and the buyer notified.

Future tax. A term used in accounts with reference to tax calculated on the profits of the accounting year but not payable until some distant date and then only if the business was still in existence. The item was made obsolete by the Finance Act 1965 and the introduction of CORPORATION TAX.

Futures. FORWARD SALES or FORWARD PURCHASES, often by SPECULATORS who have no intention of taking up or providing the GOODS personally.

Futures, dealing in. Buying and selling by middlemen of OPTIONS TO PURCHASE SHARES, STOCKS, or GOODS, or to sell them. This helps to put forward buyers in touch with forward sellers (the dealer of course takes a COMMISSION).

G

Gambling. An agreement whereby one party pays a sum of money if an event occurs on CONSIDERATION of the other party paying a fixed sum if it does not. Neither party has a personal interest in the event or stands to lose anything other than the money which is the subject matter of the agreement. For the legal position ⟡ WAGERING CONTRACTS ⟡ GAMING CONTRACTS.

Gaming contract. ⟡ CONTRACT, GAMING.

Garnishee order. A legal order made on a person owing money to a JUDGMENT DEBTOR instructing him not to pay the debt until the debtor has made good the claims against him. It effectively (though not legally) gives the JUDGMENT CREDITOR a LIEN on debts owed to the judgment debtor.

Gazetted. ⟡ LONDON GAZETTE.

General Agreement on Tariffs and Trade (G.A.T.T.). An agreement signed in 1947 by more than forty countries, to campaign against the imposition of TARIFF barriers and quota restrictions, and progressively to liberalize trade between the participant countries. There are provisions to discourage *blocs* within the group, and to insist on most-favoured-nation treatment for all members if for any. In many instances, governments are expected to ask permission before making drastic alterations to TARIFFS. As the Agreement is a gentleman's agreement, its provisions have no legal force, though there is not usually any advantage in flouting them.

General average loss. A term used in MARINE INSURANCE. When there is a partial loss of ship or cargo incurred for the benefit of others than the owner of the ship or that particular cargo, the loss is apportioned over all persons involved. For instance, if there is a fire in a ship and in putting out the fire, cargo other than that which caught fire is damaged, then the loss is apportioned between owners of all the cargo, the freight and the ship. In order that a loss may be a general average loss there must be an extraordinary sacrifice or expenditure, voluntarily made at a time of necessity for the purpose of preserving all the property involved in the venture. The danger must be common to all those called on to contribute; contributions will be assessed at the port of discharge; the shipowners must collect contributions from the various shippers, and it is then up to them to claim from their insurance company.

General average sacrifice. A MARINE INSURANCE term for a sacrifice made by the master of the ship for the benefit of the shipowner, charterer and cargo owners. ◊ GENERAL AVERAGE LOSS.

General certificate in supervisory studies. A certificate awarded by the national examining board in Supervisory Studies, leading to graduate membership of the Institute of Supervisory Studies.

General clearing. ◊ CLEARING, TOWN AND GENERAL.

General crossing. ◊ CROSSING, GENERAL.

General offer. An OFFER to the public at large, acceptance usually being made by some act. Communication to the offeror is not always necessary. The offer may give rise to many CONTRACTS. For instance, if A advertises that he will pay £5 for every fifteenth-century coin submitted to him, he is bound to accept each coin offered and pay the money. On the other hand, the offer may give rise to only one contract. If A offers £5 for certain information, only the first person to provide the information is entitled to the £5.

General partner. ◊ PARTNERSHIP ◊ PARTNERSHIP, LIMITED.

Gift. A voluntary transfer of property by one person to another, no CONSIDERATION being given. Promises to give freely in this way are only enforceable if they are made by DEED. When a gift is of some property other than money, it is subject to ◊ CAPITAL GAINS TAX (payable by the donor), which is levied as if the property had been sold at the date of transfer for its proper MARKET VALUE.

Gift cheques. Certain BANKS offer these for use on festive occasions such as birthdays, weddings, or Christmas. They cost one shilling, plus of course the amount of the CHEQUE.

Gill. Fourth part of a pint.

Gilt-edged securities. These are SECURITIES or investments where the risk is marginal, i.e., CAPITAL repayment and INTEREST are almost certain. Generally applied to government securities.

Giro. ◊ NATIONAL GIRO ◊ BANK GIRO.

Gold and dollar reserves. ◊ RESERVES, GOLD, DOLLAR, ETC.

Gold coins. The Exchange Control Act 1947 insisted that all gold coins or BULLION should be submitted to an authorized dealer. They may be sold through a jeweller. Collectors may retain coins which were minted before 1816, or have a greater numismatic value than their gold content.

Gold Pool. In 1961, eight countries (the United Kingdom, France, West Germany, Switzerland, Italy, the United States, Belgium and the Netherlands) informally agreed to intervene in the London Gold Market to prevent pressure on the PRICE of gold and avoid too much SPECULATION by preventing the price from rising above $35·19⅞.

This was done by forming the Gold Pool. In 1967 at the time of U.K. devaluation, France, for reasons best known to herself, opted out, and there was considerable speculation. This led to a crisis in the Gold Market (as yet unresolved), the creation of a two-tier price system, and the abandonment of the Gold Pool. ◊ RESERVES, GOLD, DOLLAR, ETC.

Golden handshake. ◊ COMPENSATION FOR LOSS OF OFFICE.

Good faith. ◊ BONA FIDE.

Goods. The definition of 'goods' is important because of the obligations imposed and the protection offered by, the Sale of Goods Act 1893. Goods are generally personal chattels, emblements, industrial growing crops, and ships, but not CHOSES-IN-ACTION or money. CONTRACTS for the SALE OF GOODS should be distinguished from contracts for work and materials, which are not governed by the Sale of Goods Act. (The test is, whether the payment was made for the work done rather than for the materials supplied. A contract for work done where the materials are incidental, e.g. the painting of pictures, will be a contract for work and materials.)

Goods on approval. A person may ask for GOODS on approval if he wishes to see them before deciding whether to buy, and the VENDOR will usually allow him a stated number of days in which to make a decision. Equally, a vendor may also send goods to a selected number of persons in the hope that they will purchase them. In the first instance, the purchaser is a voluntary ◊ BAILEE and has a duty to take care of the goods and to return them as directed. In the second instance, the person is a quite involuntary bailee and has no responsibility towards the goods, unless custom dictates otherwise. He may not destroy them, but may demand that the vendor retakes them immediately and at his own expense, or simply redirect them to the vendor, leaving him to pay. If the goods are in any way a nuisance, he may take necessary precautions.

Goods on consignment. GOODS sent to an AGENT for sale. The agent has possession but not TITLE, though he may be able to give a good title to a BONA FIDE purchaser, even when acting outside his authority. The goods are usually returnable by the agent, who works for a COMMISSION. The venture is normally made for a limited period only.

Goodwill. Johnson defined goodwill when he said 'We are not here to sell a parcel of boilers and vats but the potentiality of growing rich beyond the dreams of avarice.' It is a nebulous term for that part of the VALUE of an ASSET or business arising from factors not directly associated with the assets or business as such. For instance, goodwill may arise from the good reputation of the business or the fact that it is making profits above the average due to some particular advantage. The calculation of goodwill is somewhat complex and is a matter for bargaining (by accountants).

Government stock on the Post Office register. The POST OFFICE will buy or sell government SECURITIES. Applications for purchase or sale must be made at a POST OFFICE SAVINGS BANK. Amounts of up to £1,000 may be bought on any one day. Payment may be out of a Post Office Savings Account or by CHEQUE payable to the Post Office. The remittance should cover the estimated cost of the STOCK and the COMMISSION. The holder is given a certificate or bond book, giving details of the holding. Stock can be sold by filling in an application and depositing the certificate or bond book. Payment, less commission, will be made at a BANK or post office. (This does not apply to ◇ NATIONAL DEVELOPMENT BONDS.) Commission charges are: for securities not exceeding £10, 5p; £25, 7½p; £50, 12½p; £75, 17½p; £100, 22½p; and an additional 5p for every extra £50. Anyone can buy or sell who is over the age of seven years; younger persons may have stock purchased on their behalf. This is not normally saleable before they attain the age of seven years. Transfer can be made from one bondholder to another through the Post Office.

Graft. U.S. slang for money made in illicit dealings while employed on political or municipal business. Now sometimes applied more generally to monies made by taking illicit advantage of one's office.

Gratuity. Often referred to as a tip, this is a sum paid without obligation for services rendered. It is normally taxable in the hands of the recipient. In some industries, e.g., cab driving, catering, or hairdressing, gratuities are an important source of income and basic salaries may be adjusted accordingly. The term is often used for lump-sum payments on the termination of employment, misleadingly in the case of the Armed Forces, where such payments are actually contracted for. In the hotel industry, a charge may be added to the bill, supposedly in lieu of gratuities. This is known as a service charge, and is divided amongst the hotel staff much as prize money was divided in the romantic days of British naval supremacy.

Graving dock. A dry dock where ships are taken for repairs and maintenance, particularly to the exterior of the ship below the waterline.

Greengrocer. Generally a retail trader in vegetables and fruit.

Grocer. Generally a retail trader in provisions, particularly spices, sugar, dried fruit, etc. The name is derived from the fact that these traders originally purchased in the gross.

Gross profit. A vague term. Where the buying or selling of GOODS is concerned, it is used for the proceeds of SALE, less the cost of putting the goods into a condition for sale. Where the goods are also manufactured, this cost will include part of the OVERHEAD EXPENSES. Otherwise, overheads concerned with distributing or selling the goods and administering the business generally are charged after gross profit (also known as 'gross profit on trading') to produce net profit on trading. This will then be adjusted for exceptional items or items not connected with the major objects of the business, to produce the actual net profit.

Gross profit on trading. ⟡ GROSS PROFIT.

Ground rents. RENT paid for land as opposed to rent paid for the buildings on the land. Rights to receive ground rents can be bought and sold. At one time prior to April 1964, tax was deducted by the payer, and the payment was treated as an annual charge. Payment is now made gross, i.e. not tax-deducted.

Group. A group of interrelated COMPANIES (in fact one single business entity jointly controlled). It usually consists of one holding company and a number of ⟡ SUBSIDIARY COMPANIES, though there may be sub-subsidiary companies or associated companies (for example if A Company and B Company each own 50 per cent of C Company and A Company owns B Company, C Company is part of the group though not a subsidiary of either). Situations where A Company owns B Company owns C Company owns A Company are not permitted.

Group accounts: omission of subsidiaries. ⟡ GROUP. Where SUBSIDIARY COMPANIES are omitted from GROUP ACCOUNTS, indication of the following must be given: (1) the reason why they are not so dealt with, (2) the aggregate profit or loss of those subsidiaries, attributable to the holding company, for the current year and previous years since acquisition, (3) any qualifications by the AUDITORS in the accounts of the subsidiaries, (4) the total VALUE of SHARES in subsidiaries, and amounts owing to and from subsidiaries, (5) any shares held by the subsidiaries in the holding company.

Guarantee. An agreement to be answerable for the debt, default or miscarriage of another. This is different from an INDEMNITY, which is a CONTRACT where one party agrees to suffer the loss of the other (e.g. FIRE INSURANCE). He takes a primary liability; there may be only two persons concerned. A guarantor assumes secondary liability. He agrees to pay if the debtor defaults. He must have no interest in the contract between the debtor and CREDITOR. He is sometimes called a surety. The contract of guarantee itself must be accompanied by a memorandum in writing. Normally on default of the debtor, the creditor may take action against the guarantor without first having taken action against the debtor. If the guarantor pays he may then attempt to recover from the debtor. The liability of a guarantor may disappear if the contract between debtor and creditor is altered without his notice. The law on guarantees is fairly extensive. Points to note are: (1) the guarantor in recovering from the debtor can take over a SECURITY previously held by the creditor; (2) he may also claim contribution from co-sureties.

Guinea. Originally a U.K. gold coin made from gold mined in Guinea in Africa, but nowadays simply the sum of 21s. Professional fees are often quoted in guineas, but will probably cease to be after the introduction of the decimal system.

Gunsmith. A maker or repairer of firearms, particularly the small ones.

H

Haberdasher. Formerly a dealer in many different items, particularly caps, hats, etc. Now a dealer in clothing and dressmaking accessories, such as ribbon, lace, thread, etc.

Haggle. To cavil and wrangle when settling a bargain.

Half commission man. A STOCK EXCHANGE term for a person who being neither a STOCKBROKER nor a STOCKJOBBER, introduces clients to a broker in return for a share in the COMMISSION.

Hall-mark. A mark made on precious metals after an ASSAY test. At present there are two qualities of silver and four of gold. The British hall-mark is accepted internationally as a guarantee of standard. There are four marks: the maker's mark, the hall or assay-office mark, the quality mark, and the date letter. The hall or assay-office mark may be made at London (leopard), Chester (the arms of the city), Birmingham (anchor), Sheffield (crown), Edinburgh (castle), Glasgow (fish, tree, bell, and bird) and Dublin (Irish harp with crown).

Gold must also have the carat mark on it to indicate its quality – there are four recognized CARAT marks at present, 22 carat (i.e. 22 parts gold, 2 parts alloy), 18 carat, 14 carat and 9 carat. In Dublin there is an additional 12 carat. The date is indicated by a letter, each year having a separate letter, the letters being changed on different dates at different centres. Quality marks for silver are a lion passant for England and a thistle or a lion rampant for Scotland. All objects made of gold or silver must be stamped, but there are exceptions, which are, briefly: (1) chains, e.g. watch chains, alberts, dress chains, key chains, but not chain bracelets, etc. (articles attached to the chains are not necessarily excepted), (2) lockets, (3) the actual settings of precious stones, (4) imported articles over one hundred years old, (5 – gold only) jointed sleeper ear-rings, rings other than wedding rings, thimbles, pencil cases, or items richly engraved or set with stones that might be damaged by marking, and items too small to be marked (weighing less than 10 dwts), (6 – silver only) items too small to be marked, stamped medals, and certain items weighing a very small amount.

There are heavy penalities for selling items not hall-marked.

Hammered. A member of the STOCK EXCHANGE is hammered when he cannot meet his debts. The process is named from the three

165

strokes of the hammer delivered by the WAITER at the Stock Exchange as a prelude to the announcement of the name of the defaulter. It is said to be the only effective way of producing silence in the Stock Exchange.

Haulage. The charge made for carrying GOODS, though not usually for loading or unloading them.

Hawker. A person who sells GOODS which he carries round with him; usually one who sells from a vehicle rather than from a pack or suitcase. ⟡ SHARE HAWKING ⟡ STREET TRADER ⟡ PEDLAR.

Head lease. When property is leased to one person and then sub-let in part or whole to others, the original lease is known as the head lease.

Hedging. A trader, particularly if buying forward or selling forward in the COMMODITY EXCHANGES, may 'hedge' to protect himself from losses arising from variations in PRICE. For instance, a dealer who has sold a large quantity of GOODS forward, may want to insure against the possibility of heavy losses through a rise in price by buying early or passing on some of his FORWARD SALES to other dealers (much as a bookmaker lays off debts). ⟡ FUTURES.

Her Majesty's Customs and Excise. Objectives are: (1) to control imports and exports and the manufacture of dutiable GOODS, and to assess and collect Customs duty, Excise duty and/or PURCHASE TAX on them; (2) to collect purchase tax and betting and gaming duties, checking relevant statements of liability; and (3) to administer reliefs from, or repayments of, duties.

For collection of revenue, the United Kingdom is divided into thirty-four sections. The officials of the Customs and Excise fall into three categories: (1) officers of Customs and Excise (not uniformed) who control the landing and shipping of cargo and the manufacture of dutiable goods, and also verify purchase tax and collect betting and gaming duties; (2) executive and clerical officials who are concerned with all the background paper work, and with issuing RECEIPTS for duties paid; (3) the Customs Waterguard Service (uniformed), who are concerned with the prevention of smuggling, etc., are stationed at seaports and airports, and patrol the coast by land and sea, particularly the rivers, creeks, and harbours. They also patrol the land frontier in Ireland. ⟡ CUSTOMS etc.

Hidden reserve. ⟡ SECRET RESERVE.

High seas. The seas or oceans of the world which are not enclosed national waters, or what are known as TERRITORIAL WATERS or the '*mare clausum*'. Any ship has the right to venture on the high seas.

Higher National Certificate in Business Studies. A qualification re-

placing the Intermediate Certificate in Business Studies. It is awarded
by the Department of Education and Science. Candidates for this
(external) examination must have the Ordinary National Certificate in
Business Studies, have completed an H.N.C. CONVERSION COURSE
or passed G.C.E. A level in two subjects. Students must submit a
thesis at the end of the second year. The certificate gives partial
exemption from the examinations of certain professional bodies.

Higher National Certificate in Business Studies: conversion course. A
one-year course enabling mature students to reach the standard
necessary for starting a HIGHER NATIONAL CERTIFICATE IN
BUSINESS STUDIES course proper.

Hire purchase. Lord Greene M.R. once said that a great part of his
time on the bench was concerned, '... with people who are persuaded by persons whom they do not know to enter into CONTRACTS
they do not understand to purchase GOODS they do not want with
money they have not got'. Hire purchase is defined by the HIRE
PURCHASE ACT 1965 as 'an agreement for the BAILMENT of goods
under which the BAILEE may buy the goods or under which the
property of the goods will or may pass to the bailee'. That is, a hire
purchase agreement is in effect an agreement to hire goods for a
specified period, with an option for the hirer to purchase the goods
at the end, usually for a nominal sum. The property in the goods
does not normally pass to the hirer until the last payment is made.
Both the seller and the hirer or buyer have certain rights and obligations defined by the Act. The hirer may terminate the agreement at
any time by giving notice but must allow the seller to retake possession, and must also pay instalments due and the additional amount
necessary to bring total payments up to 50 per cent of hire purchase
PRICE (unless a lesser sum is specified in the agreement). The hirer
may also be liable for any damage done to the goods due to his
negligence. The agreement cannot restrict the buyer's right to
terminate. The seller has certain rights. He may retake the goods if
an instalment is not paid provided he serves a 'notice of default'
requiring payment within seven days, and the payment is not made.
This right is restricted insofar as after one-third of the hire purchase
price is paid, the seller cannot recover the goods except by action in
a county court. If he does otherwise the agreement is terminated and
the hirer may recover all sums paid. There must be a written agreement which must state the CASH PRICE of the goods, the hire
purchase price, the amount and date of the instalments, and a list of
the goods. The agreement must be signed by the hirer and all other
parties and must contain a notice of the right of the hirer to ter-

minate the agreement and the restriction of the seller's right to recover the goods. A copy of the agreement must be sent to the hirer within seven days. ◊ HIRE PURCHASE: CONDITIONS AND WARRANTIES.

Apart from these and other particular rules, hire purchase sales are subject to the general provisions of the Sale of Goods Act 1893.

Hire purchase is normally financed by a third party, e.g. a FINANCE COMPANY which effectively buys the debt, enabling the seller to collect the cash at the beginning rather than the end. ◊ HIRE PURCHASE FINANCE.

Hire Purchase Act 1965. This Act deals with CONTRACTS of HIRE PURCHASE, CONDITIONAL SALE AGREEMENTS where the purchase PRICE does not exceed £2,000, and CREDIT SALE AGREEMENTS of £30 – £2,000. These maximum limits can be increased by an Order in Council. The Act lays down certain conditions and specifies the form these various contracts must take. The requirements of the Act are, briefly, that: (1) the CASH PRICE must be stated in writing prior to the signing of the contract, e.g. by a ticket attached to the GOODS; (2) the agreement must state the cash price, the hire purchase price, the amount and date of instalments, and the relevant goods. It must be signed by both parties; (3) a copy of the agreement must be sent to the hirer or buyer within seven days; (4) the hirer may cancel the agreement within four days of receiving his copy where the agreement was not signed at the seller's appropriate trade premises; (5) any dealer is taken to be the AGENT of the owner, e.g. a FINANCE COMPANY, and representations made by the dealer are taken to be representations made by the owner; (6) there are various conditions and warranties (◊ HIRE PURCHASE CONTRACTS: CONDITIONS AND WARRANTIES); (7) where there is a COLLATERAL, GUARANTEE AGREEMENT the guarantor must receive a copy of the hire purchase or other agreement. (8) The hirer or buyer must be able to terminate the agreement at any time before the due date of the final payment by written notice to the person to whom he pays the instalments, though the owner or seller may then retake the goods and the hirer must pay the amount in arrears and if necessary make the payments up to one half of the hire purchase price (a court may reduce this). The hirer could be liable for damages if he has not taken reasonable care of the goods.

The seller's rights to terminate the agreement are restricted in various ways. *Inter alia*, he must give seven clear days' notice and cannot recover the goods after one-third of the hire purchase price has been paid, without applying to a county court.

Hire purchase price means total purchase price in credit sale or conditional sale agreements.

Hire purchase contracts: conditions and warranties. Certain CONDITIONS and WARRANTIES are implied by the Hire Purchase Act 1965. These apply to all HIRE PURCHASE and CONDITIONAL SALE AGREEMENTS.

The conditions are, *inter alia*, that: (1) the owner shall have a right to sell when the time comes for the property to pass; (2) the GOODS will be of merchantable quality though if the hirer or buyer has examined them he cannot complain of defects he should have discovered; (3) where the purpose is made known to the supplier the goods will be reasonably fit for that purpose; (4) where the goods are sold by SAMPLE, that the bulk will correspond to the sample and the buyer or hirer will have an opportunity to find out that this is so; (5) if the goods are sold by description, the goods will correspond to the description. None of these conditions may be excluded in the CONTRACT, with the exception of (2) where the goods are second-hand.

The warranties are: (1) the hirer or buyer shall enjoy quiet possession of the goods; (2) the goods shall be free from any charge or encumbrance in the favour of a third party when the TITLE passes.

Some of these conditions and warranties are confirmed by COMMON LAW.

Hire purchase finance. RETAILERS selling GOODS on HIRE PURCHASE or on credit, may need cash more quickly than they receive it. They may therefore employ a HIRE PURCHASE company, which will make agreements directly with the retailer's customers, who will make their payments, including INTEREST, direct to the hire purchase company. The interest is usually about 10 per cent *per annum*, and the period of repayment depends on government policy. The hire purchase company may require the retailer to GUARANTEE the debt or re-purchase the GOODS if the customer defaults. The hire purchase company will pay the retailer a proportion of the hire purchase PRICE when each CONTRACT is signed.

Alternatively, the retailer may sign hire purchase agreements with his customers and sell these agreements to a hire purchase company, which will immediately pay, say, 75 per cent of the hire purchase price, which the retailer will repay over the period of hire. The retailer collects the instalments on behalf of the hire purchase company. The charges for this type of block discounting vary according to the risk, and may be between 5 and 7 per cent *per annum*.

Hire purchase: third party liability. Where GOODS are sold to a HIRE

PURCHASE company, which hires the goods to the buyer, the buyer, although not a party to the CONTRACT, may sue the original seller for breach of WARRANTY.

Historical cost. The original cost of an ASSET as opposed to its saleable value, replacement value, or value in present or alternative use.

Historical cost accounting. A method of accounting (supported by most professional organizations) whereby ASSETS are maintained at their original cost in the books of the COMPANY or other organization, and DEPRECIATION charged accordingly. This could mean that insufficient profit is set aside for replacement of the assets in a time of rising PRICES.

Hogshead. A large cask. At one time it equalled 63 gallons of wine, or fifty-four gallons of ale. These measures are still in use in the United States.

Holder for value. A term applying to NEGOTIABLE INSTRUMENTS. 'Value' refers to CONSIDERATION given, though this may be an antecedent debt. A holder for value is a holder of, e.g. a BILL OF EXCHANGE, for which value has been given at some time. He need not have given value himself. However, he can only claim from persons who were parties to the bill, up to the time value was last given; and cannot claim a better TITLE than that of the person from whom he took the bill.

Holder in due course. This concerns BILLS OF EXCHANGE, including CHEQUES. A holder in due course is a person who has taken a bill, complete and regular on the face of it, not overdue and without notice of any previous dishonour. He must have taken it in good faith for value and without notice of any defect in the TITLE of the person from whom he took it.

The holder of a bill is presumed to be a holder in due course, unless the opposite is proved. If, however, FRAUD is proved at any stage, he must (to be recognized as holder in due course) prove that value was given after that time. The advantage of being a holder in due course is that one has the best possible TITLE, and can claim from all parties who have signed the bill.

Holding company. ⟡ SUBSIDIARY COMPANY.

Holding company, identity of. A SUBSIDIARY COMPANY must state in its accounts the name of its ultimate holding company and the country where this is incorporated, unless the subsidiary carries on business outside the United Kingdom and the DIRECTORS and the BOARD OF TRADE are agreed that disclosure would be harmful.

Honorary secretary. A person who takes on the secretarial duties of a club or organization without payment.

Honour policy. ◊ POLICY PROOF OF INTEREST.

Horizontal integration. ◊ VERTICAL INTEGRATION.

Horticulture improvement scheme. Grants of up to one-third of some costs are available to horticultural growers, landlords, and co-operatives. These are costs involved in growing, storage, preparation for market, and transport, of horticultural produce. Grants of less than £200 are not made.

Hosier. A dealer in stockings and socks.

Hotel. ◊ INN.

Hull insurance. A MARINE INSURANCE term for the INSURANCE of the vessel itself and liabilities arising from collision, etc.

Hypothecation, letter of. Shippers may borrow from a BANK, using the GOODS they are shipping as SECURITY. Until repayed, the banker has a LIEN on the goods, as they are listed in the BILL OF LADING. The lien, which of course is not a POSSESSORY LIEN, is conveyed by a 'letter of hypothecation'.

I

I.O.U. This is a note indicating a debt owed by one party to another, and has no other legal significance. It is normally a statement of liability signed by a debtor. It is not a NEGOTIABLE INSTRUMENT, needs no stamp, and can be used as evidence of an ACCOUNT STATED but not as proof of money lent.

Ignorantia juris neminem excusat. 'Ignorance of the law is no excuse.' E.g. a person making an ILLEGAL CONTRACT unenforceable at law cannot succeed by pleading that he had no knowledge of the illegality.

Illegal. An illegal act is one forbidden by law. An unlawful act, on the other hand, is one which, though not forbidden by law, is not given the protection of the law.

Illegal partnerships. PARTNERSHIPS formed for illegal purposes are void *ab initio*. Partnerships consisting of (generally speaking) more than twenty persons are illegal: such businesses must be registered as COMPANIES. Larger partnerships of accountants, solicitors and stock brokers are now permitted (Companies Act 1967).

Immediate holding company. A legal and accounting term for the COMPANY which actually holds the controlling interest in another company, even though the first company may itself be controlled by yet another company.

Imperial preference. A system whereby Commonwealth countries are given preferred treatment in dealings with the United Kingdom. Lower rates of duty are charged.

Impersonal accounts. ⟡ ACCOUNTS, NOMINAL, REAL, AND PERSONAL.

Implied terms. Terms which are not included in a CONTRACT, but which the law considers would have been included had the parties remembered or thought it necessary to do so, or which any reasonable man would have taken for granted. For instance, if a man builds a house for another, although the contract says nothing about it, it is taken for granted the house will be fit to live in. Terms may also be implied by custom or by statute (such as the Sale of Goods Act 1893). These terms may be excluded by an express clause to that effect in the contract.

Importers' entries of goods. When a ship arrives in port, details of the GOODS on board must be entered on a special form by the importers involved, who then pay the appropriate duty. The form is sent to the

Customs and Excise office and compared to the master's report, after which the goods may have to be examined. If the form is cleared it serves as a WARRANT allowing the goods out of Customs charge or to a bonded warehouse for duty-free storage.

Imports. ◊ VISIBLE IMPORTS AND EXPORTS.

Impressed stamps. Certain documents must be stamped at a stamping office. Duty is paid and the document is then impressed with the official stamp. Examples include the MEMORANDUM OF ASSOCIATION of a COMPANY, and conveyances.

In pari delicto. 'Equally guilty', used with reference to ◊ ILLEGAL CONTRACTS. Where persons are not *in pari delicto*, the less-guilty party may be able to recover monies paid in spite of the fact that the contract was illegal.

Inch maree clause. A MARINE INSURANCE clause coverings risks which are not necessarily 'perils of the sea', e.g. damage to cargo while in harbour.

Inchoate instrument. A term used with reference to BILLS OF EXCHANGE. Where a blank signed piece of paper is given to another party to be made a bill of exchange, that other party may fill in all necessary details, but he must do so within a reasonable time. Similarly, when a bill is in any way incomplete, the holder may make good the omissions, and provided this is done within a reasonable time the bill will be enforceable against prior signatories.

Income profits. Profits arising from trade, business, or one's profession; not CAPITAL PROFITS.

Income tax. Anyone receiving an income (with some exceptions ◊ NON-TAXABLE INCOME) pays tax on it. The amount is graded according to the income's size. Income tax is sometimes given other names, for instance CAPITAL GAINS TAX is an income tax, as opposed to a wealth tax, like ESTATE DUTY, or an expenditure tax, like SALES TAX or PURCHASE TAX. Many income tax ALLOWANCES are available. ◊ INCOME TAX, STANDARD RATE ◊ DIRECT TAXATION.

Income tax allowance: national insurance contributions. No allowance is now given for these contributions though it was prior to 6 April 1965. Employers can of course deduct from profits sums paid on account of employees.

Income tax allowance: purchased life annuities. If a person purchases a life ANNUITY, sums received annually will be apportioned between CAPITAL and income, only the income being taxable.

Income tax allowance: retirement annuities. Self-employed persons, controlling DIRECTORS, and persons not in pensionable employment, may deduct £75 or 10 per cent of their income before tax, to pay premiums on retirement ANNUITIES. There are also special provisions applying to persons born before 1916, which give them additional relief.

Income tax allowance: superannuation. Contributions to an approved fund may be deducted from an income before tax. These payments are not treated as life ASSURANCE premiums.

Income tax: business and professions. ▷ TAXATION OF PROFITS.

Income tax: code number. PAY AS YOU EARN (P.A.Y.E.) taxation is graded according to a code system. If the employer does not know his employee's code number, he must deduct tax at a high (emergency code) rate, though the excess can be reclaimed when the code is known (▷ INCOME TAX, REPAYMENT OF). Income tax is deducted at a fixed rate; the differences in code are determined by whatever INCOME TAX ALLOWANCES are appropriate. These allowances are claimed when completing the annual tax return (▷ TAXATION: ANNUAL TAX RETURN), so this should be done with care.

Income tax reliefs. ▷ Income tax ALLOWANCE and RELIEF headings.

Income tax, repayment of. If a person has over-paid tax he can claim repayment at any time within the following six years. Claim forms are available from the Inland Revenue. Persons who do not pay tax at the standard rate, may need to claim repayment when they receive DIVIDENDS or INTEREST from which tax has already been deducted at the standard rate (tax is deducted from nearly all interest and dividend payments).

Income tax: standard rate. The rate for 1971–72 is 39p in the pound. This is the standard rate. There is no longer a reduced rate charged after benefit is given for various reliefs and allowances. ▷ Income tax ALLOWANCE headings ▷ RELIEF headings. Incomes of less than £328 *per annum* are not taxable.

Increase of capital. A COMPANY may increase its CAPITAL where the ARTICLES OF ASSOCIATION so authorize. Additional STAMP DUTY will be payable. Notice must be given to the Registrar of Companies within fourteen days. If the articles do not permit an increase, they may themselves be altered.

Indemnity. An agreement whereby one person agrees to make good any loss suffered by a party to a CONTRACT to which he himself is a stranger. For example, A buys goods from B on credit, C states that he will see that B is paid. C indemnifies B – he takes primary liability, unlike a GUARANTOR who takes secondary liability, e.g. (C pays B if A does not). The most common contracts of indemnity are INSURANCE contracts.

174

Indenture. A form of DEED, but different from a deed poll in having serrated rather than straight edges. There were originally two copies of an indenture. They were both written on the same parchment, which was afterwards torn in half. The impossibility of matching the tear was a guard against forgery.

Index number. The index number system is used for comparing prices, incomes, etc., over a number of years (or weeks, months, etc.). The figure for one year is taken as the base figure, and figures for subsequent years are given as percentages of it. By this means, the rise or fall in prices or income can be most easily appreciated. The system can be applied to the price of a single item or to the average cost of living. ◊ RETAIL PRICE INDEX ◊ MOVING AVERAGES.

Indirect expenses. Expenses incurred in producing GOODS or services though not attributable to any goods or service in particular. The distinction between indirect and DIRECT EXPENSES is important in COSTING. ◊ OVERHEAD EXPENSES.

Indirect labour. Labour needed in producing GOODS or services though not attributable to any goods or services in particular. Administration is one example. The distinction between indirect and DIRECT LABOUR is important in COSTING.

Indirect taxation. Taxation levied not directly on income, but connected with expenditure, for instance by being added to the PRICE of GOODS or services.

Inducement to break a contract. Generally speaking if a person induces another to break a CONTRACT, he is committing an actionable wrong. This does not appear to apply to trade unions. Nor is there anything to stop one person persuading another to end a contract in a lawful manner.

Industrial and Commercial Finance Corporation Ltd (I.C.F.C.). An organization founded to help small and medium-sized businesses in Great Britain which need finance for expansion and development. It is owned by the BANK OF ENGLAND, the English clearing BANKS, and the Scottish banks. It provides long-term loans, SHARE CAPITAL, plant purchasing and leasing facilities (or all of these), amounting to £5,000 – £300,000 on first application, and up to £500,000 afterwards. It is not under government control and does not lend government money. Net new investment for 1969 was over £9,000,000, and the outstanding amount was over £125,000,000.

The I.C.F.C. does not interfere in management, and does not normally seek to appoint DIRECTORS. If it does, it chooses someone independent, not a member of the I.C.F.C. staff. Customers must satisfy certain requirements: they must *inter alia* produce detailed

175

accounts for the first five years, and obviously they must be a good risk. Address: Piercy House, 7, Copthall Avenue, London EC2.

Industrial artists and designers. Designers involved with visual communication in industry: graphic artists, product and engineering designers, or illustrators.

Industrial Artists and Designers, Society of. This was formed in 1930, and is the only professional association of designers in Great Britain. Its objects are to preserve standards of performance and professional conduct and integrity, and also to provide educational facilities and information regarding the profession. There is a code of professional conduct. Members may be Fellows (F.S.I.A.), Members (M.S.I.A.), Associates (A.S.I.A.) or Licentiates (L.S.I.A.), depending on merit and experience, but not on examinations. The Society produces a monthly, *The Designer*, and also the *S.I.A.D. Year Book*. Address: 7 Woburn Square, London WC1.

Industrial bank. ◊ FINANCE COMPANY.

Industrial Bankers' Association. This was formed in 1956 to promote high standards of industrial banking. Similar to the ◊ FINANCE HOUSES ASSOCIATION, it deals with small FINANCE COMPANIES and tends to be more dynamic. Members must have LIMITED LIABILITY and must employ 75 per cent of their total ASSETS in credit finance. Borrowing must be related to CAPITAL and limited standards of LIQUIDITY are set.

Industrial insurance. INSURANCE where premiums are collected on a house-to-house basis. Payments are made, say, weekly, and premiums tend to be higher to cover the cost of collection.

Industrial Re-organisation Corporation.* A corporation set up by the government to supervise and encourage reorganization within industry which is aimed at improving the efficiency of particular industries, and 'to search for opportunities to promote rationalization schemes which could yield substantial benefits to the national economy'. The Corporation is supposed to seek full cooperation from industry and various financial institutions: schemes initiated will 'whenever possible be put into effect either through the normal machinery of the market or in close collaboration with the market'. To this end the Corporation may buy SHARES though it should not become a holding company but should dispose of the shares at an opportune moment. Priority will be given to schemes which are advantageous to the balance of payments or which help deployment of industry in DEVELOPMENT AREAS. It may at times act in a purely

---

* In process of being wound up.

advisory capacity as opposed to buying a stake or forcing the pace. It was intended that schemes promoted by the Corporation would have prior clearance from the Monopolies Commission.

Industry. ◊ EXTRACTIVE INDUSTRY ◊ CONSTRUCTIVE INDUSTRY ◊ MANUFACTURING INDUSTRY.

Infant. ◊ MINOR ◊ CONTRACTS: INFANTS.

Inherent vice. A term used with reference to the carriage of GOODS. The carrier may not be liable for the goods he carries, if their nature makes them an exceptional risk, which is not obvious, and has not been made known to him.

Initial allowances. ◊ CAPITAL ALLOWANCES.

Injunction. A court may order someone to perform or not perform some action. This order is called an 'injunction' in England, and an 'interdict' in Scotland. Injunctions are often issued to prevent someone from continuing to act in a certain capacity, or in a manner harmful to someone else.

Inland bill. A ◊ BILL OF EXCHANGE drawn and made payable within the British Isles.

Inland waterways. A system of canals, rivers, and lochs, used both for commerce and pleasure. Inland waterway transport is governed by the British Waterways Board, Melbury House, Melbury Terrace, London NW1. The Board provides (1) storage accommodation and up-to-date handling equipment, (2) road transport fleets from depots and trans-shipment points, (3) a container service, and (4) three independent docks equipped as trans-shipment points between ocean-going vessels and inland transport. These are: Weston Point Docks (on the south bank of the Mersey; cargo capacity 1,600 tons), Sharpness Docks (on the east bank of the Severn; 5,000 tons) and Gloucester Docks (750 tons).

Inland waterway traffic consists largely of raw materials in specialized vessels (e.g. bulk liquids in tankers, or coal in compartment craft). Trains of barges may be towed by one motorized vessel. Canal transport may be slow, but the routes are usually more direct. For instance, on the Caledonian Canal, the speed limit is 6 m.p.h. on the canals (about twenty miles) though there is no limit on the lochs which make up the remaining forty miles; by using the canal, ships are saved the long and perhaps difficult voyage round the north coast of Scotland. Locks are the canals' main drawback.

Inland Waterways Amenity Advisory Council. This was set up by the Transport Act 1968 to advise the Waterways Board and the relevant Minister on the use of INLAND WATERWAYS for recreational purposes.

Inn. Traditionally a place where a jovial character known as an innkeeper offers hospitality. Originally subject to the Innkeepers Act 1878, he was bound to supply food and accommodation for 'genuine and proper' customers and their horses. The Hotel Proprietors Act 1956 has altered and clarified the position. Nowadays an establishment is either a hotel or not. Whether it is called an inn is irrelevant. A hotel is defined as 'an establishment held out by the proprietor as offering food, drink, and if so required, sleeping accommodation, without special CONTRACT, to any traveller presenting himself who appears able and willing to pay a reasonable sum for the services and facilities provided and who is in fit state to be received'. The proprietor cannot refuse accommodation without a reasonable excuse, for instance that he has no available rooms, or that the applicant is drunk or unclean (illness is no ground for refusal). If he does unlawfully refuse, he may be both civilly and criminally liable, as he may be if he charges excessive prices. He must provide food within a reasonable time and on payment, unless he has none in the house (though he may also consider the possibility of other customers arriving later).

He is liable for the GOODS of his guests as if he were an insurer, unless the loss is due to an 'act of God, an act of the Queen's enemies, or negligence of the guest'. Proprietors often post notices to guests that goods of value should be deposited for safe keeping, but these notices have no legal effect and do not diminish the proprietor's responsibility. As far as damage is concerned, the innkeeper's liability once depended on his negligence. The 1956 Act increased his responsibility, but it may still be limited to a total of £100 per guest. This limitation only applies if the appropriate notice (as prescribed by the Act) is displayed. His liability is not limited when the notice is not displayed or when the loss or damage is occasioned by negligence of himself or his servants. The proprietor is not now liable for loss or damage except where the traveller was staying the night and the loss and damage occurred during the period beginning with the preceding and ending with the following midnight, the period for which the traveller was a guest. The proprietor is no longer liable for cars, bicycles, horses, etc. – except under the ordinary law of negligence.

The proprietor has a LIEN on the guest's goods for money owed by him.

Inscribed stock. Certain STOCK, usually government stock, may be 'inscribed'. This means that certificates are not issued to stockholders but their names are inscribed in a record book. When ownership is transferred, certain formalities must be completed before one name is erased and another put in its place. This type of stock is not very common, partly because it is so difficult to transfer.

Insolvency. A person or organization is insolvent when he or it is unable to pay debts when they become due. Insolvency is not the same as BANCKRUPTCY or LIQUIDATION of a COMPANY (though they may follow from it): a very rich man can be insolvent if his ASSETS cannot be realized at the time he needs cash.

Instalments, delivery and payment. Where in a CONTRACT the promise is divisible, that is to say, delivery or payment is to be by instalments, problems arise from a failure to keep up these instalments. Failure of one instalment discharges the other party. In the case of delivery, the court will generally look to the intention of the defaulting party. If it is obvious that he intends to continue to fail to produce the instalments, then the case will be treated as one of BREACH OF CONTRACT. If there is merely a failure on one instalment in part or whole, then other things being equal, the complaining party can only hope for DAMAGES. In the case of payment, the position has been clarified by various statutes. ◊ HIRE PURCHASE ◊ CREDIT SALE AGREEMENTS ◊ CONDITIONAL SALE AGREEMENTS.

Instant. Term used in commerce, usually abbreviated to inst., referring to the present month.

Institute cargo clauses. A MARINE INSURANCE term for clauses included in policies to cover exceptional risks. The Institute referred to is the Institute of London Underwriters.

Insurable interest. To insure any property or insure against any particular event, one must have an insurable interest, i.e. must stand to lose from the destruction of the property or from the event. In life ASSURANCE the interest must exist at the time the policy is made; in MARINE INSURANCE it must exist at the time of the loss; in FIRE INSURANCE and general ◊ INSURANCE, it must exist at the time of the loss and usually also at the time of the policy, particularly where the insurance of buildings is concerned.

Insurance. The payment of a sum of money by one person to another on the understanding that in specified circumstances the second person will make good any loss suffered by the first. ◊ FIRE INSURANCE ◊ MARINE INSURANCE ◊◊ ASSURANCE.

Insurance broker. A person employed to negotiate a CONTRACT of INSURANCE. He is AGENT for both parties but PRINCIPAL for the purpose of receiving payment from the insured. He has a LIEN on the policy for the balance due. There are two governing bodies: the ASSOCIATION OF INSURANCE BROKERS and the CORPORATION

OF INSURANCE BROKERS. Brokers are not bound to belong to these, but it may be in customers' interests to deal with those who do (or with Lloyds brokers).

Insurance Brokers, Association of. A COMPANY LIMITED BY GUARANTEE. This and the CORPORATION OF INSURANCE BROKERS are the two principal organizations representing brokers, and reliable brokers normally belong to one of them (unless they are Lloyds brokers). Members of the Association must have been in practice for at least three years as principal of their business though this requirement may be waived if they have equivalent experience and/or have passed the examination of the Chartered Insurance Institute. Members must produce an annual certificate of SOLVENCY given by a recognized ACCOUNTANT and must have professional indemnity cover for a minimum of £25,000 on any one risk. Applications for membership are scrutinized carefully and inquiries are made into an applicant's standing, competence and integrity, before his admission is approved. The Association has a disciplinary committee. Address: Craven House, Kingsway, London WC2.

Insurance Brokers, Corporation of. This association, formed in 1910, ensures that members, when dealing with the public, are able, by expert knowledge and experience, together with an unbiased mind as to insurers, to place the insured risk in the right market, having regard to the real needs of the insured and the SECURITY of the insurer. Members must (1) submit to examinations and close scrutiny by the membership committee, (2) produce an annual audit certificate completed by an ACCOUNTANT from one of the categories specified by the Companies Act 1948, (3) hold a broker's indemnity policy for £100,000, (4) have been practising on their own account for three years or more, and must now have passed the qualifying examination of the Chartered Insurance Institute to Associateship level in any branch of subjects.

Members aim to assist the public in obtaining the best INSURANCE, keeping policies under review, seeing that protection is sufficient, and helping with claims. They are paid by the insurer and not the insured. Address: 15 St Helens Place, London EC3.

Insurance Export Finance Company. An organization set up to help finance exports. Members are INSURANCE companies affiliated to the British Insurance Association, and funds amount to about £150,000,000. The Company purchases long-term PROMISSORY NOTES on behalf of its members. It tends to deal with long-term finance (e.g. five years and over). Its rates of INTEREST are approximately $6\frac{1}{2}$ per cent.

Insurance, loss of profit. This policy covers loss of profit of a business which cannot operate due to, say, fire damage. A sum is paid to compensate for the loss of expected profits during the time the firm is out of business. Calculation of the amount is complicated and varies from company to company, but basically is calculated on profit in previous years.

Insurance premium. What the insured agrees to pay to the insurer annually. It is payable on a stated date though a number of DAYS OF GRACE are normally allowed.

Intangible assets. An accounting term for those INVISIBLE ASSETS which have a value to the business and perhaps also a saleable value, e.g., GOODWILL, PATENTS, TRADE-MARKS, copyrights, etc. These are sometimes called invisible assets, but should be distinguished from ◊ FICTITIOUS ASSETS.

Interdict. Scottish term for ◊ INJUNCTION.

Interest. The amount paid by a borrower to a lender in payment for a loan. Interest may be simple or compound. SIMPLE INTEREST is a fixed rate on a stated sum. The same amount is paid or accumulated each year irrespective of the amount borrowed, for instance £100 lent at 5 per cent simple interest would earn £5 a year. If the interest were not paid when due, it would not itself earn interest. But if a sum is invested at COMPOUND INTEREST and the interest is allowed to accumulate, the interest is calculated each year on capital and interest already accumulated.

Stated interest rates are often deceiving. Hire purchase interest at 10 per cent may be higher in fact, depending on the period of repayment. If a sum is borrowed at 10 per cent, the 10 per cent being calculated on the total and paid back in monthly instalments over a year, the *average* amount outstanding is only half the actual loan and therefore the interest rate is in fact 20 per cent. On the other hand interest on overdrafts is calculated on the money outstanding at a particular time.

Interest rates are always stated as per cent *per annum*. They are sometimes stated in terms of money, e.g. £5 per cent – this means £5 per £100 (= 5 per cent). Interest rates vary considerably according to risk. They are also controlled by the ◊ BANK RATE and by government policy. ◊ MONEYLENDER.

Interest on calls. INTEREST is payable on CALLS IN ARREAR, though only if the ARTICLES OF ASSOCIATION of a COMPANY so provide.

Interest on debts. ◊ MONEYLENDER. The Law Reform (Miscellaneous Provisions) Act 1934 states that INTEREST on debts recovered at law, or interest on DAMAGES, may be allowed by the court, over the period between the date when the cause of action arose and the judgment date. The Act does not apply to interest on interest, or to interest already agreed, or to the dishonour of BILLS OF EXCHANGE (see the Bills of Exchange Act 1882). Where there is no agreement to pay interest, it may still be payable (1) where there is a trade custom that interest should be paid, (2) on bills of exchange – normally at 5 per cent, (3) in CONTRACTS of INDEMNITY, and of GUARANTEE where the guarantor has paid the debt, (4) on JUDGMENT DEBTS or ARBITRATION awards – normally at 4 per cent, and (5) in any situation where the court thinks interest should be paid, over the period from cause of action to judgment.

Interest or no interest. ⟡ POLICY PROOF OF INTEREST.

Interest out of capital. The Companies Act 1948 does not permit distribution of DIVIDENDS paid out of CAPITAL, except in one instance: when the capital is for the construction of works, no profits being earned, and the payment is authorized by the ARTICLES OF ASSOCIATION and sanctioned by the BOARD OF TRADE. The rate must be fixed by the Treasury. Where INTEREST has been paid out of capital, the accounts must show both the capital involved and the rate of interest.

Interest payable by companies. The Companies Act 1967 states that the accounts must show details of INTEREST payable by COMPANIES, distinguishing between (1) BANK LOANS and BANK OVERDRAFTS, and loans repayable within five years by instalments or otherwise, and (2) all other loans.

Interests in subsidiaries not consolidated. An accounting term for the VALUE of holdings in SUBSIDIARY COMPANIES, where the accounts of the subsidiaries are not consolidated when GROUP ACCOUNTS are presented. Subsidiaries need not be consolidated, where, for example, the amounts involved are immaterial, or when the business of the subsidiary is quite different from that of the holding company.

Interim dividend. DIVIDENDS are paid on SHARES when the profits for the year are known. This may be some time after the end of the year. It is therefore common practice to declare part of the dividend, as it were on account, before the end of the year. This is known as an interim dividend. It will not normally be very large in relation to the total dividend, but it is an indication of the probable total dividend and the way business is going. The shareholder also receives something earlier than he would otherwise do.

Interim receiver. A person appointed by the court to protect the debtor's property until a RECEIVER proper is appointed.

Internal audit. The AUDIT of a business conducted by the business itself on a continuous basis. This is part of the general system of ⟡ INTERNAL CONTROL.

Internal check. In-built systems of accounting control, part of the general system of ⟡ INTERNAL CONTROL.

Internal control. The agglomeration of systems and checking devices applied by a business organization to maximize accuracy in record keeping, and minimize FRAUD.

International Bank for Reconstruction and Development. Often known as the World Bank, this was set up together with the INTERNATIONAL MONETARY FUND by the Bretton Woods Agreements of 1944. Its purpose was to help finance post-war reconstruction by making loans to governments or GUARANTEEING outside loans. The loans are for fifteen to twenty-five year periods. The Bank is a specialized agency of the United Nations. About one-third of the funds come from Europe. Members must also be members of the International Monetary Fund. Two off-shoots of the Bank are the International Finance Corporation (1960) and the International Development Association (1961). Both of these place particular emphasis on aid to less-developed member countries, which have become more demanding in recent years.

International Cargo Advisory Bureau. ⟡ BRITISH OVERSEAS AIRWAYS CORPORATION.

International Credit Unions. Reciprocal agreements between European FINANCE HOUSES. The purposes are (1) to provide credit facilities in international trade (e.g. to enable foreign buyers to stock U.K. GOODS prior to sale), (2) to facilitate the purchase of capital equipment where instalment credits are concerned, and (3) to provide ancillary services to assist exporters with their financial problems.

International Monetary Fund. One of the fruits of the Bretton Woods Agreements in 1944. The Fund was formed in 1946 and began to operate in 1947. Its object is to maintain and stabilize RATES OF EXCHANGE and facilitate multilateral clearing systems, and also to eliminate unnecessary restrictions on foreign trade. It has the power to advance money to countries in balance of payment difficulties: it will supply a country with the currency it needs in return for that country's own currency. There is a repayment period of about five years. It also gives countries credit guarantees, that is, without actually lending, it agrees to lend, if asked. These facilities are obviously only available to member countries. Members finance the fund by making contributions according to an estimate of their means. The higher the contribution the higher the voting rights. The amount paid in is partly in gold and partly in the currency of the country.

Introductions. ◊ PLACINGS.

Investigation. ◊ COMPANY: BOARD OF TRADE INVESTIGATION.

Investment allowance. An allowance made to companies, for taxation purposes, in addition to the initial and annual ◊ CAPITAL ALLOWANCES. It was not deducted from the ASSET in calculating these allowances and was used as an incentive to capital investment. It was discontinued in 1966 and has been replaced by an ◊ INVESTMENT GRANT.

Investment club. A voluntary association of persons who pool their savings, or part of them, to build up an investment portfolio, which gives them a better return per person than each could expect separately. There is no fixed form for these organizations, and they vary considerably.

Investment company. Any COMPANY which uses its funds to acquire SHARES or SECURITIES rather than engage in business on its own account. They are usually referred to as ◊ INVESTMENT TRUSTS, but theoretically this is a misnomer, as DIRECTORS of investment trusts or investment companies are not legally trustees and there is no trust instrument. True, securities are often held on trust for the benefit of others, but this is a different matter and takes the form of a trust proper rather than that of a company.

Investment grants. Government grants available to industry for specified purposes, e.g. the purchase of machinery used for certain qualifying industrial processes. The grants were introduced by the Industrial Development Act 1966. They applied to the manufacturing industries but were also available for the purchase of computers, ships and hovercraft. The grants were of 20 per cent, but of 40 per cent in DEVELOPMENT AREAS. These rates were increased to 25 per cent and 45 per cent for expenditure between 1 January 1967 and 31 December 1968. Grants have been discontinued as from 27 October 1970.

Investment income. Income from outside investments, as opposed to income from normal trading operations.

Investment trusts. COMPANIES formed to invest the collected funds of shareholders. They invest in other companies, the spread of holdings being very wide. Investment trusts help small investors by giving them the benefit of spreading their risks and enjoying the advantages of experienced management. Investment is normally in quoted SECURITIES (at the end of 1963 £1,800,000,000 out of £1,900,000,000 were in these securities) but these companies will show interest in smaller or unquoted businesses where they are offered good security. They may also underwrite issues of shares or help to form specialist FINANCE COMPANIES, perhaps with a view to investment in smaller businesses. ◊ INVESTMENT COMPANIES ◊ UNIT TRUSTS.

Invisible assets. ◊ INTANGIBLE ASSETS.

Invitation to treat. This should be distinguished from an OFFER. When a person puts goods in his window or lists goods in a catalogue, with PRICES, he is not necessarily making an offer, but merely inviting the public to make offers to him. A shopkeeper is under no obligation to sell at the prices indicated in the window. Also, a person advertising an item for sale is obviously not bound to sell to every person who wishes to buy. He is in fact asking people to make him an offer even though he states a price.

Invoice. A document issued by a VENDOR of GOODS stating *inter alia* the nature of the goods, the name of the debtor, and the sum due.

Invoice discounting. The practice of obtaining money on the SECURITY of BOOK DEBTS (i.e. money to be received). A COMPANY which finds that it has too much WORKING CAPITAL tied up in book debts may sell these debts to a FINANCE COMPANY. This is known as invoice discounting. In a typical case, the finance company would agree to advance, say, 75 per cent of outstanding debts of a certain category. The security might be either GOODS, where the debtors are HIRE PURCHASE debtors, or BILLS OF EXCHANGE accepted by the borrower. The borrower would act as AGENT in collecting the debts, and monies would be payable to the finance company, the additional 25 per cent being paid over perhaps, when the first 75 per cent is satisfied, i.e. when the bill of exchange is met. The borrower is normally responsible for all bad debts and the finance company would charge a COMMISSION, depending on the financial state of the borrower. ◊ FACTORING.

Ironmonger. A dealer in ironware and hardware, usually for domestic use.

Irredeemable debentures. ◊ PERPETUAL DEBENTURES.

Irrevocable and confirmed credit. This is similar to an IRREVOCABLE DOCUMENTARY ACCEPTANCE CREDIT: it is a credit confirmed by a London BANK, where the person opening the credit lives in a country that does not have a bank with an office in London. ◊ LONDON ACCEPTANCE CREDIT.

Irrevocable documentary acceptance credit. A credit scheme to facilitate foreign trade. An overseas customer opens a credit in the London office of an overseas BANK, or with a London bank. The bank then

185

gives the exporter an irrevocable letter of credit. The bank will then accept BILLS OF EXCHANGE drawn on it by the exporter, when he presents his shipping documents. ▷ LONDON ACCEPTANCE CREDIT.

Issued capital. The amount of CAPITAL actually issued by the COMPANY. ▷ AUTHORIZED CAPITAL. Capital is issued normally in the form of SHARES. ▷ SHARE CAPITAL. These may be ORDINARY SHARES, PREFERENCE SHARES, etc. Issued capital is not the same thing as CALLED-UP CAPITAL or PAID-UP CAPITAL.

Issuing house. A financial institution acting as intermediary between industry seeking CAPITAL and investors willing to provide it. Capital is usually provided by a public issue of shares, by a PROSPECTUS or OFFER for sale, or by the placing of STOCK. Issuing houses also deal with ▷ RIGHTS ISSUES, ▷ AMALGAMATIONS and ▷ TAKE-OVER BIDS. Many issuing houses also act as MERCHANT BANKERS, ACCEPTING HOUSES, INVESTMENT BANKERS and INVESTMENT TRUST managers. They are prominent in the export trade, giving advice to exporters on financial matters. They also offer to keep SHARE REGISTERS on behalf of limited companies.

Issuing Houses Association. Formed in 1945, the Association has fifty-six members, not only in the City but also in other parts of London and in the Provinces. It aims to represent the ISSUING HOUSES' interests in dealings with other financial institutions and with government departments.

J

Jason clause. A MARINE INSURANCE clause covering risks undiscoverable even by proper diligence.

Jerque. To jerque is to examine a ship's papers to ensure that the captain's list of any cargo agrees with that of the Customs house, and to search for any unentered cargo.

Jerque note. A certificate issued by a Customs officer when he is satisfied the cargo is in order. ◊ JERQUE.

Jerquer. A Customs officer who ◊ JERQUES.

Jerry building. Quick building by SPECULATORS aiming at profit rather than durability, and therefore using inferior materials. This kind of building was common in the BOOM years of the Industrial Revolution.

Jetsam. GOODS thrown overboard to lighten a ship.

Jettisons. A MARINE INSURANCE term for objects thrown overboard to save a ship. ◊ GENERAL AVERAGE LOSS.

Job analysis. Detailed analysis of a particular job leading to agreement on the best methods of carrying it out, and the qualities needed by whoever is to do it.

Job evaluation. ◊ JOB ANALYSIS. The assessing of the relative worth of different jobs with reference to skills, responsibility, etc. It forms the basis for wage agreements.

Jobber. ◊ STOCKJOBBER.

Jobber's turn. A STOCKJOBBER always quotes two PRICES for SHARES or SECURITIES: a buying price and a selling price. The selling price is higher than the buying price and the difference is known as the jobber's turn.

Jobbery. Originally a term of abuse for sharp practice in STOCK EXCHANGE dealings, but now used more generally.

Joint account. In banking it is an account opened in the names of more than one person, often a husband and his wife. Each can draw on the account.

Joint and several. A commercial phrase used in cases of liability. For instance, partners are jointly and severally responsible for the debts of their firm.

Joint consultation. A means of settling disputes or preventing them from arising. All sides in a disagreement come together to sort out their differences in a civilized manner and also to define policy so as to avoid any unnecessary and time-wasting argument or dislocation. This is often the only alternative to 'force majeure' in industrial bargaining.

Joint consultation commonly consists of councils composed of management representatives on one side and trade unions or clerical personnel on the other. It may concern one industry or may encompass many.

Joint holders. Where SHARES are held jointly, the holders may have them registered jointly, in which case only the first name receives notices. They may, however, split the holding and be registered separately. ◊ BANKRUPTCY: PARTNERS.

Joint stock companies. A name for ◊ COMPANIES LIMITED BY SHARES.

Joint tenants. Persons who hold property jointly in such a way that should one tenant die the other takes the property. This is unlike a ◊ TENANCY IN COMMON, where the representatives of the deceased tenant take his share.

Joint tenure. A PARTNERSHIP for a limited period, usually without a written agreement. Not now in common use.

Journal. A book-keeping term for the book or books where details of transactions are first entered. There are several, e.g. PURCHASE JOURNAL, SALES JOURNAL, private journal.

Judgment creditor. One who has proved a debt in a court of law, or won an action for the recovery of a debt.

Judgment debtor. One who has been ordered by a court to pay a sum of money to another (the JUDGMENT CREDITOR).

K

Kaffirs. A group of SHARES in South African countries, dealt with on the STOCK EXCHANGE.

Kangaroos. A STOCK EXCHANGE term for SHARES or SECURITIES in Australian land mining and tobacco COMPANIES.

Keelage. Dues paid by a ship entering and resting in certain ports.

Keep house. ⟡ BANKRUPTCY, ACT OF.

Kennedy round. ⟡ TARIFF ADVANTAGES OVERSEAS.

Key money. ⟡ PREMIUMS ON A LEASE.

Kite. A slang term for an ⟡ ACCOMMODATION BILL, particularly one raised with the express purpose of seeming affluent.

Kite flying. ⟡ KITE. The use of ⟡ ACCOMMODATION BILLS or other forms of raising money on credit, not supported by ASSETS, in order to appear affluent or credit-worthy.

Knot. One NAUTICAL MILE per hour.

L

Laches. A legal term for the delay sufficient to deprive a person of his right to SPECIFIC PERFORMANCE of a CONTRACT, or to an INJUNCTION. The statute of limitations does not apply to equitable remedies – with these a person may lose the right to such a remedy by a short delay in seeking it. The length of time is decided by the court.

Laesio enormis. The doctrine in certain continental legal systems that CONSIDERATION, when a matter of PRICE, must be fair and serious, otherwise the other party could rescind the contract. The doctrine is of Roman origin, and the cash offered had to bear some relation to the value of the object.

Lame duck. A member of the STOCK EXCHANGE who cannot meet his debts and is about to be HAMMERED.

Land waiter. Also known as a landing officer or searcher, this is a Customs officer responsible for sampling and examining GOODS liable to duty. He makes out an account of landed goods for tax purposes, and ensures that goods for export are shipped in the prescribed form.

Landed. A term used in foreign trade CONTRACTS. It applies where the exporter, in addition to EX SHIP charges, sees to the landing of the GOODS. He is not normally responsible for dock charges.

Landing book. A book kept by dock companies for noting details of all GOODS received off incoming ships. Landing accounts are made up from this book and sent to the relevant cargo owners. It gives them an indication of the state of the goods, and of when the RENT due for e.g. use of WAREHOUSES, becomes payable.

Landing officer. ◊ LAND WAITER.

Landing order. ◊ CUSTOMS: LANDING CARGO ◊ LAND WAITER.

Lands Improvement Company. A company formed by special Act of Parliament in 1853, to provide long-term loans for capital improvements to estates and farms. The improvements must be approved by the Ministry of Agriculture, Fisheries and Food. The loan is based on the rental value of the property, repaid by an ANNUITY over a period of not more than forty years. Loans can be obtained on property already MORTGAGED. CAPITAL cannot be called in and the INTEREST is fixed.

Larboard. The port or left-hand side of the ship (facing forward). The other side is called starboard.

Larceny. Obtaining GOODS from another by trickery when that other had no intention of parting with them. Where the person intended parting with the goods but the manner of obtaining them was fraudulent, this is obtaining goods on false pretences, not larceny. ♢ STOLEN GOODS.

Last in first out (L.I.F.O.). ♢ STOCK VALUATION.

Law Society. A voluntary organization with over 19,000 members, the Society maintains the Roll of SOLICITORS, issues annual practising certificates, controls enrolment of students, and supervises their education. It is the examining authority for the profession of solicitor. Although membership is voluntary, the Society has authority over all solicitors whether members or not *re* professional practice, conduct, and discipline. It administers the Compensation Fund, keeps an appointments registry, library, etc., and offers advice on professional practice and procedure. It also administers legal aid and advice schemes. It is responsible for public relations. Publications include a monthly journal *The Law Society's Gazette* and a quarterly news-sheet *Obiter*.

The history of the Society is colourful – it began as the Society of Gentleman Practisers in the Courts of Law and Equity in 1739, became the Metropolitan Law Association in 1819, and the Law Institution in 1825. When it received the first of five Royal Charters in 1831, its title was 'Society of Attorneys, Solicitors, Proctors and others not being Barristers practising in the Courts of Law and Equity of the United Kingdom'. The name Law Society was adopted in 1903. For a more comprehensive description of its functions, apply to 113 Chancery Lane, London WC2.

Lawyer. A member of the legal profession, usually a SOLICITOR or BARRISTER.

Lay days. The days allowed by custom for loading or unloading a vessel. Failure to complete the job within these days may make the guilty party liable to pay DEMURRAGE. Lay days may be counted in WORKING DAYS, RUNNING DAYS, or WEATHER WORKING DAYS. Where the number of lay days is not specified in the CONTRACT, the work must be done in a reasonable time (this might allow for delays due to strikes, etc.).

Leasehold Land. Land rented from the true owner. The lease may be for a long or short period. At the end of the period it must be handed back, together with all buildings, whether these were on the land originally or not. The tenant may also be liable for dilapidations.

It is possible to mortgage leasehold land, though the possibility will depend upon the term of the lease and any conditions imposed by the lease.

The 1967 Companies Act directs that published accounts shall show separately freehold land, land held on a long lease and land held on a short lease. A long lease for this purpose is one where there are at least fifty years to run.

Ledger. A book where an organization's individual accounts are kept. For practical reasons it is usually divided into several books: CASH BOOK, PERSONAL LEDGER, private ledger, and GENERAL LEDGER. In the past, ledgers were great tomes where information was recorded in copperplate handwriting by little men with long quills. Now they are usually trays of cards, with information printed by ACCOUNTING machines. ⟡ DOUBLE-ENTRY BOOK-KEEPING.

Leeman's Act 1867. This deals with sales of SHARES in a JOINT STOCK COMPANY. The sale is void unless the numbers of the shares as given in the SHARE REGISTER are stated in the CONTRACT. The STOCK EXCHANGE tends to ignore this provision, but a party to such a contract can still rely on the Act.

Leeward. The side of the ship facing the quarter towards which the wind is blowing.

Legal tender. Money, which being offered in payment of a debt at an appropriate time and place, must be accepted by the other party in satisfaction of that debt. If the CREDITOR refuses, the debt remains, but if the debtor is sued, the creditor will probably have to pay the costs. An OFFER of money in this way stops INTEREST running, and usually extinguishes the creditor's right of LIEN. Legal tender of money must be an unconditional offer in legal currency of the exact amount owed, to the creditor or his AGENT, the money being produced. It consists of BANK OF ENGLAND notes to any amount – silver not exceeding £2, bronze not exceeding 1s., twelve-sided threepenny pieces not exceeding 2s.

The debtor cannot demand change, though if the creditor accepts a larger amount he will be obliged to give change. It might be noted before refusing to take as change on a bus what is strictly not legal tender, e.g. 1s. 11d. in pennies on the offer of 2s. for a 1d. bus ride, that once one is on a bus one has no alternative but to get off or give the larger amount together with one's name and address and ask that the change be forwarded. A bus conductor is not obliged to give change.

Letter of allotment. ⟡ ALLOTMENT OF SHARES.

Letter of attorney. Similar to a POWER OF ATTORNEY.

Letter of credit. A document issued by a BANK or other financial institution to a prospective borrower, for an agreed amount, and for a definite or indefinite period. It allows the borrower to draw BILLS OF EXCHANGE on the institution up to that amount – the bills will be accepted automatically. The purpose for which the money is required is stated initially and the bills drawn must conform to this. Letters of credit are also used in foreign trade. The buyer arranges with his bank to open a credit in the country of the seller, who may then obtain payment by presentation of the relevant documents, when these have been accepted and returned by the buyer. When the seller is informed of the credit it becomes irrevocable.

Letter of hypothecation. ⟡ HYPOTHECATION, LETTER OF.

Letter of indemnity. When a manufacturer exports GOODS he sometimes sends a letter of indemnity agreeing to make good any loss due to faulty packing, short loading, etc. In doing this he ensures a CLEAN BILL OF LADING.

Letter of licence. An insolvent debtor may come to some agreement with his CREDITORS whereby they agree to give him some time to pay, and not to take any proceedings against him until that time has elapsed. This is known as a letter of licence.

Letter of mart and countermart. An authority formerly issued to private adventurers in time of war, empowering them to seize the ships and GOODS of enemy subjects.

Letter of regret. A letter sent to applicants for a new issue of SHARES informing them that their application has not been accepted.

Letter of renunciation. This applies to a rights issue of SHARES, where the holder who does not wish to take up the new shares, may renounce his rights, either absolutely or in favour of another person, by sending a letter of renunciation.

Liability. A general term used to describe a debt. It may be cash or only a chose in action. ⟡ LONG-TERM LIABILITIES ⟡ CURRENT LIABILITIES ⟡ CONTINGENT LIABILITIES.

Licence. A document permitting its holder to do something otherwise forbidden, and usually obtainable by paying a fixed sum. Licences are a means of raising revenue and of controlling the use or abuse of certain rights. They are needed *inter alia* for driving or conducting a bus, carrying GOODS or passengers for money, selling wines, spirits, beer or tobacco, using a premises for dancing or singing, or for hunting, shooting or fishing. Anyone in doubt as to whether or not he needs a licence should consult his local authority or the police. Conditions vary between parts of the country. Some licences are obtainable from post offices, e.g. broadcast receiving, dog, drivers', export, game, hounds, local taxation and excise, and vehicle licences; others from magistrates, e.g. for the sale of alcohol; others from various other authorities. Members of the public can oppose the issue of particular licences by magistrates, if they attend the court.

Licences: motor vehicles. All motor vehicles must be licensed before they can be used on a public road. First licences are obtained from county or county borough councils, renewals are obtainable from post offices. Additional licences are necessary if the vehicle is to carry GOODS or passengers for payment. Public service vehicles must have special licences, as must their drivers and conductors.

The driver of any vehicle must be licensed.

Licensing laws: intoxicating liquors. A complicated subject: reference should be made to the Licensing Act 1964. One or two points of general interest are: (1) Licences are granted by local justices and can be revoked by them. (2) A licensee may refuse to serve any customer without giving his reason. (3) It is an offence to serve a drunken person with liquor or to buy a drink for one. (4) It is an offence to serve a person not yet eighteen years of age with liquor, or to buy a drink for one. (5) Persons not yet fourteen years of age are not allowed in rooms where alcohol is being sold unless the sale is incidental to the provision of a meal. (6) Persons under eighteen years of age may not be employed in rooms where alcoholic liquor is being served. (7) Persons of sixteen and over can be supplied with beer, porter, cider or perry if it is consumed with a meal.

There are general regulations regarding opening and closing hours, which vary locally. Generally speaking, the opening times allowed are nine hours per day with a break of two hours in the afternoon. On Sundays, Christmas Day, and Good Friday, fewer hours are allowed. Generally, pubs close at 10.30 p.m. but licences till 11 p.m. can be issued.

The rules regarding clubs are complex: reference should be made to the Act.

Lien, equitable. This is not a POSSESSORY LIEN, although it could be. It is conferred by EQUITY and is a right to have property disposed of in a certain way, e.g. the lien of a partner on the property of a PARTNERSHIP, or the lien of the VENDOR of land for the purchase money.

Lien, general. This is a POSSESSORY LIEN which can arise from a particular CONTRACT, or in some trades and professions, by custom. It attaches to the GOODS in respect of all sums owed to the holder by the owner, not just to the sum pertaining to those particular goods. A person having a lien cannot charge for storage. He may sell the goods but the law usually requires that a reasonable time must elapse and that the SALE must be by public AUCTION.

Lien, maritime. In certain circumstances, certain persons have a lien attaching to a ship and/or its cargo which enables them to recover money owed to them. These are: BOTTOMRY BOND holders; the master, for wages and dispersement; sailors, for work done; seamen, for wages; and the owner of another ship damaged in a collision. Possession is not necessary.

Lien on shares. The ARTICLES OF ASSOCIATION of a COMPANY usually provide that the company has first lien on the SHARES of a member for his debts or liabilities. The lien may also apply to DIVIDENDS. It may be enforceable by SALE, but cannot be enforced by forfeiture.

Lien, particular. A POSSESSORY LIEN enabling the holder of GOODS to retain the goods until money due on those goods is paid. COMMON LAW affords such liens to unpaid carriers and unpaid sellers. The lien arises when goods are held for improvement rather than main-tenance. The work must be completed. The fact that the goods do not belong to the person who deposited them does not always defeat the lien.

Lien, possessory. One person's right to retain possession of another person's GOODS pending the payment of money due. The right varies according to the nature of the CONTRACT. ◊ LIEN, GENERAL ◊ LIEN, PARTICULAR, etc.

Light dues. Levies payable by ships as contributions to the maintenance of lights, beacons, buoys, or other navigational aids in rivers or roads. The dues are paid to TRINITY HOUSE, through HER MAJESTY'S CUSTOMS AND EXCISE. The shipowner pays them on the basis of ten home trade voyages, eight foreign ones, or a com-bination of each.

Limitation of actions. The law holds that if an action is to be brought it must be brought within a reasonable time. The Limitation Acts 1939, 1954, 1963 prescribe, *inter alia*, that an action should be brought within the following periods after the cause first arose: by MONEY-LENDERS for the recovery of money and INTEREST, within one year; by persons claiming damages in CONTRACT or in tort for personal injuries, within three years; actions generally in contract, tort, or concerning trusts, etc., within six years; actions on certain SPECIALITY CONTRACTS or to recover land, or MORTGAGE money secured on land, or personal property, or actions to do with claims on personal estates, within twelve years. The period normally runs from the date when the cause arose, or the date when the plaintiff was or could have been aware of the existence of the claim. Part payment of the debt or acknowledgement of the claim by the other party could start the time running again.

Limited. Every COMPANY with LIMITED LIABILITY must put the word 'Limited', or the abbreviation 'Ltd', after its name. Companies formed to promote the arts, science, etc., are exceptions to this rule.

Limited company. ◊ COMPANY.

Limited liability. This applies to COMPANIES LIMITED BY SHARES or companies limited by guarantee. No MEMBER can be asked to pay more than the nominal value of his SHARES or the amount of his GUARANTEE. Holders of fully-paid shares have no liability whatever. The MEMORANDUM OF ASSOCIATION must contain a clause stating that the members' liability is limited. The word 'Limited' or the abbreviation 'Ltd' must always appear as part of the name of the company. ◊ COMPANY, NAME OF.

If a company carries on business for more than six months with less than seven members (two for a PRIVATE COMPANY), members knowing this fact become liable for all the company's debts.

Linguists, Institute of. This can be of help to exporters by putting persons in touch with reliable translators of sales literature and instructions.

Liquid ratio. The ratio of quick CURRENT ASSETS to CURRENT LIABILITIES. Quick current assets are cash, and items readily convertible into cash, but not STOCK or WORK IN PROGRESS, though stock could be included if it consisted of GOODS bought for resale for cash rather than credit. ◊ CURRENT RATIO.

Liquidation. This is effectively the BANKRUPTCY of a COMPANY. There are two forms – voluntary and compulsory (these terms are self-explanatory). When a company is wound up, ASSETS are realized and debts paid as far as possible. Certain debts have preferential treatment. ◊ LIQUIDATION: PREFERENTIAL DEBTS. If any monies remain these are distributed between the owners of the company according to their respective rights.

Liquidation: admission and rejection of proofs. The LIQUIDATOR must settle a list of CREDITORS. He fixes a date before which the creditors must prove debts. This must be advertised to every creditor mentioned in the statement of affairs. Debts must be proved by AFFIDAVIT and SECURITIES must be stated. It may be necessary to produce vouchers, i.e. INVOICES, etc. Trade discount must be deducted but not cash discounts over 5 per cent. Future debts may be proved and must be discounted at 5 per cent; wages may be proved *en bloc*. The liquidator must examine all proofs and admit or reject with reasons within twenty-eight days. The creditor can object to rejection within twenty-one days by application to the court. On the first of each month, the liquidator files a list of proofs received during the previous month, indicating whether they have been accepted or rejected.

Liquidation: committee of inspection. In the case of a COMPULSORY WINDING-UP the ◊ LIQUIDATOR is subject to the control of the committee of inspection or the BOARD OF TRADE. The committee consists of MEMBERS OF THE COMPANY and CREDITORS. It meets monthly and any member may summon a meeting. A QUORUM is a majority. Any member may resign or be removed. He is in a fiduciary position. The sanction of the committee is necessary in certain circumstances. ◊ LIQUIDATOR.

Liquidation: meetings of creditors and contributaries. These are called by the LIQUIDATOR in a ◊ VOLUNTARY WINDING-UP. In a winding-up by the court, first meetings of CREDITORS and CON-TRIBUTARIES are summoned by the OFFICIAL RECEIVER one month after the winding-up order, or six weeks where a special manager has been appointed. Notice is given to creditors and members – the notice to creditors gives the latest date for lodging proofs of debts. It also gives a summary of the STATEMENT OF AFFAIRS of the COMPANY and reasons for failure. Notice is also given to DIRECTORS.

Meetings may also be summoned at any time to ascertain the wishes of creditors and contributaries. They must be summoned when required by persons holding one-tenth (in VALUE) of SHARES or creditors for one-tenth of the debts. The liquidator must also call meetings to fill vacancies in the COMMITTEE OF INSPECTION. Meetings are summoned with seven days' notice in the LONDON GAZETTE and one local paper, and by notice to all persons recorded as creditors or contributaries. Motions are passed by majority in number and value, present in person or by PROXY. Where there is no definite majority the court will decide. Creditors that have not proved cannot vote. SECURED CREDITORS can only vote *re* that part of the debt which is not secured. All resolutions passed at meetings must be filed with the registrar of the court.

Liquidation: preferential debts. The order of payment of debts in a LIQUIDATION is that ◊ SECURED CREDITORS are paid first, then UNSECURED CREDITORS, PARI PASSU. There are, however, certain categories of unsecured creditors entitled to payment in full before this is done. Debts with priority are: (1) cost of liquidation, this being a first charge, (2) rates and taxes but not for more than one year (the relevant authority can choose the year), (3) wages of clerks, servants, workmen or labourers for not more than four months and not more than £200 each, (4) amounts ordered to be paid under the Reinstatement in Civil Employment Act 1944, (5) accrued holiday pay due to any persons in category (3) on termination of employment, (6) employers' contributions under the various National Insurance Acts (for a period of twelve months), (7) compensation due to workmen, the relevant date being the date of the winding-up order or the date of the appointment of a provisional LIQUIDATOR. All these debts rank *pari passu* amongst themselves. Where a person has advanced money to the COMPANY to pay wages that would have had priority, the person may claim priority by SUBROGATION. Crown debts have no priority as such.

Liquidation: proof of debts. These rules are similar to those in BANK-RUPTCY cases. ◊ WINDING-UP, CONDUCT OF.

Liquidation: special manager. ◊ SPECIAL MANAGER.

Liquidator. An official who supervises the WINDING-UP of a COMPANY. He takes over the company's property, though it does not vest in him unless a court says so. He acts rather as a receiving manager. Generally speaking he does anything necessary to conduct the winding-up: *inter alia* calling meetings where necessary (◊ LIQUIDATION: MEETINGS OF CREDITORS AND CONTRIBUTARIES), fixing a date for the proof of claims, admitting or rejecting proofs (◊ LIQUIDATION: ADMISSION AND REJECTION OF PROOFS), settling lists of CONTRIBUTORIES, making calls and disclaiming property. If the company is INSOLVENT, the COMMITTEE OF INSPECTION settles his remuneration, otherwise the members of the company do. If the winding-up is compulsory, payment is usually a COMMISSION based on property realized and DIVIDENDS paid.

The liquidator's powers and duties vary according to whether the winding-up is compulsory or voluntary. If compulsory, he is subject to court control (and the court or the BOARD OF TRADE can remove him at any time, for instance if he becomes bankrupt, and can appoint additional liquidators if necessary). He is also subject to the control of the COMMITTEE OF INSPECTION on questions of (1) bringing or defending actions in the company's name, (2) carrying on the company's business, (3) paying any class of CREDITORS in full, (4) compromising with debtors, creditors, or contributories, or (5) appointing a SOLICITOR. The liquidator must advertise his own appointment and that of the committee of inspection. He must report to the Registrar of Companies on the progress of liquidation, at the end of the first year and after each subsequent six months. If he carries on the business of the company, he must keep a separate trading account which is regularly audited by the committee of inspection. Creditors and contributories have certain rights to inspect books and receive summaries of accounts. The liquidator must give notice of winding-up to creditors, and tell them when proofs must be lodged if they are to receive a share of the dividend (i.e. distribution). He declares dividends to creditors by giving not more than two months' notice to the Board of Trade, sending a list of proofs. The liquidator must pay all monies into the company's liquidation account at the BANK OF ENGLAND, or else as directed by the Board of Trade. When the liquidation is complete, he applies to the Board for his release. Various formalities must be observed. The liquidator must usually give SECURITY.

If the winding-up is voluntary, the liquidator is not controlled by the Board of Trade in quite the same way. He must advertise his appointment, deal with proof of debts and make statements to the Registrar of Companies. Monies, though, need not be paid into the company's liquidation account unless they are retained for more than six months, or after the dissolution. The liquidator must generally submit some form of accounts for AUDIT and his costs may be taxed.

Liquidators, appointment of. In the case of a VOLUNTARY WINDING-UP, the LIQUIDATOR is appointed by the members of the COMPANY (or by the CREDITORS in a creditors' voluntary winding-up). In the case of a winding-up by the court, the court appoints the OFFICIAL RECEIVER as provisional liquidator. He then calls meetings of creditors and CONTRIBUTORIES to decide whether to apply for the appointment of a liquidator proper and/or a COMMITTEE OF INSPECTION.

Liquidator's accounts. The LIQUIDATOR of a COMPANY must keep accounts in a form prescribed by the BOARD OF TRADE. A private copy is then sent to all CREDITORS and CONTRIBUTORIES. If the liquidator carries on the business he must keep a separate trading account to be verified by AFFIDAVIT at least once a month and submitted to the COMMITTEE OF INSPECTION.

Liquidity. A term for the ease with which funds can be raised by the sale of ASSETS. In any business, cash is needed at various times for various purposes, but on the other hand idle cash earns no money. Cash may therefore be used to purchase assets, e.g. BILLS OF EXCHANGE, SECURITIES, market investments, or may be deposited for short periods, so that INTEREST is earned but the asset is quickly realizable. These funds are said to be near-liquid.

Liverpool Cotton Exchange. The Liverpool Cotton Exchange is reputed to be the largest in the world. Most of the cotton is American, and buying is done by BROKERS normally on behalf of cotton spinners. An official PRICE list is issued daily.

Livery companies. The relics of the medieval craft guilds of the City of London – one of the oldest being the Merchant Taylors' Company. They are companies formed by Royal Charter – those that cannot produce their charters are assumed to have received them at one time or other. Today there are eighty-three, and the senior companies, referred to as the Great Twelve, are the Mercers', Grocers', Drapers', Fishmongers', Goldsmiths', Skinners', Merchant Taylors', Haberdashers', Salters', Ironmongers', Vintners', and Clothworkers'. Some of the guilds have formed their own schools, not necessarily for educating children into their own crafts, though that might have been the original intention. The Mercers' Company was prominent in this field. It formed the Mercers' School in 1542 and was also responsible for supporting St Paul's School. The guilds united to form the City and Guilds of London Institute in 1878, to help with technical education. In 1907 they helped form the Imperial College of Science and Technology. The Livery companies have elaborate dress for ceremonial occasions, and also some fine banqueting halls. Most of them are now little more than social organizations, but some still play an active part in their trade; for instance the Fishmongers' Company still looks after Billingsgate and seizes any bad fish.

Lloyds. The popular name for the Corporation of Lloyds. It started in a coffee house in Tavern Street in 1689, and moved, via Lombard Street and Pope's Head Alley, to the Royal Exchange in 1774. Subsequently it moved into its own building, where it remains. Members are BROKERS or UNDERWRITERS. Each is a sole trader although they normally operate in syndicates. The Corporation itself has no liability for the defaults of its members. However, a member must deposit a substantial sum of money before he is accepted, and premiums recived by underwriters are placed in a trust fund. Claims are paid out of this fund. Annual AUDITS are compulsory. The Corporation provides standardized documents, shipping intelligence services, a daily newspaper (LLOYDS LIST AND SHIPPING GAZETTE), a claims bureau, and LLOYDS AGENTS in nearly every important port in the world. LLOYDS REGISTER OF SHIPPING classifies vessels and gives comprehensive information regarding them. Lloyds deal with a vast part of all annual INSURANCE in this country though not with life ASSURANCE. Its main business has been, is, and probably always will be, MARINE INSURANCE.

Lloyds agents. AGENTS throughout the world appointed by LLOYDS.

They supply information regarding shipping, aviation, etc., to Lloyds, and also appoint surveyors to report on damage or loss. They may also be authorized to settle claims. There are about 1,500 Lloyds agents and sub-agents.

Lloyds List and Shipping Gazette. Founded in 1734 and previously *Lloyds List*, this is a daily paper providing a mass of shipping information, particularly on the movement of shipping.

Lloyds medals. These are awarded for extraordinary exertions in saving life at sea or preserving vessels or cargoes. There is also a Lloyds War Medal for exceptional gallantry at sea, and a medal awarded for outstanding service to LLOYDS itself.

Lloyds Register of Shipping. A society formed to survey and classify ships for the benefit of insurers and other interested parties. If a ship is constructed under the supervision of Lloyds surveyors it is marked with a Maltese cross. Ships are generally given periodic surveys. The society is responsible for an annual publication known as *Lloyds Register of British and Foreign Shipping*. This contains details of all vessels afloat of 100 tons or more. ◊ A1.

Loading broker. An AGENT acting for a ship-owner with a view to obtaining cargo.

Loan capital. That part of the CAPITAL of a COMPANY or other organization subscribed for a fixed period; or for a period determinable by either party; or on the happening of a stated event. It is entitled to fixed INTEREST and may be secured on the property of the business or on a GUARANTEE by a third party. It must be distinguished from SHARE CAPITAL. The most common form of loan capital is a ◊ DEBENTURE.

Loans to directors. A COMPANY may not make loans to its DIRECTORS unless: (1) it is an EXEMPT PRIVATE COMPANY (these companies were abolished by the Companies Act 1967), (2) the director is a holding company, (3) the money is necessary to enable the director to perform his duties to the company and the loan is approved by the company in general MEETING, or (4) the loan is made in the ordinary course of business by a company whose ordinary business includes lending money. Particulars of loans must be shown in the ACCOUNTS.

Loans to employees. COMPANIES may make loans to employees though there are certain restrictions concerning DIRECTORS and other officers of the company (◊ LOANS TO DIRECTORS). Where loans are made for the purpose of purchasing SHARES in the company, they must be shown in the accounts. The 1948 Act provides that loans to officers of the company and details of those made during the year, must be shown in the accounts, unless the loans are made in the ordinary course of a business which includes the lending of money, or the loans are of less than £2,000.

Local Employment Acts. ◊ DEVELOPMENT AREAS.

Locus poenitentiae. A legal term applying to ILLEGAL CONTRACTS. Where money is paid for an illegal purpose the parties may be allowed a '*locus poenitentiae*' – an opportunity to change their minds. Once the illegal purpose is carried out no action at law can be maintained.

London acceptance credit. An exporter's credit with a London ACCEP-TANCE HOUSE or BANK, which enables him to draw BILLS OF EXCHANGE on certain conditions, e.g. payable within three months and up to a stated amount. Credits may be indefinite or for a fixed period. If the latter, maturing bills will often be replaced by others, and this is known as a revolving credit. SECURITY is usually though not always necessary, and may take the form of LETTERS OF HYPOTHECATION, tender of shipping documents, etc. By this means the exporter obtains cash immediately on order, perhaps before the GOODS are made, or when they are shipped. He is obliged to put funds at the disposal of the ACCEPTOR when the bills are due for payment.

London Association for the Protection of Trade. An organization giving status reports *re* the credit-worthiness of potential customers, principally within the London area. There are branches in certain other towns and also affiliated organizations.

London bank export credit. Similar to ◊ LONDON ACCEPTANCE CREDIT, except that the U.K. exporter draws BILLS OF EXCHANGE on the overseas buyer and the BANK collects these bills.

London Gazette. A weekly bulletin enjoying the unique distinction of being 'published by authority'. Any information published in the *London Gazette* (or in Scotland, the EDINBURGH GAZETTE) is notice to the world, or rather to the nation, and no one can deny knowledge of it, even though he has neither heard of, nor seen, the publication. Matters included in the *Gazette*, apart from certain traditional items, are notification of public appointments, etc., details of winding-up orders, BANKRUPTCIES, meetings of CREDITORS, changes of names of COMPANIES, PARTNERSHIPS, and individuals, changes in the constitution of partnerships, and all other matters which the law requires to be gazetted.

London metal exchange. The exchange has about 110 members, and deals in copper, tin, lead, and zinc. The dealing methods are traditional and somewhat complicated. Dealings are partly for cash and partly forward – most are in three-month FUTURES and are by word of mouth, CONTRACTS being drawn up afterwards. An official price list is issued daily.

Long-term liabilities. An accounting term for amounts borrowed by a business and not repayable within the next ACCOUNTING PERIOD.

Loss leader. A retailing term for GOODS deliberately sold at a loss in order to attract customers. ◊ RESALE PRICE MAINTENANCE.

Lost capital. ◊ REDUCTION OF CAPITAL.

Lost share certificates. ARTICLES OF ASSOCIATION generally provide that where a MEMBER OF THE COMPANY loses a SHARE certificate the COMPANY will replace it but be indemnified by that member.

Lump sum, freight. FREIGHT payable irrespective of the amount of GOODS loaded.

Luncheon vouchers. Vouchers or slips of paper (issued for instance by employers to their staff) which are exchangeable for meals but not for cash. The employer purchases the vouchers from an organization specializing in this kind of business. This organization later re-purchases them from the restaurant, making its profit from the discount offered by the restaurant and the COMMISSION paid by the employers. Luncheon vouchers are a means of giving employees additional benefit in kind and are tax free up to 15p per day. Not all restaurants accept them.

Lutine bell. In 1799, the *Lutine*, insured at LLOYDS, went down in the North Sea with a large cargo of bullion, much of which was never recovered. The Lutine Bell is a bell suspended above the rostrum in the underwriting room at Lloyds, which is rung when important announcements are to be made to the Market. Two strokes mean good news, one stroke bad. Nowadays it is not often used, not because of the scarcity of news, but because more sophisticated means of communication have been developed.

M

Mail order firm. A FIRM selling a very wide selection of GOODS, but by post rather than through retail premises. It employs AGENTS who take orders, which are dealt with by a central organization. The agent has an elaborate catalogue and is paid a COMMISSION on his sales. The goods are sold at competitive PRICES, the economies in MARKETING enabling the firm to allow the customer to pay in instalments without necessarily charging him a higher price.

Maintenance. A CONTRACT or agreement whereby one party assists another in a lawsuit without having sufficient legal or moral interest. Contracts concerned with maintenance are illegal.

Making a price. A STOCK EXCHANGE term for the double quotation given by a STOCKJOBBER. The jobber quotes the buying and the selling price without knowing if the STOCKBROKER approaching him wishes to buy or sell.

Making up day. A STOCK EXCHANGE term for the first settlement day. ◊ ACCOUNT DAYS ◊ PAY DAY ◊ MAKING UP PRICE.

Making up price. A STOCK EXCHANGE term for the price at which bargains are carried over from one account to another. ◊ ACCOUNT DAYS. It is normally the market price at noon on that day.

Mala fide. ◊ BONA FIDE.

Management accounting. The control of a business by refined and economic means: collecting relevant information, analysing it and applying the results for the benefit of the business. Various techniques include ◊ STANDARD COSTING and ◊ BUDGETARY CONTROL.

Management, British Institute of. An independent, non-political, non-profit-making COMPANY, LIMITED BY GUARANTEE and not having a SHARE CAPITAL. It was established in 1947 on the recommendation of the Baillieu Committee, set up by the BOARD OF TRADE, and is the national clearing house for information on management policies, practices, and techniques, and management development including education and training. Its members include industrial and commercial COMPANIES, nationalized industries, government departments, BANKS, FINANCE HOUSES, trade and employers' associations, trade unions, MANAGEMENT CONSULTANTS, professional bodies, educational institutions and individuals. It has a library and a consulting services information bureau. Its publications include the monthly *Management Today*, the bi-monthly *British*

Institute of Management Notes for Collective Subscribers, the quarterly *Management Abstracts*, and also various specialist books. The Institute holds courses, conferences and seminars. Individual members may be Fellows (F.B.I.M.), Members (M.B.I.M.) or Associate Members (A.M.B.I.M.). Qualification for Fellowship is eminent achievement in the practice of management, for Membership, general management experience at board or general management level and for Associate Membership, a Diploma in Management Studies or equivalent qualification in management subjects, and one year's acceptable experience. Persons with long experience in management may be admitted to an Associate Membership without a Diploma. Individual subscriptions: Fellows and Members £8·40, others £6·30. Address: 80 Fetter Lane, London EC4.

Management consultant. A person whose business is to advise on management problems: on making more effective use of resources employed; and also on problems involving basic organization, administration and reorientation. Consultants advertise as their range of services (1) over-all policy and planning, (2) cost reduction and utilization of resources, (3) personnel function and industrial relations, (4) management techniques, and (5) overseas services. ⟡ MANAGEMENT CONSULTANTS' ASSOCIATION.

Management Consultants' Association. An association founded in 1956 to establish high standards of ethical conduct and technical competence throughout the management consultancy profession in this country. Most leading firms belong to it. Advice is given on which firm is most suitable to a customer's needs. The basic conditions of membership are: (1) the firm must have been in business in the United Kingdom as consultants for five years and 25 per cent of the consulting staff must have had five years' experience with the member firms; (2) the principals' personal experience must be approved as adequate by the council, and the staff must also have had suitable experience; (3) members must employ, in the United Kingdom and full time, at least five consulting staff; (4) 80 per cent of staff must hold graduate degrees or equivalent qualifications, or belong to a recognized professional institution. Members must adhere to the Association's code of professional conduct. There is an annual report reviewing activities of members and of the Association. There are also occasional papers on topics of interest to managers. Address: 23–4 Cromwell Place, London SW7.

Managing director. The DIRECTOR of a COMPANY with specific responsibility for management. Apart from the CHAIRMAN, he is normally the senior person in the company.

Manchester Ship Canal. A very important canal linking Manchester with the sea and making Manchester in effect a port.

Manifest. A detailed list of a ship's cargo which must be sent to AGENTS abroad, and to Customs authorities, within six days of clearance outwards. ◊ EXPORTERS' DECLARATIONS.

Man-of-war. Any ship commanded by a person in a nation's recognized armed navy. For instance, any ship commanded by an officer of the Royal Navy would theoretically be a man-of-war.

Manufacturer's agent. An AGENT who obtains CONTRACTS for manufacturers. He works within a specified area for a COMMISSION, and probably has the sole agency for a manufacturer within that area.

Manufacturing industry. That branch of industry concerned with the manufacture of GOODS by the application of labour to raw materials supplied by the EXTRACTIVE INDUSTRIES.

Margin. A margin is strictly the difference between the cost of an ASSET or investment and the amount that a lender of money is willing to advance for its purchase; or (and this is much the same thing) the amount of money a SPECULATOR puts down in FORWARD DEALINGS. Where a person wishes to buy or speculate in a property he may not intend to take it up, but the margin or deposit is an earnest of his intentions. The term is particularly used with reference to forward dealings in commodities or even currencies. Dealings in margins occur when a speculator, having secured a certain quantity at a fixed price in the future, sells the margin by selling the OPTION, at a profit or loss.

Margin dealing. ◊ MARGIN.

Marginal cost. The extra cost of producing an item above and beyond the agreed output level. The figure for this cost (usually DIRECT EXPENSE only) is used to decide whether the additional production is justified. Other considerations such as GOODWILL apart, the additional sales revenue should equal or exceed the marginal cost.

Marine insurance. A marine insurance CONTRACT is concerned with a marine adventure: with insuring ships, cargo, passengers, etc. Marine insurance is rather a complex matter. Policies are long and couched in language both colourful and obscure. The relevant act is the Marine Insurance Act 1906.

The risks insured against include damage by fire, storm and tempest; detention by foreign princes, seizure under legal process and dangers occasioned by 'men-of-war, fire, enemies, pirates, rovers, thieves, jettisons, letters of mart and countermart, surprisals, takings at sea, arrests, restraints, and detainments of all kings, princes, and people of what nation, condition, quality so ever, BARRATRY of the master and mariners, and of all other perils, losses, and misfortunes, that have or shall come to the hurt, detriment or damage of the said goods and merchandises, and ship, etc., or any part thereof'. 'Pirates' includes passengers who mutiny and rioters who attack the ship from the shore, but 'thieves' does not include clandestine thefts by one of the crew or a passenger. This is a general list: any particular policy may exclude some of them or include others.

The insurer must have an INSURABLE INTEREST, i.e. he must personally suffer from the loss. The interest must exist at the time of the loss, though it need not when the policy is signed. Gambling policies where the insured has no interest at any time are likely to be void. The policy holder may even be prosecuted. ⟡ POLICY PROOF OF INTEREST.

Marine insurance policies are policies UBERRIMAE FIDEI. The contract must take the form of a marine insurance policy and must be signed by the insurers. It must state: (1) the name of the insured, (2) the subject matter, (3) the risk, (4) the voyage or time, (5) the sum insured, (6) the name of the insurers. Policies may be VOYAGE POLICIES, time policies, or a mixture of the two. They may also be valued or unvalued. A valued policy specifies the agreed VALUE of the subject matter, an unvalued policy does not. On a total loss the holder of an unvalued policy would receive a sum related to the value of the subject matter at the time of the loss. The holder of a valued policy receives the sum insured irrespective of the value at time of loss. A floating policy is a general policy leaving the name of the ship or ships, etc. to be given subsequently. There are various express and implied WARRANTIES and if these are not complied with by the insured, the policy may be ineffective. For instance, the ship must be seaworthy at the commencement of the voyage, and also fit to carry the GOODS. With voyage policies the ship must sail from the place specified. It must not deviate from the course nor delay unduly. (This does not apply to deviations or delays due to factors outside the master's control or deviations to help ships in distress, where human life is in danger.) There are other DEVIATIONS allowed (these are specified in the Act), e.g. for the safety of the ship or other insured matter, or for obtaining medical aid. Marine policies can be assigned by ENDORSEMENT unless this is prohibited by the policy. The assignee must have an interest. It is immaterial whether or not the loss has occurred. There are different forms of loss, and liability varies accordingly.

Marine insurance: third party risk. Although the doctrine on ⟡ PRIVITY OF CONTRACT is fairly sacrosanct, there are certain exceptions. Road INSURANCE is one, MARINE INSÚRANCE is another. The CONSIGNEE of goods named in a BILL OF LADING and an endorsee of the bill have the same rights and liabilities as the original party to the CONTRACT of carriage.

Market overt. An antique term with a rather specialized meaning. Generally speaking, a person who has not a TITLE to GOODS cannot pass a title (i.e. cannot sell them). If the sale is made between sunrise and sunset in market overt, when the goods are exposed publicly, in bulk (a SAMPLE is insufficient), and are of the class usually dealt in by the seller, then a good title can be passed to the purchaser in good faith, irrespective of the title of the seller. In the City of London, market overt is held daily (except on Sunday) in all shops and markets. In the country, it is held on special days in special places according to charter, custom or statute. ◊ STOLEN GOODS.

Market rate of discount. The rate of DISCOUNT charged in the money market for discounting BILLS OF EXCHANGE.

Market Research Society. A professional association for persons using survey techniques in market, social, and economic research. Founded in 1947, it seeks to promote and protect the interests of its members and those employing their services. It also attempts to publicize the profession. Members are bound to observe a standard code of practice in conducting scientific sample surveys and reporting results. Various conferences are held to exchange information, and liaison with government departments, universities, scientific institutions, etc., is preserved. Members may be Full Members (M.M.R.S.) or Associates (A.M.M.R.S.), the former having obtained full professional standing. They now must also have been Associates for more than two years. Full Members pay £7·35, Associates £4·20 *per annum*.

Various organizations offer market research in particular areas on behalf of exporters. Plans are sometimes offered without obligation. The Market Research Society has a register of members and will provide the address of the nearest association.

Details from 39 Hertford Street, London W1.

Market value. A term (often used in published accounts) for the amount that an ASSET would realize if sold in a completely free market. (◊ SHARES: MARKET VALUE ◊ STOCK-IN-TRADE.) Distinction should always be made between value in present use and value in alternative use. The latter may be very much greater, for instance where factory land could profitably be developed for housing. The Companies Act 1967 states that where the market value of land held by a company is substantially higher than its book value, the directors should draw attention to this fact. However, the Act does not say whether 'market value' means value in present or alternative use.

Marketing. A term defined by the ◊ INSTITUTE OF MARKETING as 'the management function which organizes and directs all those business activities involved in assessing and converting customer purchasing power into effective demand for a specific product or service to the final consumer or user so as to achieve the profit, target, or other objectives set by a company' (that is, the presentation and distribution of goods and services in the manner best designed to benefit the producer, the distributor, and the public).

Marketing, Institute of. This was incorporated in 1911 as the Institute of Marketing and Sales Management (◊ MARKETING), in order to provide its members with opportunities to develop their skill and judgment and to educate their successors in marketing theory and practice. Members may be Fellows (F.Inst.M.S.M.), Members (M.Inst.M.S.M.), Associates (A.Inst.M.S.M.) or Graduates (G.Inst.M.S.M.), and are elected by the Council of the Institute at its absolute discretion. Conditions of membership are experience, or a Diploma in Marketing. The Institute publishes a monthly: *Marketing*, and also the journal of the College of Marketing, *Marketing Forum*. Address: Marketing House, Richbell Place, Lamb's Conduit Street, London WC1.

Marketing research. Marketing research is distinguished from MARKET RESEARCH in that while the latter deals with the pattern of a market, the former deals with problems involved in marketing a particular product. It starts with market research and then studies practical difficulties in selling and deciding, for instance, what lines might be pushed in particular areas and what special problems might be met in any particular region. It is concerned with the problems attached to selling a particular product for a particular manufacturer, while market research on the other hand would tend to study the state of consumers' demand in relation to perhaps a group of products of very similar kind. Thus market research might be used by a group of manufacturers to obtain a field study whereas marketing research would be used by a particular manufacturer to discover the best way of selling his own particular GOODS.

Marriage brokage contracts. Some persons offer for reward to provide a partner in marriage. These CONTRACTS are illegal. The LOCUS POENITENTIAE rule does not apply and money may be recovered even after part performance or marriage itself.

Master porter. A dock company employee responsible for supervising the unloading of a ship.

209

Mate's receipt. ◊ SHIPPING NOTES.

Mean (arithmetic). A statistical term for the average of a series of numbers, obtained by totalling the series and dividing this total by the number of items in the series.

Mean (geometric). A statistical term for the average of a series of numbers. In a series of *n* numbers it is the *n*th root of the product of those numbers.

Mean price. When SECURITIES are quoted on the OFFICIAL LIST, two PRICES are given: the STOCKJOBBERS' buying and selling prices. The mean price is the average between the two. It is also the market price of an investment.

Medium-term capital. Funds raised for a stated and limited period, not repayable at call. The period is normally less than five years. Funds raised for longer periods would be LONG-TERM CAPITAL.

Meeting, annual general. Every COMPANY must hold a meeting of its MEMBERS once in every calendar year. This meeting is known as the annual general meeting (and must be specified as such in the notices calling it). Not more than fifteen months may elapse between one annual general meeting and the next, though if the first is held within eighteen months of incorporation, no meeting other than the STATUTORY MEETING need be held in the year of incorporation or in the following year. Normally the annual general meeting considers the accounts and the reports of DIRECTORS and AUDITORS, the fixing of the AUDITORS' REMUNERATION, the declaration of a DIVIDEND, and the appointment or re-appointment of auditors or directors. Notice must be given individually to each member, and must specify any business (other than that stated above) to be discussed at the meeting. If a member is unable to attend he must be given the opportunity to appoint a PROXY to attend in his stead.

Meeting, extraordinary. This is a meeting other than the ANNUAL GENERAL MEETING. It may be called by the DIRECTORS at any time, either of their own volition or after being requisitioned by the holders of not less than one-tenth of the PAID-UP CAPITAL (voting). (The ARTICLES OF ASSOCIATION of the COMPANY may increase this percentage.) The requisition must be signed by the requisitionists. If the directors do not act within twenty-one days the requisitionists (or more than half of them) may call the meeting themselves. A printed notice of the resolution passed must be sent to the registrar within fifteen days.

Meeting, notice of. Each MEMBER OF A COMPANY must receive notice of every meeting (the ARTICLES OF ASSOCIATION normally state that notice may be sent by post and need not be sent to anyone not resident in the United Kingdom). The notice must contain details of any special business to be transacted. For the ANNUAL GENERAL MEETING twenty-one days' notice is required; for other meetings (but see below) fourteen days. Where the meeting is to remove a DIRECTOR or authorize a director of seventy to act, or to remove the AUDITOR, the company must receive twenty-eight days' notice of intent to move the resolution, and must pass this notice on to the members, with the notice of the meeting. The director and the auditor have a right to make representations at the meeting. If wrong notice is given the meeting is invalid, unless: (1) at the annual general meeting all members, who are entitled to, attend and vote; (2) at other meetings members holding 95 per cent or more of the SHARES' NOMINAL VALUE agree otherwise.

Meeting, ordinary. The ◊ ANNUAL GENERAL MEETING as opposed to an EXTRAORDINARY MEETING.

Meeting, statutory. A meeting that must be held within a period of not less than one month, and not more than three months, from the date on which a COMPANY commences business. At this meeting members may inspect a list showing names, descriptions and addresses of members, together with the number of SHARES held by each. The meeting discusses matters relating to the FORMATION OF THE COMPANY or to the ◊ STATUTORY REPORT.

No notice is necessary of any resolution, unless the ARTICLES OF ASSOCIATION state otherwise. Failure to hold the meeting is a ground for folding up the company.

A PRIVATE COMPANY need not hold a statutory meeting.

Member bank. Another name for a commercial BANK (i.e. a JOINT STOCK BANK, MERCHANT BANK, etc.), usually a member of the Clearing House Association.

Members of companies. A person becomes a member of a COMPANY when his name is entered in its register of members. Subscribers to the MEMORANDUM OF ASSOCIATION become members automatically. Other persons are entitled to registration when allotted SHARES on application, or when shares are transferred to them. Strictly speaking, anyone whose name does not appear on the register is not entitled to the rights of membership. A court may order RECTIFICATION OF THE REGISTER if a person's name is wrongly omitted. On the other hand, entries in the register are not conclusive and a person may have his name removed if it has been wrongly entered, though application to the court may be necessary first.

Members' voluntary winding-up. ◊ WINDING-UP, VOLUNTARY.

Memorandum of agreement. ◊ HIRE PURCHASE.

Memorandum of Association. A document filed with the Registrar of Companies on the formation of a COMPANY, open for inspection at any time by any person at Bush House. It contains (1) the NAME OF THE COMPANY, (2) the nationality (normally whether the ◊ REGISTERED OFFICE is to be in England or Scotland), (3) the ◊ OBJECTS OF THE COMPANY, (4) a statement that the members have LIMITED LIABILITY, (5) the amount of AUTHORIZED CAPITAL and the number and amount of SHARES into which it is divided (the greater the AUTHORIZED CAPITAL the greater the STAMP DUTY payable). These details must be followed by what is known as an association clause and subscription. This states *inter alia* the names, addresses, and descriptions of subscribers and the number of shares taken by each. This is normally a formality, but it is necessary to indicate there are at least seven members (two for a PRIVATE COMPANY); the persons stated take at least one share each.

A company is bound by its memorandum but may alter it, generally by SPECIAL RESOLUTION. The alteration must be made known to the Registrar. ◊ COMPANY: OBJECTS OF.

Memorandum of satisfaction. A document stating that a MORTGAGE or charge on property has been discharged by repayment of the money lent. It should be signed by all parties concerned. A copy should be sent to the Registrar of Companies if the mortgage has been made by a COMPANY and registered.

Mercantile agent. ◊ FACTOR.

Mercer. Traditionally a dealer in fine cloths and fabrics.

Merchant bank. A rather vague term for 'BANKS who are not merchants, merchants who are not banks, and, houses who are neither merchants nor banks'. Nevertheless, in the City the term is applied to members of the ◊ ACCEPTING HOUSES COMMITTEE and the ◊ ISSUING HOUSES ASSOCIATION.

Merchant shipper. A person who buys directly from manufacturers with a view to selling overseas. These merchants are also known as export merchants and most belong to the EXPORT HOUSES ASSOCIATION.

Merchantable quality. A term used with reference to the ◊ SALE OF GOODS. There is an implied CONDITION that GOODS are of merchantable quality, which means that a reasonable person, after full examination, would accept them in satisfaction of his CONTRACT. Where there is more than one use of the GOODS, and the buyer has not made his intentions known, it might be sufficient that they are suitable for one of the purposes.

Merchantman. A ship engaged in trade or commerce, not for war-like purposes.

Merger. The amalgamation of two or more business organizations, with a view to becoming more efficient or creating a MONOPOLY. Nowadays mergers may be subject to the approval of the Monopolies Commission. ◊ TAKE-OVER BID ◊ CITY CODE ON TAKE-OVERS.

Middle market price. ◊ MEAN PRICE.

Middle market value. ◊ CLOSING PRICE.

Middle man. A person who, rather than produce GOODS, puts producers in touch with consumers.

Milliner. At one time a dealer in fancy wares and apparel, particularly from Milan (hence the name), but now a dealer or maker of women's hats or trimmings.

Minimum subscription. The amount stated in the PROSPECTUS which the DIRECTORS consider the minimum that must be raised for the COMPANY to be launched.

Minor. A person who has not attained his majority, i.e. is not yet eighteen years of age. Before 1 January 1970 the age of majority was twenty-one years of age.

Minority shareholders. Persons holding SHARES in a COMPANY which is a ◊ SUBSIDIARY COMPANY, though not themselves the holding company or nominees of it.

Misfeasance summons. A summons which may be taken against any DIRECTOR, PROMOTER, LIQUIDATOR, or OFFICER OF A COMPANY in a WINDING-UP where it is believed that he has misapplied or retained money or property, or has been guilty of misfeasance or breach of trust. He may be publicly examined and ordered to repay the money.

Misrepresentation. If a person induces another to form a CONTRACT by falsifying certain information, he is guilty of misrepresentation. This may be innocent or fraudulent. If the person who made the representations can show that he believed them correct, the misrepresentation is innocent. In this case the injured party cannot always claim DAMAGES, though he can rescind the contract if he can show (1) that he has not implicitly accepted the misrepresentation, (2) that he has acted promptly, (3) that no innocent third parties have obtained rights in the subject matter for value (i.e. some kind of payment), and (4) that the parties can be restored to their former positions. The injured party could claim damages for innocent misrepresentation if (1) an AGENT has misrepresented his authority, (2) misrepresentations have been made in a PROSPECTUS, (3) misrepresentation is in the

213

form of a CONDITION or WARRANTY, or (4) there is a special relationship between the parties (a SOLICITOR or banker, for instance, has a legal duty to take care) though in this case there would have to be negligence. The MISREPRESENTATION ACT 1967 gives additional aid to vicitms of innocent misrepresentation in certain cases.

Fraudulent misrepresentation entitles the injured party to damages and rescission. ◊ FRAUD.

Misrepresentation Act 1967. The law dealing with innocent ◊ MISREPRESENTATION in CONTRACT has been altered by the Misrepresentation Act 1967, which states *inter alia*: (1) DAMAGES may be obtained even for innocent misrepresentation, unless the person making the representation proves that he had reasonable ground to believe, and did believe up to the time the contract was made, that the facts represented were correct (representation must still be of a fact and not an opinion); (2) where a contract could be rescinded for innocent misrepresentation and the court thinks rescission would cause hardship, it may award damages in lieu; (3) in certain circumstances, contracts can be rescinded on the grounds of innocent misrepresentation, even though they have been performed; (4) in the case of contracts for the sale of specific goods, the Sale of Goods Act 1893 has been amended so that the contract may be rescinded, on grounds of breach of condition, even though property has strictly passed to the buyer. Provisions in a contract which attempt to avoid this Act may be treated as void by the court.

Mistake. Generally speaking, when two persons enter into a CONTRACT it is taken for granted that they know what they are doing. The law will therefore not interfere, and if one party fails to perform his part he will be liable for BREACH OF CONTRACT. Mistakes nevertheless do happen. They may be mutual or unilateral; they may be mistakes of fact or of law. If there is mutual mistake fundamental to the contract, whether about the existence or the nature of its subject matter, or about some other matter material to the contract, the contract will be void *ab initio*, for it does not represent the intention of either party and the court will not enforce it. This will not apply where the mistake is superficial, where the parties are getting substantially what they bargained for – though there may be grounds for an action for DAMAGES.

Where the mistake is unilateral the position is rather difficult. Where there has been ◊ MISREPRESENTATION on the part of one party, whether fraudulent or innocent, particular rules apply. Where there has been no misrepresentation the doctrine of CAVEAT EMPTOR will probably apply. However, even where no representations have been made, there are situations where unilateral mistakes can invalidate contracts. For instance, if one party is mistaken on something material to the contract, whether the person with whom he is contracting, or a term in the contract, or the nature of the document, and if the fact that he is mistaken is known to the other party (who need not have contributed to the mistake himself) the contract will not be enforced.

Mistakes of law are usually irrelevant as everybody is expected to know the law: '*Ignorantia juris neminem excusat*'. However, money paid where there is a mistake of law can sometimes be recovered if it would be inequitable for the other party to retain it, e.g. if the payee knew of the mistake.

Mitigation of damage. In an action for BREACH OF CONTRACT, where the plaintiff is claiming DAMAGES, the court will consider whether he has taken all steps necessary to minimize damage. For example, a seller must dispose of GOODS if there is an available market. The court will not award damages that could have been avoided by reasonable action, though the plaintiff is not expected to go out of his way to help the defendant. None of this applies to ANTICIPATORY BREACH OF CONTRACT.

Mock auction. Under the Mock Auctions Act 1961, a mock auction is one where during the course of SALE (1) any lot to which the Act applies is sold at a PRICE lower than bid, or any part of the price is repaid or credited to the bidder, (2) the right to buy is restricted to those who have bought or agreed to buy one or more articles, or (3) any articles are given away or offered in the form of GIFTS. Anyone running or helping to run a mock auction could be fined £1,000, imprisoned for not more than two years, or both. ⟨⟩ CHEAP JACK.

Mode. A statistical term for a form of average. When the numbers are arranged in increasing order, the mode is that number which is exactly half way up the scale.

Money at call and at short notice. An item on a BALANCE SHEET of a BANK. Money at call is money that must be repaid on demand. Money at short notice may be money borrowed for, say, twenty-four hours, at a very low INTEREST rate. There is a great deal of money at short notice circulating in the city. When more money is offered than required, money is said to be 'easy' – when the reverse is true, money is said to be 'tight' in Lombard Street.

Money broker. A person who puts BANKS, etc., with money to lend from day to day, in touch with persons or institutions wishing to borrow on such terms, e.g. a DISCOUNT HOUSE looking for an

OVERNIGHT LOAN. The broker neither lends nor borrows: he is an intermediary receiving a COMMISSION.

Money had and received. A particular form of action where money paid by one party to another is claimed, not so much because the second party has failed to perform his part of the CONTRACT properly, but rather because there has been total failure of CONSIDERATION, or because the money was obtained under false pretences or under duress and it would be unconscionable for the second party to retain it.

Money market. DISCOUNT HOUSES, BANKS, etc., handling the credit and finance of the country in the City of London.

Moneylender. A person whose business is lending money. These are bound by strict regulations, *inter alia*, that they: (1) must not carry on business except in their own names, (2) must hold a moneylender's certificate and annual Excise licence, and (3) must not charge COMPOUND INTEREST.

Rates of INTEREST may vary, but a court may not allow recovery of interest that it considers excessive. A rate of interest over 48 per cent is *prima facie* excessive. Moneylending CONTRACTS and SECURITIES relating to them are unenforceable unless a note in writing is made and signed personally by the borrower. The note must be made before the loan. It must include the date, the amount of the loan, and the rate of interest.

Monger. Once just a dealer or trafficker in GOODS. Now a person carrying on some disreputable trade.

Monopoly. A monopoly is said to exist where at least one-third of a local or national market is controlled by one person or a group of persons working together. The relevant Acts are the Monopolies and Mergers Acts 1948 and 1965. There is a Monopolies Commission, appointed by the BOARD OF TRADE, which has from four to twenty-five regular members, and is designed to protect the public interest. The Commission may be ordered by the Board of Trade to investigate and report on apparent monopolies in the production or supply of GOODS and services, or on prospective MERGERS between two or more enterprises. It may also report on unregistered restrictive practices. Agreements which must be registered are listed in the Restrictive Trade Practices Act 1956. Registration of these agreements debars investigation by the Commission. Mergers may be referred to the Commission where a monopoly situation may result, or where the value of ASSETS taken over exceeds £5,000,000. Reference must be made within six months and the Commission must report within another six months plus any extra time (limit three months) allowed by the Board of Trade. The Board of Trade has power to nullify agreements on the basis of the Commission's investigations. It may also order the break up of a business and has further powers over the regulation of PRICES.

There are special provisions relating to newspaper mergers, again for the protection of the public. These mergers, if they result in one proprietor's controlling an average daily circulation of 500,000 or more copies, must (with limited exceptions) be investigated and must receive the written consent of the Board of Trade.

Moral obligation. This is not good CONSIDERATION for the formation of a CONTRACT.

Morcock doctrine. ◊ FUNDAMENTAL TERMS.

Mortgage. Any transaction by which land is given as SECURITY for repayment of a loan. The rules are governed by the Law of Property Act 1925. Mortgages may be legal or equitable. A legal mortgage may be of two kinds: (1) A DEED granting a lease for a stated number of years to the mortgagee – the lease to end on repayment of the money at the end of that period, with the possibility of a second mortgage granting a lease for the same number of years plus one day. The mortgage is usually accompanied by the deposit of title deeds. The mortgagee may insist on this. Possession of title deeds means that the mortgage need not be registered as a land charge. (2) A charge by way of legal mortgage. This dates from the 1925 Act. It is similar to (1), but not strictly a lease and can therefore be used for mortgaging household land when the lessor is not supposed to sub-let.

In both types of mortgage the mortgagor always has a right to redeem – this cannot be taken from him by clauses in the deed (◊ EQUITY OF REDEMPTION). It may however not be possible until the term of the mortgage (or some lesser time) has run.

Equitable mortgages may be made by deposit of title deeds or written charge. No strict form is necessary. Possession of title deeds is good security but if there is a charge then this should be registered at the Land Registry, or else it will not be valid against a purchaser for value in good faith. Equitable mortgages rank in the order of their registration and not in the order in which they were made.

Mortgagee, rights of. The rights of the mortgagee where the mortgagor has defaulted are: (1) to sue on the personal covenant to repay; (2) to enter and take possession – though this is dangerous as a mortgagee must account scrupulously for income and expenses; (3) to foreclose, which involves asking the court to order repayment within a specified time with a view to obtaining permanent ownership of the property; (4) to sell the property. There is an implied power of sale in all mortgages by DEED – unless anything is said to the contrary. Sale can only take place after the date of repayment and with three months' notice, or when INTEREST is two months in ARREARS or some other covenant breached. The mortgagee, after paying expenses and himself, holds the BALANCE on trust for the mortgagor, or other lenders; (5) to appoint a RECEIVER. This is an alternative to selling. The receiver is the AGENT of the mortgagor although appointed by the mortgagee. He pays charges on the property, INTEREST on loans, etc., and applies the balance of income to reducing the loan.

Motor insurers' bureau. A bureau set up by various INSURANCE offices for the protection of the general public, when a motorist involved in an accident is not properly insured against third party risks. The bureau pays out and then attempts to recover from the motorist.

Moving average. A statistical term used to show trends in a series of figures. It attempts to iron out casual fluctuation by showing the movement in an n year average: for example, if total ASSETS are shown for fifty years, the average for the first, say, five years would be taken. The second figure would be the average after dropping the first year and adding in the sixth, the process continuing until the fiftieth year is included. This type of average is rather rudimentary and tends to be of value only when the series is particularly long. In any event the initial figures are usually unreliable.

Multiple store. A shop which, rather than specialize in one type of article, sells a multiplicity of items which may range from pencils to ladies' underwear.

Muster roll. A book kept to record details of all persons on board a ship.

Mutual life assurance company. A mutual COMPANY is one where there are no shareholders. These companies developed from friendly societies, and were formed by large numbers joining together for their mutual interest. The CAPITAL of the COMPANY is made up of premiums paid in.

Mutuality. This concerns actions for BREACH OF CONTRACT. The court will not give a decree of SPECIFIC PERFORMANCE unless there is mutuality, that is to say, unless the remedy would be available to both parties. For instance, a MINOR will never obtain specific performance of CONTRACTS which cannot be enforced against him because of his infancy.

Name day. ⟡ TICKET DAY.

Names of directors. ⟡ DIRECTORS' REPORT.

National Association for Quality and Reliability. An organization aiming to promote high standards of quality and reliability in British industry. It consists of forty government agencies, industrial organizations, and professional bodies. It is serviced by the British Productivity Council, and cooperates with the BRITISH STANDARDS INSTITUTION. October 1966–October 1967 was made 'Quality and Reliability Year'.

National Association of British Manufacturers. ⟡ CONFEDERATION OF BRITISH INDUSTRY.

National Bus Company. This is being set up by the Transport Act 1968. It is to operate in England and Wales as a public authority (there is a separate authority for Scotland: the Scottish Transport Group). The Company is required to supervise the provision of adequate bus services throughout the country and to cooperate where necessary with the Scottish Transport Group, the London Board, the Railways Board and local authorities.

It is authorized to carry passengers by road in or outside England and Wales and also by ship or hovercraft where ancillary. It is also authorized to hire out vehicles for carrying GOODS, and to act as a travel agent. It may use existing services and will in fact take over the SECURITIES of most of the larger bus companies in the country. The provisions which refer to the National Bus Company are many and complicated. Anyone interested should consult the Act.

National Chamber of Trade. This was formed in 1897, and is a comprehensive organization for the retail trade. Members are either individual or affiliated organizations, the latter consisting of local chambers of trade and commerce (approximately 875) and national trade organizations (approximately 41). The objects are to advance the prestige of the distributive trades as a whole by safeguarding and promoting the interests of traders, merchants, and others with common or similar interests. It works with local authorities and county councils, and aids members in: (1) encouraging local shopping, (2) dealing with local authorities, (3) providing information on legislative changes, (4) representing trade interests in political matters. Its publications include a monthly *National Chamber of Trade Journal*

219

and various specialized documents and booklets. Address: Enterprise House, Hyde Park Place, London W2.

National debt. The debt the government owes to the general public, made up of long-term and short-term loans. It began in 1694 when it was reputed to be about £49,000,000. By 1918 it was £7,800,000,000 and at present it is in the region of £30,000,000,000.

National development bonds. These were introduced in 1964 in connexion with Section 2 of the National Loans Act 1939. They are a government SECURITY obtainable at a post office or a TRUSTEE SAVINGS BANK, issued in multiples of £5, with INTEREST at $5\frac{1}{2}$ per cent *per annum*, and payable on 15 January and 15 July. The interest is taxable and tax is not deducted at source. Anyone may hold the bonds, including COMPANIES, clubs, charities, etc. Bonds may be bought for children under seven by an adult, but cannot be cashed until the child is seven; the interest must be credited to a savings bank account in the child's name. The maximum holding is £2,500 (in addition to holdings of previous issues of 5 per cent National Development Bonds). Repayment is made at the rate of £102 for each £100 of Bonds on the interest date following the fifth anniversary of purchase. The £2 is free from INCOME TAX, SURTAX and CAPITAL GAINS TAX. A month's notice is necessary for withdrawal.

National Film Finance Corporation. This was established in 1949 (under the Cinematograph Film Production Special Loans Act), with authority to borrow up to £6,000,000 from the BOARD OF TRADE with additional temporary borrowing powers of £2,000,000. The money is lent to the film industry at 2 per cent over BANK RATE, plus a share in the profits; the purpose is to aid the production of good films for cinema or television (mostly cinema). About 25 per cent of British films are assisted by the Corporation. The British Film Fund Agency was formed to distribute monies collected as a levy at the box office, to supplement the grants of the Corporation. The President of the Board of Trade has power to make regulations *re* the collection by the Board of a Customs and Excise levy from exhibitors.

National Freight Corporation. This was set up by the Transport Act 1968 to cooperate with the Railways Board in promoting properly integrated services for the carriage of GOODS by road or rail within Great Britain; and also to see that goods are carried by rail whenever this is efficient and economic. The Corporation is intended *inter alia* (1) to carry goods by road in or outside Great Britain, (2) to cooperate with the Railways Board in carrying goods either as

AGENTS for the Board or on its own account, (3) to store goods, (4) to operate harbours, (5) to provide transport services by sea where these are provided by organizations taken over by the Corporation, (6) to operate jointly with private individuals if necessary, (7) to provide hovercraft services, (8) to let vehicles out for hire. The Freight Corporation is not a COMMON CARRIER in respect of any activity.

It takes over the SECURITIES of *inter alia*, BRITISH ROAD SERVICES Ltd, British Roadrailer Services Ltd, Pickfords Ltd, Tartan Arrow Service (Holdings) Ltd, and Transport Holding Company Trustees Ltd.

National giro. A system of settling accounts similar to the CURRENT ACCOUNT facilities available at JOINT-STOCK BANKS. It is operated by the POST OFFICE. Anyone can open an account by depositing a sum of money, at least £5, at any post office. The account is kept at the National Giro Centre. Account-holders do not draw CHEQUES but may make out an order directing the National Giro to pay a certain sum of money to another person. If that person is an account-holder, the amount will automatically be transferred to his account. He will be notified by the payer that this has been done. If he is not an account-holder the centre will send him a payment order and he may cash this at a post office. For amounts over £50 the post office will be specified.

An account-holder may draw money on his own account at the post office nominated. The limit is £20 every other day. Persons who are not account-holders may use the Giro system by paying cash in at a post office and by filling in the necessary form. Non-account-holders pay a charge. Transactions between account-holders are normally free.

There are numerous other facilities including automatic debit transfer, whereby a RETAILER could instruct his wholesaler to send all his bills direct to Giro; the wholesaler would notify the retailer and Giro would debit the retailer's account if it received no instruction to the contrary during a specified period. Standing orders are possible. There is even a possibility of an international Giro system. A statement of account is sent to a business every day its balance changes, and to a private person every day his account is credited. The statement is accompanied by supporting documents.

The Giro system will obviously compete strongly with the BANKS. One advantage is that whereas there are many post offices in every town, there are not so many branches of one bank. Again, the Giro is a central organization and this will give it the advantage of economy and speed. Instructions are dealt with on the day they are received at the Giro Centre and statements are despatched on the same day. It may be that suppliers will append a tear-off strip to an INVOICE containing full instructions so that it may be sent directly by the recipient to the Giro and the necessary transfer effected. Alternatively, the recipient may take the slip with cash to the post office.

National Marketing Council. This was established in 1965 by the British Productivity Council. It has committees on PROMOTION, education, regional activities, research and export. Its aim is to spread knowledge of MARKETING techniques both nationally and internationally.

National Research Development Corporation. This was established by the BOARD OF TRADE in 1949. Its purpose is to develop and exploit inventions arising from research by government departments and other public bodies. It may also help in independent research, where this seems to be in the public interest, and this aspect of its work was emphasized by the Development of Inventions Act 1954. Funds are obtained by borrowing from the Board of Trade, and adding incomes from ROYALTIES and PATENT rights. Grants up to £1,000 may be made. If more is required, Board of Trade sanction is necessary

National Savings Bank. ◊ POST OFFICE: SAVINGS BANK.

National Savings Certificates. A government SECURITY introduced in 1916 (when it was called a War Savings Certificate) and obtainable at post offices. No INCOME TAX or SURTAX is payable on INTEREST from these Certificates (it need not be specified in a U.K. tax return); nor does CAPITAL GAINS TAX apply to an increase in their VALUE. A current (Twelfth Issue) Certificate costs £1 and will be worth £1·25 in five years: in the first year 2½p is added, in the second year 1p is added every four months, in the third, fourth and fifth years 2p is added every four months. COMPOUND INTEREST is £4·56 per cent per annum, equivalent to a gross £7·76½ per cent to people paying the standard rate of tax.

Certificates are available in multiple units. They may be bought by anyone in his own name or that of another. There is a limit to the number any one person may hold at one time (£1,500 at the moment). Each holder has a number. A signature is necessary except for children under seven, for whom the date of birth suffices instead. Repayment follows from written application to the Director of Post Office Savings, Manor Gardens, London N7. Forms are obtainable at most post offices, and normally eight working days' notice is necessary.

National Savings Gift Tokens. These are available at post offices and TRUSTEE SAVINGS BANKS in units of £1, £3 and £5. They cannot be cashed at a post office.

National Savings group schemes. Group schemes for purchasing NATIONAL SAVINGS CERTIFICATES or saving money in POST OFFICE SAVINGS BANKS, organized by the National Savings Movement for the benefit of firms, schools, etc. They enable small amounts to be saved weekly, and accumulated. Inquiries should be sent to: National Savings Committee, Alexandra House, Kingsway, London WC2.

National Savings Stamps. These may be purchased at post offices and TRUSTEE SAVINGS BANKS at 10p each, and may be used to purchase NATIONAL SAVINGS CERTIFICATES, NATIONAL DEVELOPMENT BONDS or PREMIUM SAVINGS BONDS. They may also be paid into an account at a POST OFFICE SAVINGS BANK.

Nationalized industries. These are industries owned by the public, i.e. in the direct control of the government. There are no shareholders apart from the government, though to raise money to buy the SHARES (or just to provide additional finance) the government has sometimes issued BONDS at fixed INTEREST. Certain industries may be acquired by the back door, by purchasing shares gradually, and sometimes, rather than purchase an industry outright, the government acquires sufficient interest to enable it to direct policy – a modified form of nationalization.

Nautical mile. ◊ ADMIRALTY MEASURED MILE.

Near money. Not quite cash in the BANK or in hand but nevertheless near liquid, such as ◊ MONEY AT CALL AND AT SHORT NOTICE.

Necessaries. Articles reasonably needed and suitable to the station in life and standard of living of the person wanting them. The word is significant in ◊ INFANTS' CONTRACTS. A married woman has an implied authority to pledge her husband's credit for necessaries. He can only escape liability by showing that he has forbidden his wife to do so and has given notice to those persons whose bills he has paid in the past. If the husband had already supplied the wife with sufficient GOODS, then naturally she cannot claim the goods purchased to be 'necessaries'.

Negligence of auditor. An AUDITOR, in the performance of his duty, may be negligent and so liable for BREACH OF CONTRACT. This CONTRACT is with the audited COMPANY and it is the company which has the course of action. Difficulties arise when third parties rely on audited accounts and suffer loss. In the past it has been held that auditors have no liability to third parties. Now the attitude of the courts seems to be changing and in any event when the auditor knows, or can infer, that the accounts are to be shown to another person who may, say, lend money to the company, he may be liable for negligence.

Negligence of directors. Generally speaking, DIRECTORS are not liable for CONTRACTS made on behalf of the COMPANY where they are not acting ULTRA VIRES. They have, however, a duty to take care, and this could involve them in a charge of negligence. A director may be liable for the acts of his fellow directors if he habitually abstains from attending board meetings. He is not liable, when he acts in good faith, for errors of judgment. Also, provided he acts honestly and reasonably, the court can relieve him from responsibility for *ultra vires* transactions.

Negotiable instrument. A document of title that can be freely negotiated. It usually concerns CHOSES-IN-ACTION. Title can be transferred by delivery, and no particular form is necessary. BILLS OF EXCHANGE, CHEQUES, PROMISSORY NOTES, are all negotiable instruments.

Net assets. A term often used in published accounts for the total of fixed plus net ⟡ CURRENT ASSETS, or fixed plus current assets less current liabilities. ('Fixed assets' means here all ASSETS which are not CURRENT ASSETS.) The significance of this total may be somewhat doubtful depending on whether one considers it equal to ⟡ CAPITAL EMPLOYED. It is often described as this.

Net book amount. A term often used in published accounts, concerning FIXED ASSETS. The Companies Act 1948 stated that fixed assets should be shown at cost or valuation, less amounts written off by way of DEPRECIATION (the depreciation figure being shown separately). Where the original cost was not known, or could only be discovered at great inconvenience, the COMPANY was allowed to show fixed assets at net book amounts in July 1948. This figure was the WRITTEN DOWN VALUE of the assets at that time.

Net present value. A term used with particular reference to investment control. When a project is being considered, various devices are employed to discover whether it is profitable. One method is to take the net present value of expected income, i.e. the net income for the years the plant will be productive. This is discounted back at a rate of INTEREST consistent with the risk involved, to the date of investment. There will be a figure for each year. If the total exceeds the CAPITAL to be invested, the project may be profitable. Another similar method is to find the rate of interest that would reduce the anticipated income to the amount invested. The project is then assessed according to the adequacy of the interest rate. The first method is known as the net present value (N.P.V.) technique, the second as the discounted cash flow (D.C.F.). Both methods are in common use. There are also other more sophisticated techniques but they are basically variations of these two, i.e. worked on the theory of COMPOUND INTEREST.

Net price. The amount a buyer pays after all discounts, etc., have been deducted. This is also called 'net cost'.

Net weight. The actual weight of GOODS, after deducting the weight of all packing materials.

Net worth. An accounting term for the total of SHARE CAPITAL and RESERVES or rather the difference between total ASSETS and outside liabilities. ◊ CAPITAL EMPLOYED.

Night safe. A facility offered by BANKS (and available at most branches) whereby money can be dropped into the bank strong room through a form of letter box after banking hours. The money is in a bag containing details of the customer's name, etc. A customer using a night safe does not legally bank the money and it is left there at his own responsibility. He collects it the following morning and banks it properly.

No claims bonus. An incentive to policy holders in certain types of INSURANCE, not to make claims for small amounts. The premium is progressively reduced provided that no claims are made. It applies to motor insurance more than to any other: these premiums may be reduced to, say, 40 per cent of the original amount.

Nominal accounts. ◊ ACCOUNTS, NOMINAL, REAL, AND PERSONAL.

Nominee shareholders. SHARES need not be registered in the name of their beneficial owner. They may be registered in the name of a nominee or TRUSTEE. In this way the true ownership of perhaps substantial holdings may be concealed. The Companies Act 1948 gave the BOARD OF TRADE drastic powers to investigate true ownership where necessary. They may appoint inspectors, of their own volition, to investigate the membership of a COMPANY and discover who is financially interested in its success or who is able to control it. The Companies Act 1967 makes it necessary for DIRECTORS to give full details of shares held by themselves, or by other persons for their benefit, or by persons closely related to them, such as wives and children. ◊ DIRECTORS' SHAREHOLDINGS.

There is also a provision in the 1967 Act for the disclosure to the company of substantial individual interests in SHARE CAPITAL carrying unrestricted voting rights. This relates to persons controlling not less than one-tenth of the nominal value of the share capital. The word 'person' is closely defined so that not only the shares held by a person in his own name are included, but also those held by another person or corporation which he controls (it is sufficient to have one-third of the voting rights at a company meeting to control the company for this purpose). Shares which he is entitled to take up at any time, or that he has contracted to buy, are also included.

Non-taxable income. Incomes not liable to INCOME TAX include wounds pensions and disability pensions, bounty payments to army volunteers, widows, war pensions regarding children, the Korea gratuity, annuities paid to Victoria Cross and George Cross holders, INTEREST on NATIONAL SAVINGS CERTIFICATES, certain interest on POST OFFICE SAVINGS BANK accounts, interest on the new contractual savings scheme, COMPENSATION FOR LOSS OF OFFICE if less than £5,000, scholarship income, payments regarding employment, sickness benefits, etc., and certain payments in kind (though this does not generally apply to DIRECTORS or employees earning over £2,000 per year). Certain incomes earned abroad may not be taxable if not remitted to this country. ⬦ POST WAR CREDITS.

Not negotiable. If the words 'not negotiable' are written across a BILL OF EXCHANGE, a person taking the bill cannot get a better TITLE than the person from whom he took it. This does not prevent the bill from being negotiated but the bill is no longer a NEGOTIABLE INSTRUMENT proper. ⬦ CROSSINGS: NOT NEGOTIABLE.

Notary, public. Usually a SOLICITOR, and specifically appointed to deal with such matters as ⬦ NOTING AND PROTESTING BILLS OF EXCHANGE, attesting DEEDS, etc. A notary's word is acceptable as evidence in most foreign courts.

Note circulation. ⬦ BANK OF ENGLAND. Note issue is controlled by Parliament, through the Issuing Department of the BANK OF ENGLAND. The Bank of England has a monopoly of note issue in England and Wales. At one time notes were backed by gold; this is no longer so. The note issue is now almost entirely a FIDUCIARY ISSUE. The gold held by the Issue Department was transferred to the EXCHANGE EQUALISATION FUND. Profits on note issue, and any surpluses or deficiencies on weekly revaluation of SECURITIES, etc., which are held by the Issue Department, are also paid to this Account.

Notes in circulation at present are in denominations of £1, £5, and £10. £1 notes have been issued by the Bank of England only since 1928, though introduced by the Treasury in 1914. £1 notes and £2 notes were issued in 1797 but ceased to be issued in 1821. Apart from these, the Bank's notes, until 1928, were limited to £5 and upwards. The £5 note dates from 1793, the £10 note from 1759. Notes of £10, £20, £50, £100, £500 and £1,000 were discontinued in

1943 for political reasons, but the £10 note was revived in 1964. Other denominations issued at one time were £15, £25, £30, £40, £60, £70, £80, £90, £200, £300 and £400. Only the £200 note survived the nineteenth century, and this was abolished in 1928. The number of notes in circulation at any time, though limited by the fiduciary issue, depends upon conditions of supply and demand. Over two million new notes are issued each year, and a similar number of dirty or damaged notes destroyed. The average life of a £1 note is about nine months, of a £5 note, fifteen months. It is hoped to increase the life of notes, for obvious reasons. Banks in Scotland and Northern Ireland may continue to issue their own notes. All but a very small number of these must be fully covered by holdings of Bank of England notes, gold, or silver coin.

Notice in lieu of distringas. This is used in company law to prevent the wrongful transfer of SHARES. The notice is issued by the shareholder to the COMPANY, which must then inform him of any attempt to transfer his shares.

Notice of abandonment. Notice must be given to the insurer when a ship is abandoned as a CONSTRUCTIVE TOTAL LOSS. ⟡ ABANDONMENT.

Noting and protest. Where a BILL OF EXCHANGE is not accepted or paid when presented, the holder, to protect himself and prove that the rules regarding presentment have been observed, should take the bill to a NOTARY PUBLIC, who, either himself or through an AGENT, re-presents it on the day of dishonour or the next successive business day. He also makes an entry in his register and 'notes' on the bill or a document attached to the bill, various particulars including the reason for dishonour. This is known as noting.

The protest is a document containing: (1) an exact copy of the bill, (2) details of the persons protesting and protested against, (3) the time and place of the protest, (4) a statement that acceptance or payment was refused and the reasons given. The signatures and seal of the notary appear on the document.

If a notary public is not available, the bill may be protested by any householder or substantial resident in the presence of two witnesses. Protest should be at the place of dishonour, unless the bill has been presented and returned by post, or is payable at some place other than the place of acceptance, when the protest should be made at the place of payment. Noting and protest are only legally necessary with (1) FOREIGN BILLS, (2) INLAND BILLS as a preliminary to an ACCEPTANCE SUPRA PROTEST. Noting and protest is obviously unnecessary on inland bills dishonoured by the acceptor.

Novation. ⟡ CONTRACT OF NOVATION.

Obsolescence. In accounting, obsolescence is the ending of an ASSET's useful life for reasons other than deterioration. A machine may become obsolete when a new invention makes its use no longer economic, and this may happen soon after purchase. Businesses commonly set aside profits to protect them when large amounts of capital equipment have to be written off through obsolescence.

Off licence. A shop licensed to sell intoxicating liquor for consumption off the premises.

Offer. A term used in the law of CONTRACT. The offer is the first step. Other things being equal, acceptance of the offer can bind the offeror. The offer may be conditional or unconditional. The acceptance must be in the same terms as the offer. An offer is not operative until communicated to the other party. Posting a letter, for instance, is not sufficient. An offer should not be confused with an invitation to make an offer. A shopkeeper who marks his GOODS with a PRICE in the window is not offering to sell at that price, or to sell at all: he is inviting persons to come into the shop and offer to purchase the goods.

An offer does not necessarily have to be in writing. ♢ INVITATION TO TREAT.

Offer and acceptance by post. An OFFER by post is not final until communicated to the offeror and therefore can be revoked until that time. Acceptance is complete when the letter is posted, and proof of posting is proof of acceptance. (Delivery to a postman is not posting – the letter must be placed in the post box.) The offeror may be bound even though the acceptance does not reach him.

Offer by tender. ♢ TENDER: CAPITAL ISSUES.

Offer of shares for sale. Instead of issuing a PROSPECTUS, a COMPANY may sell all its SHARES to an ♢ ISSUING HOUSE, which will then offer the shares to the public. This offer must be in the form of a prospectus.

Office Management, Institute of. The institute was established over fifty years ago, and has a membership of over 5,000. It caters for specialists in office management, full time office managers and persons with senior office responsibilities. Members may be Fellows (F.I.O.M.), Ordinary Members (M.I.O.M.) or Associates (A.I.O.M.).

An ordinary member must be over twenty-seven, and either have a
Diploma awarded by the Institute, be responsible for at least a large
section of his COMPANY'S office, be a specialist in office management,
or teach the subject. Associate Members must be over twenty-three,
be engaged in responsible work in office management, or hold the
Institute's Certificate. Fellows must have been ordinary members for
five years and occupy senior positions in general or office management, or have rendered outstanding service to the Institute. Companies
can become patrons: the minimum donation is £30. There are local
and national meetings, and publications of books, pamphlets, and
a quarterly, *Office Management*. There is an information service
including a library, and a research and information committee.
Courses are offered in technical colleges leading to (1) a Diploma in
Office Management, (2) a Diploma in Organization and Methods,
(3) a Certificate in Office Supervision, (4) an Intermediate Certificate
in Organization and Method Studies. To obtain a diploma, members
must either be already members of the Institute or have gained a
suitable degree or professional qualification. Address: 167 Victoria
Street, London SW1.

Officer of a company. In LIQUIDATION proceedings it is sometimes
important to know who are the officers of a company. The Companies
Act 1948 allows the court to investigate the conduct of officers with
a view to their being compelled to repay money or property by
means of a MISFEASANCE SUMMONS (which can be made against
any DIRECTOR, PROMOTER, or officer of a company). The term
'officer' includes directors, managers, SECRETARIES and, when they
are acting on behalf of the company, sometimes AUDITORS and
SOLICITORS.

Official List. The list published by the ◊ STOCK EXCHANGE at the
end of each day's dealings, giving PRICES of SHARES, BONDS, etc.

Official quotations. Figures quoted by the ◊ STOCK EXCHANGE on
the ◊ OFFICIAL LIST.

Official receiver. A public official appointed by the BOARD OF TRADE
to supervise the winding-up of a bankrupt's or a COMPANY'S
affairs unless or until a trustee or ◊ LIQUIDATOR is appointed.

Oligopoly. Control of a market by a few independent organizations.
◊ CARTEL.

On demand. A BILL OF EXCHANGE is payable on demand when it is
payable on presentation. An uncrossed CHEQUE is a bill payable on
demand.

On the berth. In shipping terminology, a vessel loading, unloading, or
waiting to do either.

Oncost. ⟡ OVERHEAD EXPENSES.

Open cheque. A ⟡ CHEQUE that is not crossed and therefore does not need to be paid into an account but may be cashed over the counter. A crossed cheque can be opened (by the drawer) by writing 'pay cash' over the CROSSING.

Open cover. ⟡ OPEN POLICY.

Open credit. Credit facilities afforded to a customer, without immediate proof of credit-worthiness. There may or may not be a limit.

Open general licence. Importers must obtain LICENCES. There are usually restrictions on some GOODS imported from some areas, but where no restrictions apply, open general licences are available.

Open indent. When someone in another country wishes to purchase U.K. goods, he may use an export AGENT in the United Kingdom. The export order is known as an indent; an open indent gives the agent *carte blanche* in selecting the manufacturer. A closed indent indicates the manufacturer.

Open-jaw trip. An air-transport term for a (usually long-distance) circular tour whose starting and finishing points do not coincide.

Open market. Open markets are those where OFFERS to buy or sell are made to the public at large and not to a restricted number or behind closed doors. ⟡ MARKET OVERT.

Open market operations. Operations by the central bank intended to stabilize INTEREST rates, or adjust the quantity of money in circulation. For example, the BANK OF ENGLAND may increase the quantity of money enormously by buying SECURITIES on a large scale in the OPEN MARKET. The money it spends will increase the BALANCES of the clearing banks, and this will enable them to lend an even greater amount to the public.

Open policy. A MARINE INSURANCE term used where GOODS are insured though the VALUE of the goods is not known or not fixed when the policy is effected. A provisional sum is agreed and the premium adjusted when the value of the goods *is* known.

Operating statement. An imprecise term for a statement showing the cost of running a business and the profit earned by a business or one of its departments.

Operation of law. A CONTRACT may be discharged by operation of law. A judgment obtained by a party to a contract discharges the contract – the contract becomes merged in the judgment. Again, a contract, or the obligations of a contract, may be discharged by the lapse of time. ⟡ LIMITATION OF ACTIONS.

Operational research. Study of resources: what they are, and how best to use them, particularly in situations where demand for a product varies considerably. Problems dealt with include those concerning (1) the level of service facilities which will minimize idleness in machine and labour time, and (2) the most economical level of stock, with reference to when, and how much, to re-order.

Operator's licence. Under the Transport Act 1968, an operator's licence (obtainable from a local licensing authority) must be held by any person using a GOODS vehicle on a road for carrying goods either for hire or reward or in connexion with any trade or business carried on by the owner. This only applies to vehicles of more than 30 cwt unladen weight. Others do not now need any additional licence. The provisions of the Act are rather complex and users of goods vehicles are advised to study them.

Option. An agreement whereby one person grants another the right to buy or sell certain GOODS or CHOSES-IN-ACTION at an agreed PRICE, at or within a stated future time. The term is usually used with reference to dealings on the STOCK EXCHANGE. Options to sell are known as deals for the 'put', options to buy are deals for the 'call'. It is possible to have a double option, i.e. to buy or sell.

It is a criminal offence for a DIRECTOR of a COMPANY to deal in options to buy or sell SHARES or DEBENTURES of his company or of associated companies. For this purpose a director includes his wife or children.

Options to purchase shares. A person may be given an ⬦ OPTION to take up SHARES in a COMPANY at a stated PRICE provided he does so before a given date. Whether he does so or not depends on how the market price has moved or is moving. He could make a large profit immediately by selling the shares as soon as he takes them up. For this reason, options often have to be paid for. This is not true of options given by the company itself. These would be privileges given to employees without any demand for payment.

Options to purchase given to PROMOTERS must be stated in the PROSPECTUS. There are special rules on options given to DIRECTORS.

Oral evidence. Evidence given by word of mouth in court. Generally speaking oral evidence cannot be admitted to change a written agreement, though there are certain exceptions to this rule. These are: (1) Where the whole CONTRACT is not in writing, when oral evidence may be allowed to supply additional terms, (2) where it is necessary to show trade usage or custom or that the sub-contract was subject to a condition precedent, or (3) to explain that words are used with a meaning other than their everyday meaning (trade usage perhaps).

Originating bank. A term used in foreign trade. Where a system of ◊ DOCUMENTARY CREDIT is used and/or a foreign buyer works through the London branch, say, of an overseas BANK, the overseas bank is the originating bank and the London branch is known as the correspondent bank.

Outcry market. A term used with reference to COMMODITY EXCHANGES. In an outcry market dealings are by private CONTRACT but every deal must be shouted out so that it can be recorded.

Output. Quantity of GOODS produced. Not a very precise term.

Outside brokers. STOCKBROKERS who are not members of the STOCK EXCHANGE.

Outward manifest. ◊ EXPORTERS' DECLARATIONS.

Over-capitalized. A business is over-capitalized when it has more CAPITAL than it can profitably use.

Overdrafts. ◊ BANK OVERDRAFTS.

Over entry certificate. A Customs term used with reference to importing. Duty is paid initially on the basis of ◊ PRIME ENTRY. It is sometimes found that too much duty has been paid and an over entry certificate is issued. If the duty paid was insufficient, a post entry is paid.

Overhead expenses. Sometimes known as oncost, these are expenses incurred in manufacture, though not directly identified with any particular item produced. Examples are administrative expenses, selling expenses, etc. ◊ DIRECT LABOUR ◊ DIRECT EXPENSES.

Over-insurance. Property is over-insured if insured for more than it is worth. There is no advantage in this as an insurer will never pay more than the true VALUE of the property.

Overnight loan. A loan made by a bank to a bill BROKER enabling him to take up BILLS OF EXCHANGE, the loan being repayable on the following day. It is usually renewed: if not, the broker must turn to the BANK OF ENGLAND and would then be forced to pay BANK RATE. As this is higher than that charged by the clearing banks, general discount rates may be affected by the broker's assessment of this possibility.

Over-riding commission. A COMMISSION paid to BROKERS who find persons willing to UNDERWRITE the issue of SHARES.

Overseas companies. COMPANIES incorporated outside Great Britain but with a place of business in the United Kingdom. They must deliver to the Registrar of Companies (1) a certified copy of their charter or MEMORANDUM OF ASSOCIATION and ARTICLES OF ASSOCIATION, (2) particulars of DIRECTORS and SECRETARY, (3) the name and address of person or persons resident in the United Kingdom authorized to accept service of process and notices,

(4) an annual statement in the form of a BALANCE SHEET and PROFIT AND LOSS ACCOUNT, conforming with the provisions applicable to U.K. companies.

These companies must mention their country of origin in all prospectuses and all official publications. They must also register charges on English property. If liability of the members is limited, this must be stated.

Over-subscribed. SHARES are said to be over-subscribed when more are applied for than are offered. In these cases, applications are usually scaled down *pro rata*, though sometimes small applications are met in full and only large ones (above a stated limit) are scaled down. This depends on the democratic attitude of the organization.

Overtime request. Customs officers are sometimes requested to supervise cargo outside ordinary hours, in which case special charges must be paid.

Over-trading. A business is said to be over-trading when it tries to do more business than its WORKING CAPITAL will allow, i.e. when too much money is tied up in STOCKS and debts, and cash is not coming in quickly enough to pay CREDITORS, or the normal expenses of running a business, like wages, RENT, etc.

P

Packaging. A MARKETING term for the presentation of GOODS, i.e. the manner in which they are wrapped or displayed. The wrapper can be a vital selling factor, apart from a platform for ADVERTISING. Where the weight of the goods must be stated, the weight of the wrapping should not normally be included: 'net weight' means the weight of the goods without the packaging.

Adequacy of packaging may be important when goods are to be sent by post, and the Post Office has set certain standards. These are explained in the POST OFFICE GUIDE. ◊ TRADE PROTECTION ACT.

Paid-up capital. That part of the CAPITAL of a COMPANY, both CALLED-UP and paid-up. The difference between called-up capital and paid-up capital will represent calls in arrears.

Paper money. Documents with a VALUE stated on them but having no value in themselves (unlike coins).

Par value. A ◊ SHARE'S NOMINAL VALUE.

Parent company. ◊ SUBSIDIARY COMPANY.

Pari passu. A legal term meaning 'ranking equally'. For instance, all shares of one class in a COMPANY rank *pari passu* as to receipt of DIVIDENDS and return of CAPITAL.

Part load. A term used with reference to transport, normally road transport. Rather than hire a vehicle, someone wishing to send GOODS may buy space in a vehicle already going to a particular area without a full load. This can be a cheap way of sending goods.

Part payment. In CONTRACTS for repayment of money lent, or also where money is due, if one party offers part payment, and the other accepts, this is no satisfaction of the debt unless the CREDITOR receives an additional advantage, such as payment before the due date. The offer of part payment cannot be enforced as a separate contract unless there is separate CONSIDERATION.

Part performance. A CONTRACT needs to be evidenced in writing before either party is able to enforce it, but this evidence may be waived where one party has by his actions indicated that the contract is actually made. This is known as part performance. It must be proved by a party claiming redress or SPECIFIC PERFORMANCE. DAMAGES cannot be awarded as a remedy where there is no written evidence.

Participating preference shares. ◊ PREFERENCE SHARES with a right to an additional share of the profit, when the holders of ORDINARY SHARES have received a certain amount.

Particular average loss. A MARINE INSURANCE term for a loss which is not a GENERAL AVERAGE LOSS, but one caused by damage to a particular cargo, and borne by the insurers of that cargo, not shared by the insurers of the rest of the cargo. Certain policies are free of particular average, i.e. do not cover particular average losses.

Partner, active. A partner in a FIRM who works for the firm and is not merely a SLEEPING PARTNER.

Partner, general. A partner in the full sense of the word, without restrictions on his liability. ◊ PARTNERSHIP ◊ PARTNERSHIP, LIMITED.

Partner, infant. An infant partner is bound by the PARTNERSHIP deed until he repudiates it. Repudiation must take place on coming of age or soon after. He cannot be made bankrupt. Regarding his relations with the public, his liability is that of an ◊ INFANT.

Partner, limited. A partner whose liability is limited by law. ◊ PARTNERSHIP, LIMITED.

Partner, nominal. A person who allows his name to be part of the name of a firm, perhaps for purposes of GOODWILL, but has no real interest in the business. He is nevertheless fully liable as a partner. He may be ◊ ESTOPPED from denying personal liability.

Partner, sleeping. A partner who provides money but takes no active part in the management or organization of the business. He may or may not be a LIMITED PARTNER. The word has no legal significance.

Partners, incoming and outgoing. Incoming partners are not liable for debts incurred before they become partners, though they could be liable if they agreed to be. Outgoing partners are liable for all debts incurred when they were partners. They could also be liable for subsequent debts if they have not given proper notice that they are no longer partners. They can avoid liability for past debts by a CONTRACT OF NOVATION.

Partnership. Two or more people involved in the ownership and control of a business. This form of organization is governed by the Partnership Act 1890. The relationship between partners, and their individual rights and duties, are governed by the agreement that they draw up. In the absence of an agreement all partners are equal as regards profits and losses: each partner may act on behalf of the FIRM and bind the firm providing he is acting within his apparent authority, and each partner must indemnify every other partner doing so. (This obviously does not apply to matters outside the normal business of the firm.) A partner is not entitled to INTEREST on his CAPITAL nor to remuneration (in addition to his share of the profits). Each partner may take part in the management and differences are decided by a majority. No changes may be made in the nature of the partnership without the consent of all the existing partners. A partnership CONTRACT is a contract UBERRIMAE FIDEI: partners must account for private profit and must not compete with the firm. Subject to agreement, partnership is automatically dissolved on the death or BANKRUPTCY of any partner.

Partnership may be construed where it does not officially exist, when persons act together so as to give an impression that they are in partnership.

Partnership, assignment of share in. There is nothing to prevent a partner assigning his share in profits to another person, though that other person has no right to interfere in the business.

Partnership at will. A partnership where there is no particular written agreement. If a PARTNERSHIP's written agreement expires, and the partners continue to act, they are partners at will. Relationships of this kind are governed by the Partnership Act 1890.

Partnership, limited. A PARTNERSHIP governed by the Limited Partnership Act 1907. Intended originally as an alternative to a limited COMPANY, it is similar to an ordinary partnership except that certain partners have a LIMITED LIABILITY. The liability is limited to the amount the limited partner contributes on becoming a partner. He cannot dispose of his share or withdraw it, take part in the general management of the business, or bind the firm. He cannot dissolve the partnership or object to the introduction of another partner. The limitation of his actions is obviously a considerable price to pay for the limitation of liability. The general partners have the last word in just about everything. There must be at least one general partner with unlimited liability. A limited partnership must be registered with the Registrar of Companies and the registration must be accompanied by certain particulars. These are: (1) the FIRM's name, (2) the general nature of the business, (3) the principal place of business, (4) the full names of the partners, (5) the term of the partnership, (6) the date of commencement, (7) a statement that the partnership is limited, which also names the limited partners, (8) the amount paid in by each limited partner, and the manner of payment (cash or otherwise).

Passenger coupon. That part of an air-passenger's ticket which constitutes the passenger's written evidence of the CONTRACT of travel.

Passengers' luggage. Passengers on railways may normally take a reasonable amount of luggage free of charge. The railways will be responsible for the loss of this luggage up to £50 where the loss is due to their negligence, but certain valuables must be declared before they will be liable. These are specified in the Carriers Act 1830 and include, for example, precious stones, watches, and furs. There is no liability if the passenger himself is negligent. A passenger is not negligent if he leaves his luggage to go to the restaurant car.

The luggage must be personal luggage, not merchandise or items connected with the passenger's work. It has been held that a SOLICITOR'S briefcase is not personal luggage, nor an instrument carried by a professional musician.

Passing a name. A STOCK EXCHANGE term for stating the name of a buyer on ACCOUNT day.

Passive bonds. BONDS on which no INTEREST is payable, the holder being entitled to some other benefit.

Patent. A patent gives the patentee the sole right to make, use, or sell, his invention during the period the patent remains in force. This period is sixteen years from the date of filing, subject to the payment of fees. These are: an initial fee when the patent is registered; and renewal fees payable annually, at present £6 per year until the fifth year, then gradually increasing to £30. British patents only apply to the United Kingdom. Protection in other countries can only be obtained by applying for patent. When a person wishes to apply for patent, he must apply to the PATENT OFFICE. Before an invention will be patented it must be proved to contain an element of novelty. Patents are not given if the invention, or its use, is contrary to law or morality, or if it consists of foodstuffs or medicine with no other properties than the ingredients are already known to contain. No financial assistance or advice is given. Information on whether patents are still in force, and in whose name they are registered may be obtained on application to The Patent Office, 25 Southampton Buildings, Chancery Lane, London WC2.

When applying for patent it is often advisable to employ a patent agent – a list of registered patent agents can be obtained for 1s. from the Chartered Institute of Patent Agents (C.I.P.A.), Staple Inn Buildings, London WC2.

An International Convention for the Protection of Industrial Property helps to obtain patent rights abroad by giving the holder of the patent in a member country priority in obtaining similar patents in another country. Most well-known countries belong to this Convention, including: the U.K., the U.S.A., the U.S.S.R., and most Commonwealth and European countries.

Patent office. The government office responsible for the grant of PATENTS and the registration of TRADE MARKS and designs.

Pawnbroker. A dealer in pledges, licensed to carry on a money-lending business on the SECURITY of GOODS taken into pawn. The loans are governed by the Pawnbrokers Acts 1872, and 1960, provided the money involved is less than £50. If the amount is over £50, the Acts do not apply and COMMON LAW rules prevail. There may be special CONTRACTS for loans over £5 when a special pawn ticket must be given and signed, and a duplicate signed by the pledgor. INTEREST on loans below £5 is limited to ½d. per 2s. per month. (Less than fourteen days equals half a month, more than fourteen days equals one month.) For amounts over £5, substitute 2s. 6d. for 2s. The goods pledged are redeemable within six months, with seven days' grace. After this, the pawnbroker may then dispose of the goods at a public AUCTION. Until he does the goods are still redeemable. In the case of pledges for more than £2 the pawnbroker must retain any money the goods make (beyond what he is owed) for three years, and hand it over. Pledges of less than £2 he can take absolutely at the end of the six months and seven days. Tickets must always be issued – if lost they may be renewed by a magistrate (the old ticket then becomes void). The pawnbroker must not deliver the goods to any person other than the one with the ticket. When the pawnbroker sells goods pawned, he may on no account buy them himself.

Pay As You Earn (P.A.Y.E.). An ◊ INCOME TAX system whereby tax is deducted from wages or salaries by the employer, before payment. This saves the employee the trouble of saving money to make tax payments at regular intervals. It only applies to full-time employees. When a person terminates his employment he will receive a form from his ex-employer, which will state his gross pay to date in the tax year, tax deducted to date, and his CODE NUMBER.

SURTAX is never deducted by P.A.Y.E.

Pay day. A STOCK EXCHANGE term for the SETTLING DAY on which payment is actually made.

Pay roll. The list prepared by a firm each week or month, giving details of wages and salaries. It states the name or number, or both, of the employee, and the amounts paid. It may also give information on how the net pay is calculated. For instance: basic pay, plus overtime; minus lost time, gross pay, INSURANCE and other deductions; tax paid, and net pay. When prepared on a machine, pay slips for inclusion in wage packets may be prepared at the same time – the one being a carbon copy of the other. The term 'pay roll' is normally reserved for the list of weekly wages, and the salaries of those who have not achieved what might be called an executive status. The salaries of these are normally closely guarded secrets, and the equivalent pay roll is compiled quietly, separately and privately.

Pay roll tax. ◊ SELECTIVE EMPLOYMENT TAX.

Pay slip. A slip of paper included in a pay packet, giving details of how the net pay has been calculated. ◊ PAY ROLL.

Payable to bearer. A BILL OF EXCHANGE is payable to bearer when no particular payee is named, or where it is endorsed in blank. (◊ ENDORSEMENT.) A holder, by adding his name, could make the bill PAYABLE TO ORDER.

Payable to order. A BILL OF EXCHANGE is payable to order when the name of a payee is stated, and where there are no restrictions on transfer. ◊ ENDORSEMENT.

Payback period. A term used in assessing investment projects. It refers to the period over which the net income from the investment equals its original cost.

Paying-in book. A book used by a BANK customer, recording details of cash, CHEQUES, etc., paid in to his account at the bank, over the counter.

Payment for honour supra protest. Where a BILL OF EXCHANGE is not paid and is protested (◊ NOTING AND PROTEST) it may be taken up to be honoured by a party whose name is not on the bill.

Payment in advance. An accounting term for money paid for GOODS or services not yet received, where the cash normally cannot be recovered. Examples are: rates and RENTS paid for a period ending after the date to which the accounts are made up. Payments in advance are usually included with debtors in accounts.

Payment on account. Part payment of a debt. This should be distinguished from a DEPOSIT.

Peculation. Embezzlement of money or GOODS, particularly public money or goods, by a person to whose care they have been entrusted.

Pedlar. Someone who sells from door to door for cash. He needs a LICENCE, which he can obtain from the police if he has been resident in the district for one month, and can provide two testimonials. Once he has a licence, the pedlar can sell anywhere. The licence costs 5s. and is renewable annually. ◊◊ HAWKER.

Pegging the exchanges. Dealings on the foreign exchange market by, say, the EXCHANGE EQUALISATION FUND, intended to stabilize RATES OF EXCHANGE.

Penalty clause. A clause in a CONTRACT stating that a certain sum should be paid by any party who breaches the contract. The sum should not be an attempt to estimate the possible damage, but

239

merely a penalty imposed by one party on another. It is generally unenforceable but where DAMAGES are very difficult to assess in advance, it may be customary to include lump sum payments in the contract by way of compensation and the court may uphold these where, in the circumstances they appear to be reasonable, e.g. ◊ DEMURRAGE. ◊ DAMAGES, LIQUIDATED.

Peppercorn rent. A nominal RENT purely to establish the fact that the property is leasehold, not freehold.

Per contra. A book-keeping term meaning 'on the other side'.

Perfecting the sight. ◊ BILL OF SIGHT.

Performance bond. A SURETY given by, say, a BANK, on behalf of a person doing CONTRACT work for, for instance, a government department. It is a guarantee that the work will be done properly.

Period bill. A BILL OF EXCHANGE not payable AT SIGHT but on a particular date.

Perishable goods. GOODS which deteriorate if not used within a specified time, e.g. food.

Perishing of goods. In a CONTRACT for the SALE OF GOODS, it happens sometimes that the GOODS perish either before the contract was made, or before delivery. Goods 'perish' when they cease to be substantially the goods contracted for or described. The perishing of unspecified goods is unimportant because then the seller must provide some from another source. Where the sale is of specific goods, if they have perished before the contract was made, the contract is void; if they perish after the contract was made but before the ◊ RISK passes to the buyer, the contract may still be avoided. The perishing must be the fault of neither party.

Permission to deal. When a COMPANY issues a PROSPECTUS it often states that permission has been obtained, or is to be sought, for the SHARES to be dealt with on a recognized STOCK EXCHANGE. Any ALLOTMENT OF SHARES is void if either permission has not been applied for before the third day after the issue of the prospectus, or permission is refused before three weeks after the closing of the subscription lists. The monies must then be returned.

Perpetual debentures. DEBENTURES which the holder cannot redeem by demanding repayment are called perpetual debentures. When they cannot be redeemed in any event, they are called irredeemable debentures.

Perpetual inventory. A method of continuous stock-taking. Rather than take STOCKS at the end of the financial period, it is possible to check them continually throughout the year, partly by checking quantities with bin cards and stores records, and partly by comparing quantities and stores records with records maintained at head office.

Perpetual succession. A COMPANY has perpetual succession if its existence is separate from that of those who promote or direct it and from members at any one time. Being a separate 'person', it continues to exist until wound up in the manner prescribed by the law (◊ LIQUIDATION). In a company with perpetual succession, each person controlling the organization is responsible for the CONTRACTS of his predecessor.

Personal accounts. ◊ ACCOUNTS, NOMINAL, REAL, AND PERSONAL.

Personal loan. A loan made to a person rather than a business. Recently certain BANKS have taken to issuing 'personal loans' known as such. They are made to customers for a specified purpose and SECURITY is not always necessary.

Personnel management. Defined by the ◊ INSTITUTE OF PERSONNEL MANAGEMENT as 'that part of management concerned with people at work and with their relationships within an enterprise. Its aim is to bring together and develop into an effective organization the men and women who make up an enterprise and, having regard for the well-being of the individual and of working groups, to enable them to make their best contribution to its success'. It is concerned *inter alia* with manpower planning, recruitment and selection, education and training, terms of employment, standards of pay, working conditions, consultation at and between all levels, wage negotiations, etc.

Personnel Management, Institute of. A voluntary association with over 7,000 members, aiming to encourage high standards of qualification and performance, and promote investigation and research. There are five grades of membership, based on experience, examination success, or both. There are two corporate grades (corporate membership can be gained by experience only, though academic qualification may be a help): Member, and Associate Member. Three non-corporate grades are: Graduate Member, Affiliate Member, and Student Member. Graduate Members must have passed the Institute's examinations. The Institute publishes a quarterly, *Personnel Management*, and a monthly, *I.P.M. Digest*. Address: 5 Winsley Street, Oxford Circus, London W.1.

Petties. A term sometimes used on INVOICES, etc., for minor charges not enumerated separately.

Petty cash. Money kept on a COMPANY's premises for payment for petty items immediately necessary, reimbursement of incidental expenses, etc. This should be distinguished from cash taken during the day but not banked.

Petty cashier. A person responsible for keeping ◊ PETTY CASH and the petty cash book.

Placings. A method of issuing SHARES, normally used where small amounts are involved. The shares are placed by an ISSUING HOUSE or a BROKER, with investors who may be interested. The broker makes a profit from the difference between the buying and selling PRICE of the shares. This form of issuing shares is common with PRIVATE COMPANIES converting to PUBLIC COMPANIES. It is like an introduction, except that in that case the broker or ISSUING HOUSE does not purchase a stated number of shares, but agrees to introduce them gradually on to the market. STOCK EXCHANGE control is necessary.

Plant hire. ◊ EQUIPMENT LEASING. The Companies Act 1967 provides that the amount paid for plant hire should, where material, be shown in the accounts.

Plant machinery register. A business's register, giving details of all items of plant and machinery. There is usually one card or page for each item, giving date and details of purchase, annual DEPRECIATION, and date and details of SALE (or scrap).

Plant purchase scheme. A scheme operated by the ◊ INDUSTRIAL AND COMMERCIAL FINANCE CORPORATION, to help customers buy industrial plant, machinery, and commercial vehicles on HIRE PURCHASE over five years.

Plantation House. The most important COMMODITY EXCHANGES are situated in Plantation House, Mincing Lane, London EC3. ◊ RUBBER EXCHANGE ◊ TEA AUCTIONS ◊ WOOL AUCTIONS.

Plate glass insurance. A specialized form of INSURANCE dealing with the replacement of shop windows, etc. The emphasis is on speed. Although the cost of a shop window is high, INSURANCE PREMIUMS may be fairly low as breakages are comparatively rare.

Ploughed-back profit. That part of the profit for the year not distributed but retained in the business, normally for development.

Policy proof of interest. In MARINE INSURANCE, P.P.I. policies are those where the insured has not the necessary ◊ INSURABLE INTEREST in the subject matter or BONA FIDE expectation of acquiring one by the time of loss. Strictly speaking these are void under the Marine Insurance (Gambling Policies) Act 1909, which inflicts both fines and imprisonment on offenders. However they are used in commerce quite frequently, and treated by insurers as CONTRACTS of honour.

Political and charitable contributions. The Companies Act 1967 makes it necessary for companies to give details in accounts of any such contributions made by themselves or their SUBSIDIARIES. Total political, or total charitable contributions, if more than £50, must be shown. Also, if a political contribution amounts to more than £50, the name of the party must be given.

Poll. The vote at a shareholders' meeting. It is usually taken by ballot, and MEMBERS have votes in proportion to the number of SHARES they hold. Preliminary voting is by SHOW OF HANDS, but the ARTICLES OF ASSOCIATION may provide that a certain minimum number of members may demand a poll on any matter except the election of CHAIRMEN or adjournment. A member with several shares may vote one way with some shares and another with others. A PROXY can vote in a poll but not on a show of hands unless the Articles provide otherwise.

Port. ◊ LARBOARD.

Port clearance. ◊ EXPORTERS' DECLARATIONS ◊ CUSTOMS AND EXCISE ◊ CUSTOMS: FINAL CLEARANCE INWARDS AND ENTRY OUTWARDS.

Post entry. ◊ OVER ENTRY CERTIFICATE.

Post Office. At one time a government department, made into a public CORPORATION on 1 October 1969. It deals with inland and overseas communications, written, printed, or spoken – apart from radio broadcasting. It is also responsible for numerous ancillary services such as the issue of LICENCES, government BONDS, telephone directories, postal and money orders, distribution of social security benefits, etc., runs the POST OFFICE SAVINGS BANK and has recently inaugurated the ◊ NATIONAL GIRO. In the following pages, some attempt has been made to list, and give details of, the services offered. Rates have been stated, as also have certain limitations on size, weight, and nature of articles the Post Office will accept. These, particularly the rates, are constantly being changed and it is advisable to consult the POST OFFICE GUIDE, available for 20p from any post office.

Post Office: air mail. Letters and postcards to Europe normally go by air if this will result in an earlier delivery. There is no special charge and no labels are necessary. There is no second class air mail service to Europe. Letter rates are: to Gibraltar and Malta, 2p for 1 oz., 1p for each additional ounce; to the rest of Europe, 4p for 1 oz., 2p for each additional ounce. Postcards cost 2p to anywhere in Europe. Small packets, printed papers, phonopost packets, newspapers, and samples should be sent at letter rate if quick delivery is necessary. Insured mail is sent only by surface routes.

Mail to countries outside Europe must have an air mail label at the top left-hand corner of the addressed side, though on letters, the words 'by air mail' will do instead. Air letters are obtainable from post offices for 4p each, but nothing may be enclosed in them. Newspapers normally travel at reduced rates. The letter rate varies according to zone (A, B, or C, depending principally on distance; for instance, Australia is in zone C, the U.S.A. in zone B, most of North Africa in zone A). These rates are:

	A	B	C
Letters, per ½ oz.	5p	7½p	9p
Postcards, each	2½p	4p	4p
Printed papers, per ½ oz.	2½p	3p	3½p
Phonopost packets (where accepted) per ½ oz.	3p	3½p	4p
Samples, per ½ oz.	2½p	3p	3½p
Small packets (where accepted) per ½ oz. (minimum 7½p)	2½p	3p	3½p
Insured boxes (where accepted) per ½ oz. (minimum 14½p, plus insurance)	2½p	3p	3½p
Newspapers and periodicals (if registered at the G.P.O.) per ½ oz.	1p	1½p	2p
Literature for the blind, per 2 oz.	1p	1p	1p

If the correct rates have not been paid, there is a surcharge of twice the difference. If less than 75 per cent of the correct rate has been paid, the item may travel surface mail. Packets, etc. may have to pay Customs duty (consult the post office). There is a weight limit of 4 lbs. and size limits are as those of surface mail.

Reply-paid postcards do not return by air mail unless the other party specifically sends them by air.

Post Office: airway letters. Letters carried by air on certain routes. They are handed in at one airport and collected or posted at the other. The weight limit is 1 lb., and the cost, ordinary postage rate plus, for letters not over 2 oz. 18p, 4 oz. 22p, 1 lb. 26p. This service is only available inland, not to the Irish Republic. Registration is not possible.

Post Office: articles for use of the blind. A list of permissible articles, e.g. aids for the blind, can be obtained from the post office. These can be sent free by inland mail (first class). There is a weight limit of 15 lb. The size limits are the same as those for letters. Packets must be left unsealed and labelled 'articles for the blind'.

Literature for the blind may be sent overseas. There is a weight limit of 15 lb., and the size limits are again the same as those for letters.

Post Office: business reply service. This enables a person or firm to receive cards or letters from clients without prepayment of postage. The postage, together with a fee of $\frac{1}{2}$p on each item, is paid by the person using the service. He must obtain a LICENCE for £5 from the local head postmaster, and will usually have to deposit a sum of money sufficient to cover the charges likely to accrue. The reply coupon should take the form of a card, envelope, folder or label of a special design. A folder could be incorporated in a newspaper advertisement. Postal charges are made on all replies received. If they are not of post-office-preferred size, an additional charge may be made.

Post Office: cash-on-delivery (inland). Parcels and registered letters may be sent cash-on-delivery to any address in Great Britain, Northern Ireland, the Channel Islands or the Isle of Man. The trade charge (i.e. the VALUE of the GOODS being paid for on delivery) must not exceed £50. Special labels are available – the package must be marked with name and address of addressee and of sender, and the amount of the trade charge. Present cash-on-delivery fees (in addition to postage and registration) are in the range of 25p for £50. A certificate of postage can be obtained. The cash is collected by the postman where less than £20; otherwise the addressee is notified and collects from the post office. On no account will the parcel be handed over or opened until the trade charge is paid. There are no special rules, so maximum compensation is £5 if the parcel is not registered.

Post Office: cash-on-delivery (overseas). There are facilities for sending cash-on-delivery parcels abroad, but not all countries accept them. The maximum trade charge (i.e. the VALUE of the GOODS to be paid for on delivery) is £40, less in some countries. No currency declaration is necessary. The Customs examination is the same as for normal post. The addressee's name must be followed by the word '*remboursement*' and the trade charge. The sender must fill in a trade charge card, pay a cash-on-delivery fee, and obtain a certificate of posting.

Post Office: certificate of posting. These can be obtained, at a cost of 1p per item, when posting unregistered packages at a post office. If a package is lost, the certificate holder is entitled to compensation, though not to more than he would receive if the package had been put in a letter box.

Post Office: collections. Letters and parcels may be collected free, by application to the local postmaster, where (1) there are more than 1,000 letters, or postage amounts to more than £25, (2) there are more than fifty parcels, or (3) there are batches of more than ten parcels each to be collected regularly. Three hours' notice is preferable, and applications by letter should be marked 'immediate – van order'.

Apart from free collections, letters should be posted in the normal way; parcels, packets, and letters in considerable numbers, should be handed in at a post office neatly tied in bundles. Letters and parcels should never be handed directly to a postman, except perhaps in country districts where there is no post box or post office near.

Collections are made from private post boxes, for instance in hotels. The Post Office Act 1953 states that a special notice should be affixed to these, pointing out that they are private, and that the general rule that proof of posting is evidence of receipt does not apply. The fee for a private post box is £4 per year for one daily collection, plus an extra £2 for each additional daily collection. Private post boxes must conform to the approved pattern.

Post Office: compensation. Compensation is available for loss of, or damage to, registered packets, unregistered parcels, recorded-delivery packets, and express-postal packets conveyed entirely by post office messenger, but only if specified packing requirements have been complied with (for instance, money must be sent in the prescribed manner, and fragile goods must be marked 'fragile – with care' even if registered). The Post Office must be satisfied that the damage occurred in the post. Damaged articles should be retained for inspection.

Compensation is always limited to the MARKET VALUE of the articles involved. Otherwise, for registered packets ⟡ POST OFFICE: REGISTRATION. Limits on unregistered post are: parcels £5, recorded-delivery packets £2, express-postal packets £5. Certain articles, such as jewellery, must be registered, if any compensation at all is payable.

The Post Office is not legally liable to pay compensation on parcels sent abroad (including to the Irish Republic). It will however pay up to £3·40 for registered packets lost when in the hands of the British Post Office. Many other countries take a similar responsibility.

Post Office: datel services. The POST OFFICE provides facilities for the transmission of information in a form suitable for computer services. Information is transmitted either by telephonic or by telegraphic means. There are various types of conversion equipment supplied for a rental by the Post Office, e.g. for translating audio signals. The services are continually being elaborated and improved.

Post Office: delivery. In towns, apart from normal deliveries, anyone may collect letters from the post office. There is a charge of 5p payable by those who are neither private box holders nor entitled to use poste restante. The fee is payable for the search whether or not the letter is found. Similar rules apply in country districts but packets are obtained freely where they arrive by mails that are not connecting by normal delivery to the addressee. Rural residents may also, for a fee of 5p, have packets reserved to be called for. Registered and recorded delivery packets may be reserved at any post office for a fee of £2 per year.

Delivery is made to the address on the envelope but packets may be delivered regularly to another address for a fee of £20 per year. Where one premises has two styles of address, an additional fee is also payable. Postal packets may be retained at the post office at holiday periods, without charge, or for long periods on payment of a fee.

Letters and parcels to be called for may be addressed to the post office but not a town sub-office. They must have the words 'to be called for' or 'poste restante' as part of the address. This service is for the convenience of travellers and therefore facilities are only available in the same town for three months. Generally speaking, letters not collected within fourteen days are treated as undeliverable. Postal packets addressed to fictitious names, or with only christian names or initials, and no surname, are treated as undeliverable.

Post Office: delivery (private boxes and bags). Private boxes may be hired. They are kept at delivery offices and mail is collected by the hirer at his convenience. The annual charge is generally £10 for letters and £10 for parcels. Private bags may also be used for collection and delivery – these are taken to and fro by the hirer. The charge is £6 if the bag is collected, but £12 if collected and delivered. Special rules apply to country districts.

Post Office: evasion of postage. It is not permissible to evade postage by enclosing one letter inside another, unless they are both addressed to the same person. If this happens and is detected, the post office may take out the second letter and send it separately, charging postage.

Post Office: express delivery (inland). This varies according to place and time. Services available include:

(1) Express. This is conveyance by post office messenger from point A to point B at the sender's request, and also from the delivery office at the addressee's request. This service is available on weekdays only from telegram post offices and one or two others in large towns. The charge is 20p per mile or part of a mile, plus any charge for public or private transport used at the sender's request. If there is more than one packet the charge is increased. There is also a waiting fee at the other end of 5p for ten minutes. Packets must be marked 'express'

in red in the left hand corner and must not be put in a letter box. The messenger will wait for a reply if the words 'wait reply' or 'wait further service' are written on the packet. The charge is necessarily increased. There are special messenger facilities for sports writers, from the sports ground to the nearest telegraph office. Where the express service is requested by the addressee, special application must be made and part of the charge prepaid.

(2) Railex. This is delivery by post office messenger to the railway station, dispatch by the first available train and delivery by the first available messenger at the other end. This service is available between any two stations in Great Britain or Northern Ireland. The package must be handed in during normal times of business at a post office dealing with express delivery. Registered and recorded delivery packets are acceptable, and charges are £1 for up to 1lb. (unless to or from Northern Ireland or the Channel Islands where the weight limit is 2 oz.). No packet will be accepted for this service where it appears to be registerable or marked 'for recorded delivery'.

Post Office: express delivery (overseas). Letters can be sent express for an extra charge of 10p (or more if the addressee is outside the normal delivery area). They must be marked 'express' in red. Some countries do not accept express delivery, but these are very few and rather remote. Express deliveries can be sent from these countries but the fee is payable in Great Britain. Similar rules apply to parcels though in some places the addressee is merely notified, by express, and must collect the parcel himself.

Post Office: franking machines. These are frequently employed by businesses. A LICENCE must be obtained from the local head postmaster. Some money must be paid in advance and readings must be submitted to the POST OFFICE weekly. The machines are not supplied by the Post Office but by private firms. They are however subject to frequent Post Office inspection.

Post Office Guide. A booklet issued by the Post Office Corporation annually, with supplements. It gives information about POST OFFICE services available at the time of going to press, and costs 20p.

Post Office: H.M. forces. There are special rates for and regulations concerning mail to servicemen at home and abroad. Consult the POST OFFICE GUIDE.

Post Office: insurance. This provides cover for possible loss or damage to parcels or letters in overseas areas where there are no facilities for registration, though it does not apply to all countries. The limit is £400, though less in some countries. There are three categories:

insured letters, insured boxes (provided by the Post Office for jewellery, etc.), and insured parcels. Insured items could take longer than ordinary mail.

There are regulations concerning packing and sealing. A certificate of posting must be obtained, the packet must be sealed, and the amount of insurance cover stated on the envelope or packet. For various special conditions, consult the POST OFFICE GUIDE.

Post Office: late posted packets. Letters (by first class mail) can be posted after normal hours at any railway station where there is a travelling post office. Wherever the mail train stops, the letter can be put straight into it if handed in five minutes or more before its departure. There is an additional charge of $\frac{1}{2}$p, or, in the case of registered or recorded-delivery mail, $7\frac{1}{2}$p.

Post Office: letter services. These regulations apply to letters, cards. and what were once known as printed papers (there are special rules for newspapers) sent between places in Great Britain, Northern Ireland, the Channel Islands, the Isle of Man, and also the Irish Republic. There are two delivery services available: first and second class. First class rates are: 3p for 4 oz., 5p for 6 oz., 7p for 8 oz., 2p for each additional 2 oz. up to 1 lb. (15p), 20p for $1\frac{1}{2}$ lb., 30p for 2 lb. with 15p for each additional 1 lb. Second class rates are: $2\frac{1}{2}$p for 4 oz., $4\frac{1}{2}$p for 6 oz., 1p for each additional 2 oz. up to 1 lb., $10\frac{1}{2}$p for $1\frac{1}{2}$ lb. There is a weight limit of $1\frac{1}{2}$ lb. on second class mail, but no limit on first class. Size limits are: 2 feet by 18 inches by 18 inches; in the case of rolls, the length plus double the diameter must not total more than 3 feet 3 inches, and no dimension may exceed 2 feet 8 inches. The minimum letter size allowed is 4 by $2\frac{3}{4}$ inches.

Overseas rates are higher. They vary between air and surface mail. ▷ AIR MAIL RATES. Surface rates are: in the British Commonwealth, 2p for 1 oz. and 1p for each additional ounce; other countries, 4p for 1 oz. and 2p for each additional ounce. There is a general weight limit of 4 lbs. Size limits are the same as those for inland mail. Postcards cost 2p to any country. There are special rates and conditions for printed papers, samples, small packets, phonopost packets, and literature for the blind.

Post Office: licences. Certain LICENCES are obtained from the Post Office. These are:

(1) Broadcast receiving licences: T.V. and sound radio (£6), colour T.V. and sound radio (£11). There are concessions for blind persons. Motor car radios need separate licences, though one licence covers all the sets in one private house (though not sets

in separate lodgings or flats). Separate licences are necessary for sound transmission to the public. These licences are all renewable annually. There are special savings schemes.

(2) Vehicle licences: these licences, and their cost, vary according to the class of vehicle. They are all renewable annually.

(3) Miscellaneous: dog licences (37½p per dog), game licences (red £6, green £4, blue £4), game licences (occasional) for fourteen days (£2), game dealer licences (£4), game keeper licences (£4), hounds licences (37½p per hound). All these are renewable annually, except the third.

Post Office: money orders (inland). These may be purchased and are payable at any post office in Great Britain, Northern Ireland, Channel Islands, or the Isle of Man. They may have any value not over £50. Poundage (cost per order) 25p. A form must be completed giving the name and address of PURCHASER and payee. The money order may or may not be crossed. Notice of payment will be given for a fee of 7½p. It is possible to defer payment. An order will not be paid unless the payee signs the order and gives the name of the remitter. It is possible to stop payment of an order. The POST OFFICE is not liable when an order is lost. Money orders may also be remitted by telegraph. There are special regulations concerning overseas money orders and money orders to H.M. forces abroad. Consult the POST OFFICE GUIDE.

No poundage is payable for certain orders addressed to commissioners of Customs and Excise, the Inland Revenue, or the Minister of Finance in Ireland.

Post Office: newspapers. ♢ POST OFFICE: PRINTED PAPERS.

Post Office: non-delivery (inland). Letters and parcels which cannot be delivered are returned direct and unopened if the sender's address is on the outside. If not, they are opened by a special officer and, if an address can be found, returned (unless they only contain magazines, newspapers, or commercial advertising material, in which case they are destroyed). If no address can be found, they are destroyed unless they contain important material. Parcels are normally disposed of after three months. Letters and parcels marked 'newspaper rate' (which entitles them to a rebate) are automatically destroyed.

Post Office: non-delivery (overseas). The rules which apply are similar to the inland ones, except that charges may be made.

Post Office: parcels (inland). Postage rates for parcels sent between places in the British Isles (but excluding the Irish Republic) range from 15p for parcels weighing up to 1½ lbs. to 65p for parcels between 18 and 22 lbs. These rates are reduced by 5p for parcels sent to addresses within the same delivery area (i.e. in the same POST TOWN). Parcels may not weigh more than 22 lbs.; length and girth combined may not exceed 6 feet; length alone may not exceed 3 feet 6 inches. The POST OFFICE GUIDE makes various recommendations on packing and addressing. Parcels should be marked 'parcel post'. They should not be put in a letter box, unless intended for letter post. Parcels may be registered; certificates of posting are available for unregistered parcels (but compensation is limited to £5). Large numbers of parcels may be collected free. There are special regulations on sending perishable foodstuffs and on sending parcels to and from the Isle of Man.

In the Irish Republic there is no postage forward parcels service, no cash-on-delivery service. Compensation is limited to £4 and not given at all for perishable items. There are various Customs regulations, quota restrictions, and import restrictions. Gift parcels worth less than £2 are admitted duty free, provided they do not contain tobacco, alcohol, watches, or clothing. Consult the POST OFFICE GUIDE.

Post Office: parcels (overseas). Postage rates for parcels sent abroad vary considerably according to distance and cost of handling. Some countries charge a fee for delivery. Size and weight limits are the same as those for inland parcels. There is also a minimum size limit of 4 by $2\frac{3}{4}$ inches for one area (unless the parcel has an attached label measuring $6\frac{1}{4}$ by $1\frac{1}{2}$ inches). Parcels in the form of a roll must measure at least $6\frac{3}{4}$ inches in length plus doubled diameter. There is a maximum size limit of 3 feet 6 inches for length, and 6 feet for length and girth combined. There is also a weight limit of 22 lbs.

It is necessary to fill in a Customs declaration form for each parcel, and advisable to state the contents on the outside to facilitate inspection. Customs duty is payable on a long list of items, and various items are banned by some countries (they may be confiscated if sent). Some goods may only be exported under licence. There are currency controls to be observed, and forms to be filled in where items exceed a certain value. Certain privileges are enjoyed by gift parcels containing licensable goods worth less than £25, if sent by and to private individuals. For details of all these restrictions, it is best to consult the POST OFFICE GUIDE or a post office official.

Post Office: pensions and allowances. Certain pensions and allowances are payable at a post office, for instance sick pay, family allowance, old age pension. The relevant order book should be presented on the due date, or within a certain period afterwards.

Post Office: postage forward parcels service. This deals with parcels as the business reply service deals with letters, and is used mostly by businesses for the benefit of their customers. Users must have a LICENCE, which can be obtained from a postmaster. There is an additional postage charge of 4p per parcel. A special form of label is necessary. These parcels cannot usually be redirected.

Post Office: postage prepayment in cash. Postage may be prepaid in cash, rather than by pre-stamping letters or parcels, where there are a large number of packages to be handled (120 or more letters, twenty or more parcels). These facilities exist at all head post offices and certain others (at *all* post offices following application to the head post office).

Post Office: postal orders. These may be purchased and are payable at most post offices in Great Britain, Northern Ireland, the Channel Islands, and the Isle of Man. They are also paid in the Irish Republic. They may also be sent to H.M. Forces abroad. They are available at values of 5p, increasing by $2\frac{1}{2}$p steps to 25p, and from there by 5p steps to £1, and then at £2, £3, £4, and £5. Stamps worth up to $4\frac{1}{2}$p may be affixed to postal orders. Poundage (i.e. the charge per pound) varies between $2\frac{1}{2}$p and 5p. Postal orders are available in bulk. The name of the payee should be filled in, also where possible the name of the post office for payment. Postal orders are not NEGOTIABLE INSTRUMENTS. They may be crossed like a CHEQUE and are then only payable into a BANK. They may be repaid though poundage is retained. They are valid for six months but may be renewed on payment of a new poundage. Application *re* loss of postal orders should be made to the district postmaster or the local head postmaster; the counterfoil should be submitted. The POST OFFICE is not normally liable once a postal order has been paid. Postal orders cannot be sent overseas except to H.M. forces and persons in the STERLING AREA.

Post Office: poste restante (overseas). Incoming post from abroad is similar to poste restante Britain. Outgoing post varies. The packet must give the name of the addressee: initials, figures, christian names only, etc., are disallowed. Some countries charge an additional fee. In Belgium, France, and Spain, the parcels service is operated by the railways and not the post office, so the words '*en gare*' should be used instead of 'poste restante'.

Post Office: postcards. ⇨ POST OFFICE: LETTER SERVICES.

Post Office: printed papers. ⇨ POST OFFICE: LETTER SERVICES.

Post Office: private letter boxes. Recommended specifications: 8 inches by $1\frac{1}{2}$, and 3 feet 6 inches from the ground.

Post Office: **private tele-communication services.** These include direct lines, facilities for the transmission of pictures, music, fire alarms, data for computers, ◊ POST OFFICE TELEPHONE PROLONGED CALLS UNDER CONTRACT, and ◊ POST OFFICE TELEX SERVICES. They are all operated either by telephone or teleprinter.

Post Office: **prohibitions.** The POST OFFICE will not handle certain articles. These include dangerous articles and what are known as embarrassing packets. For full details it is best to consult the POST OFFICE GUIDE.

Post Office: **radiophone service.** This is available in the Greater London area and in South Lancashire. Subscribers must have the necessary equipment in their cars and they can then make calls throughout the United Kingdom. The subscription is £7·50p per quarter, plus normal call charges and a radio charge of 6p for three minutes.

Post Office: **railway letters.** Letters can be handed in at some stations, instead of at post offices, ◊ POST OFFICE: EXPRESS SERVICES (INLAND). These letters go by the first available train, and on arrival, can be left at the station to be collected or transferred to the nearest letter box. (The sender could arrange for a post office messenger to meet the train and deliver the letter.) Rates for railway letters are: normal first class postage, plus 10p for 2 oz., 15p for 4 oz., 20p for 1 lb. (1 lb. is the maximum weight allowed).

The charges etc. are not applicable to Northern Ireland.

Post Office: **railway parcels.** These may be handed in at any express delivery office to be taken by a post office messenger to a station. If necessary, a messenger will also meet the train and deliver the parcel. The charges are: railway charges plus 20p for each mile the messenger travels, plus 5p for each ten minutes he has to wait. The parcel must not contain a letter.

Post Office: **recorded delivery.** For a fee of 4p, the delivery of postal packets (though not of AIRWAY LETTERS, RAILWAY LETTERS, RAILEX, or CASH-ON-DELIVERY packets) can be recorded. Delivery is not made to the addressee *in person*. The item goes by normal post, but a receipt is obtained and kept by the POST OFFICE. For an additional fee, the sender can be advised of delivery. Packing regulations are similar to those for registered items. Compensation is limited to £2. Money and jewellery must not be sent recorded delivery. Inquiries about losses are made on official forms which cost 1s.

Post Office: **redirection.** This is possible without additional charge provided: (1) the letter, postcard, paper, etc., is redirected not later than the following day (Sundays and public holidays are not included), (2) the packet has not been tampered with, and (3) if a new address label is put on the packet, the name of the original addressee is not obscured. Parcels may only be redirected if the new address is in the same delivery area. They will not be delivered, without payment of additional postage, to persons who have already refused them. Business reply packets can only be redirected by an official of the Post Office. Letters and parcels to H.M. Forces and ships, on service, may be redirected without charge. Registered packets may be redirected but only by taking them to a post office. Recorded delivery packets must also be taken to a post office.

Mail can be redirected at a post office. This is frequently necessary when a person changes his address. The necessary form should be completed and handed to the post office or the postman. The service is free for three months after removal (but additional postage is necessary on parcels). If the service is still necessary after three months, a fee is payable. The Post Office reserves the right to decline to redirect post in any instance and to discontinue at any time. Redirection of parcels abroad is not possible.

Post Office: registration. Any first class letters, parcels, or packets can be registered, but not AIRWAY LETTERS, RAILWAY LETTERS or RAILEX. The fee is 20p, covering a loss of not more than £150; higher fees are payable where higher ◊ COMPENSATION would be necessary (up to 30p for £500). The sender is responsible for seeing that an adequate fee is paid on top of postage. Personal delivery to an addressee is not possible. Registered packets etc., must be handed in at the post office and must be sealed – parcels, where tied with string, must be sealed with wax. Used envelopes can rarely be used for registration. Money sent by registered post should be sent in special envelopes provided by the POST OFFICE, as should uncrossed POSTAL ORDERS, DIVIDEND WARRANTS, savings stamps, etc. If these envelopes are opened and found unregistered, they will be registered compulsorily. Perishable articles must not be sent. The envelope should be marked 'registered' and where a higher fee is paid this should be stated on the envelope. Inquiries for loss of registered packets must be made on official forms – a fee of 5p is payable. Advice of delivery can be obtained. Registration applies to letters overseas with one or two exceptions. The liability of the British Post Office is limited to £3·40 for total loss when it is in the hands of the British Post Office. When the letter has been passed into the hands of another country the compensation depends on the other country. With reference to loss of contents, or damage to the contents, compensation is only paid when the packet is posted to certain countries. Registration of overseas parcels is not possible but there are facilities for INSURANCE.

Post Office: reply coupons. These enable anyone sending letters abroad to prepay replies. The coupons can be exchanged for stamps covering the minimum postage (surface mail) from that country to this. Coupons can be purchased and exchanged in most large post offices. There are two sorts: international, and Commonwealth reply coupons. International reply coupons cost 6p each; those received from abroad can be cashed for 4p. Commonwealth reply coupons cost 3p each; those received can be cashed for 2p.

Post Office: samples. Inland, these are charged as letters. SAMPLES sent overseas (surface mail) cost $1\frac{1}{2}$p if not over 2 oz. plus 1p for each additional 2 oz. The weight limit is 5 lb. to Commonwealth countries, 1 lb. to others. Size limits are: 3 feet in length and depth combined (the greatest dimension being 2 feet); or for rolls, 3 feet 3 inches for length plus twice diameter (the greatest dimension being 2 feet 8 inches). There are certain minimum charges. Samples must not include printed material. They must not be sealed and must be marked 'sample'.

In addition there are special charges for sending small packets to certain countries. This enables GOODS dutiable or otherwise to be mailed as if printed papers. There are also special rates for the transmission of gramophone records, tapes, etc.

Post Office Savings Bank. Since 1 October 1969, the National Savings Bank. Anyone over seven years of age may open new accounts at any savings-bank post office, by depositing a sum of 25p or more and signing a simple form. Relatives or friends may open accounts for children under seven. Persons may also open accounts jointly; and accounts may also be opened by clubs (but not by COMPANIES or business organizations). There are two types of account: ordinary accounts and investment accounts.

In ordinary accounts amounts up to £10,000 may be deposited. Certain organizations may apply for permission to deposit larger sums. The minimum deposit is 25p. Up to £20 may be withdrawn on demand at a savings-bank post office, but the book will be retained by the post office if more than one demand for over £5 is made in any period of seven days. Only one demand may be made on any one day. Larger amounts can be withdrawn by filling in a notice of withdrawal, obtainable at the post office. Urgent withdrawals may be made by telegraph (for a fee). Transactions are recorded in a bank book which must be sent to Savings Bank Headquarters (1) for INTEREST to be entered, (2) when a warrant is required, (3) when two pages, or the whole book, have been filled with entries, or (4) when two demands for more than £5 have been made in seven days. Interest is at £3·50 per £100 per annum. Interest begins to accrue on the first day of the month following deposit. Interest must be stated in tax returns: the first £15 is free of INCOME TAX (but not of SURTAX); husband or wife are entitled to £15 each. Certain firms operate savings group schemes which may be affiliated to the National Savings Movement.

Investment accounts are available to persons with at least £50 in an ordinary account. The minimum deposit is £1, the maximum £10,000. One month's notice of withdrawal is required. Interest rates vary.

Post Office: special delivery. Delivery by post office messenger from the delivery office after transmission by post. Special-delivery post travels by next ordinary mail but is given priority, i.e., is specially picked out at the delivery office and at any intermediate office. This is a weekday service, it is not available on public holidays. Similar facilities are available on Sundays, but only between certain large towns. The special delivery charge is 20p.

Post Office: stamp duty. Certain Inland Revenue and Judicature stamps are available at the post office. These stamps include, stamps for BANKRUPTCY court fees, COMPANIES WINDING-UP fees, CONTRACT NOTES, district AUDITS, judicature fees. Postage stamps may be used for stamping BILLS OF EXCHANGE, and INSURANCE policies.

Post Office: stamps and stamped stationery. Stamps are available in denominations between ½p and £1. Books of stamps are available at 10p, 25p, 30p and 50p. Rolls of postage stamps are also available. Postcards are available impressed with a 2½p stamp, at 3p each or 10 for 29p. Packets of 100 postcards cost £2·90. Letter cards are available impressed with a 2½p stamp, at 3½p each or 10 for 32½p; or with a 3p stamp at 4p each or 10 for 37½p. Embossed envelopes come in two sizes, 5¾ by 3¾ inches, and 9¼ by 4¾ inches. They cost, with a 2½p stamp, 3½p each; or with a 3p stamp, 4p. Discounts are available for bulk purchases. Stamped registered-letter envlopes are available in three sizes. Air letter forms are available at 4p each. Postage stamps may be impressed on customer's own stationery, or may be perforated with customer's initials.

Stamps issued in the reigns of Victoria or Edward VII are no longer valid for the pre-payment of postage, and are not repurchased by the POST OFFICE. Other stamps may be repurchased on certain conditions. The Post Office runs a philatelic bureau for the benefit of collectors. It issues a monthly bulletin giving details of new issues, etc. Its address is: Philatelic Bureau, G.P.O., 2–4 Waterloo Place, Edinburgh. There is an independent Post Office Users' Council at the G.P.O. headquarters, St Martin's Le Grand, London EC1. For details of local Post Office advisory committees, apply to the local head postmaster.

Post office telegrams: express messenger. Subscribers may obtain the services of express messengers for the delivery of TELEGRAMS.

Post office telegrams (inland). Inland telegrams are those sent within Great Britain, Northern Ireland, the Channel Islands and the Isle of Man. The normal charge is 25p for twelve words or less, plus 2p for each additional word. There is a surcharge of 12½p on Sundays, Good Fridays and Christmas Day. De Luxe and standard greetings cards are available. De luxe cards include wedding, birth, birthday and twenty-first birthday cards and cost 35p for twelve words, plus 2p for each additional word. Standard greetings cards (for all purposes) cost 27½p plus 2p for each additional word. When counting the charge, all the words are counted separately, including the address. Telephone and telex addresses are charged as two words. Compound and hyphenated words are charged as one word, as are abbreviations in common use. Figures are counted separately.

Telegrams should be written in block capitals and can be handed in at any post office or railway station which does telegraph business. They may be in plain language, code, or cipher. They may also be sent by telephone or telex. Senders' names and addresses should appear on the reverse of telegrams handed in.

Delivery is not personal. The telegram is put through the letter box, unless the sender gives special instructions. Telegrams may be delivered at any time of the day or night, unless the sender asks for morning delivery: delivery will then not take place between 11 p.m. and 7 a.m. Telegrams can be delivered to people on trains (they should be addressed to a station master) or to the crew of aeroplanes or ships. Greetings telegrams may be handed in for delivery on a specified day. Bundles of telegrams may be delayed unless the post office is notified before noon on the day before they are to be delivered.

Overnight telegrams are those sent between 8 a.m. and 10.30 p.m. for delivery normally by first post the following morning. If there is no delivery, they are held till the next delivery. The word 'overnight' must be written before the address. The charge is reduced to 1p for each additional word. This does not apply to telex numbers, greetings telegrams, multiple address or telegraph money order services, nor to priority telegrams.

A multiple-address telegram, to be sent to many addresses in the same area, is available at reduced rates. Redirection of telegrams is possible, for 25p if in the same area, and for the original rate of the telegram if not. For economy, businesses may adopt telegraphic addresses, which consist of perhaps one word, and are registered with the Post Office for £3 per annum.

Prepaid-reply telegrams are available. The sender can use special instructions, e.g. can mark the envelope confidential. There is no charge for this.

Priority telegrams are available at an additional charge of 10p. Certificates of acceptance of telegrams are available free of charge. Telegrams to the Irish Republic are a special case. There are special facilities for press telegrams.

Weather forecasts can be obtained by pre-paid telegram.

Post office telegrams (overseas). Ordinary telegrams may be written in plain language or code and are charged per word. The minimum charge is for seven words. There are special definitions regarding words and figures. It is possible to send urgent telegrams to most countries – these have priority in transmission and are charged double rate. The word 'urgent' should precede the address. There are also cheaper telegrams known as letter-telegrams. European letter-telegrams are available for Europe and North Africa: delivery takes place not less than five hours after handing in. In other countries delivery takes place the day after handing in. In both instances time may be longer where destination is remote. The letters E.T.L. or L.T. should precede the address.

Another class of telegram is the Commonwealth social telegram. Plain language must be used and only greetings and family news sent. The minimum charge varies according to the country, but the minimum number of words is eleven. Delivery normally takes place on the following day. The letters G.L.T. should precede the address. De luxe telegrams are delivered on ornamental forms, which vary according to the country. The letters LX should precede the address. There are special rates for telegrams to H.M. Forces.

Telegrams may be delivered by telephone at the sender's request. The letters T.F. should be written before the address and the name and address should follow the telephone number. Telex addresses may be used and also multiple addresses. If a telegram is to be forwarded the letters F.S. should precede the address.

The sender's name and address must be provided. Delivery of telegrams cannot be guaranteed within any particular period of time.

Normally ordinary rates are delivered within a few hours but a telegram which arrives at its destination at night will probably be delivered the following morning. The words *jour* or *nuit* can be inserted where the sender wishes to specify day or night delivery. For further details see the POST OFFICE GUIDE.

⇗ POST OFFICE TELEGRAMS (INLAND).

Post office telegrams by telephone. TELEGRAMS may be given over a telephone by a subscriber or from a call office. They may also be delivered by telephone and addressed to the other party's telephone number.

Post office telephone: bills. These are issued three-monthly. The rental is three months in advance, and call charges three months in arrear.

Post office telephone: credit cards. Credit cards are available for persons using telephones frequently. The cards cost about 25p per quarter. The subscriber may have more than one card for handing out to employees, etc. The card number is given to the operator – it can be used for both telephone calls and TELEGRAMS. The cost is added to the subscriber's private bill. Calls are charged at appropriate rate plus 2½p per call.

Post office telephone: directories. These are supplied free to subscribers. Classified directories are available free to businessmen. Additional copies obtainable from local telephone managers.

Post office telephone: fixed time calls. Trunk calls can be booked in advance for a particular time, but the time is not guaranteed. The charge is 10p in addition to the normal fee.

Post office telephone: information services. The POST OFFICE offers many information services, some varying locally. Details of them can be found in TELEPHONE DIRECTORIES. Typical are: the time-services, whereby the subscriber can obtain the correct time, the test-match service giving the latest score and details of the game, the recipe service including the dish of the day, the road-weather service, the summer road condition service, weather information and forecast, and the teletourist service giving 'what's on' information in London in English, French, German and Spanish.

Post office telephone (inland). The POST OFFICE controls the telephone system throughout Great Britain except for Hull, Northern Ireland and the Isle of Man. Also it does not control the local system in the Channel Islands. Charges are based on a fixed rental, being at present £5 per quarter, plus a charge for the calls themselves. It is possible to have internal extensions – the cost depends on distance and varies from 40p to £2·75 per quarter. There are shared services where two subscribers share one line; each person has a separate number, but no indication is given to the one party when the other receives or makes a call. In addition to the charges mentioned above there are connexion charges of up to £25. ◊ POST OFFICE: PRIVATE TELECOMMUNICATION SERVICES.

The cost of telephone calls varies considerably. On Subscriber Trunk Dialling (S.T.D.) which is fully automatic, all dialled calls are charged in units of 1p (2p for pay-on-answer coin box lines). The cost is based on distance and for one's 1p or 2p one can speak on dialled trunk calls for 24 seconds up to 35 miles, 12 seconds for 35 to 50 miles, 8 seconds for other calls. Times are doubled for coin box calls. Local calls are 1½p or 2p for 4 minutes. There are certain times when cheap calls are available (times are more than doubled thereby reducing the cost). Cheap times are 6 p.m. to 8 a.m. and all day Sunday. There are also cheap rates available on Saturdays from 8 a.m. to 6 p.m. though the reduction is rather less. These times do not apply on certain public holidays. Where trunk calls are made through the operator, the charge depends on distance and is based on three minute units costing from 10½p for 35 miles to 25½p for 50 miles. These rates are again lower, though still more than half, in cheap periods. After the first three minutes calls are charged on a minute by minute basis. This does not apply to calls from coin boxes where an additional charge per call is made. When requested to do so, the operator will advise duration charge after the call has been made. Where S.T.D. is not available the cost of a local call is 1½p, or 2p from a call office. Trunk calls are charged as above.

The minimum charge for a trunk call is for three minutes. The Post Office reserves the right to restrict the duration of a call if it needs the line. The duration and cost of a trunk call will be notified to the subscriber for a fee of 2½p.

Post office telephone: morning and alarm calls. One may arrange to be called by the POST OFFICE at any time of the day or night. The charge is 10p. Certain country districts do not offer this facility.

Post office telephone (overseas). This applies to calls from Great Britain, the Channel Islands, Northern Ireland and the Isle of Man. The minimum charge is for three minutes, unless direct dialling is available. Supplementary fees for personal and transferred-charge calls, which are usually only available for Europe and the U.S.A. Timing ends when the calling party gives a clearing signal to the exchange. There are special facilities for booking calls and for cancellation. There are also special regulations for coin box calls: these are not normally possible to places overseas outside Europe, though for this purpose Europe includes the U.S.S.R., Algeria, Morocco, Tunisia, Turkey and various islands. Personal calls are possible. For further details see the POST OFFICE GUIDE.

Post office telephone: personal calls. A personal call may be made, enabling the caller to ask for a particular person, one of a number of persons, a person referred to by title only, two persons specified, or a person brought from one place to another to take the call. The caller may give his name and number. If the person is not available, a message will be left for them to ring back as soon as possible or at a particular time. The call is cancelled after twenty-four hours. The charge is 10p. Distance is irrelevant, but the fee is payable whether or not the call is successful. For charge purposes the time begins when the caller is connected to the person he is calling.

Post office telephone: prolonged calls under contract. Where lines are available it is possible to make prolonged calls of over two hours. Where the CONTRACT allows for calls each of more than fifteen minutes duration and totalling more than five hours, the charges are at present: three-quarters of ordinary rates for the first half-hour (or part), and half of ordinary rates for subsequent periods.

Post office telephone: transferred charge calls. Charges may be reversed if the other party agrees to accept the call. The charge is 2½p. There are no transfer calls to the Irish Republic.

Post office telex service. This is the communication of information which includes the use of a printing device at both ends of a line. The U.K. telex service is automated and operated by direct dialling to any subscriber in this country and also to certain European countries and throughout the world. The service is available day and night. Messages may be received even when the teleprinter is un-attended – this helps where there are substantial time differences when dealing with overseas subscribers. Rental charges are about £160 per annum, which includes maintenance. There is an additional charge where the premises are more than thirty miles from the nearest telex centre in the country and the charge is based on the number of miles distant. Call charges vary from 1p per minute upwards. To the Irish Republic charges are slightly higher. Telex directories are supplied free. The telex system can be used for sending telegrams.

Phototelegraphic services are also available for transmitting drawings, plans, photographs, etc. in facsimile over line and radio links to many places in the world. There are various regulations on size.

Post office telex service (overseas). This service is available to most countries. Europe, the U.S.A., Canada, and New Zealand, may be reached by direct subscriber dialling, other countries via the London exchange. There is a twenty-four hour service to Europe, but other countries vary. Overseas telex directories are available from the telephone manager.

The telexogram service allows for telegrams to be sent to the telex service in another country. There is also a phototelegraph service – for details see the POST OFFICE GUIDE. There are also special regulations regarding ship's radio-telephones.

Post Office: unpaid and underpaid incoming packets. Charges are double the deficiency.

Post town. A town with a post office.

Post war credits. During the years 1941–6, additional tax was levied, with a promise that it would ultimately be paid back. So far, it has only partly been paid, but since October 1959 the government has paid INTEREST on the amount still due. On application to a local tax inspector, repayment in full can be obtained, but only by men over sixty, women over fifty-five, those who can prove special hardship, and the successors of a holder who has died.

Poste restante. ♢ POST OFFICE: DELIVERY ♢ POST OFFICE: POSTE RESTANTE (OVERSEAS).

Power of attorney. A form of instrument authorizing the holder to act on behalf of another, i.e. to sign DEEDS, etc. This is often used when the principal is in a different country.

Precedent, rule of. ♢ COMMON LAW.

Pre-emption. Before an OFFER is made generally, a prior right to purchase given to a person or an organization. This is called pre-emption.

Preferential debts, companies'. When a company is wound up, debts must be paid in a certain order: SECURED CREDITORS are paid first, unsecured creditors second. While generally speaking all unsecured creditors rank equally, certain debts must be given preference: *inter alia* (1) rates and taxes for one year, (2) wages of clerks, workmen, etc. for not more than four months and not more than £200 per person, (3) accrued holiday remuneration payable on termination of employment, (4) employers' contributions payable within twelve months of the commencement of the winding-up and relating to the Unemployment Insurance Act 1935, the National Health Insurance Act 1936, the Widows', Orphans' and Old Age Contributory Pensions Act 1936, the National Insurance Industrial Injuries Act 1946, and the National Insurance Act 1946.

Preferential debts have priority over debts secured on a FLOATING CHARGE that has not crystallized. Crown debts have no priority as such.

Preliminary expenses. These are the expenses necessarily incurred in the formation of a COMPANY, for instance the expenses of promoting the company, issuing a PROSPECTUS, issuing SHARES, obtaining the STATUTORY BOOKS etc. Details of these expenses must be given in the STATUTORY REPORT.

Premium. A sum paid in addition to the nominal VALUE of an item, in recognition of some additional value received, for instance a SHARE PREMIUM, or one for GOODWILL. The annual payment on an INSURANCE policy is also known as a premium.

Premium on a lease. Very often when property is leased, the lessee, in addition to paying a RENT for an agreed period, pays a lump sum. This is known as a premium, or sometimes as 'key money', and was once intended to avoid taxation and disguise the true rent. Premiums for leases granted for fifty years or less are now taxable. For tax purposes the premium is reduced by 2 per cent for every complete twelve months of the lease's length after the first twelve months.

Premium savings bonds. A government SECURITY introduced in 1956, on which no INTEREST is paid: all interest is put into a prize fund and distributed by monthly prize draws. The prize fund is equal to one month's interest at $4\frac{5}{8}$ per cent *per annum* on the eligible bonds. The rate of interest or the prizes may be changed with three months' notice in the *London*, *Edinburgh*, and *Belfast Gazettes*. Premium bonds are available at most post offices and BANKS. They are issued in units of £1, but can be bought in multiple units. The purchaser must fill in an application form giving name, address, and signature. They may be bought by anyone who is sixteen or more, but cannot be held by clubs or corporate bodies. Bonds may be bought for children under sixteen, but only by a parent or legal guardian. Bonds become eligible for prizes after being held for three clear calendar months. Prize draws are made monthly by Ernie (Electronic Random Number Indicator Equipment) and the prizes vary between £25 and £50,000. There is an additional weekly draw for the £25,000 prize, and a monthly draw for the £50,000.

Prizes are free of U.K. INCOME TAX, SURTAX, and CAPITAL GAINS TAX. No one unit can win more than one prize in any one draw. Prize winners are notified by post at the last address recorded in the Post Office. Prize numbers are published monthly in the *London Gazette* and in main post offices, but winners' names are not disclosed. It is necessary to produce the bond when claiming the prize. Unclaimed prizes are kept until their winners remember to tell the Post Office that they have changed their address. Bonds may be cashed at any time, usually at six working days' notice. They are not transferable and will be repaid only to the person in whose name they were issued. Change of address should be reported to the Premium Savings Bonds Office at Moorland Road, St Anne's on Sea, Lancashire. Women who marry, or people who lose their bonds, should also notify the office.

Prepayments. ⟡ PAYMENTS IN ADVANCE.

Present value. ⟡ DISCOUNTING BACK ⟡ NET PRESENT VALUE.

Prevention of Fraud (Investments) Act 1939. ⟡ SHARE PUSHING.

Price. Very generally, the total amount of money that must be handed over in exchange for an article or service that is being purchased. This does not necessarily have anything to do with the VALUE of the item. ⟡ MARKET VALUE ⟡ COST PRICE ⟡ HIRE PURCHASE ⟡ MIDDLE MARKET PRICE ⟡ CLOSING PRICE ⟡ CASH PRICE.

Price-earnings ratio. A term used in investment analysis for the ratio between the MARKET VALUE of SHARE CAPITAL and the profit for the year. The taxed profit is divided theoretically between a number of ORDINARY SHARES; the result is called earnings-per-share. This is then divided into the market price as quoted by OFFICIAL LIST. The result is known as the price-earnings ratio. The figure is high when the ⟡ YIELD is low, i.e., when the demand for the shares has forced the PRICE up, relative to the profits being made, and possibly also the DIVIDENDS being paid. This happens when the prospects of the organization are highly rated, rightly or wrongly, by the investing public.

Primage. Part of the cost of loading or unloading a ship. This varies from port to port, and is included in the FREIGHT charge.

Prime costs. The prime costs of production are direct materials, direct labour and direct expenses, i.e. materials, labour, and expenses that can be directly associated with the cost of producing a specific item.

Prime entry. ⟡ CUSTOMS ENTRY ⟡ CUSTOMS BILLS OF ENTRY.

Prime entry, books of. A book-keeping term for the books containing the original records of transactions. ⟡ DAY BOOKS.

Principal activities of a company. ⟡ DIRECTORS' REPORT.

Private banks. A rather vague term. Strictly, it means all BANKS not state owned, but it is more generally used for banks which are not members of the banks' clearing house. ⟡ CLEARING HOUSE: BANKERS.

Private carrier. A private carrier is a carrier making no general OFFER to the public but carrying goods on specific CONTRACTS. He is subject to the general law relating to BAILMENTS, NEGLIGENCE, etc. ⟡ COMMON CARRIER.

Privateer. A ship and its crew authorized by its government to attack and loot the ships of certain other nations. These were common in the sixteenth and seventeenth centuries.

Prize money. The proceeds of the sale of property, particularly of ships, seized in war, and distributed among the captors in proportions that at sea seem to have favoured the senior members of the crew considerably.

Pro forma invoice. A preliminary INVOICE stating the VALUE of GOODS and notifying the recipient that they have been dispatched. It is not a demand for money, and might for instance accompany goods sent off on approval.

Pro rata freight. A proportion of the agreed ⟡ FREIGHT payable when GOODS are delivered at a port, short of the agreed port of discharge, with the consent of the owner of the goods.

Procuration. The power given to another person to sign documents and act on behalf of the person giving it. Hence 'p.p.'. Authority is given by ⟡ POWER OF ATTORNEY.

Produce exchanges. ⟡ COMMODITY EXCHANGES.

Professional valuation. A term sometimes used in BALANCE SHEETS or PROSPECTUSES. ASSETS are said to be at professional valuation, which means that they have been valued by a person who professes to have the expertise necessary to value them, or whose profession or job suggests that he is competent to do so. The valuation is usually written and signed, and the valuer could be guilty of negligence if it is not made properly.

Profits tax. This was a tax levied in addition to INCOME TAX on COMPANIES but not on individuals or PARTNERSHIPS. It was a flat-rate tax on profits after adjustments in addition to those necessary for income tax purposes. It was abolished when CORPORATION TAX was introduced.

Programme evaluation and review technique (P.E.R.T.). Closely related to ⟡ CRITICAL PATH ANALYSIS, this is a continual review of the procedures developed by critical path analysis, with a view to maximizing efficiency and making necessary alterations at the earliest opportunity.

Programming. A fairly general term for information processing by computers. A computer will only do what it is told to do. The instructions given to a computer are known as a programme, and devising these instructions as programming.

Promissory note. Defined by the Bill of Exchange Act 1882 as an 'unconditional promise in writing made by one person to another, signed by the maker, engaging to pay, on demand or at a fixed or determinable future time, a sum certain in money to, or to the order of, a specified person, or to bearer'. The note must be delivered to the payee or bearer. The person making the note must pay it to a HOLDER IN DUE COURSE: he has no right to deny the existence of the payee or the capacity of the payee to endorse.

Notes payable on demand should be presented within a reasonable time – how long that is depends on the custom of the trade.

Promoter. The person responsible for the formation of a COMPANY.

Promotion. A word with several meanings: (1) increasing SALES of specific GOODS or services by means of MARKET RESEARCH, ADVERTISING, etc., (2) upgrading an individual in his employment, (3) forming a limited COMPANY (◊ PROMOTER).

Prompt day. ◊ WOOL AUCTION ◊ TEA AUCTION ◊ FUR MARKET.

Proposed dividends. ◊ DIVIDENDS proposed to be paid. When the ANNUAL ACCOUNTS of a COMPANY are printed they usually contain an item for dividend on ORDINARY SHARES. This is the amount recommended by the DIRECTORS, but it does not become payable until it has been approved by the shareholders at the ANNUAL GENERAL MEETING.

Proprietary insurance company. An INSURANCE company organized in the same manner as an ordinary limited COMPANY, that is, not a MUTUAL company.

Prosecution: agreements to stifle. Generally speaking, agreements to stifle prosecution are illegal, being against public policy. There are one or two exceptions: for instance a man may not disclose a fraud if he hopes that by doing so he will enable other frauds to be detected; or where there are both civil and criminal remedies, an innocent party may sometimes go for the civil action where this is to his benefit. The threat to bring legal proceedings, or give evidence leading to prosecution, could constitute ◊ DURESS in equity, where the purpose of the threat is not to serve the purposes of the law but rather those of the threatener.

Prospectus. Defined in the Companies Act 1948 as: 'any prospectus, notice, circular, advertisement or other invitation offering to the public for subscription or purchase any SHARES or DEBENTURES of a COMPANY'. It is in fact an OFFER of shares to the public – by 'public' is meant all or any section of the public.

Prospectuses must be issued publicly, with the intention of awakening the interest of the public, or part of it, in the company. Statements by 'experts' contained in the prospectus are included with the written permission of the expert. A prospectus must be registered with the Registrar of Companies and comply with the Fourth Schedule of the

Act; the directors must see that it does so. This does not apply to offers of shares to existing members, e.g. RIGHTS ISSUES, or to the issue of shares ranking equally with shares already issued.

Where a prospectus is not issued a statement in lieu of one must be registered; this applies when a company is formed.

Protected transactions. ◊ RELATION BACK, DOCTRINE OF.

Protest. ◊ NOTING AND PROTEST.

Provincial clearing. ◊ CLEARING TOWN AND GENERAL.

Provision. An accounting term defined in the Companies Act 1948 as 'any amount written off or retained by way of providing for DEPRECIATION, renewals, or diminution in VALUE of ASSETS, or retained by way of providing for any known liability of which the amount cannot be determined with substantial accuracy'. If the amount is more than the DIRECTORS consider strictly necessary, the difference should be treated as a RESERVE and not as a provision.

Provision for renewals. An accounting term for the replacement of minor items of the fixed assets variety. Instead of charging each year's replacement costs as they fall due, a company may include in its accounts an average year's expenses.

Provisional liquidator. When a winding-up order is made the court appoints the OFFICIAL RECEIVER as provisional liquidator pending the appointment of a LIQUIDATOR proper.

Proxy. A person acting in place of another. A MEMBER OF A COMPANY can nominate another person (who need not be a member) to attend a meeting and if necessary vote. The proxy can only vote if the member has power to vote, and only on a POLL, not on a SHOW OF HANDS unless the Articles provide otherwise. Notices calling meetings must state that a member may appoint a proxy. The appointment is usually made in writing on a form provided by the COMPANY. It must be deposited with the company before the meeting, but the company cannot insist that it be deposited more than forty-eight hours before.

There are various forms of proxy: a general proxy with power to vote at any meeting, and a special proxy (for a particular meeting). Special proxy forms may be: (1) at the discretion of the proxy holder: he may vote as he thinks fit, (2) two-way proxies: these are printed so that the member can state whether he wants the proxy to vote for or against the resolution, and (3) three-way proxies, basically a combination of the first two. The STOCK EXCHANGE insists that companies wanting QUOTATIONS must provide for the issue of two-way proxies. If the member attends the meeting as well as the proxy, the proxy might just as well not be there. It is common practice for

DIRECTORS to issue proxy forms naming themselves as proxies for the members.

Public house. A house licensed to sell intoxicating liquor for consumption on the premises, and differing from a hotel or INN in that it does not offer accommodation. A pub offering accommodation to casual customers will probably be a hotel within the definition of the Hotel Proprietors Act 1956 and the various Innkeepers Acts.

Public relations. This concerns the relationship between a business or individual and the general public. A public relations officer or FIRM is employed to create GOODWILL towards the business or individual, to put forward its point of view in a manner which is likely to appeal, and to keep a careful watch on public opinion, taking steps to alter it if necessary.

Puisne mortgage. A legal MORTGAGE without the deposit of TITLE deeds. It is registerable at the Land Charges Registry. If there are other mortgages, priority will be given to those first registered.

Punched cards. Cards used for recording information. This is done by punching holes in the cards at positions determined by various cyphers, which are numbers or letters. When the cards are fed into a machine, it will then reproduce the information in full. The cards are punched perhaps twice to avoid error. They can be automatically sorted, e.g., if each card represents a sales INVOICE, the cards may be automatically sorted into alphabetical order according to customer. The cards are usually small and easily handled and can contain a great deal of information. Their uses depend upon the sophistication of the equipment. They can be used in connexion with computers, and are a popular form of putting information into the computer, though they are giving way to other methods of recording, such as magnetic tape.

Puncheon. A liquid measure of 84 gallons.

Pupil. The word used in Scottish law for INFANT.

Purchase journal. A book-keeping term for the book in which details of all purchases are first entered. Under the DOUBLE-ENTRY BOOK-KEEPING system, the information is afterwards transferred to the personal and general LEDGERS. The journal gives the name of the PURCHASER, a description of the GOODS, the date of purchase, the PRICE charged, trade discounts, etc. Nowadays it is common for these journals to be kept mechanically: they may perhaps be no more than a copy of INVOICES issued, the journal being the backing sheet where invoices are typed.

Purchase tax. A tax levied on certain GOODS manufactured in this country, either to raise revenue or to restrict the manufacture of the goods. It is not payable on goods exported. Manufacturers must keep special records and these are open to the inspection of Customs officials at any time. Persons manufacturing goods subject to tax must be registered with the Customs and Excise authorities and receive a LICENCE from them.

Purchase tax relief. Customs and excise allows export from tax free STOCK, to persons registered with the Customs and Excise. Persons not registered may obtain credit for tax paid, on application to the relevant authorities. Documentary evidence of export is almost always needed.

Purchaser. In common usage a person who buys GOODS from another, but legally any person taking a TITLE to goods from another person, whether cash passes or not.

Purchaser for value. A person who has purchased GOODS and given value for them, i.e. paid for them either in cash or in kind.

Purser. A person on board ship who keeps the cash account, and is responsible for cash payments.

Q

Qualified acceptance. This is an ACCEPTANCE of a ◊ BILL OF EX-
CHANGE which varies the effect of the bill as drawn. It only affects
the rights of those previously liable on the bill. Normally the drawer
presents the bill for acceptance and need not accept the qualification.
If the bill has been negotiated before acceptance the holder is not
bound to take a qualified acceptance when he presents the bill, and
may treat the bill as dishonoured. If he takes a qualified acceptance
he releases from liability all previous signatories who did not assent.
Partial acceptance, i.e. only part of the sum specified, does not
release the previous signatories providing they are notified.

Quality of bills of exchange. In the MONEY MARKET, ◊ BILLS OF
EXCHANGE are graded into various qualities according to their
reliability. There are three principal qualities: (1) ◊ TRADE BILLS,
(2) ◊ AGENCY BILLS, and (3) ◊ BANK BILLS.

Quantity surveyor. Among various definitions are 'the economist of the
construction industry' and 'one who advises on all cost and contractual arrangements and acts as the ACCOUNTANT of the project'.
A quantity surveyor is concerned with construction and provides a
link between the ARCHITECT and the contractor. He is consulted by
the architect or engineer responsible for the design and advises on
probable costs, perhaps considering alternative possibilities of
structure, lay-out or materials. When the design is complete, he
prepares a bill of quantities concerning labour and material required.
This is concerned with quantity and not PRICE. A copy is sent to
each contractor tendering for the work, who then quotes a price.
The quantity surveyor may also be required to assess progress
payments made to contractors and final settlements. Quantity
surveying can be specialized, particularly in the case of civil engineering, or work done for government departments and local authorities.
The quantity surveyor may work in a private capacity or for a
contractor. Specialization may concern both type and condition of
work. A quantity surveyor will belong to one of the recognized
institutes, either the ◊ ROYAL INSTITUTION OF CHARTERED
SURVEYORS or the ◊ INSTITUTE OF QUANTITY SUR-
VEYORS.

Quantity Surveyors, Institute of. This was founded in 1938, and aims
(1) to develop the science and techniques of QUANTITY SURVEYING,

(2) to recruit suitable persons to the profession, (3) to help members in the performance of their task, (4) to give them recognized status, (5) to protect the public by ensuring that only suitable persons should be allowed to use their distinguishing letters and designation, (6) to maintain satisfactory standards of professional etiquette. The Institute publishes the bi-monthly *The Quantity Surveyor*, and has its own library and appointments register. Membership is open only to quantity surveyors proper, and not to general surveyors. Members must pass the examinations set out in its regulations and syllabus. There are various grades of membership, the more important being Associate Member (A.I.Q.S.) and Fellow (F.I.Q.S.). Associates must be at least twenty-one, with three years in practice; Fellows must be thirty-five, with five years in practice. Address: 98 Gloucester Place, London W1.

Quantum meruit. This applies when someone does not complete work he is contracted to do and may perhaps claim payment *quantum meruit*, that is, 'as much as he has earned'. For instance, someone supplying the wrong quantity of GOODS can claim payment in proportion, if the purchaser does not decide to refuse delivery altogether.

Quarter days. The four days taken by custom to mark the quarters of the year. On these days, tenancies begin and end, and RENTS and other quarterly charges become due. In England and Ireland the quarter days are: 25 March, 24 June, 29 September, and 25 December – or, Lady Day (the Feast of the Annunciation), Midsummer Day, Michaelmas (the Feast of St Michael), and Christmas Day. In Scotland they are: 2 February, 15 May, 1 August, and 11 November – or, Candlemas Day (the Feast of Purification), Whitsuntide, Lammas (Loaf Mass – harvest festival), and Martinmas (the Feast of St Martin).

Quasi-contracts. These occur when, although no proper ◊ CONTRACT exists, a court considers that one person has an obligation to another. One could arise for instance from an ILLEGAL CONTRACT, where the court allowed one party to recover money paid even though the contract was void.

Queen's Award to Industry. An annual award announced on 21 April of each year. The closing date for applications is about six months earlier. Winners of the award may display the emblem on the GOODS they produce. The award is given in recognition of outstanding achievements in industry, either in increasing exports or in making technological innovations. They are generally given to FIRMS, but government agencies, research associations, and educational institu-

271

tions are also eligible. Applications should be sent to: 1 Victoria Street, London SW1.

Quintal. A term used in Liverpool and the U.S.A. for 100 lb. *avoirdupois*.

Quorum. The number of persons who must be present at a meeting in order that the meeting can officially take place. With COMPANIES, the quorum for MEMBERS' meetings is fixed by the ARTICLES OF ASSOCIATION. TABLE A specifies 'three members present in person', but one member could be a quorum if the articles said so.

Quotation. ◊ SHARES of PUBLIC COMPANIES cannot be dealt with officially on the ◊ STOCK EXCHANGE unless they have been granted a quotation. This is applied for on formation of a company, but before it is granted, stringent conditions laid down by the Stock Exchange and the Companies Act 1948 must be satisfied. A company must also supply regular information regarding MEETINGS, DIVIDENDS, DIRECTORS' EMOLUMENTS, half-yearly profit statements, etc. Even when a quotation has been granted, it can always be withdrawn again if the company ceases to satisfy the conditions, or if the Exchange becomes dissatisfied with its integrity. Shares may be subscribed for on condition that a quotation is obtained. The monies would be repayable if it were not. In certain circumstances permission to deal on the Exchange may be given without a quotation, but of course the shares would not feature in the OFFICIAL LIST.

Quoted investments. An accounting term for investments in ◊ SHARES or ◊ DEBENTURES which are quoted on a recognized ◊ STOCK EXCHANGE. The amount at which the quoted investments are shown in accounts is normally their cost at the time of their acquisition. However the law requires that the MARKET VALUE be given, and also the Stock Exchange value where this is different.

Quoted price. Usually, the PRICE of a ◊ SHARE, etc., as stated in the ◊ OFFICIAL LIST.

Racking. A Customs term for the drawing off of wines and spirits from casks.

Rack rent. Property is said to be let at a rack rent, when the RENT is equal to the total income from the property, and is therefore only just worth paying.

Railex. ◊ POST OFFICE: EXPRESS DELIVERY (INLAND).

Railway advice. A document issued by British Rail indicating that GOODS are waiting for collection and stating ◊ DEMURRAGE terms.

Railway parcels. ◊ POST OFFICE: RAILWAY PARCELS.

Rate of exchange. When one currency is to be converted into another, the PRICE quoted to those wishing to convert is known as the rate of exchange. Official exchange rates between all major currencies are fixed in terms of the dollar with the exception of members of the STERLING AREA whose currencies are fixed in terms of STERLING (though this makes little difference as sterling is tied to the dollar). Day to day fluctuations within narrow limits are permitted depending on conditions of supply and demand. If there is to be a major change in the rate of exchange, or such a change is thought necessary, the proper procedure is to apply to the INTERNATIONAL MONETARY FUND for permission to revalue. A new official rate of exchange is then quoted. In practice revaluation is often accomplished without obtaining permission as it is obviously important that no leakage should occur that might cause a rush on currency concerned.

Currencies are also controlled internally by government restrictions on the purchase of certain foreign currencies, or on taking of money out of the country.

Rate of turnover. An accounting term for the speed with which stock is turned over. In a retail business, for instance, if stock averaged £10,000 and sales £75,000, the stock would be turned over seven and a half times PER ANNUM.

Ratification of agents' contracts. If an ◊ AGENT acts outside his actual authority, the principal can ratify the CONTRACT and become bound by it. That is, if A purports to act for B without B's knowledge, then providing A states himself to be an agent for B, B can ratify and adopt the contract. But ratification cannot be used to introduce a stranger to a contract: if A contracts with C on a private basis, B cannot claim afterwards that A was acting as his agent.

When a contract is ratified, rights and obligations are related back to when the contract was made.

If the agent is acting within his apparent authority and has been held out by the principal as his agent, ratification is not necessary.

Real accounts. ⟡ ACCOUNTS, NOMINAL, REAL, AND PERSONAL.

Realization account. An account opened for convenience when a business is being wound up. ASSETS are debited to it, liabilities and proceeds of SALE are credited, and the BALANCE is called the profit (or loss) on realization.

Receipt. A document issued by a CREDITOR to acknowledge payment of a debt. At one time it was demanded as proof of payment. Now, if payment is by CHEQUE made out to the creditor and paid into his account, no receipt is legally necessary.

Received for shipment. A ⟡ BILL OF LADING containing these words indicates that the GOODS have been received alongside, but not that they have been shipped. Such bills are not popular, though they can be sent to a third party more quickly than a SHIPPED BILL.

Receiver. A person appointed by a court, or some other competent authority, to take over the property of another person, usually a debtor, for the purpose of receiving the income and paying off the debt. He does not usually manage the business, but is there in a supervisory capacity. DEBENTURE holders are often given power to appoint a receiver. ⟡ OFFICIAL RECEIVER.

Receiving order. An order obtained from a court by the CREDITORS of an INSOLVENT debtor. The effect of the order is to put the ⟡ OFFICIAL RECEIVER in charge of the debtor's estate. The Receiver summons creditors' meetings, and if no scheme can be found which is satisfactory to both them and the court, application is made to the court to have the debtor declared BANKRUPT. A receiving order against a firm applies to all partners equally and personally. A sealed copy of any receiving order is sent to the Official Receiver, who serves another sealed copy on the debtor. The registrar of the court gives notice to the BOARD OF TRADE. The Official Receiver gives notice to a local paper and to the Chief Land Registrar. The receiving order is also published in the LONDON GAZETTE.

The receiving order has three principal consequences: (1) though the Official Receiver does not become the owner of the debtor's property, the debtor cannot dispose of any of his property prior to adjudication, and may be deprived of possession, (2) remedies enjoyed by creditors with provable debts are barred (this does not apply to SECURED CREDITORS), (3) actions or proceedings against the debtor's property are stayed.

The order may be rescinded for various reasons. For instance: (1) the court may agree to a scheme which is also acceptable to the creditors, (2) the creditors may be paid in full, (3) it may be decided that the order should not have been made because (a) the debtor is an undischarged bankrupt and has no assets, (b) he has no prospect of acquiring assets, (c) he is a professional bankrupt, (d) the creditors assent.

Recognizance. A CONTRACT made with the Sovereign. It only applies in a limited number of instances, for instance where a promise is made to pay a sum of money if an accused person does not answer to bail.

Reconstruction of companies. ◇ COMPANIES: RECONSTRUCTION, REORGANIZATION, AND AMALGAMATION.

Record of designers. ◇ COUNCIL OF INDUSTRIAL DESIGN.

Recourse agreement. In HIRE PURCHASE transactions, this is an agreement the seller makes with the hire purchase company, to retake the goods if the hirer defaults.

Rectification of register. Where a person convinces a court that his name should be on the register of MEMBERS OF A COMPANY but is not, the court may order the register to be rectified at the cost of the person responsible for the error. Similarly, when the court thinks a person's name should be removed from the register it may order that to be done.

Redeemable preference shares. Preference SHARES which the COMPANY reserves the right to redeem. The fact that the shares are redeemable must be stated in the BALANCE SHEET, together with the earliest and latest dates for redemption and any premium payable. The shares may only be redeemed out of distributable profits or the proceeds of a further issue of shares. Where redemption is made out of profits, a sum equal to the amount redeemed must be put into a capital reserve, and this cannot be distributed.

Redemption yield. Similar to the EARNINGS YIELD or DIVIDEND YIELD, except that this concerns BONDS with a fixed redemption date, or more particularly with a premium on redemption – it takes these factors into account, e.g. rate of INTEREST acceptable 10 per cent; bonds earning 5 per cent on nominal value; market price would tend to be £50 on dividend yield. Were the bonds redeemable at par in, say, a year, the gain on the redemption of £50 over the dividend yield price has to be taken into account before a market price can be established. The yield shown by relating the dividend and capital gain to the market price would be the redemption yield.

Redundancy. A person is redundant when his work is no longer necessary. Many firms make private arrangements to compensate those suffering financial loss through redundancy. Attention seems to be directed more to senior personnel but the Redundancy Payments Act 1965 has provided for payments by employers to employees for the benefit of those employed for more than three weeks and then made redundant. Redundancy, and the appropriate scale of payment, are defined in the Act. Both employers and the State make contributions into a central redundancy fund. In certain circumstances the employer can then claim from the fund when he makes redundancy payments.

Refer to drawer. This may be written across a CHEQUE by a BANK when the person drawing the cheque has insufficient funds.

Re-finance credits. Credits obtainable by an overseas buyer, where the exporter cannot provide credit and the buyer does not wish to pay cash. A credit is opened at the branch of the overseas BANK in London in favour of the exporter. The exporter is paid on a SIGHT DRAFT drawn on the buyer's credit; the advising bank in London (this being a recognized London bank) accepts a BILL OF EXCHANGE on the buyer; the bill is discounted and the proceeds credited to the account of the foreign bank that issued the credit, thus off-setting the amount paid to the exporter. The buyer pays nothing until the bill drawn on the London bank matures.

Register of charges. All charges on the property of a COMPANY by way of MORTGAGES, fixed or floating DEBENTURES, BILLS OF SALE etc. must be registered with the Registrar of Companies. If not, they will be void, and so not enforceable against LIQUIDATORS or CREDITORS. The company itself also keeps a register containing full details of each charge: the property, the persons involved, and the amount of the charge. This must be kept at the offices of the company and must be open for inspection by MEMBERS OF THE COMPANY and creditors at a fee not exceeding 1s.
Certain charges must also be registered with the Land Registry. ♢ MORTGAGE.

Register of companies. A Register kept at Bush House. All COMPANIES must file certain documents with the Registrar of Companies before they can obtain a certificate of incorporation. Companies may be struck off the register if the Registrar has reasonable cause for believing that they are not in business. He ascertains this by sending a letter. If he receives no reply within a month, he sends a registered letter. After another month, if there is still no reply, or if the company replies that it is not in business, he may notify it that it is to be struck off the Register, unless good reason can be given why this should not be done. The company will then be dissolved after three months. Notice that the company has been struck off must be published in the LONDON GAZETTE, or the *Edinburgh* or *Belfast Gazette* where applicable.

Register of debentures. ◊ REGISTER OF CHARGES. Each COMPANY must keep a register of all MORTGAGES and charges affecting its property. It must also keep copies of all mortgages and charges that must be registered with the Registrar of Companies. It need not keep a register of DEBENTURE holders but will usually do so.

Register of directors. Every COMPANY must keep a register of ◊ DIRECTORS giving names, former names, addresses, nationalities, business occupations, dates of birth and other directorships held. A copy of this register is sent to the Registrar of Companies, who must also be notified of any alterations.

Register of directors' shareholdings. Under the Companies Acts, 1948 and 1967 every COMPANY must keep a register showing the number, description and amount of SHARES and DEBENTURES of the company or its SUBSIDIARY COMPANIES held by its ◊ DIRECTORS, or held in trust for them, or of which they have some right to be holders. Directors are obliged to notify the company in writing of all shares and debentures, and interest in shares and debentures, that they hold, cease to hold, or acquire the right to purchase, in the company or a subsidiary. A person in accordance with whose instructions a director is accustomed to act is considered to be a director for these purposes. Interest in shares and debentures is construed fairly widely. If the shares are held by a body corporate, the director is interested if he holds a third or more of the voting power at a general meeting of that body. He is also interested if he can at any time require the shares to be registered in his name or to call for delivery of the shares to himself. Interests of wife or infant sons and daughters are interests of the director.

It is the responsibility of the director to inform the company of all relevant facts within a very short period. There are very heavy penalties for failing to comply with the Acts. The register must be kept at the REGISTERED OFFICE or wherever the Register of Members is kept, and shall, during business hours, be open to the inspection of any member without charge and any other person for 1s. or less. It need not be open all day but must be for at least two hours.

Register of members. ⟡ SHARE REGISTER.

Registered land certificate. Certain land in the country is registered with the Land Registry. The title deeds can be exchanged for a certificate, which facilitates transfers, as any charge not registered at the Land Registry will be void, and so not enforceable against a purchaser for value. The certificate will give details of the land, the owner, and any charges.

Registered office. The official house of a COMPANY. Any document which the law requires to be delivered to the company must be delivered to the registered office. The Registrar of Companies must be notified of any change of address.

Registered stock. This is (1) similar to ⟡ INSCRIBED STOCK, or (2) ordinary STOCK, converted from SHARES. A stock register may be kept, just as SHARE REGISTERS are.

Registration of business names. Certain names must be registered under the Registration of Business Names Act 1916. Names of PARTNERSHIP FIRMS must be registered if they do not consist solely of the names of the existing partners themselves. A COMPANY must register its name within fourteen days of commencing business: registration is made in a prescribed form. The company must state: (1) the business name, (2) the general nature of the business, (3) the NAME OF THE COMPANY, (4) the REGISTERED OFFICE, (5) the principal place of business, (6) the date of commencement of business, (7) any other business names used. The statement must be signed by a DIRECTOR or the SECRETARY. Undesirable names will be refused registration. Where the business is controlled by a person or persons in another country – the names, nationality, etc., of the true owners must be registered within fourteen days. Any person can, on payment of a small fee, inspect the filed documents and obtain certified extracts.

Registration of debentures. ⟡ REGISTER OF CHARGES ⟡ REGISTER OF DEBENTURES.

Regulated companies. An obsolete type of COMPANY originally formed to regulate particular trades, as professional associations do today.

Reinsurance. The insuring of a risk by an insurer, as a bookmaker lays off a bet.

Relation back, doctrine of. In cases of BANKRUPTCY and LIQUIDATION, the power of a trustee or LIQUIDATOR relates back to the commencement of the bankruptcy and liquidation. This means that he can ignore all transactions that are made between the commencement and his appointment and recover monies paid. He is entitled to all the property that existed at the commencement. There are,

however, certain protected transactions. These are generally transactions made by the debtor in good faith and for value (e.g. some
kind of payment).

Relief, age. Persons over 65 with an income not exceeding £900 may
obtain a deduction from tax of two-ninths for unearned income.
This applies to married couples where one is sixty-five and total
income does not exceed £1,000. Marginal relief is also available. Age
relief is an alternative to AGE ALLOWANCE.

Relief: earned income. For purposes of INCOME TAX, earned incomes
are subject to a reduction of two-ninths up to an earned income of
£4,005, and a further reduction of one-ninth on the following
£5,940. Earned income is income arising from work done, rather
than money invested, but it also includes pensions, family allowances, and some INSURANCE benefits. Any allowable expenses must
be deducted before tax.

Relief, small income. The Chancellor affords certain protection to the
recipients of small incomes. At the moment, provided one does not
earn more than £450 *per annum*, the two-ninths deduction can be
claimed on all income whether earned or unearned. Marginal relief
amounts to one-half. The purpose of this relief is to help retired or
disabled persons living on investment income. AGE ALLOWANCE
is more advantageous: those over sixty-five pay no tax provided
their incomes do not exceed £425. For married couples, the figure is
£680.

Relief, wife's earned income. A married man with a working wife is
entitled to an additional allowance in respect of his wife's earned
income. This allowance is £325 or one-ninth of those earnings,
whichever is the lowest. The wife is also entitled to reduced rate
relief on income after deducting earned income relief. Family
allowances do not count as wife's earned income.

Rendu. ◊ FRANCO, RENDU, OR FREE CONTRACTS.

Rent. The sum received by a person who hires his property out to
another.

Rent roll. A list of all RENTS receivable from an estate.

Renting back. A term current in COMPANY finance. Where a company
has valuable property, i.e. real property, and is also in need of funds,
it may sell the property to, say, an INSURANCE company with a
collateral agreement that it shall rent the property over a long
period. Profits will obviously fall by the amount of the RENT, but
the money raised may more than compensate for this.

Reorganization of companies. ◊ COMPANIES: RECONSTRUCTION,
REORGANIZATION AND AMALGAMATION.

Replacement cost. An accounting term for the cost of replacing an ASSET, as opposed to HISTORICAL COST. Assets are sometimes valued at replacement cost, perhaps to show FIXED ASSETS at a more realistic VALUE in a BALANCE SHEET or perhaps to charge the cost of materials or GOODS against SALES in the manufacturing or trading account. ◊ STOCK VALUATION.

Replevin. The restoration of GOODS to an owner after the goods have been distrained, and while the court is deciding whether the DISTRAINT was right and proper.

Repudiation. A CONTRACT is repudiated when one party makes known to the other his intention not to fulfil his part.

Reputation, loss of. Generally speaking, in the law of CONTRACT, DAMAGES are not available for loss of reputation. However, a banker may be sued by an account holder for loss of reputation if he bounces a CHEQUE when there are funds to meet it. There is also the question of the reputation a contract itself would have brought: an actor suing for BREACH OF A CONTRACT for a leading part, may obtain damages for the loss of the prospective reputation.

Reputed owner. The person who appears to be the owner of property even though it may in fact belong to some other party. The phrase has a particular meaning in BANKRUPTCY: if A has allowed B posseession of GOODS knowing that third parties might assume B to be true owner of them, then A may be estopped from denying this if B were to go bankrupt. ◊ ESTOPPEL.

Resale price maintenance. The penalties or restrictions imposed by manufacturers on the PRICES at which, or conditions on which, thĕir GOODS should be sold. Most of these agreements are now subject to the Restrictive Trade Practices Act 1956 and the Resale Prices Act 1964. The second Act attempted to abolish resale price maintenance: suppliers cannot now state the prices at which goods are to be sold. They cannot state minimum prices, nor withhold supplies from persons selling below a particular price. They can withhold the goods however if the customer is using them as LOSS LEADERS, but loss leaders are not clearance sales. Withholding supplies includes refusal to supply on customary terms or on terms available to dealers generally. Certain goods are exempted. In order that goods should be exempted the supplier must satisfy the Restrictive Practices Court: (1) that price maintenance is necessary to avoid any falling off in the quality of goods or number of places where they could be obtained or; (2) that prices would tend to be increased or; (3) that goods would be sold in such a way as to endanger health or; (4) that necessary ancillary services would no longer be supplied. Exempted goods must be registered with the Registrar of Restrictive Practices and lists of these goods are published from time to time.

Rescission. This is what happens when a ◊ CONTRACT is, as it were, wound up, and both parties restored to their original position. It is the usual remedy in cases of MISREPRESENTATION. It is only allowed, though, where the parties *can* be restored to their original position, where no third parties are involved, and where the claimant has acted within a reasonable time.

Reserve capital. A COMPANY may pass a SPECIAL RESOLUTION stating that a portion of its CAPITAL not already called up shall not be capable of being called up except in the event of the company's being wound up. This capital is called the reserve capital and sometimes reserve liability. It cannot be turned into ordinary capital without permission of a court and it cannot be charged by the DIRECTORS.

Reserve for obsolescence. A sum of money set aside by a business out of profits to guard against the possibility of sudden OBSOLESCENCE of FIXED ASSETS. In accounting an asset becomes obsolete when a new model or a new method is invented which renders the old asset uneconomic.

Reserve liability. ◊ RESERVE CAPITAL.

Reserve price. A term used with reference to AUCTIONS. A lot which is subject to a reserve price, is one which the owner does not wish sold below this price. If the AUCTIONEER sells below this figure, the SALE is void provided the catalogue does indeed state that there is a reserve price (it need not of course say what the price is). If there is no indication in the catalogue then, if the auctioneer has signed the memorandum (which he does if the CONTRACT must be evidenced in writing), the TITLE will pass to the purchaser. The owner's remedies are to stop the SALE before the memorandum is signed or to sue for BREACH OF WARRANTY OF AUTHORITY.

Reserves, capital. As opposed to ◊ GENERAL RESERVES, these are funds in a COMPANY which belong to the shareholders but may not be distributed, or are not in the DIRECTORS' opinion available for distribution. Examples are the SHARE PREMIUM account, revaluation reserve, etc. The term is not peculiar to company accounts but could apply to those of any business.

Reserves, general. As opposed to ◊ CAPITAL RESERVES, profits accruing to the owners of a business but not distributed to them for reasons of policy.

Reserves: gold, dollar, etc. All nations have what might be called last-ditch reserves to settle debts due to other countries or international organizations. These reserves must of course be held in an internationally acceptable currency. Reserves are accumulated either through trade surpluses, or by the national output of gold. In settling an adverse balance of payments with one country, e.g. Germany, deutchmarks would be acceptable, but one cannot necessarily rely on deutchmarks for settling payments due to countries other than Germany. It is therefore essential to have in reserve some currency that *is* internationally acceptable. For some reason gold has served the purpose of an international currency for a very long time and the wealth of a country in terms of its reserves is often indicated by the amount of gold it holds. Since the end of the 1939–45 War the dollar has been equivalent to gold in that it has been acceptable throughout the world, and that the United States could always be relied on to change it for gold if asked to do so. Reserves have then generally been called gold and dollar reserves. The position is now rather more delicate, as public faith in the American economy is less strong and also there is some doubt of stability of the PRICE of gold. If it increased the dollar would be worth less in terms of gold.

The gold reserves of any country, and in fact the total reserves of all currencies, are directly related to international trade and surpluses and deficits. It is possible to cover temporary shortages by borrowing from other countries or more usually from the INTERNATIONAL MONETARY FUND. Britain tends to do this frequently. The trouble with borrowing is that not only does the money have to be repaid in gold or a stipulated currency, but INTEREST charges have an adverse effect on the balance of payments when the imbalance was probably the reason for the loan.

Reserves, movements on. The Companies Act 1967 makes it necessary for COMPANIES to show details of movements on all reserve accounts which are not DEPRECIATION reserves, showing reasons for increases and decreases.

Reserves, revenue. A general heading for all reserves which are not ◊ CAPITAL RESERVES. They are monies available for distribution but for various reasons not yet distributed, e.g. GENERAL RESERVES, or the BALANCE on a PROFIT AND LOSS ACCOUNT.

Resolution, extraordinary. This is usually a resolution concerned with the WINDING-UP of a COMPANY. To be passed it requires a majority of three-quarters of the total votes cast. Notice of the resolution must be included in the notice of the meeting.

Resolution, notice of intended. MEMBERS OF COMPANIES who represent one-twentieth of the total voting rights of those entitled to vote at the meeting, or 100 or more members holding SHARES on which a minimum of £100 has been paid, can claim at their own expense to have notice of an intended resolution sent to members, together with a statement of not more than 1,000 words. The requisition must be deposited at the registrar's office not less than six weeks before the meeting.

Resolution, ordinary. Any resolution passed by a majority of persons present at a general meeting.

Resolution, special. This is a resolution passed *inter alia*, to alter the ARTICLES OF ASSOCIATION or objects of a COMPANY, to change its name, or reduce its CAPITAL. It needs a three-quarters majority of total votes cast. Twenty-one clear days' notice must be given to shareholders, stating that a special resolution is to be proposed. A private copy of the resolution, if passed, must be sent to the registrar within fifteen days.

Respondentia bond. A shipping term for a loan raised by the master of a ship on the SECURITY of the cargo.

Restitution. Restitution has never played a big part in English Law. Its main application is in EQUITY. Similar remedies are for MONEY HAD AND RECEIVED, and tracing. It applies in INFANTS' CONTRACTS where money or property in the possession of an infant which cannot be recovered in contract may be recovered by an order for restitution.

Restraint of trade, contracts in. These, unless there are special circumstances, are contrary to public policy and so void. Restraints are only reasonable if they are in the interests of the contracting parties and also of the public. ◊ RESTRICTIVE COVENANTS.

Restrictive covenants. Terms in a CONTRACT which restrict the right of one party to contract freely after determination of the contract or during its continuance. They occur in contracts of employment where the employee agrees not to compete with the employer or practise his trade within a given area or time after leaving his employment. They may also appear in the contract for the SALE of a business where the VENDOR agrees not to compete with the purchaser, perhaps within a given area, or in any way diminish the value of the GOODWILL. Another instance would be a contract for the sale of GOODS which restricts the rights of the buyer to purchase elsewhere. Such covenants are disliked by the law and are generally only enforceable when they are thought necessary for the protection of the party concerned, and are not against the public interest. ◊ RESTRICTIVE TRADE PRACTICES.

Restrictive endorsement. ◊ BILLS OF EXCHANGE may be endorsed in a way which restricts the freedom of the endorsee to negotiate them.

Restrictive practices court. This was set up in 1956 to deal with matters arising from the Restrictive Trade Practices Act, i.e. to investigate trading agreements. Since 1964 it has also had responsibility for matters arising from the Resale Prices Act.

Restrictive trade practices. At one time these were the province of the COMMON LAW ($\Diamond$ CONTRACTS IN RESTRAINT OF TRADE), but under the Restrictive Trade Practices Act 1956 and Resale Prices Act 1964 a great number of trading agreements must now be registered by the Registrar of Restrictive Trading Agreements. These are: those between two or more persons carrying on business in the United Kingdom, concerning GOODS, PRICES, conditions of sale or supply, the way in which the goods are to be manufactured, restrictions on quantities to be sold, processed, or manufactured, or restrictions as to areas where goods are to be sold or supplied. The 1956 Act does not apply to agreements dealing with exports. Particulars to be registered are names of persons or parties involved and details of the agreement. It is irrelevant whether or not the agreement is in writing. Any person may apply to the Restrictive Practices Court to investigate these agreements. Where the agreement is considered to be against the public interest the Court may prohibit it or order it to be rectified. The Court may also, when prohibiting an agreement, prevent further agreements being substituted for the prohibited one. The 1964 Act also provides for the enforcement of certain agreements that are in the public interest. Very often what are known as sole distributor agreements are allowed. The matter is somewhat complicated and the Act very detailed.

Retail Trading-Standards Association (R.T.S.A.). Founded in 1935, and incorporated by the Board of Trade in 1937, this is a voluntary organization, with members including retail traders, ADVERTISING AGENCIES, trade associations, newspapers, periodicals, and manufacturers. Its aims are to preserve acceptable standards in the description of GOODS by the retail trades. There is a booklet or general code entitled *Standards of Retail Practice*, and members agree to observe the code or to notify the R.T.S.A. if they think some amendment is necessary. Complaints are passed on to members by the Association. The Association also publishes a bulletin at irregular intervals. The Association's objects are described in its MEMORANDUM OF ASSOCIATION, clause 3(a), as 'to formulate and establish schemes for promoting and regulating uniformity in the standard of retail practice, and in the conduct of persons engaged in the retail trades; and in particular for the purpose of ensuring the use . . . of descriptions, terms, and names, corresponding with the quality, nature, and VALUE of the merchandise and goods to which the same relate'.

There is a Council consisting of between twelve and twenty members, and a membership fee which varies according to the type of the member and size of the organization.

The R.T.S.A. is looked upon as an authority on the ◊ TRADE DESCRIPTIONS ACT 1968 and will advise members. In addition to looking after its members, the Association protects the public against its own members, and also by dealing with confusing and misleading advertisements. It also helps its members by investigating complaints of unfair competition. Address: Retail Trading-Standards Association (Incorporated), 356 Oxford Street, London W1.

Retailer. A person selling GOODS directly to the public. These goods have normally been purchased from a WHOLESALER, or from a manufacturer by means of an order placed with his representative.

Retention money. In certain types of CONTRACT, particularly building contracts, part of the PRICE is kept back for a period after the contract is complete in order to give the purchaser time to inspect the work done and discover any bad workmanship.

Retiring a bill. A BILL OF EXCHANGE is retired when it is paid on the due date (or earlier) at a DISCOUNT.

Return load. When a vehicle is hired to carry GOODS to a particular area, the haulier, rather than bring the vehicle back empty, will advertise for return loads.

Return on capital. A rather nebulous phrase. In the terminology of investment analysis and accounting it means the profit earned by CAPITAL. If the profit were £10 and the capital £150, the return would be $\frac{10}{150}$, i.e. 6⅔ per cent. However, there are so many ways of defining both capital and profits, and so many difficulties involved in each definition, that it is doubtful if the phrase has any valuable meaning. It is often stated as return on ◊ CAPITAL EMPLOYED. In company accounts return on capital is often the ratio that the profit bears to the total EQUITY funds or shareholders' funds employed, but because definitions vary so widely, it is better to read the wording rather carefully in the accounts. The phrase 'return on capital' is frequently used when what is really meant is ◊ DIVIDEND YIELD, or ◊ EARNINGS YIELD.

Revaluation of assets. The ASSETS of a COMPANY are often revalued, either because they become worth more than when they were acquired, or else because it is necessary to take account of inflationary changes. The surplus (or deficiency) would probably be transferred to a

285

surplus on revaluation account and included amongst CAPITAL or GENERAL RESERVES. It is a CAPITAL PROFIT and could not as such at one time be distributed in the form of dividend, though this is possibly no longer so. If realized it would be subject to CAPITAL GAINS TAX.

Revenue account. Another term for PROFIT AND LOSS ACCOUNT, or INCOME AND EXPENDITURE ACCOUNT. It should be distinguished from CAPITAL account.

Reversible lay days. If the LAY DAYS ⬦ are reversible, then if a shipper loads his cargo in a shorter time than agreed he may be allowed to add the time saved on to the days allowed for unloading.

Revocable credit. A term used in foreign trade. Credit, given by a banker willing to accept BILLS OF EXCHANGE up to a certain value which is revocable at any time without notice. ⬦ DOCUMENTARY CREDIT.

Revolving credit. ⬦ LONDON ACCEPTANCE CREDIT.

Rigging the market. Operations designed to create an artificial market to benefit the operator. Everyday examples are BULL and BEAR activities on a large scale.

A COMPANY may, by increasing DIVIDENDS, etc. raise the market price of its SHARES prior to a new issue. This issue may then be put out at a higher SHARE PREMIUM, but, unless the dividend is maintained, the issue PRICE will be artificially high. The Treasury is often accused of 'rigging the market' when, prior to a new issue of BONDS, it instructs the BANK OF ENGLAND to buy heavily, thus creating an artificial demand and enabling the new issue to be made at more favourable terms.

Right of resale. In certain circumstances a seller of GOODS may resell, for instance after STOPPAGE IN TRANSITU, or because of a LIEN. Neither stoppage nor lien rescinds the CONTRACT but the seller can, if the goods are likely to perish, resell the goods and give a good TITLE. He may also resell if the buyer does not pay within a reasonable time after the seller has announced his intention to resell. As the title remains with the buyer the surplus on resale belongs to him, after the seller has reclaimed any expenses.

This does not apply where in the contract the seller reserves the right of resale: then the contract *is* rescinded.

Rights issue. An invitation to existing shareholders to acquire additional SHARES in the COMPANY. The right will be, e.g. one new share for each two shares previously held. The price is usually lower than it would be in the OPEN MARKET, and the shareholder can normally sell the right to buy to a third party, thus making a profit for himself.

From the point of view of the company it is an easy way of raising new CAPITAL – for obvious reasons.

Ring trading. A term used with reference to dealings in FUTURES. Dealers come together around what is known as a ring, and bids and OFFERS are called and PRICES marked up.

Risk. ◊ SALE OF GOODS: RISK.

River dues. Amounts payable for use of rivers by vessels.

Road haulage. Road haulage in the United Kingdom is partly in the hands of the ◊ NATIONAL FREIGHT CORPORATION, and partly in the hands of private ROAD HAULIERS. There is no definite distinction between the work done by the National Freight Corporation and the others. The services offered are various and are generally a matter of private negotiation.

The principal advantage of road transport appears to lie in the fact that GOODS are taken directly from the sender to the recipient without needing to move the goods from one vehicle to another, as is the case with rail or water transport. Express services are available for long distance transport. There is an organization, the ROAD HAULAGE ASSOCIATION, which supplies details of reliable road hauliers in any particular area, who are members of the Association.

Road transport is governed by general laws relating to the carriage of goods, e.g. the Carriers Act 1830, and the liability of a road haulier depends on whether he is a ◊ COMMON CARRIER or a ◊ PRIVATE CARRIER. The National Freight Corporation is not a common carrier. The Road Transport Act 1964 relates to carriage of goods by road between two separate countries and lays down regulations on compensation for losses, etc. The Transport Act 1968 has altered the competitive advantage of road transport by establishing the National Freight Corporation.

Road Haulage Association. ◊ ROAD HAULAGE. The Road Haulage Association has about 17,000 members. Its aims are to protect the interests of members and provide the public with a list of reputable ROAD HAULIERS. It gives members advice on law, INSURANCE, etc., and also offers opportunities for financial aid. It publishes a monthly: *Roadway*. Address: 22 Upper Woburn Place, London WC1.

Road haulage contract hire. Facilities offered by, e.g. the NATIONAL FREIGHT CORPORATION for hiring a fleet of vehicles or even just one vehicle. Each vehicle can be dressed in the customer's livery and is to all intents and purposes the customer's own property. Drivers can be supplied, the vehicle can be housed by the customer or the true owner. The CONTRACT is normally based on a monthly rental.

287

The advantages are obviously that CAPITAL outlay is avoided and that vehicles are maintained and serviced by the lessor.

Road haulier. A person offering to carry goods by road. ◊ ROAD HAULAGE. He may be a COMMON CARRIER or a PRIVATE CARRIER.

Rolling stock. A general term for railway engines, carriages, trucks, etc.

Rotation of directors. A number of DIRECTORS normally retire each year and offer themselves for re-election (the number or proportion is usually stated in the ARTICLES OF ASSOCIATION). This is to give shareholders an opportunity of changing the directors without going through the procedure necessary to dismiss them. In TABLE A it is required that at a COMPANY'S first ANNUAL GENERAL MEETING all directors retire and at subsequent annual general meetings one-third of them do.

Roup. The Scottish term for ◊ AUCTION.

Royalties. The sum paid for the right to use another person's property for productive purposes. For instance, royalties may be paid for working mines to the owner of the land, or by a publisher to an author. There are special taxation rules for dealing with royalties where they apply to books, the object being to spread the income over the period of expenditure. Thus the income may be spread back over the time the book was written.

Rubber exchange. This is situated at Plantation House, Mincing Lane, London EC3. Dealings are carried on daily from 10 a.m. to 5 p.m. The selling dealer sells to a BROKER acting for an undisclosed principal. The broker GUARANTEES payment. Dealings are made by private CONTRACT and not by AUCTION. Most dealings are for cash. There are also dealings in FUTURES. These are known as settlement house contracts. Settlements are normally made every fortnight. All sales of rubber are made on the floor of Plantation House.

Rule in Foss v. Harbottle. This is a rule observed by the court *re* limited COMPANIES. It will not interfere with the running of a company at the instance of any particular shareholder, if it considers that the shareholder has his own redress within the rules of the company itself. Generally speaking, majority decisions within a company are upheld, assuming there is no FRAUD on the minority.

Rule in Hadley v. Baxendale. In BREACH OF CONTRACT cases, a court will only award DAMAGES for loss which arises out of the breach itself, and which might have been contemplated by the parties at the time at which the CONTRACT was made.

Rule in Royal British Bank v. Turquand. In COMPANY law, where

DIRECTORS of a company act within their apparent powers (as indicated in the MEMORANDUM OF ASSOCIATION and ARTICLES OF ASSOCIATION) another party to a CONTRACT is not expected to discover whether internal regulations have been complied with, e.g. whether a company has power to borrow, or whether specific loans must be authorized by a resolution of DIRECTORS. Provided a loan is within limits set by the memorandum, the borrower need not make sure that the resolution has been properly passed.

Rummage. H.M. Customs preventative officers rummage a ship (i.e. search it) for all contraband, dutiable, or prohibited GOODS. There are often a number of unannounced searches.

Running broker. A BILL BROKER who acts as an intermediary.

Running days. Consecutive days including Sundays – not only WORKING DAYS.

Running down clause. A MARINE INSURANCE clause whereby the insurers agree to indemnify the shipowner against DAMAGES arising from a collision where the insured ship is in some way to blame.

Rural Industries Bureau. Now taken over by the COUNCIL FOR SMALL INDUSTRIES IN RURAL AREAS. A bureau offering technical and advisory services to industries employing up to twenty skilled workers either in the countryside or in towns with a population of less than 10,000. Priority is given to exporting firms. It is financed by government funds. Address: 35 Camp Road, Wimbledon, London SW19.

Rural Industries Loan Fund Ltd. ▷ COUNCIL FOR SMALL INDUSTRIES IN RURAL AREAS.

S

Safe custody. Documents and personal possessions in deed boxes or sealed packages may be deposited in the BANK for safe keeping.

Sale. In the Sale of Goods Act 1893, a CONTRACT of sale is defined as 'a contract whereby the seller transfers, or agrees to transfer, the property in goods to the buyer, for a money CONSIDERATION called the PRICE'.

Sale of goods. At one time the doctrine of CAVEAT EMPTOR applied to the sale of GOODS, but this has now been modified by various statutes, the most important of these being the Sale of Goods Act 1893. This gives various implied ◊ WARRANTIES and ◊ CONDITIONS concerning the sale of goods. These will apply unless specifically excluded (◊ EXEMPTION CLAUSE).

The implied conditions are: (1) that the seller has a good TITLE and will be able to pass a good title; (2) where the sale is by description that the GOODS actually comply with the description; (3) where the sale is by SAMPLE, that the goods comply with the sample, and that the customer will have a reasonable time to make a comparison; (4) where the customer relies on the skill and judgment of the VENDOR and the goods are of a kind that the vendor usually supplies, that the goods will be fit for the purpose for which they are required. (This is modified by the fact that where the buyer relies on a trade name there is no implied condition.) It is not necessary that the buyer should state that he is relying on the seller's judgment: this may be inferred. If a man buys chips in a chip shop, it may be taken for granted the seller knows the purpose for which they are required; (5) that the goods should be of MERCHANTABLE QUALITY. Where the customer has had opportunity to examine the goods this does not apply to defects that an examination should have revealed.

The implied warranties are: (1) that the buyer should have and enjoy quiet possession of the goods; (2) that the goods are free from any charge in favour of a third party. A condition can be reduced to a warranty in certain circumstances, e.g. where the customer delays in making a claim.

The tendency for the law today is to afford the customer further advantages: there have been two Consumer Protection Acts and probably more to come based on the Moloney Report. There are also of course independent ⟡ CONSUMERS' ASSOCIATIONS and a state subsidized ⟡ CONSUMER COUNCIL. ⟡ MISREPRESENTATION.

Sale of goods: risk. Generally speaking, risk passes with TITLE. If there is a delay in delivering the GOODS themselves, the risk will remain with the party responsible for delay. In marine CONTRACTS, the seller must also give the buyer sufficient information to enable him to insure the goods. If he does not, they will remain at the seller's risk.

Sale of goods: sub-sales. When GOODS are sold by a purchaser to a third party, this is known as a sub-sale. In an action for damages for BREACH OF (the original) CONTRACT, the claimant may hold that valuable sub-contracts have been lost and that this has increased his monetary loss. Whether or not an action will lie for the recovery of these losses will depend on the circumstances and the loss that might have been anticipated when the original contract was made. It was decided in Victoria Laundry (Windsor) Ltd v. Newman Industries Ltd that as the defendants knew that failure to deliver certain machinery must result in loss of profits, they were responsible for loss of normal profits, but not for particular losses arising from some particularly lucrative contract that they could not have foreseen.

Sale of goods: title. It is often important to know when the title to GOODS passes. When the SALE is of ascertained GOODS, title will normally pass according to the intention of the parties. Sale of Goods Act 1893 states that where the contrary is not defined in the CONTRACT, if specific goods are named and are in a deliverable state, then the property passes immediately the contract is made. When the contract is for specific goods, and something remains to be done to them before they can be delivered, then title passes when that something is done and the buyer is notified of it. Goods are in a deliverable state when they are in such a state that the buyer would be bound to accept them.

Where goods are unascertained, e.g. where an order is made for a quantity of goods, and the specific goods are not named, the intention of the parties is still relevant but generally speaking title passes when goods are appropriated to the contract with the assent of the buyer and the buyer has been notified. The assent may be implied, and may even be given before goods are appropriated. Where goods are on sale or return, title passes when the buyer either signifies his assent to the contract, or retains the goods for an unreasonable length of time.

So far as the title of the seller is concerned, there is an implied CONDITION in the Sale of Goods Act that the seller is entitled to the goods and is able to sell them, or will be when the time of sale comes.

Generally speaking a person without a title to goods cannot pass a title to a third party. There are exceptions to this rule. For instance (1) where, in a contract for sale, the buyer has possession of the documents of title, or the goods, with the assent of the true owner, the buyer is able to give a good title to an innocent third party. Also, where the seller retains the documents of title or the goods, after the ownership has passed to the buyer, the seller can give a good title to an innocent third party. Other exceptions are (2) sales by ◊ FACTORS, (3) sales in ◊ MARKET OVERT, (4) the Hire Purchase Act 1965 gives special protection to innocent persons buying cars privately where they are subject to HIRE PURCHASE agreements. They can obtain a good title.

Sales agent. A MARKETING term for the person employed by a COMPANY or manufacturer to control or supervise the distribution of his goods in a particular area. The sales agent strictly negotiates CONTRACTS between the manufacturer and a third party, and is not himself a contracting party. It is however a vague term and often used very much more widely to describe persons selling a particular manufacturer's GOODS, regardless of whether they act as principal or ◊ AGENT. ◊ FACTOR.

Sales journal. A book-keeping term for the book in which details of SALES are first entered. It is similar to a ◊ PURCHASE JOURNAL.

Sales representative. A MARKETING term for a person employed by an organization to sell its GOODS and to make CONTRACTS on its behalf concerning these SALES.

Salvage. The reward given to persons who save, in part or whole, a ship or its cargo from shipwreck. The person rendering assistance must show that he did so voluntarily, that there was danger involved and that he showed enterprise, that the ship was in need of help and that some benefit did arise from what he did. Salvage money cannot be claimed by those already responsible for the care of the ship. The reward is given by the owners of the ship and cargo.

Sample. A proportion of bulk sent to a prospective customer so that he may decide whether to make a purchase. If he purchases on the basis of the sample, the bulk that he receives must correspond to it. If it does not he may return it, but he must do so promptly or he will be presumed to have accepted it. The Sale of Goods Act 1893 imposes three conditions on a CONTRACT for the SALE OF GOODS by sample: (1) The buyer must have a reasonable chance of comparing the bulk with the sample. (2) The bulk must correspond with the sample in quality. (3) The goods must be free from any defect not apparent in the sample but making them unmerchantable.

Sampling order. An order enabling the holder to take away samples of GOODS retained at WAREHOUSES.

Sandwich courses. Courses run at technical colleges, etc., based on the idea that practical experience and theoretical knowledge should be obtained at the same time but that part-time day-release and evening classes arc not a satisfactory method of education. The student spends a period of three or six months in college followed by a similar period with the COMPANY for which he works. The course is planned so that he may take the various exams, leading to the qualifications he wants. The student usually receives full pay while at the college but also agrees to work for his sponsor for a certain period after qualifying.

Sans recours. ◊ WITHOUT RECOURSE.

Savings bank. ◊ TRUSTEES SAVINGS BANK ◊ POST OFFICE SAVINGS BANK.

Scheduled territories. ◊ STERLING AREA.

Scotland: company law. Generally speaking Scottish Company Law and English Company Law correspond. There are, however, differences in terminology. For instance, the word 'interdict' is used instead of 'INJUNCTION', 'pledge' or 'bond and disposition in security' instead of 'MORTGAGE', 'heritable property' instead of 'real property', etc. Again, the *Edinburgh Gazette* takes the place of the LONDON GAZETTE in issuing official notices. Other differences stated in the Companies Acts are that:

(1) a COMPANY is registered in Scotland, not England,

(2) it is possible for trusts to be indicated in the SHARE REGISTER,

(3) there is no such thing as a NOTICE IN LIEU OF DISTRINGAS,

(4) the Limitation Act 1939 does not apply to Scotland but unpaid calls and unclaimed DIVIDENDS become barred by the long negative prescription after twenty years,

(5) it is doubtful whether a valid mortgage of SHARES can be affected by the deposit of the SHARE CERTIFICATE under blank transfer,

(6) borrowings are slightly different, the principal methods being: (a) a pledge of movable property (this is only effective if the property is actually transferred to the CREDITOR). Floating DEBENTURES were rarely issued; possession could not be given. The position was changed by the Companies (Floating Charges) (Scotland) Act 1961. This gave limited power to make, and to register, floating charges over property, even in England, (b) PROMISSORY NOTES, BILLS OF EXCHANGE, etc., as in England, (c) debentures fairly similar to English

293

debentures; they may be payable to a registered holder or to bearer. The 1948 Companies Act makes the latter valid and makes them NEGOTIABLE INSTRUMENTS. Debentures may be secured or unsecured. Because of the difficulties indicated in (c) the inability to create floating charges, registered debentures are usually accompanied by a trust deed so that the TRUSTEES can take possession. RECEIVERS are not appointed – Scottish law does not recognize receivers but the trustees have power to appoint managers, (d) a bond and disposition in security (similar to a mortgage). A DEED acknowledging a sum of money and setting out interest payable and repayment terms. It must be recorded in the Division of the General Register of Sasines for the appropriate county. The provisions *re* registration of mortgages do not apply to Scotland but do apply if a Scottish company has a place of business or operates in England or if the property mortgaged is situated in England. Similarly, an English company must register charges in the General Register of Sasines when the property charged is Scottish. Equitable Mortgage by deposit of title deeds is ineffective in Scotland and creates no obligation as to repayment or security.

(7) WINDING-UP rules are similar. A winding-up is often called a liquidation. The rules as to landlords are slightly different. Creditors can claim interest from the date of winding-up. Invalidation of floating charges does not apply, obviously. There is no OFFICIAL RECEIVER but the court may appoint someone equivalent to a LIQUIDATOR.

Scottish Country Industries Development Trust. This is similar to the ◊ RURAL INDUSTRIES BUREAU. Address: 27 Walker Road, Edinburgh 3.

Scrip issue. An issue of SHARES to existing shareholders made possible by the capitalization of RESERVES. No payment is necessary, so it is often called a bonus issue. In a case where one new share was issued for every two previously held, the shareholder would be receiving an acknowledgement that his capital had increased by 50 per cent. However if the old rate of DIVIDEND were not maintained the share PRICES would be depressed and the shareholder might not find himself financially better off. If the dividend were maintained he would have received something that he could sell. The proceeds, being capital, would not be subject to DIVIDEND TAX. It may be a good policy to capitalize profits rather than distribute them in the form of dividends, but unless profits are increasing, it will not be possible to maintain dividend rates on an expanding capital.

The issue of bonus shares used to be looked on as an alternative to a cash dividend, giving the recipient a saleable ASSET, the profits not being taxable. This gap was closed by the introduction of CAPITAL GAINS TAXES and also by the Finance Act 1968, which provided that where a shareholder could opt for cash or additional shares, the additional shares were to be treated as a distribution in cash, and therefore would be subject to dividend tax. This did not apply to REDEEMABLE PREFERENCE SHARES.

Scrivener. An obscure word. Originally it meant a scribe. Now it can also mean a person acting as a money broker.

Seal. Documents and other items can be secured by a seal. A small pool of soft wax is run over the join, and before it hardens this is impressed with a metal design, which should be peculiar to the sealer (signet rings were originally meant for this purpose). When the seal is hard, the document cannot be opened without breaking it. DEEDS which are sealed are effective even though no CONSIDERATION has been given. Various other legal documents, for instance conveyances, also require seals. Today wax is not normally used: sometimes a thin wafer is, but more often a document is simply impressed with the mark of the sealer.

Searcher. ◊ LAND WAITER.

Searching the register. The inspection of, say, the Register of Land Charges, to ascertain whether or not there is any charge on a property to be purchased.

Second via. A copy of a ◊ BILL OF EXCHANGE sent by a different route in case the original is mislaid.

Secret profits. Profits made by a person who is in a fiduciary relationship with another, and makes the profits by reason of the relationship, or arising out of it, without disclosing them to the other person. When they are discovered, they must be shared and in certain circumstances the guilty party may also be sued by the innocent party. Examples of secret profits are profits made by an AGENT while working for his principal, profits made by one partner while about PARTNERSHIP business, profits made by DIRECTORS of COMPANIES from CONTRACTS with other organizations in which they have an interest.

Secret reserves. An accounting term for RESERVES kept by a COMPANY or business but not disclosed to the public in the BALANCE SHEET, being hidden in the wrongful valuation of ASSETS or liabilities. For instance, a company may over-depreciate assets or refrain from revaluing them when they increase in VALUE, thus showing them at a value far smaller than their true one. Were these assets to be realized, the company would make a profit not apparent from the accounts. Limited companies may not have secret reserves, although BANKS are given favourable treatment and allowed them as it is thought that this may help public confidence, and help the banks to meet rainy days.

Secretaries, Corporation of. This was founded in 1922 as an organization for secretaries and administrative OFFICERS OF COMPANIES or similar organizations. Members must satisfy certain examination requirements: To be Fellows they should be not less than twenty-four and must have been practising for three years as secretary, assistant secretary, or similar, and have passed preliminary, intermediate and final examinations (though certain exemptions are possible for those holding other similar professional qualifications). For Associates conditions are similar but the jobs held need not have such high standing. Fellows may use the letters F.C.C.S. and Associates, A.C.C.S. The Corporation's governing body provides professional supervision over members and protects and promotes their interests and the interests of their profession by various means from parliamentary petitions to conferences. It also runs an Appointments Bureau. Present membership is approximately 11,000. It publishes a monthly: *Secretaries Chronicle*. For information apply to Corporation of Secretaries, 13 Devonshire Street, London W1. ◊ CHARTERED SECRETARIES, INSTITUTE OF.

Secretary. The person who deals with the general administration of an organization, particularly with clerical work such as correspondence, taking minutes at meetings, and keeping records. It is often a full time occupation. ◊ COMPANY SECRETARY.

Secretary, personal. A person employed as an assistant to deal with correspondence and other matters not needing the employers' personal attention.

Secretary, private. A PERSONAL SECRETARY, but acting for one person only instead of many people within an organization.

Secretary, private confidential. A PRIVATE SECRETARY with greater responsibility than normal and so allowed to deal with confidential matters.

Secured creditor. A creditor whose debt is secured, e.g. by a charge on the property of the debtor: this may take the form of a DEBENTURE where a company is concerned. The charge may be a fixed or a floating charge. A fixed charge is one where the actual property is specified; a floating charge is one which attaches to the property of the debtor generally – the actual property only becomes known when the debt is payable, when it is said to crystallize.

Security. A misused term often applied indiscriminately to SHARES, DEBENTURES, etc. In fact a security is something given or GUARAN-

TEED by the borrower as a safeguard for a loan. The term is often applied to debentures and similar loan stock, and to NEGOTIABLE INSTRUMENTS. Certificates of liability are known as securities, so sometimes are government stocks or any loans whose repayment is guaranteed. The term should not be applied to shares.

Selective employment tax (S.E.T.). A tax introduced in 1966 whereby firms are taxed according to the number of persons they employ. The bias is weighted against SERVICE INDUSTRIES and in favour of MANUFACTURING INDUSTRIES. The rates, which differ according to the sex of the employee, were increased by 50 per cent in 1968 and again by 33⅓ per cent in 1969, and were reduced by 50 per cent in 1971. Certain COMPANIES receive a refund (equal to the tax paid) and at one time certain companies received additional premiums. Thus there were three categories.

There has been a great deal of difficulty in deciding which category individual businesses belong to. The premium over and above the amount paid was abolished in 1967 at the time of devaluation, though certain exceptions were made in favour of ◊ DEVELOPMENT AREAS. In the Finance Act 1968 additional reliefs were given to hotels in certain areas.

Self-service store. A retail establishment where the customer serves himself from shelves, where the GOODS are priced, and pays on leaving the shop.

Self-balancing ledger. An accounting term for a personal LEDGER containing a CONTROL ACCOUNT.

Self-liquidating. An ASSET is said to be self-liquidating where its original cost is paid for out of its earnings.

Sellers' market. A situation where market conditions are favourable to sellers, usually because demand is running ahead of supply.

Sellers over. A term used in the City for market conditions when there are more sellers than buyers.

Selling out. A STOCK EXCHANGE term which applies when a purchaser cannot take up SHARES, etc., at the proper date. The owner may then sell as best he can and the original buyer must pay expenses.

Selling price. Generally, the cash PRICE which a customer must pay for an article.

Semi-variable costs. Costs partly fixed but partly variable, e.g. costs which are fixed until a certain level of output is reached, and then fixed again, at a higher level until another level is reached. TWO-PART TARIFFS are another example of semi-variable costs (for instance, there is a fixed charge for the installation of, say, a telephone, and then a variable charge for its use).

Sequestration. The legal appropriation of property by a third party pending the settlement of a dispute.

Service charge. ⟡ GRATUITY.

Service contracts. ⟡ DIRECTORS' SERVICE CONTRACTS.

Service industry. An organization offering services to EXTRACTIVE INDUSTRIES, CONSTRUCTIVE INDUSTRIES or MANUFACTURING INDUSTRIES or to the public, for instance plant hire, car hire, or catering. These organizations do not actually make anything: they provide a service by putting producers in touch with consumers.

Set of bills. A BILL OF EXCHANGE or BILL OF LADING with various copies.

Set-off. A right of set-off can occur when two parties are indebted one to the other. One debt can only be set off against another when the parties concerned are acting in the same capacity. For instance a personal debt from A to B cannot be set off by B against monies he owes to A acting as TRUSTEE for a third party.

Settling days. ⟡ ACCOUNT DAYS.

Severable contracts. This phrase often occurs in CONTRACTS for the SALE of GOODS, particularly where the goods are to be delivered in instalments. It is possible to treat separate instalments as separate contracts, but not necessary – in a BREACH OF CONTRACT case the court would look to the intention of the parties. Failure to deliver, or pay for, one instalment, might be a breach of the whole contract. On the other hand, the contract might be treated as severable, and an action brought for only the one particular failure to deliver or pay. ⟡ INSTALMENTS: DELIVERY AND PAYMENT.

Share broker. ⟡ STOCKBROKER.

Share capital. The total of SHARES issued, or authorized to be issued, by the COMPANY. The CAPITAL stated in the MEMORANDUM OF ASSOCIATION is the AUTHORIZED CAPITAL. The company cannot issue more than this amount unless it first passes a RESOLUTION at a general MEETING.

The amount of capital usually appears in the company's BALANCE SHEET, followed by a list of shares, of various categories, actually issued, under the heading 'issued share capital'. Another term is PAID-UP CAPITAL: this is the amount called up on shares issued.

Share certificate. This is evidence of ownership of SHARES, but not a NEGOTIABLE INSTRUMENT nor strictly a document of TITLE. Ownership is determined by the entry in the company's SHARE REGISTER.

If a person is in possession of a certificate properly issued, a COMPANY may be ESTOPPED from denying that he is the owner of the relevant shares.

Share hawking. At one time it was possible to hawk SHARES from door to door, but nowadays nobody may deal in SECURITIES or SHARES unless they are licensed dealers or exempt dealers. Exempt dealers are e.g.: (1) members of recognized STOCK EXCHANGES or recognized associations of dealers in securities, (2) the BANK OF ENGLAND, (3) statutory or municipal corporations, (4) TRUSTEES of authorized unit trusts. Licensed dealers obtain licences annually from the BOARD OF TRADE, leaving a deposit of £500. The Board of Trade has made rules to which dealers must conform regarding issuing books, forms of CONTRACT notes. ⟡ SHARE PUSHING ⟡ HAWKER.

Share index. An INDEX NUMBER based on the PRICES of a particular parcel of SHARES supposed to be representative, and intended as a guide to overall market fluctuations. It may refer to share prices generally or to the particular group of shares. Among the better-known share indices are the *Financial Times* 'Industrial Ordinary Share Index', The Dow Jones Index, and the *Daily Mail* 'Index of 440 Shares'.

Share premium. A sum may be charged on an issue of SHARES, over and above the nominal value, if their profitability indicates that their real VALUE is in excess of their nominal value. Share premiums are put to a special account (the share premium account), which is a CAPITAL RESERVE, and cannot be distributed to members. It can however be capitalized and form the basis of a SCRIP ISSUE.

Share pushing. SHARES were once touted, sometimes from door to door, by share pushers who made unsubstantiated statements regarding the shares. The matter was dealt with by the Prevention of Fraud (Investments) Act 1939. Now no one can deal in shares without a Board of Trade licence, except for members of the STOCK EXCHANGE, etc. (⟡ SHARE HAWKING). Misleading statements, etc. may be an offence, and circulars inviting persons to purchase shares must comply with the provisions of the Companies Act, 1948, i.e. they must take the form of a PROSPECTUS.

Share register. The register kept by a limited COMPANY giving the names and addresses of MEMBERS and particulars of their SHARE holdings. Where shares are held jointly both names are entered. Where there is a trust, the names of the TRUSTEES are entered (the company is not bound to take any notice of the fact that they are in fact acting as trustees: ⟡ NOTICE IN LIEU OF DISTRINGAS).

The register also records the dates of beginnings and endings of memberships, and the amounts paid up on shares (⟡ PAID-UP CAPITAL). Entry in the register is *prima facie* evidence of membership, or liability if the shares are not fully paid. The share register must normally be kept at the REGISTERED OFFICE and it must be open, to members gratis and to non-members on payment of a nominal sum. Extracts from the register must also be obtainable at, say, 2½p per 100 words.

Share transfer. This is accomplished through a broker or BANK. A share transfer form must be completed and sent with the seller's SHARE CERTIFICATE to the REGISTERED OFFICE of the COMPANY. The name of the buyer is then entered in the company's books in place of that of the seller. The transfer form is signed by the seller. The company will destroy the old certificate and issue a new one to the buyer. The buyer normally pays transfer duty on the CONSIDER-ATION. This varies from 1p where the consideration does not exceed £1·25, to 50p where it is £300, then 5p per cent from then on. There is commonly a company registration fee of 12½p payable by the buyer. The buyer pays the broker's COMMISSION of, say, 1p in the pound (with certain minimum charges), and also the STAMP DUTY on the CONTRACT NOTE, perhaps 10p on amounts of £100 to £500. The seller also pays a commission to the broker.

Share warrant. A SHARE CERTIFICATE that does not contain the name of the member, so that title is transferable by delivery. It is not a NEGOTIABLE INSTRUMENT. Warrants can only be issued when shares are fully paid. The member's name is struck off the register when the warrant is issued. The ARTICLES OF ASSOCIATION usually allow the warrant holder to vote at meetings on presentation of the warrant. ⟡ COUPONS are usually attached.

Shares. The owners of a COMPANY are its shareholders, that is, the people who have promised to subscribe a sum of money to the company's CAPITAL in return for a portion of the profit. The SHARE CAPITAL is divided into shares of, say, £1 each. These shares are transferable, freely in PUBLIC COMPANIES, though PRIVATE COMPANIES usually restrict the right to transfer. Transfers are usually effected through a STOCKBROKER. There is no limit to the number of shares an individual or organization can hold in a company. Theoretically a public company must have at least seven shareholders, and a private comapny at least two. ⟡ SHARES headings ⟡ STOCK. Each company keeps a SHARE REGISTER, which members of the company may inspect. A copy is kept at Bush House, Aldwych, London WC2, and is available for inspection by members of the public. However, as shares are often held in the names of nominees, it is not always possible to ascertain true ownership this way.

Shares, 'A' ordinary. ⟡ ORDINARY SHARES without voting rights.

Shares, deferred ordinary. A special category of SHARE, often issued to the founders of a company. These shares normally give the owner special DIVIDEND rights, and often entitle him to all profits after a certain percentage has been paid on the other classes of shares. This type of share is not very common in public companies as it tends to arouse suspicion.

Shares, forfeiture of. When a shareholder does not pay the calls (⟡ CALLED-UP CAPITAL) due on his shares, they may be declared forfeited by the DIRECTORS provided the ARTICLES OF ASSOCIATION of the COMPANY allow. Forfeited shares may be reissued.

Shares held by subsidiaries. The Companies Act 1948 prevents subsidiary companies holding shares in the holding company, except in certain circumstances (⟡ COMPANY: PURCHASE OF OWN SHARES). When shares are held by subsidiaries or nominees, or such persons have the beneficial interest in those shares, details must be given in the annual report of the holding company.

Shares issued at a discount. It is *prima facie* illegal for a COMPANY to issue SHARES at a discount, except where (1) the issue has been sanctioned by a court, (2) the shares are issued within a month of the court sanction, or within any other period the court specifies, (3) the issue has been authorized by a resolution at a general meeting, (4) this resolution specifies the maximum rate of discount, and (5) more than a year has elapsed since the company became entitled to commence business. Details of the discount, or that part of it not written off, must be published in every PROSPECTUS, BALANCE SHEET, ANNUAL RETURN, etc.

Shares: lien. The ARTICLES OF ASSOCIATION of a COMPANY normally give a first LIEN on the SHARES of each member, for debts and liabilities, to the company. The lien usually applies to DIVIDENDS due: the company cannot enforce it by forfeiting the shares.

Shares: management. ⟡ DEFERRED SHARES ⟡ FOUNDERS' SHARES.

Shares: market value. The PRICE at which SHARES are available on the OPEN MARKET. The price of QUOTED INVESTMENTS will be found in the OFFICIAL LIST, published daily. For other shares it is a matter of negotiation. Any restrictions on the transferability of shares could influence the price.

Shares: nominal value. The nominal value of a SHARE is the value stated in the MEMORANDUM OF ASSOCIATION and on the SHARE CERTIFICATE. The MARKET VALUE of the share may be quite different.

Shares: no par value. These are SHARES having no nominal value. All monies payable are similar to SHARE PREMIUMS and would be put into a stated CAPITAL account. These shares are not permitted in this country at present.

Shares: ordinary. These have no particular right to DIVIDEND but are entitled to all the profits after prior demands, such as loan INTEREST, or preference dividends. However, whether and when they receive the profits is at the discretion of the DIRECTORS, who may if they wish put all profits into RESERVE. The ordinary shareholders are the true owners of a COMPANY. The directors are, strictly speaking, stewards. The shareholders meet at least once a year and may put forward any resolution that they wish, provided certain legal conditions are complied with.

The company cannot, except under special circumstances and with court permission, redeem or in any way reduce the number of ordinary shares. It has been common to issue what are known as 'A' ORDINARY SHARES, which are normally non-voting. This practice is frowned upon by the STOCK EXCHANGE, and it offends against the principle of LIMITED liability, as those taking the greatest risks should have the greatest amount of control. The ordinary share capital is often referred to as the equity of the company.

Shares, placing of. A method of issuing SHARES. The shares, rather than be offered to the public by the COMPANY or through an ISSUING HOUSE, are 'placed' by a reliable BROKER, i.e. sold in perhaps substantial blocks to selected customers: probably financial institutions. These clients will then sell to the public when dealings in the shares begin, i.e. when a QUOTATION has been granted by the STOCK EXCHANGE. If the quotation is not obtained, of course no dealings will be possible.

Shares, preference. These SHARES have a preferential right to DIVIDEND, i.e. they are entitled to a fixed sum before anything is paid to holders of ORDINARY SHARES. The dividend may or may not be cumulative. In any event, dividends are paid at the discretion of the DIRECTORS and the shareholders cannot insist on them.

The voting rights of preference shareholders are normally strictly limited: they can usually only vote when their dividends are in arrear.

Shares are occasionally also preferential as to return of capital, and are also sometimes redeemable at the company's option. Occasionally one finds preference shares with additional dividend rights (e.g. a right to a further share in profits after ordinary shareholders have received a certain percentage). These are usually known as participating preference shares. The rights of preference shareholders can vary considerably and will be detailed in the company's ARTICLES OF ASSOCIATION ◊ REDEEMABLE PREFERENCE SHARES.

Shares, preferred ordinary. ORDINARY SHARES with additional rights. They rank before other ordinary shares when it comes to payment of DIVIDENDS or repayment of CAPITAL.

Shares, qualification. SHARES taken up by the DIRECTORS of a COMPANY as a qualification of directorship. The Companies Act, 1948 does not insist on a director holding shares but the ARTICLES OF ASSOCIATION often provide that he must. The shares must be paid for.

Shares, surrender of. Where SHARES could have been forfeited, a COMPANY, if its ARTICLES OF ASSOCIATION permit, may accept a surrender if this is more convenient. A surrender, like a forfeiture, is void if its intention is to make the company a shareholder, or to relieve the shareholder of his liabilities.

Ship broker. An AGENT acting for the ship-owners to obtain cargo and cargo space. He also deals with passengers, INSURANCE, FREIGHT, BILLS OF LADING, CHARTER PARTIES, etc.

Ship-chandler. One who supplies ships with necessary provisions.

Ship Mortgage Finance Co. Ltd. This was founded in 1951 to assist British ship-owners by making loans on completed ships against a first MORTGAGE. Capital of £1,000,000 was provided by big INSURANCE companies etc., and by the Ship-building Conference. This was later increased to £4,000,000, and a further £5,000,000 was issued in DEBENTURES. The TRANSPORT SHIP-BUILDING CREDIT SCHEME, by taking part of this business away, persuaded the company to broaden its interests, though its aim is still to help the shipping industry. The Company is managed by the ◊ INDUSTRIAL AND COMMERCIAL FINANCE CORPORATION LTD.

Ship-owner's lien. The LIEN that a ship-owner has for FREIGHT and other charges attaching to the GOODS that he carries. This lien may even exist when the goods have been warehoused if notice has been given to this effect. The lien for freight or general average contributions is a POSSESSORY LIEN. The lien for other expenses in protecting the goods is a MARITIME LIEN.

Shipped bill. A BILL OF LADING beginning 'shipped in apparent good order and condition'. It merely attests that the goods have been loaded on the ship. ◊ RECEIVED FOR SHIPMENT.

Shipper. A manufacturer or merchant who sends GOODS abroad.

Shipping agent. A GENERAL AGENT specializing in the export or import of GOODS by sea. He deals with shipping documents,

303

INSURANCE, and Customs, and sees that cargo-space is available as needed. Some are connected with particular steam-ship companies and these often circulate information about available space.

Shipping bill. A document used for claiming ◊ DRAWBACK from the Customs authorities. ◊ EXPORTERS' DECLARATION.

Shipping claims tribunal. Established in 1939 to deal with compensation for requisitioned ships, the Tribunal was never really active. It exists now only theoretically. Each year the Registrar checks that entries in reference books are correct.

Shipping company. From the point of view of the BOARD OF TRADE, shipping companies are those which own ships, or include among their activities the management or operation of ships, and have satisfied the Board of Trade that it is in the national interest that they should be treated as shipping companies.

Shipping intelligence. Shipping intelligence received at Lloyds from the LLOYDS AGENTS, coast radio stations, ship-owners, etc., is collated and distributed to newspapers, etc. Within Lloyds the intelligence is edited and published, by various departments, in LLOYDS LIST AND SHIPPING GAZETTE, *Lloyds Shipping Index*, *Lloyds Shipping Index Supplement*, *Lloyds Weekly Casualty Reports*, and *Lloyds Loading List*. There are also other publications, such as *Lloyds Maritime Atlas*, *Lloyds Calendar*, *Lloyds Survey Handbook*, and *Lloyds List Law Reports*.

Shipping notes. The various documents that are involved in exporting GOODS. ◊ EXPORTER'S DECLARATION. One of these documents is the mate's receipt – signed by the mate when the goods are received on board.

Ship's articles. The CONTRACT signed by seamen when taking up employment on a ship.

Ship's certificate of registry. A document giving all the relevant details of a ship: its name, owner, tonnage, master, and country of registration.

Ship's clearance inwards and outwards. ◊ CUSTOMS: FINAL CLEARANCE INWARDS AND ENTRY OUTWARDS.

Ship's husband. An AGENT acting for the owner of a ship and taking care of it when in port.

Ship's master. The captain of a merchant vessel.

Ship's papers. Various documents carried by a ship, including its CERTIFICATE OF REGISTRY, MANIFEST, charter agreement, SHIP'S ARTICLES and log book.

Ship's passport. A document carried by the master of a neutral merchant vessel in time of war, to prove nationality.

Ship's protest. A declaration on oath made by the master and crew of a damaged ship or cargo, concerning the damage and how it arose, etc.

Ship's report. The captain of a ship, or his representative, must give a report of his ship and its voyage, cargo, etc., to the collector of Customs at a port. The report contains details of the cargo and where it was loaded, of the ship's stores, and of unusual objects encountered on the voyage, such as shipwrecks or icebergs.

Ship's store bond. ⟡ CUSTOMS: SHIP'S STORES.

Shop. A building wherein GOODS are sold, or offered for sale, to the public, on credit or cash terms. The law relating to shop-keeping will be found in, *inter alia*, the Shop Act 1950, the Shops and Railways Premises Act 1963, the Sale of Goods Act 1893, the Resale Prices Act 1964, and the various hire-purchase acts.

Shop assistant. A person selling GOODS from behind a shop counter, as AGENT for the shop-owner. He can CONTRACT on the owner's behalf, for instance in selling on credit, provided he is acting within the scope of his apparent authority.

Shoplifting. Taking GOODS from shop counters without any intention of paying for them. This is a criminal offence and should be distinguished from obtaining goods on credit knowing that one will be unable to pay for them.

Shops' closing-hours: general. Shops must be closed for the serving of customers after a certain time in the evening, e.g. not later than 9 p.m. on a late day or 8 p.m. on any other day. Local authorities can vary these hours within limits, but they cannot force shops to close before 7 p.m. Customers may be served after hours if they were in the shop before closing time. There are special regulations allowing the SALE OF GOODS after the specified hours where the goods are: (1) meals or refreshments for consumption on the premises, (2) newly cooked provisions to be consumed off the premises, (3) alcohol to be consumed on or off the premises, (4) tobacco, table waters, or matches sold on licensed premises, (5) tobacco, table waters, confectionery sold in theatres, cinemas, etc., (6) medicine or medical appliances, (7) newspapers, periodicals and books on station bookstalls, (8) transactions of post office business.

The provisions of the Shop Act 1950 may be modified with regard to holiday resorts and sea fishing centres. Local authorities may dictate hours of opening suitable to local conditions if asked to do so by a majority of shop-keepers. All shops must be closed for the serving of customers on a Sunday. This does not apply to transactions metioned in the Fifth Schedule of the Shops Act 1950.

Shops: early closing. Every shop must close not later than 1 p.m. on one day in every week. The day is fixed by the local authority, and different days may be allocated to different classes of shops, different districts, or different periods of the year. If Saturday is chosen, the occupier may opt for another day by giving notice to customers. Where any other day is chosen the occupier may opt for Saturday.

Persons may be served after the specified closing-time (1) if they were in the shop before that time, (2) if it is necessary because of illness, or (3) where the GOODS are needed for ships arriving or departing. (For details see the Shop Act 1950.)

Certain shops need not have an early closing day. These are shops dealing with the goods mentioned in the First Schedule of the Act (these are listed under SHOPS' CLOSING-HOURS: GENERAL), and also, during certain periods of the year, shops in holiday resorts and sea fishing centres.

Short bill. A BILL OF EXCHANGE payable on demand, AT SIGHT, or within a very short period (less than ten days).

Short interest. A MARINE INSURANCE term for the difference between the VALUE of the GOODS and the amount for which they are insured. Where the latter is greater the difference is known as short INTEREST and the excess premium may be reclaimed.

Short ton. A measure used infrequently, being 2,000 lbs. and not 2,240 lbs.

Shorthand. One of various recognized forms of abbreviated writing. Shorthand is used in business, to take notes in court, to take records of parliamentary proceedings, and so on.

Shorthand typist. A person trained to write ⟡ SHORTHAND and use a typewriter, and so able to take down dictation and type. 120 words per minute is a good shorthand speed, 50 a good typing speed. Of course there are other qualities to be considered. A well-trained shorthand typist will have had tuition in other commercial subjects and may act as a ⟡ PRIVATE SECRETARY.

Shorthand writer. A person who makes a profession of writing in ⟡ SHORTHAND. He may be permanently employed in a court or in Parliament, or wherever verbatim accounts of any legal or other proceedings are necessary.

Short-term capital. CAPITAL raised for short periods, perhaps to cover temporary fluctuations in fortune. BANK OVERDRAFTS are an example.

Short-term deposits. Monies deposited with BANKS, FINANCE HOUSES, etc., on terms which allow them to be withdrawn at short notice. Generally speaking, the shorter the loan, the lower the INTEREST rate, and the greater the LIQUIDITY.

Show of hands. A method of voting at meetings. Each company share-holder has one vote on a resolution passed on a show of hands. When there is a POLL voting powers vary with the number of SHARES held so that one person may have more than one vote. The ARTICLES OF ASSOCIATION of a COMPANY normally state that voting at all meetings shall be on a show of hands but the articles usually also provide (and in fact must do so) that a poll may be demanded for all resolutions apart from the election of a CHAIRMAN or an adjourn-ment. They usually state that the number of members demanding a poll must be over a given minimum, but when a poll is demanded it often gives an opportunity for persons not present to vote. ♢ PROXIES cannot vote on a show of hands, but may demand a poll.

Shunter. A person in provincial STOCK EXCHANGES who marries transactions in those exchanges with transactions in the London Stock Exchange.

Sight draft. A name given to a ♢ BILL OF EXCHANGE payable AT SIGHT, i.e. payable when presented irrespective of when it was drawn.

Silence. A seller does not have to make any representations with reference to his goods. Silence does not constitute MISREPRESENTA-TION unless the circumstances are exceptional. When a person makes an offer, he cannot state that silence will be taken as an acceptance. However, in CONTRACTS which are UBERRIMAE FIDEI there is a duty to make all relevant facts known.

Simple interest. INTEREST calculated on the original CAPITAL sum, and not including interest on unpaid interest.

Sinking fund. An accounting term for cash set aside for a particular purpose, and invested so that the correct amount of money will be available when it is needed.

Sister-ship clause. A MARINE INSURANCE clause covering claims for damages following a ship's collision with another ship belonging to the same owner. Without this clause, an owner might not have any claim, as he cannot sue himself.

Sliding scale. ♢ AD VALOREM.

Slip. A slip can be attached to an INSURANCE, particularly a MARINE INSURANCE policy and each UNDERWRITER writes on this slip the amount for which he agrees to be liable until the amount of the insurance is reached.

Slump. The point in the ♢ TRADE CYCLE when PRICES and employ-ment are at their lowest. To escape from a slump and move towards ♢ BOOM conditions is not easy. It is a gradual process and depends upon the slow return of confidence.

Small farmers scheme. The Ministry of Agriculture makes grants to small farmers for improvements tending to make their farms more profitable. The schemes must first be approved by the Ministry. There are two types of grant: the field husbandry grant and the farm business grant. Not more than £1,000 will be granted to a farmer for any one scheme. Field husbandry grants, however, may be given in addition to other grants already obtained for this type of work. Farms must consist of between 20 and 125 acres of crops and grass (this does not include rough grazing). Labour requirements should be between 250 and 600 standard man days.

Sola. A ⬦ BILL OF EXCHANGE with no other copies in circulation.

Sold note. ⬦ CONTRACT NOTE.

Sole trader. A person who trades on his own account, rather than in PARTNERSHIP or as a member of a COMPANY.

Solicitor. A person working within the precincts of the law. Basically, he is the intermediary between the public and the dispensers of justice. His work consists for the greater part in advising clients on their legal rights, dealing himself with smaller matters from conveyancing to proceedings in magistrate's courts, and putting the client in touch with a BARRISTER where legal action is to be taken at a higher level. The charges made by a solicitor, e.g. for conveyancing, are dictated by the LAW SOCIETY, which keeps a watchful eye over the profession. A solicitor who engages in nefarious activities, offends against accepted modes of conduct, or misuses his client's monies, may be subjected to severe penalties.

A solicitor must be articled to a firm of solicitors for a defined period (two years for graduates, up to six years for others) and pass certain examinations set by the Law Society.

Solicitor's letter. Colloquially, a letter sent by a SOLICITOR – usually for a fixed charge – to a debtor who has not paid his debt within a reasonable period of time. It is usually a last resort before taking the matter to court. In a subsequent court action the cost of the letter will be paid by the debtor.

Solvent. ⬦ INSOLVENCY.

Source and disposition of funds. A statement often included with published accounts showing the cash coming in and the cash going out during the financial year, or alternatively, explaining in a slightly different way the alteration in the WORKING CAPITAL.

South sea bubble. Towards the end of the seventeenth century COMPANIES were formed in vast numbers and for quite bizarre purposes, such as importing jackasses from Spain, or in one case for 'purposes to be revealed at a later date'. It was a get-rich-quick period. There was little legal control over companies and no LIMITED LIABILITY. The climax came when the famous South Sea Company, originally formed to explore the South Seas, essayed to buy the NATIONAL DEBT and issued SHARES for this purpose. To do this cheaply it attempted to increase the VALUE of its own shares by creating a fictitious market. For a long period it did nothing but lend money for the purchase of its own shares (which were issued at frequent intervals). Very soon the whole country became involved, and large fortunes were both made and lost. Thomas Guy built Guy's Hospital with the profit he made. Little was done to stop the process, as both Parliament and the king were involved financially. The company failed in 1720 when public confidence suddenly disappeared because money lent out and profits made, rather than come back in for the acquisition of shares, were used for the purchase of land. This company formed in 1711, the biggest this country has ever seen, suddenly disappeared from the scene (as did the SECRETARY) leaving behind financial chaos and a great deal of misery. It was over a hundred years later that parliament allowed the formation of companies again and then only on very strict conditions.

Sovereign. A British coin made of 22 ◊ CARAT gold equal to £1 sterling. The standard weight is 123.27 grains. The coin is not LEGAL TENDER.

Special buyer. BANK OF ENGLAND official responsible for OPEN MARKET OPERATIONS in TREASURY BILLS. The Bank does not itself enter the market but works through a DISCOUNT HOUSE. The special buyer is an AGENT of the discount house.

Special delivery. ◊ POST OFFICE: SPECIAL DELIVERY.

Special deposits. These are deposits made with the BANK OF ENGLAND by JOINT STOCK BANKS, at the direction of the government. This is a means of restricting credit in a period of inflation. The joint stock banks lend in proportion to the money deposited with them, that is, credit given is directly in proportion to total cash held, e.g. 1–20. The special deposits are a means of reducing this cash and therefore reducing the amount of credit accordingly. Special deposits are distinct from current balances which the joint stock banks have with the Bank of England.

Special endorsement. BILLS OF EXCHANGE are sometimes endorsed to a named person.

Special manager. For the LIQUIDATION of a company, the OFFICIAL RECEIVER, with the approval of the court, may appoint a special manager if the nature of the business calls for specialized knowledge, or the CREDITORS or CONTRIBUTORIES require protection. His remuneration is fixed by the court and he must give security. He must account to the Official Receiver. He has the powers of an ordinary RECEIVER and manager, or other powers that the court decides. A special manager may also be appointed by the Official Receiver in a BANKRUPTCY where a creditor asks him to do so and can show that it is necessary to the carrying on of the business. When a TRUSTEE is appointed the special manager's duties finish. His remuneration is fixed by the creditors. He can be removed by the Official Receiver or by a special resolution of the creditors.

Special resolution. ⟡ RESOLUTION, SPECIAL.

Speciality contract. A CONTRACT BY DEED, signed, sealed and delivered.

Speciality debt. A debt which is not barred until twelve years have elapsed, e.g. a DIVIDEND, a call on shares.

Specie. Term used for coins as opposed to BULLION or BANK NOTES.

Specific performance. A court may order a CONTRACT to be completed rather than award damages to the party who has claimed that he has suffered loss. This is an equitable remedy and will only be awarded where the contract is fair between the parties, enforceable by both, and capable of supervision by the court.

Specifications. ⟡ EXPORTERS' DECLARATIONS.

Speculation. A sophisticated form of GAMBLING, often on business dealings.

Speculator. One who invests money in a risky venture in the hope of earning a high profit or capital gain: a sophisticated kind of gambler. The attractions of SPECULATION at one time lay in the fact that capital profits were not taxable. This of course no longer applies. ⟡ CAPITAL GAINS TAX.

Spit. A weapon used by Customs authorities to discover whether dutiable GOODS are hidden in other cargo.

Spot transactions. Dealings in cash rather than in credit or for FUTURES, particularly on the STOCK EXCHANGE.

Stag. A STOCK EXCHANGE term for an individual who buys heavily on a new issue of STOCKS or SHARES in the expectation that the price will rise very quickly, and earn him a large profit. He normally holds shares only for a very short time.

Stakeholder. A person involved in a ⟡ WAGERING CONTRACT or ⟡ GAMING CONTRACT who holds the money pending the outcome of the wager with the view to paying it over to the winner. Generally speaking, these contracts are void and no legal action can be taken to recover money on a bet, but it is possible to recover money from a stakeholder before he has paid over the winnings.

Stale cheque. A cheque drawn a long time previously which a bank will no longer accept.

Stamp duty. Many documents must be stamped at a local stamping office. These include certain agreements to sell land or interest in it, ANNUITIES, ARTICLES OF ASSOCIATION, TRUSTEE appointments, leases, MEMORANDUMS OF ASSOCIATION, POWERS OF ATTORNEY, and PROXIES (all 50p); conveyances, covenants, DEEDS, DIVIDEND WARRANTS, CONTRACT NOTES and INSURANCE POLICIES (AD VALOREM). The amount of money raised on stamp duty is quite considerable.

Standard costing. A costing technique which uses predetermined standards. A product is costed on the basis of a budgeted output. Where the output has been fixed, the amount of material then needed is known, as is the amount of labour. The amount of OVERHEADS is taken to be fixed. Each product then has a fixed material cost, a fixed DIRECT LABOUR cost and an overhead charge probably related to DIRECT EXPENSES. There is therefore a standard profit for the period. Actual cost will not correspond to budgeted cost, but the differences are handled through accounts known as variance accounts and the amount charged to any particular job or product is not altered until the standards are altered.

Standard deviation. A statistical term for the average deviation of numbers in a series, from the MEAN. It is normally found by squaring and summing the differences between the numbers and the mean, dividing this total by the number of numbers and taking the square root.

Standing order. An instruction to a BANK to pay a certain sum at certain intervals, for instance subscriptions or HIRE PURCHASE instalments.

Starboard. ⟡ LARBOARD.

Statement in lieu of prospectus. A statement that must be issued and delivered to the Registrar of Companies in the form prescribed by the Fifth Schedule to the Companies Act 1948, where SHARES or DEBENTURES are to be allotted by a COMPANY and no PROSPECTUS is being issued. The statement must be issued three days before the ALLOTMENT.

Statement of affairs. Any statement of accounts which shows the financial position of a person or organization at a particular time. A BALANCE SHEET is a good example.

Statement of affairs: bankruptcy. ⟡ BANKRUPTCY: STATEMENT OF AFFAIRS.

Statistic. A collection of figures arranged to illustrate a particular point.

Statistics and Market Intelligence Library. A specialized service for exporters, providing trade and other economic statistics on foreign and commonwealth countries. It also provides catalogues of overseas manufactures and overseas trade directories. Address: Board of Trade, Hillgate House, 35 Old Bailey, London EC4.

Status inquiry. An inquiry addressed to, for example, a BANK by a person who wishes to discover the credit-worthiness of a prospective customer.

Statute law. That part of the law that owes its origin to Acts of Parliament. It should be distinguished from Common Law, which is built on custom and precedent. ◊ COMMON LAW.

Statute-barred debt. A debt that cannot be recovered at law because its time limit has elapsed. The time limit within which action must be taken is set out in the Limitation Act 1939: it is six years for an ordinary debt, or twelve years for a debt under seal. The time runs from the end of the credit period. ◊ LIMITATIONS OF ACTIONS.

The time can begin to run again if the debtor acknowledges the debt. This may be by making a part payment, or by acknowledging the debt in writing. The debt may also be revived if the debtor does anything which admits the continuing existence of the debt.

Statutory books. The books which a COMPANY is bound by law to keep. These are *inter alia* (1) a REGISTER OF MEMBERS, (2) a REGISTER OF DIRECTORS and secretaries, (3) a REGISTER OF CHARGES, and (4) minute books.

The company must also keep 'proper books of account' where all its transactions are recorded and which generally speaking, must be sufficient to enable annual accounts to be properly produced.

Failure to keep these books in the manner directed, can lead to heavy fines for the OFFICERS OF THE COMPANY who happen to be in default.

Statutory companies: transfer of shares. ◊ CONTRACT BY DEED.

Statutory report. This states (1) the number of SHARES allotted, distinguishing those paid for or partly paid for in cash from those paid for or partly paid for in kind (the method of payment must be given), (2) total cash received by the COMPANY in respect of shares, (3) details of receipts and payments of the company to a date within seven days of the report, distinguishing receipts from shares, DEBENTURES and other sources; and also an estimate of the ◊ PRELIMINARY EXPENSES of the company, (4) names, addresses and descriptions of the DIRECTORS, AUDITORS if any, managers if any, and SECRETARY, (5) details of any CONTRACT to be modified at the meeting, with details of the modifications. The report should be certified by the auditors, if any, and must be delivered to the Registrar of Companies. It must also be sent to each member fourteen days before the statutory meeting. These regulations do not apply to PRIVATE COMPANIES.

Stay of proceedings. During the WINDING-UP of a COMPANY, the court may suspend proceedings pending against the company after a petition has been presented. ⟡ CESSER OF ACTION.

Stepped costs. Another name for SEMI-VARIABLE COSTS.

Sterling. The currency of the United Kingdom: the unit is the pound sterling.

Sterling area. The group of countries with Great Britain at the head agreeing to permit fairly free transfer of funds amongst themselves and to operate joint control over exchanges of sterling area currencies for external currencies. The currencies of the sterling area countries are officially linked to the pound. For the purposes of the Exchange Control Act 1947, the countries are known as the Scheduled Territories.

Sterling area countries. These are countries using U.K. currency as a trading or reserve currency. In 1969 these were: the British Commonwealth (except Canada and Rhodesia), the Irish Republic, British Trust Territories, British Protectorates and Protected States, Iceland, Jordan, Kuwait, Libya, South Africa, South West Africa, and Western Samoa.

Sterling balances. Reference is often made to an influx or inflow of money into this country. This means that persons are buying ⟡ STERLING on the London Market in exchange for their own currencies. Similarly selling sterling on the London Market in exchange for foreign currencies is called an outflow of money, or even a 'flight from sterling'. Whether or not foreigners wish to hold sterling balances depends on the confidence they have in the stability of the pound and also in the interest rates being offered in London (which are governed by the BANK RATE). Sterling balances may obviously arise initially from an unfavourable balance of trade.

Steward. One who manages the provision on board ship, or one who manages an estate on behalf of another.

Stipend. Another word for salary.

Stock. As opposed to STOCK-IN-TRADE, a stock is similar to ⟡ SHARES. The difference is that whereas shares are issued in specified amounts e.g. £1, £10, etc., stock is sold in undefined quantities. Shares cannot be converted into stock unless they are fully paid. The word 'stock' is also used to describe government loans.

Stock exchange. The London Stock Exchange, founded in 1773 at the corner of Threadneedle Street and Screetings Alley, by ⟡ STOCK-

BROKERS who were rather tired of meeting in coffee houses. Its members are ⟡ STOCKJOBBERS and stockbrokers. It is essentially a place where STOCKS, SHARES, and SECURITIES are bought and sold. PRICES fluctuate according to supply and demand. The Stock Exchange publishes an OFFICAL LIST of share prices daily. To obtain a QUOTATION in the Stock Exchange certain conditions, stated to be for the benefit of the public, must be fulfilled.

There are local exchanges (for instance, at Cardiff and Birmingham), but 'the Stock Exchange' usually means the London one. It has a visitors' gallery open from Monday to Friday from 10 a.m. to 3.15 p.m., admission free. There are guides in attendance, and also a cinema where colour films about the Stock Exchange are shown. Its motto is '*Dictum meum pactum*' – 'My word is my bond'.

Stock-in-trade. An accounting term which appears in many BALANCE SHEETS, sometimes abbreviated to 'stocks'. It applies to the quantities of raw materials or finished goods in hand, and is often coupled with ⟡ WORK IN PROGRESS.

Stock valuation. Valuation of STOCK-IN-TRADE for accounting purposes. Where any one business is concerned, the most important thing is consistency. There are various methods of valuation, among them: (1) unit-cost: the fundamental method – each item is priced at its actual cost; (2) F.I.F.O. ('first in first out'): GOODS are priced on the assumption that the first goods purchased are the first goods used and therefore that stock-in-hand should be valued at current PRICES; (3) average cost: goods are valued by averaging the cost of goods brought forward, with the cost of goods purchased during the ACCOUNTING PERIOD; (4) STANDARD COST: a predetermined or budgeted cost per unit; (5) L.I.F.O. ('last in first out'): goods are valued on the assumption that those purchased most recently are the first to be used, and that the goods in stock are likely to be old and so will not be valued at the current buying price, but at the first recorded cost of purchase; (6) base stock: often used in retail businesses – the assumption is that stock is constant in quantity and therefore given a fixed value, based on its original cost, this VALUE being used for all accounting purposes; (7) adjusted selling price: sometimes used in retail businesses – stock is valued at selling price less expected profit and selling expenses.

None of these methods is entirely satisfactory. Where the present selling price of the stock is less than the figure any valuation method reveals, the selling price should be used instead.

Stockbroker. An intermediary between the public and the STOCK-JOBBERS. He acts as AGENT for his clients and works for a fixed

COMMISSION (normally about 1p in the pound for shares and rather less for government STOCKS). All recognized stockbrokers must be members of one of the STOCK EXCHANGES. There are about 3,000 of them. A list can be obtained from the Stock Exchange. Members of the Stock Exchange are not allowed to advertise for business.

Stockbroker, default of. Members of the London STOCK EXCHANGE occasionally find themselves INSOLVENT, and are HAMMERED. For the protection of clients who may otherwise suffer, the Stock Exchange has set up a central fund from which compensation may be paid. This fund is subscribed by members.

Stockist. A MARKETING term for a person who agrees to hold certain minimum stocks of a specified manufactured product in return for special buying terms, entitling him perhaps to a particularly favourable discount.

Stockjobber. Originally a trader in STOCKS and SHARES. Traditionally these met in the Royal Exchange and the coffee houses of the City of London. In 1773 the Stock Exchange replaced these meeting places. Jobbers now act as wholesalers dealing in stocks and shares and are approached by the public through STOCKBROKERS. Jobbers must be members of the STOCK EXCHANGE.

There are about 620 jobbers in the London Stock Exchange. They tend to specialize in types of shares. They quote shares at two prices: a buying price and a selling price. The difference is known as the JOBBER'S TURN. Stockjobbing as a separate trade from broking is peculiar to England. Quoted share prices are normally the jobbers' MEAN PRICES.

Stolen goods. If GOODS are obtained by LARCENY, the thief has no TITLE to pass to any person and therefore the goods can be reclaimed at any time by the true owner. Where stolen goods are sold in MARKET OVERT, the property reverts when the thief is convicted. Where the goods have not been stolen but obtained by false pretences, for instance from an owner who was misled as to the credit-worthiness of a so-called purchaser, then that purchaser could give a good title to an innocent third party.

Stop for freight. Orders given to a dock authority by a shipowner or broker, not to allow delivery of GOODS until FREIGHT has been paid.

Stop order. A customer may give a STOCKBROKER instructions to sell should PRICES fall below a certain level.

Stopover. A break in a journey agreed to in advance by the carrier.

Stoppage in transitu. The seller of GOODS or documents of TITLE may retake them from the carrier before the buyer has taken possession, though only if the buyer has become INSOLVENT.

Straight line method. In calculating DEPRECIATION, the cost or agreed value of an ASSET is written off over its expected life by charging equal amounts against profit each year.

Stranding. A MARINE INSURANCE term once defined as: 'a taking of the ground by the vessel, which does not happen solely from those natural causes which are necessarily incident to the ordinary course of the navigation in which the ship is engaged either wholly or in part, but from some accidental or extraneous causes'.

Street trader. A person who sells out of a suitcase in a street, usually with a delightful line of patter. His main object is to dispose of his GOODS (whose quality he rarely guarantees) before being asked to move on. He may need a LICENCE – this will depend on local by-laws. ◊ CHEAP JACK ◊ HAWKER ◊ PEDLAR.

Stubb's Gazette. A weekly trade paper giving information of value to businessmen on the movements of their CREDITORS and charges made on property by COMPANIES or other persons: in particular, details of creditors' meetings, DEEDS OF ARRANGEMENT, BILLS OF SALES, county court judgments and information on WINDINGS-UP and BANKRUPTCIES.

Sub-agent. ◊ AGENT ◊ DELEGATUS NON POTEST DELEGARE.

Subdivision of capital. ◊ CONSOLIDATION OF CAPITAL.

Subpoena. A court order to appear at a specific place at a specific time.

Subrogation. A term used in CONTRACTS of INSURANCE, GUARANTEE, etc. It refers to the right of the insurer, etc., to stand in the shoes of the person whose claim he has paid and to take over not only what is left of the property, but all the legal and equitable rights of the insured person, including the right to sue a third party for damages. If an insurer pays for a total loss he may take over the subject matter and rights attaching to it; in a partial loss he may take over the rights but not the subject matter.

Subscriber. A person who puts his name to the MEMORANDUM OF ASSOCIATION of a COMPANY. A PUBLIC COMPANY must have at least seven and they must take at least one SHARE each. They must be named and described (they may be MINORS or aliens) and their signatures must be witnessed. Their duties are to pay for their shares, to sign the ARTICLES OF ASSOCIATION, to appoint the first DIRECTORS and to act for the directors until they are appointed. The subscriber becomes a member by signing; neither allotment nor registration is necessary. He must take his share directly from the company and not from another subscriber.

Subscriber capital. ◊ AUTHORIZED CAPITAL ◊ ISSUED CAPITAL.

Subsidiary company. By the Companies Act 1948, a COMPANY is a subsidiary of another company: (1) if that other company is a member of it and controls the composition of its board of DIRECTORS, (2) if that other company holds more than half (in nominal value) of its equity SHARE CAPITAL, or (3) if it is a subsidiary of any company which is a subsidiary of the first company. The parent company is known as the holding company.

Subsidy. Effectively, a method of supporting a PRICE. The Government subsidizes prices when it allows GOODS to be sold at a price lower than the market price, by giving the seller the difference between the SELLING PRICE and a viable one. The term subsidy is also used for a sum of money given by one person to another to help him over a difficult period.

Substantial and individual interest in shares. ◊ NOMINEE SHAREHOLDERS.

Subvention payments. EX-GRATIA payments made by one COMPANY in a group to another, possibly to show a better profit picture. At one time these were important for tax purposes, but their importance is now very much less.

Sue and labour, clause. A MARINE INSURANCE clause allowing the insured to take any steps necessary to mitigate a loss.

Suez Canal clause. A MARINE INSURANCE clause stipulating that taking ground in the canal is not stranding. However, the insurers will be responsible for loss resulting directly from doing this.

Supercargo. A person travelling with a merchant ship to look after the cargo and perhaps obtain additional cargo *en voyage*.

Supermarket. A misused term often used for self-service MULTIPLE STORES. Strictly it is an organization where many traders do business on their own account under the same roof, i.e. where there are a number of shops on the same premises. The owners of the premises take their profit from the charges made to the traders, rather than from the turnover. They supply the premises and all the various services for the benefit of traders and shoppers. Supermarkets are popular obviously because the housewife can complete her shopping in one building.

Supervening impossibility. ◊ FRUSTRATION OF CONTRACT.

Surety. ◊ GUARANTEE.

Surrender value. An ASSURANCE term for the amount a person will receive if he cashes in his policy before the date of its maturity. In life ASSURANCE policies that have not run for a very long time, it will often be less than the amount actually paid.

Surtax. A tax paid by those earning over £2,000 *per annum*. This taxable figure is reached after adding income from various sources. DIVIDENDS, etc., must be shown gross, but long-term capital gains are not included. Deductions may be made for *inter alia*: (1) ANNUITIES but not payments under DEED OF COVENANT, (2) INCOME TAX losses, (3) interest to BUILDING SOCIETIES, (4) the various personal allowances other than the single allowance of £255: e.g. marriage allowance less single allowance, children allowance, dependent relative allowance etc., (5) EARNED-INCOME RELIEF (but not WIFE'S EARNED-INCOME RELIEF), (6) an earnings allowance of £2,000 or a sum (if less) that would reduce the earned income, after earned-income relief, to £2,000. Where all income is earned, these allowances mean that surtax is not payable on incomes below £5,000.

The tax is payable in arrears on 1 January following the year of assessment (a husband or wife may apply for separate assessment). The maximum rate at present is 10s. in the pound.

Surveyor of customs. The superintending officer of a Customs house station or WAREHOUSE.

T

Table A. An appendix to the Companies Act 1948 giving a prototype for the ARTICLES OF ASSOCIATION of a COMPANY. It may be, and often is, adopted in part or whole.

Takers-in. Persons prepared to carry over commitments for BULLS by taking up the STOCK that the bull does not wish to, or cannot, pay for at that particular time.

Take-over bid. An OFFER made to the shareholders of a COMPANY by a person or organization intending to gain control of the company. If the company is quoted on the STOCK EXCHANGE the bidder is expected to observe certain recommendations. ▷ CITY CODE ON TAKE-OVERS. These have no legal force but failure to observe them is not always advantageous.

If a person owns a certain proportion of the SHARES of the company, a minimum of 90 per cent, he can apply to the court for an order entitling him to purchase the shares he does not already hold at a PRICE approved by the court. Similarly the shareholders may insist that their shares are purchased.

Bids may be conditional or unconditional: the bidder may offer a price for the shares but make the offer conditional upon receiving a sufficient number of acceptances to give him control. When he is satisfied that he has received sufficient acceptances, he may then make the offer unconditional.

Tally. A piece of wood once used for recording a debt or payment, and once also a formal receipt given for a loan to the Exchequer or sovereign. It is also a distinguishing mark on an item or bale of merchandise.

Tallyman. This could be (1) one who sells GOODS on credit to be paid for by instalments, (2) a form of ACCOUNTANT, or (3) a person who checks off a ship's cargo against a list.

Talon. This concerns SHARE CERTIFICATES or loan certificates. It is a slip of paper to be sent to the COMPANY, or other authority to obtain new dividend COUPONS when the supply of them has been exhausted.

Tare. An allowance for packing, etc., made in establishing the weight of GOODS. Tares may be actual, agreed by custom, or estimated.

Target. The monthly publication of the British Productivity Council. It prints, *inter alia*, case histories to prove British Productivity

Council slogans. It is non-political and free of government control.

Tariff. Generally a list of charges established by an organization for services or GOODS. For instance, a hotel tariff is the list of charges for various rooms, meals, accommodation over a period, etc.

The word also has specialized meanings: (1) The Customs authorities issue a tariff showing dutiable goods together with the amount of duty payable. (2) There are what are known as two-part tariffs, where a set basic charge is made together with an additional charge which varies with the CONTRACT. For instance, a subscriber pays a set rental for a telephone, plus an additional charge which varies with the number of calls. (3) The term is also applied where one rate is charged up to a certain maximum and a higher or lower rate for purchases or orders above this level.

Tariff advantages overseas. There are various tariff advantages available in different areas overseas. The more important are: (1) those associated with the ◊ EUROPEAN FREE TRADE ASSOCIATION, (2) Commonwealth tariff advantages (◊ IMPERIAL PREFERENCE), (3) Kennedy Round tariff cuts: a fairly recent agreement to reduce tariffs substantially in important overseas markets, e.g. the EUROPEAN ECONOMIC COMMUNITY, Japan and the United States. The reductions are to be staggered over the years 1968–72. The agreements are supervised by the ◊ GENERAL AGREEMENT ON TARIFFS AND TRADE. For detailed information apply to the Board of Trade, Exports Services Branch, Hillgate House, 35 Old Bailey, London EC4, or to Her Majesty's Stationery Office, (4) advantages available in the Irish Republic. There was an agreement in 1966 to eliminate almost all protection over ten years.

For information apply Board of Trade, Commercial Relations and Exports Department, 1 Victoria Street, London SW1.

Tariff offices. INSURANCE companies or offices which charge rates set by an organization to which they belong, for instance the Accident Offices Association. Non-tariff offices are free to quote their own rates of INSURANCE PREMIUM.

Tasting order. An order given to a specified person to taste wines, spirits, etc., stored in dock WAREHOUSES before making any purchase or SALE.

Tax deduction card. This is concerned with P.A.Y.E. (◊ PAY AS YOU EARN). When an employer deducts tax from wages or salaries, details of gross pay, tax deducted, net pay, and contributions to the graduated pensions scheme, are entered on a tax deduction card. These cards are submitted to the Inland Revenue at the end of the tax year.

Tax equalization account. ⟡ DEFERRED TAXATION.

Tax reserve certificates. Certificates may be purchased from the State and surrendered in payment of tax. This is to enable persons or businesses to have money available to pay tax when the tax is due. They may be cashed at any time. They earn INTEREST but the interest is greater when the certificate is used for payment of tax. The interest is exempt from INCOME TAX, SURTAX, CAPITAL GAINS TAX and CORPORATION TAX.

Taxation: income tax annual return. Every person is obliged to notify the tax inspector of any income he receives, or any changes in his source of income. Nor will he obtain INCOME TAX ALLOWANCES unless he claims them from the tax inspector: to do this he must complete an annual return. Where P.A.Y.E. (⟡ PAY AS YOU EARN) is concerned, the employee will have a code number based on his allowances. If he has made no return, he will have no code number and will be taxed at an emergency rate: this can lead to over-taxation and the fuss and bother of making a repayment claim.

Taxation: marriage. There is no tax on marriage – at one time the State made its own contribution to the festivities by affording certain tax advantages in the year of marriage. Until April 1968, the husband (ignoring the possibility of separate assessment) could claim a full year's marriage allowance, even though the wedding took place only a few days before the end of the tax year. In addition, the wife could claim a full year's allowance on her income before marriage. What is more, the husband could obtain additional personal relief if his wife continued to work after marriage. Consequently, in choosing a wedding date, it was advisable where possible to allow the wife to earn more than her total allowances as a spinster before marriage and also allow her to earn more than the additional personal relief after marriage.

These benefits have been considerably reduced by the Finance Act 1968. The marriage relief which the husband can claim (the excess of the marriage relief over the single relief) is reduced by one-twelfth for every month between the beginning of the tax year and the date of the marriage. The husband can elect to be treated as a single person for that year, if it proves more advantageous.

Taxation: net United Kingdom rate. U.K. tax paid by a company where, due to the fact that it is paying overseas tax plus U.K. tax, the net or average rate is less than the U.K. standard rate. ⟡ INCOME TAX: STANDARD RATE.

Taxation of interest. ⟡ MORTGAGE INTEREST ⟡ BUILDING SOCIETY INTEREST ⟡ BANK INTEREST.

Taxation of profits. Any person earning profits from any business activity, whether these are CAPITAL PROFITS, or income profits, must pay tax on them. Taxation of capital profits is dealt with by ◊ CAPITAL GAINS TAX. COMPANY profits are taxed at present by means of CORPORATION TAX plus DIVIDEND TAX. For any other type of business, not a company and not a non-profit-making association, tax is assessed on the persons owning the business. They may pay tax, partly on the salaries they draw – these will be Schedule E (◊ TAXATION SCHEDULES) and tax will probably be paid by P.A.Y.E. (◊ PAY AS YOU EARN) – and partly on the profits shown by their annual accounts (after deduction of salary). The profits taken as taxable are those of the accounting year ending in the year preceding the year of assessment, e.g. the profits for the year to 31 December 1967 would form the basis for the tax year 1968–9. Special provisions apply to the opening years of a business and to its closing years. The profits shown by the accounts may have to be adjusted as not all items deducted from income for business purposes are allowed for tax purposes. Losses can usually be carried forward to following years or may be set against income from other sources. If the business is a PARTNERSHIP, tax is payable on total profits by the firm after account has been taken of the allowances due to individual partners. The tax is collected from the firm but any partner could be sued personally for the total.

Taxation schedules. Headings used to facilitate the collection of INCOME TAX. The Schedules are:

(A) now obsolete, but previously dealing with land and buildings,

(B) woodlands managed commercially, unless the owner prefers to be assessed under Case (1) Schedule (D),

(C) INTEREST or DIVIDENDS on government, public authority, and certain overseas funds,

(D) Case (1) trades and businesses; Case (2) professions and vocations; Case (3) interest where tax is not deducted at source etc., Case (4) SECURITIES overseas; Case (5) possessions overseas; Case (6) profits, etc., not included in any other Case or Schedule; Case (7) short-term capital gains; Case (8) income from land or property,

(E) income from employment, normally P.A.Y.E.,

(F) company distributions.

Taxation: separate assessment. A husband and wife are normally taxed as one person. However, either may claim to be separately assessed. The claim must be made within six months before 6 July of the year of assessment. Allowances and reliefs are apportioned between the two parties and both are responsible for paying their own tax.

Taxation: taxable income. All income arising in the United Kingdom is taxable; income from abroad received by persons considered resident in the United Kingdom is also taxable. Where a person is not resident in the United Kingdom but domiciled abroad or, being British, is ordinarily resident abroad, only overseas income actually remitted to the United Kingdom is taxed. A visitor to the United Kingdom is considered resident if present there for more than six months. Persons may also be considered resident if, although they spend less than six months *per annum* in the United Kingdom, they make frequent visits or maintain a place of residence there.

Taxi. A vehicle licensed to ply for hire, that is, to roam the streets looking for passengers wishing to be conveyed privately to destinations previously unspecified. A taxi normally has a meter showing the cost of the journey.

Taxis should be distinguished from vehicles operated by CAR HIRE firms. Certain firms have vehicles licensed to carry passengers which can be ordered (e.g. by telephone) for a specific journey, but these are not allowed to ply for hire. They may often be called taxis but it is illegal for them to stop in the street at the request of a passer-by.

Tea auctions. Auctions held three times a week at Plantation House, Mincing Lane, London EC3. Tea is sampled by selling BROKERS and buyers – the buyers making notes on their catalogues. Buying brokers must give the names of their principals within twenty-four hours of any purchase and the seller must approve the name. Brokers sometimes act as both selling and buying brokers. Payment consists of a deposit paid to the selling broker in exchange for a weight note, plus the balance paid on prompt day, three months after the sale. Indian tea is auctioned on Monday and Wednesday and Ceylon tea on Tuesday.

Technical Development Capital Ltd. This was formed in January 1962 by Commonwealth INSURANCE companies, MERCHANT BANKS, etc. Its CAPITAL was to be £2,000,000. Administration is the responsibility of the INDUSTRIAL AND COMMERCIAL FINANCE CORPORATION. The purpose is to help industrialists with projects which have passed the research stage but which lack finance to put them into production. Generally speaking the project must be shown to be workable and if necessary could be patented. Technical Development Capital Limited normally takes a share in the equity though with the intention of selling out at the appropriate time; it does not insist on control.

Telegrams. ◊ POST OFFICE: TELEGRAMS.

Telegraphic address. Because telegrams are paid for according to the number of words, including the address of the recipient, it is customary for organizations, particularly the larger ones, to apply to the POST OFFICE for a telegraphic address. This may consist of one word and is sufficient to identify the organization. A fee is payable.

Telephones. ◊ POST OFFICE: TELEPHONES.

Telex service. ◊ POST OFFICE: TELEX SERVICE.

Teller. A BANK clerk who gives and takes money across the counter.

Temporary exports. Certain GOODS to be used as SAMPLES or exhibits and to be reimported may be initially exported free of duty if certain Customs procedures are observed. ◊ CARNET.

Tenancy in common. A situation where persons held land in common, but could deal separately with their shares. Tenancies in common have been virtually abolished by the Law of Property Act 1925, but are still possible in this instance only: where land is to belong to a number of persons in common, it is vested in, say, the first four persons mentioned in the DEED, and these hold it in trust for all the persons interested. Those four persons are legally tenants in common. This does not apply to charities.

Tender: capital issues. ◊ SHARES are occasionally issued by tender. The COMPANY issuing the shares asks for tenders for them, at PRICES above a certain minimum. Tenders will be made at various prices. If an OFFER is made for all the shares at the highest price, this will be accepted. Otherwise the shares will be issued at the highest practicable price, so that all shares will be disposed of. This means that persons offering the highest prices may receive the shares for less. This method of share issue has a certain popularity – it minimizes the possibility of ◊ STAG dealings.

Tender: sale of goods. ◊ INVITATION TO TREAT: ◊ OFFER.

Tenor. A BILL OF EXCHANGE may be payable sometime in the future. The length of this time is known as the tenor of the bill.

Terminal costing. A cost accounting term for the costing of building and engineering contracts, etc.

Terminal markets. A market, particularly a commodity market, which deals in FUTURES.

Territorial waters. Those waters next to the coast of a country over which sovereignty is claimed. This is intended to prevent ships of other countries from, for instance, fishing in these waters. There is some doubt as to the limit of these waters: some countries claim three miles, some six, some twelve; sometimes different areas are claimed for different purposes, for instance twelve miles for fishing, six miles for other purposes.

Third class paper. ◊ BILLS OF EXCHANGE, particularly commercial bills, tend to be graded. The grades vary with the reputation of the acceptors, so that there are first class, second class, and third class bills.

Third party insurance. When a person takes out a policy of INSURANCE against a risk that involves damage to a third party, i.e. someone not himself a party to the CONTRACT, this is known as third party insurance. It is compulsory for road vehicles, it is also common in contracts concerning employer's liability, public liability, etc. When necessary, the third party can sue the insurance company if the person paying the premium fails to do so. This is an exception to the general rule that a person not a party to a contract has no cause of action.

Third party's liabilities to and from. ◊ THIRD PARTY INSURANCE ◊ CONTRACT, PRIVITY OF ◊ RESALE PRICE MAINTENANCE ◊ NEGLIGENCE OF AUDITORS.

Threadneedle Street. The BANK OF ENGLAND has been known familiarly as the Old Lady of Threadneedle Street since the eighteenth century. The street was associated, at one time, with the tailoring trade, and contained the Merchant Taylors' Hall. Already in 1598 the name of the street appears to have been Threadneedle Street.

Ticket. A ticket should be distinguished from a RECEIPT. Tickets are issued (for cash) particularly for transport or entertainment. They are usually an essential part of the CONTRACT, and contain conditions of the OFFER or else refer to the existence of these conditions and state where they are to be found. The contract is not closed until the customer accepts the ticket and hands over the money.
A RECEIPT on the other hand is an acknowledgement of payment of a debt already due, and cannot contain further conditions applicable to the contract.

Ticket day. A STOCK EXCHANGE term for the day when the STOCK-BROKERS give the names of the buyers to the sellers for the purpose of settling transactions. The slip of paper on which the name is given is known as a ticket. This is also sometimes called Name Day. ◊ ACCOUNT DAY.

Time and motion study. This is one part of ◊ WORK STUDY.

Time bargain. A STOCK EXCHANGE term for dealings in FUTURES.

Time card. A card used to record hours worked by an employee who is paid on a time basis. ◊ CLOCK CARD.

Time clerk. Person working in a ◊ TIME OFFICE.

Time charter. The hiring of a ship, or space in it, for a particular time. The ship might make any number of voyages within that time.

Time office. That office in a factory concerned principally with recording the hours worked by employees who are paid on a time basis.

Tip. Either (1) slang for information passed by one person to another, enabling him to profit financially, or (2) a ◊ GRATUITY.

Tithe. Strictly 'a tenth part'. At one time people were expected to give a tenth part of their income to the Church, for the upkeep of their parish church and priest. These tithes were the principal means of support of the clergy and a living was often judged by the tithes attached to it. In course of time they have tended to become fixed payments made at regular intervals and unrelated to the income of the payer.

Title. ◊ SALE OF GOODS: TITLE.

Token coins. Coins, the actual value of whose metal is less than their token value.

Tolls. Charges made for using certain roads, bridges, canal locks, etc. The monies collected are intended to pay for their building and upkeep.

Tommy shops. At one time it was the practice for wages to be paid partly in kind and partly in tokens. These tokens could only be used at the COMPANY'S or factory's shop and good value was not normally given. These shops became known as tommy-shops. It was a much abused practice and abolished by the Truck Acts 1831. This is probably the origin of the words 'tommy rot'.

Tonnage. The cubic capacity of a ship, not necessarily related to its carrying capacity. A ton is 100 cubic feet. Tonnage dues are payable when a ship enters or leaves port.

Tort. That branch of the law dealing with civil actions arising from breach of a duty imposed by common law or statute and dealing with injuries to the person or his property. It should be distinguished from the law of contract which deals with breaches of duties arising out of transactions entered into by mutual consent. Examples of offences in tort would be trespassing, deceit.

Total assets. The total of all the ASSETS employed in a business. This must be distinguished from ◊ NET ASSETS. ◊ CAPITAL EMPLOYED.

Tote system (British Rail). The basis of this is the tote bin, a container specially designed for bulk handling and transport of materials in granular, powder or liquid form. The bins are made of heavy-duty aluminium, in three sizes designed to fit compactly into railway wagons. They are weather-proof, dust-proof, and proof against spillage. Materials are put directly into the bins by the manufacturer and moved by fork-lift trucks to the loading bay for transfer to railway vehicles which then take them to the rail terminal. The same system operates at the other end. Tote bins can be purchased or hired – the weight of the bin is not included in the FREIGHT charge.

Towage. The charge made for towing a ship.

Town and Country Planning Association. Founded in 1899, this is an independent, non-sectarian, all-party body concerned with every aspect of town and country planning. It seeks a national policy of land-use planning aimed at improving living and working conditions, advancing industrial and business efficiency, safeguarding green belts and the best farm land, and enhancing natural, architectural, and cultural amenities. It also supports maximum freedom for private and local initiative. Membership fees are a minimum 3 gns *per annum* for individuals, 5 gns for organizations. Monthly journal: *Town and Country Planning*. Details can be obtained from the Planning Centre, 28 King Street, Covent Garden, London WC2.

Town clearing. ◊ CLEARING, TOWN AND GENERAL.

Trade bill. A BILL OF EXCHANGE drawn on and accepted by traders. Whether these bills are marketable depends on the standing of the ACCEPTOR. Such bills are normally discounted with BANKS rather than DISCOUNT HOUSES, and INTEREST rates may vary.

Trade creditor. An accounting term for a person to whom money is owed in the course of trade.

Trade cycle. PRICES and employment do not remain stable but tend to move upwards (◊ BOOM) and downwards (◊ SLUMP) in an irregular pattern. This movement is known as the trade cycle.

Trade Descriptions Act 1968. This replaces the Merchandise Marks Acts 1887 and 1953. The Act contains various provisions prohibiting *inter alia* 'misdescriptions of GOODS, services, accommodation and facilities provided in the course of trade' and 'false or misleading indications as to the PRICE of goods'. A trade description may refer *inter alia* to quantity, size, gauge, history of ownership, fitness for purpose, performance, accuracy, testing, approval by some other organization and authority, method or place of manufacture. The trade description may be attached to the goods in fact, or by implication, or may be contained in an advertisement. It may be in writing or oral. It is false if false to a material degree, or misleading. It is also an offence to imply royal approval without having it. Penalties for offences are (1) on summary conviction, a fine not exceeding £400, and (2) on conviction on indictment, a term of imprisonment not exceeding two years, in addition to the fine. ◊ RETAIL TRADING-STANDARDS ASSOCIATION.

Trade investments. Investments by one business in another with an end in view such as controlling sources of raw material, or SALES outlets. Trade investments often form a separate heading in the accounts of limited COMPANIES, though this is not legally necessary.

Trade mark. A particular mark or motif employed by a manufacturer to identify and often to advertise his GOODS. Trade marks may be registered at the ◊ PATENT OFFICE. There is a registration fee and an annual renewal fee, but registration protects the manufacturer against wrongful use of the mark by competitors.

Trade price. The PRICE paid by a retailer to a wholesaler for GOODS to be resold.

Trading certificate. The certificate issued to a PUBLIC COMPANY by the Registrar of Companies enabling it to commence business. A public company can only commence business if it has satisfied certain conditions. These are: (1) SHARES must have been allotted up to the minimum subscription and paid for in cash; (2) DIRECTORS must have taken up and paid for their shares; they need not have paid for them in full if the total amount on that type of share has not been called; (3) no monies may be due for repayment to applicants for shares or DEBENTURES; (4) a certificate must be filed stating that these conditions have been fufilled.

Trading profit or loss. This could be the BALANCE on the ◊ TRADING ACCOUNT. It is normally referred to however as gross profit on trading. The term 'trading profit' is often used in published accounts to mean the profit for the year before charging or crediting exceptional items of expenditure or income, or before including items not directly connected with the primary object of the business.

Trading stamps. Stamps used to encourage purchases. Some shops, etc., issue them to persons in proportion to the VALUE of their purchases. They can then be exchanged for GOODS or money, either at a shop or by post. Stamps are issued by trading stamp companies (these companies also exchange the stamps for goods). Their profit is made by selling the stamps to the retailer for more than the PRICE of the goods. Trading stamps are a RETAILER'S method of giving a discount to customers. The issue, use and redemption of the stamps is governed by the Trading Stamps Act 1964. This restricts the categories of persons who may carry on business in trading stamp schemes. It also states that trading stamps must show a value on the face, together with the name of the issuing company. The holder has a right to obtain cash for stamps within limits. There are WARRANTIES applied to the goods exchanged for stamps: these are similar to those in the Sale of Goods Act 1893. Catalogues and stamp books must contain the name of the PROMOTER. Shops, etc., must display notices enabling the customer to ascertain the number of stamps to which he is entitled; the notice must also state the cash value of the stamps. Shops must supply catalogues for reference purposes.

Tramp steamer. A ship carrying GOODS and offering itself to general hire, not belonging to any particular shipping organization.

Transire. A shipping document used by coasting vessels, listing the GOODS carried, and signed by the master of the ship. There are two copies: one is given up to the Customs authorities as a clearance certificate on leaving port; the other is used as a certificate of entry at the next port.

Transmission of shares. Effectively, the automatic transfer of SHARES not by transfer deed but by what might be called operation of law. Executors, for instance, have a right to be registered as shareholders on production of probate; the Trustee in BANKRUPTCY may have a right to be registered instead of the bankrupt.

Transport shipbuilding credit scheme. A credit scheme which existed from May to October 1963; £75,000,000 was made available to British ship-owners, repayable over ten years at reasonable INTEREST rates.

Trans-shipment. Where GOODS are moved from one ship to another certain Customs regulations must be observed. These vary according to whether the goods are dutiable or not.

Traveller's cheques. These are issued by BANKS for the convenience of persons travelling at home or abroad. They are issued for various amounts, e.g. £1, £5, etc. and can be changed into the currency of the country where the person happens to be.

Treasure trove. Gold and silver found in some hiding place. The word 'trove' derives from the French 'trouve'. Treasure trove must be reported to the police, the Director of the British Museum or the nearest coroner; failure to do so is a criminal offence. The finder is awarded the saleable VALUE of the find, but the treasure itself goes to the legal owner, if traceable.

A jury meets to decide whether the find is really treasure trove, who found it, and to whom it legally belongs. If the owner cannot be traced it belongs to the crown. In Scotland, all treasure trove belongs to the crown.

Treasury bill. A BILL OF EXCHANGE issued by the government and payable in three months. Issued by tender every week in very large amounts. DISCOUNT HOUSES make OFFERS, quoting PRICES. Rates of INTEREST are usually very low. By far the greatest amount of bills dealt with by discount houses are treasury bills: discount houses sometimes sell to the clearing BANKS, but the banks never tender directly. Treasury bills are sometimes allotted to central banks of other countries.

Trial balance. A list of all balances contained in the LEDGER (or ledgers, including the cash book). It is a two column list, DEBIT balances and credit balances being listed separately. The purpose is to check that the totals of each column agree and therefore show that the rules of DOUBLE ENTRY BOOK-KEEPING have been observed. It does not indicate any error arising from a total omission, or an incorrect amount recorded correctly.

Trial of the Pyx. Coins are tested annually at the Royal Mint to ensure they contain the correct ingredients. The test is made by a jury of the Goldsmiths' Company and is known as the Trial of the Pyx.

Trinity House. An organization superintending navigation in British waters. It is responsible for beacons and lighthouses and for appointing pilots. It also conducts the examinations of mariners and is responsible generally for supervising the marine interests of the country.

Troy weight. As opposed to ⟡ AVOIR DUPOIS, this is mostly used in weighing precious stones and gold. Twelve troy oz. = 1 troy lb.; 20 pennyweights = 1 oz.; 24 grains = 1 pennyweight; 7,000 grains = 1 lb. avoir dupois.

Truck. The old practice of forcing workmen to accept GOODS rather than money in payment of wages, often to the employer's advantage. ⟡ TOMMY-SHOPS.

Truckage. A charge made for the use of railway trucks, apart from carriage charges.

True and fair. An auditing term. A BALANCE SHEET is expected to give a true and fair view of a business's state of affairs at the end of the financial year, and the PROFIT AND LOSS ACCOUNT is expected to give a true and fair view of its profit and loss. This is specified in the Companies Acts 1948 and 1967 in the case of limited companies, but it is generally thought to apply to most businesses.

Trust. The merger of interests by a number of COMPANIES in the same field, with the object of creating a joint MONOPOLY. The term is more common in the United States than in this country, and such groupings are now subject to what are known as the anti-trust laws. ⟡ MONOPOLY ⟡ CARTEL.

Trust deed. ⟡ DEBENTURES.

Trustee. A person who handles monies or property on behalf of another in a trust. He usually has the TITLE to the property but in fact acts merely as a STEWARD and all the benefits belong to persons known as the beneficiaries. Because he has the legal title he can dispose of the property to an innocent third party without the consent of the true owner; this would be known as a breach of trust. It is therefore essential that a trustee is one whose integrity is undisputed.

Trustee savings bank. Anyone can open any number of accounts, in his own name, or jointly with others. Accounts can be opened for children or by TRUSTEES, also by friendly societies, BUILDING SOCIETIES, trade unions, sports clubs, social clubs, etc. Accounts can be opened for as little as 5p. The maximum which can be held in the ordinary department is £10,000. There is a special investment department for persons holding at least £50 in the ordinary department. At most trustee savings banks a CHEQUE account service is available to persons who hold £50 or who have been depositors for more than six months. Withdrawals of up to £50 can be made on demand, but notice may be required for larger amounts. Withdrawals can be made at other branches (1) of £5 per day on demand up to £20, (2) of £30 at three days' notice, (3) by cashing trustee savings bank travel drafts. INTEREST is computed monthly at 2½ per cent, and added to the principal on 20 November; higher rates are payable in the special investment department. Tax relief is the same as for POST OFFICE SAVINGS BANKS. Cheque payments can be made by application to the savings bank; the bank will also take standing orders and items may be left for safe custody. The Trustee Savings Bank also cooperates with the National Savings Movement, and savings clubs may be opened. It also buys and sells government STOCK for customers, as does the POST OFFICE.

Trusts, notice of. On the question of SHARES, a COMPANY is not bound to take notice of trusts. The shares are registered in the names of TRUSTEES. Trustees may deal with the shares and the company need not ask whether they are dealing properly with them. The beneficiary can protect his interests by issuing a NOTICE IN LIEU OF DISTRINGAS.

Turn. ◊ JOBBER'S TURN.

Turnover. An accountancy term for gross takings or total SALES before any deductions.

Turnover, disclosure of. The Companies Act 1967 makes it necessary for a COMPANY to disclose its turnover, if it exceeds £50,000. The turnover must be subdivided between the company's various classes of business.

Two part tariff. ◊ TARIFF.

Tycoon. Slang expression for a person who has accumulated a large sum of money in industry or commerce.

U

Uberrimae fidei. 'Of the utmost good faith' (contrast with BONA FIDE). Certain CONTRACTS may be void or voidable unless the party complained of has acted in the utmost good faith, i.e. has disclosed all facts relevant to the contract whether or not he has been asked to do so. The most common are contracts of INSURANCE and PARTNERSHIP: a party to be insured must tell the insurer everything that may affect his decision in issuing a contract. Again, a partner must be quite open in his dealings and must not make SECRET PROFITS, etc.

Ullage. This word is used in two senses. Originally it meant the difference between the capacity of a cask and its actual contents; in Customs terminology it is now used for the actual contents (the difference is called the vacuity). In MARINE INSURANCE the difference is still known as 'ullage', is not usually considered a loss, and is not covered by the INSURANCE policy.

Ultimo. 'Of the previous month.' This word is common in correspondence, where it is normally abbreviated to 'ult.'

Ultra vires. 'Beyond the powers of', used mostly with reference to limited COMPANIES, which are bound by the powers set out in their MEMORANDUM OF ASSOCIATION. Any acts not consistent with this would be void, as *ultra vires*, and the public would be presumed to know that this was so.

Umpire. ⟡ ARBITRATION.

Unabsorbed cost. Where OVERHEAD EXPENSES are allocated according to a budgeted output, each unit produced has a fixed overhead charge – perhaps a percentage of its cost. When the output aimed at is not reached then not all of the overheads are charged to production. The BALANCE remaining is known as unabsorbed cost.

Unappropriated profits. That part of the profit of a business not paid out in DIVIDEND or allocated to any particular use.

Unauthorized acts by directors. ⟡ RULE IN ROYAL BRITISH BANK V. TURQUAND.

Uncalled capital. That part of the issued SHARE CAPITAL of a COMPANY not yet called-up. ⟡ CALLED-UP CAPITAL.

Uncollected goods, disposal of. Where GOODS left for repair are not collected, the repairer has certain powers either by custom or by statute. The most important statute is the Disposal of Uncollected

Goods Act 1952, which states that if the goods are not collected or paid for within a reasonable time, the ◊ BAILEE may give notice that the goods are ready for collection. If he receives no reply to his notice after twelve months, he may give another notice stating his intention to sell. If no reply is received within two weeks, he may sell the goods, but only by public AUCTION. The proceeds of the SALE must be retained and after deduction of costs, including storage, etc., the monies must be handed over to the bailor. A notice that the provisions of the Act apply must be prominently displayed on the bailee's premises.

Unconscionable bargains. The law in EQUITY affords protection to poor and ignorant persons who are taken advantage of in an unconscionable way when they have no opportunity of taking or using competent advice. For instance, a person who buys valuable land from a poor and ignorant man for a song may find that the transaction is set aside in equity. ◊ DURESS ◊ UNDUE INFLUENCE.

Undated stocks. Government STOCKS with no stated date for redemption. They may be permanent funds the government has no intention of ever redeeming, such as consolidated stock. Because they are undated, they are often the best indication of the movement of INTEREST rates, as their PRICE is influenced only by the prevailing rate of interest on risk-free investments.

Underwriter. A person (or more often a FINANCE COMPANY or ISSUING HOUSE) who agrees to underwrite an issue of shares by a COMPANY. This means that in return for a COMMISSION he (or they) agree to take up a certain proportion of the SHARES, if those shares are not subscribed by the public. The amount they agree to take up is very often related to the MINIMUM SUBSCRIPTION stated in the PROSPECTUS.

Underwriter at Lloyds A member of the Corporation of LLOYDS concerned mainly with MARINE INSURANCE, but also with car INSURANCE, etc. Members have unlimited liability and come under the heading of ◊ TARIFF OFFICES. The name originates from the fact that when a CONTRACT of insurance for a marine adventure is required, various persons would agree to take liability for a certain proportion of the total insurance required. They would write their name under the details of the contract, which were written on what was known as a slip. As an example: A wishes to insure two ships for £6,000,000, and applies to Lloyds, where B signs for £200,000, C for £50,000, etc. Losses would be apportioned accordingly.

Although theoretically SOLE TRADERS, the underwriters tend to work in syndicates.

Undisclosed factoring. A type of ◊ FACTORING used by a customer who prefers that the public, or those with whom he deals, are not aware that he is making use of such facilities. Technically, the distinction is that the factor, rather than buy the debts, buys the GOODS and appoints the seller to resell and collect payment on his behalf. The customer is the AGENT and the factor the UNDISCLOSED PRINCIPAL. The factor is responsible for bad debts; the rate he charges will vary up to about 10 per cent *per annum*.

Undisclosed principal. If an AGENT acts without indicating that he is acting as agent, third parties on discovering the true state of affairs may elect to treat the PRINCIPAL or the agent as the contracting party, i.e. they may treat the agent as principal. If the identity of the principal is sufficiently important to him, the third party may be able to avoid the CONTRACT.

Undue influence. A form of moral pressure. A CONTRACT will not be enforced by a court if it can be shown that the defendant was in a position that prevented him forming a free and unfettered judgment. Undue influence will not be presumed unless certain relations, e.g. parental or confidential, exist between the parties.

Unearned income. Income that does not arise from employment, i.e. not wages, salary, or profit.

Unenforceable contracts. These are strictly speaking not CONTRACTS at all, either because they are promises not supported by CONSIDERATION, or because the formalities of the law have not been observed. ◊ CONTRACTS IN WRITING ◊ LIMITATION OF ACTIONS ◊ CONTRACTS EVIDENCED IN WRITING.

Unfunded debt. Various short-term government loans, e.g. WAYS AND MEANS ADVANCES, TREASURY BILLS, etc. It is also known as floating debt.

Unilateral. 'One-sided'. A unilateral agreement is a promise to do something, the promise not being supported by any CONSIDERATION. A unilateral mistake is a mistake by only one party to a CONTRACT.

Unilateral contracts. Strictly speaking these are not CONTRACTS at all, but promises. If someone promises to do something provided something else is done, no other person being named or put under obligation, he is only bound if the condition is fulfilled. For instance, if someone promises to pay £12,000 to anyone who will build a new ward for a hospital, he is only bound if the ward is built.

Unit cost. ◊ STOCK VALUATION.

Unit trust. An organization for the collective purchase of SHARES, SECURITIES, etc. By spreading the investment risk over a large portfolio of investments, this risk is minimized; and by appointing experienced managers, profit, by way of DIVIDEND, INTEREST or profit on sale, may be maximized for each individual member or unit holder. A unit trust is different from an INVESTMENT company because it is a mutual organization where the amount of capital can be varied according to the number of units in circulation, and because the shares or securities are held on trust for members and not as income-earning ASSETS of a COMPANY.

Units are purchased initially in multiples of, say, 25p, an invitation being made to the public to take up units. The shares or securities are registered in the names of TRUSTEES, perhaps BANKS. There is a special management company responsible for buying and selling the shares and managing the affairs of the trust. This company makes its money from a percentage of annual income plus a percentage of the capital value of units issued. The company will normally belong to the Association of Unit Trust Managers. Every day it will state a buying and selling price for units. Units can be bought and sold by the management company itself: this again distinguishes the unit trust from the investment company as a company cannot buy its own shares. Prices of units are usually quoted in the daily papers. Some unit trusts specialize in playing for high income, others are more interested in capital APPRECIATION, others again deal only in, say, PREFERENCE SHARES, thereby hoping for a steady average high return. There are also differences in choice of industry, e.g. some trusts may specialize in certain types of manufacturer or producer, some may restrict themselves to Commonwealth countries, or some may look to the EUROPEAN ECONOMIC COMMUNITY. The relative value of each to the investor depends on his point of view. There is a new development in the unit trust movement aiming at attracting wider membership and also at competing with life ASSURANCE companies. Units are offered at prices which include life cover for the whole time that the units are held. The Finance Act 1968 has made these schemes somewhat more complicated as far as tax saving is concerned.

Unlawful. An act or CONTRACT which the law does not recognize and on which no action can be based. Most contracts involving wagering are unlawful.

Unlimited company. Less common than limited COMPANIES. All MEMBERS are liable for debts while they are members. These companies need not have SHARE CAPITAL but must have ARTICLES OF ASSOCIATION and these must state the number of original members and share capital if any. An unlimited company can purchase its own

SHARES but cannot borrow money on the SECURITY of these shares. It can reduce CAPITAL or pay share capital back to the members without having to apply to the court. It must make an annual return. No AD VALOREM stamp duty is payable on the capital. It does not have to file annual accounts. With the 1967 Companies Act and the abolition of the status of the EXEMPT PRIVATE COMPANY, these companies could become more popular as also could LIMITED PARTNERSHIPS. The Companies Act 1967, Section 43, provides a straightforward process for converting a limited company into an unlimited one. The conversion does affect the status of the company but apart from this it continues in being, i.e. there is no question of the WINDING-UP of the old company and the formation of a new, thus CONTRACTS of employment continue.

Unload. A slang term in commerce for dumping a large quantity of GOODS on the market at a low PRICE, to make a quick SALE. The supplier is prepared to accept a low profit margin – this gives him competitive advantage.

Unquoted investments. An accounting term for investments in SHARES or DEBENTURES which are not quoted or dealt with on a recognized STOCK EXCHANGE. The VALUE at which these are shown in published accounts is normally cost at time of acquisition, less any amount written off (this being stated separately). There are also legal provisions for giving some indication of the current ⋄ MARKET VALUE of these shares.

Unsecured creditors. CREDITORS of a COMPANY or other business whose debts are not secured. In a WINDING-UP or BANKRUPTCY they are paid PARI PASSU after SECURED CREDITORS. If a creditor is entitled to a rate of INTEREST tied to the profits of a company then he is not repaid until other unsecured creditors have been.

Unsecured debentures. DEBENTURES not secured on any property of the COMPANY. ⋄ UNSECURED LOAN STOCK.

Unsecured loan stock. An accounting term for loan CAPITAL raised without SECURITY, e.g. UNSECURED DEBENTURES.

Upset price. An auctioneering term for the lowest PRICE at which the VENDOR would allow bidding to begin, or the object to be sold. ⋄ RESERVE PRICE.

Usance. ⋄ BILLS OF EXCHANGE may be drawn as usance – these will be bills between two foreign countries with separate currencies. They are short-term bills and 'usance' means the time allowed by custom for payment. For instance usance for bills drawn in New York upon Europe is sixty days.

Usufruct. The right to use the property of another person without

either the rights attaching to ownership or the right to diminish its
VALUE.

Usury. Lending money in return for payment of INTEREST. At one
time this was considered a rather nefarious occupation and was much
frowned upon by the Church: interest was considered something
received for nothing. The occupation was pushed into the shadows
and consequently abused for, being outside the law, the lender
would charge unfair rates of interest and treat the debtor rather
unkindly. For this reason the term 'usury', now that the lending of
money is acceptable, is reserved as a term of abuse and used mainly
in adjectival form, e.g. usurious rates of interest.

V

Vacuity. ◊ ULLAGE.

Value. The PRICE which an item would fetch in an open MARKET. Distinction should be made between value in present use and value in alternative use. For instance, a factory building may be worth £500 to a person wishing to use it as a factory but £50,000 to a person wishing to redevelop the land. Value is also determined by various other factors ranging from sentiment to long-term speculation; so it is in fact a rather imprecise term. ◊ MARKET VALUE ◊ VALUE IN USE.

Value added. A term for the increment added by each person or organization involved in the manufacture of a particular item, becoming part of its price. As an example, A provides raw materials at 25p, B works on the materials and passes them on to C at 37½p, so B has added 12½p to the value.

There have been various suggestions for a tax on value added as an alternative to a sales tax.

Value in use. The VALUE of an item to the person using it. This may be quite different from the sale PRICE. A piece of equipment or machine might have no saleable value, due to the difficulty of dismantling it, perhaps. However, to the person using it, it may have considerable value as it produces GOODS for sale.

Valued policy. A MARINE INSURANCE term for a policy which contains a stated sum insured. ◊ OPEN POLICY.

Variable costs. An accounting term for costs that vary according to the level of output. ◊ FIXED COSTS ◊ SEMI-VARIABLE COSTS.

Variation of written contracts. ◊ ORAL EVIDENCE ◊ RECTIFICATION OF CONTRACT.

Vendor. A person selling GOODS.

Vendue. Another name for a public ◊ AUCTION.

Verba chartarum fortius accipiuntur contra proferentem. A legal maxim which points out that where any doubt arises as to the precise meaning of a written CONTRACT it will be construed more strongly against the person who drew up the contract. This can be quite important where ◊ EXEMPTION CLAUSES are concerned.

Vertical integration. The linking up of a number of business concerns each operating at a different stage in the same industry. This is opposed to horizontal integration, being the linking up of a number of firms at the same stage.

Vested interest. Interest now in being, as opposed to interest anticipated. It is a term frequently used in law with regard to the TITLE to GOODS or land. Property is said to vest when the absolute owner is finally established, and his interest is in no way capable of being terminated by anyone but himself.

Viability. The ability to support oneself, or the ability of a country to support itself.

Vicarious performance. Generally speaking, when one person CONTRACTS with another, he anticipates that that other will perform the contract. Where the contract relies on the particular skill of the other person, that person cannot delegate the work: an artist if asked to paint a picture must paint it personally and paint the whole of it personally. In certain types of contract however, delegation of all or part of the work must be anticipated, particularly in building contracts where a great part of the work is sub-contracted. Sub-contracting should be distinguished from assignment of contract. The liability for BREACH OF CONTRACT still remains with the original contracting party. ◊ DELEGATUS NON POTEST DELEGARE.

Victualling bill. A list of all bonded or DRAWBACK goods that a ship takes on for use during the voyage. It must be presented to the Customs authorities for clearance.

Vigilantibus non dormientibus jura subveniunt. Equitable maxim stating that if anyone has, or thinks he has, a claim, he should proceed with it without delay. Delay can result in a loss of certain remedies. ◊ LACHES.

Vintner. A wine-dealer.

Visible imports and exports. GOODS actually shipped or otherwise sold, as opposed to invisible exports or imports which are services earning or costing foreign exchange, e.g. shipping, INSURANCE, etc. The United Kingdom has thrived for many years on invisible earnings and very rarely has a favourable balance on visible trade.

Volunteer. In law, this is a person who performs some act without any obligation to do so. Generally speaking, if he suffers loss through this he can obtain no redress. Claims cannot be followed even in EQUITY: 'Equity does not assist a volunteer.'

Voting rights. These must be stated in the PROSPECTUS of a company. The rights of various shareholders to vote will also be contained in the ARTICLES OF ASSOCIATION. ◊ MEETINGS ◊ PROXIES ◊ SHOW OF HANDS.

Voucher. In accounting, this is a document supporting entries in a JOURNAL or LEDGER.

Voyage charter. A charter agreement which applies to a particular voyage. The charter may be of the ship or of space in it, but ceases on completion of the voyage. There are various obligations imposed on both ship-owner and charterer. The owner must bring the ship to the agreed port at the agreed time and must deliver the GOODS at the specified port at the specified time. The ship-owner WARRANTS that the ship will be sea-worthy at the commencement of the voyage though not necessarily during the continuation of the voyage. Where the ship calls at a number of ports, it must be sea-worthy on leaving each port. The ship must also be properly equipped and must be ready to proceed with due dispatch. It must not deviate from its course (for exceptions ⟡ MARINE INSURANCE). The charterer must load or unload within the specified ⟡ LAY DAYS. The ship-owner does not usually accept liability for losses such as arrest and restraint of princes, rulers and people, fire, BARRATRY, gales, STRANDING, other damages of navigation (i.e. those most applicable to voyage by sea), or acts of God or the queen's enemies. The liability of the ship-owner is, apart from this, that of a COMMON CARRIER.

Voyage policy. A ⟡ MARINE INSURANCE term for a policy insuring cargo and ship on a particular voyage.

W

Wagering contract. A CONTRACT between two parties whereby either may win or lose a sum of money, or other valuable ASSET, dependent on the outcome of some investigation or on the happening of some future event in which neither has any personal interest except in so far as he stands to win or lose. Each party is pitting his own skill or luck against the other. Wagering contracts should be distinguished from contracts of INSURANCE for the insured must always have an INSURABLE INTEREST. All wagers were made void by the Gaming Act 1845 – this covers wagering contracts and GAMING CONTRACTS. It makes it, impossible to regain money paid or SECURITIES given. Wagering contracts are void but not illegal; a fresh promise to pay for a fresh CONSIDERATION is also caught by the statute. If a person who has lost money in a wager attempts to recover it, he cannot succeed even though by law he has no necessity to pay it. Where money is lent by one person to another to enable that other to enter into a wagering contract, he may or may not be able to recover the loan. If the loan was to enable the debtor to pay, e.g. betting debts, he may be able to recover. He will not recover if he pays the debt himself. Money lent for gaming is never recoverable unless the gaming was to take place in a country where it is lawful.

Wagering policy. A MARINE INSURANCE policy where the insurer has no acceptable INSURABLE INTEREST. These CONTRACTS are GAMBLING contracts and are illegal. ◊ POLICY PROOF OF INTEREST.

Waiters. Attendants at the STOCK EXCHANGE who take messages, run errands, and generally take care of the details of the day to day running of the Exchange. The word is a relic of the days when dealings took place in coffee houses, and the waiters took messages.

Waiting time. In business parlance, time which an employee spends idle, though not through his own fault, e.g. time spent waiting for a machine to be repaired or set up ready for use. It is obviously worthwhile to minimize this time.

In some services, for example TAXI driving, a charge may be made for waiting time.

Waiver. Where one person waives his rights in a CONTRACT, this is known as a waiver. Though an alteration of an existing contract, it is in effect a new agreement and requires CONSIDERATION. ◊ DISCHARGE OF CONTRACT.

Waiver clause. The clause in MARINE INSURANCE policies allowing either party to take steps to minimize a loss without thereby prejudicing rights.

Wall Street. The location of the New York STOCK EXCHANGE.

Warehouse. Generally speaking, a place where GOODS are stored prior to their being sold or used. The word is more restricted in shipping terminology, where it means a public warehouse where goods are stored on being landed from a ship. These warehouses are often responsible for sorting, examining, and delivering goods as well as storing them. The goods may be for home consumption or re-export. Some warehouses are bonded warehouses, where duty need not be paid on the goods until they are actually removed from the warehouse. ◊ BONDED GOODS.

Goods are released on production of a warehouse keeper's order issued by the Customs.

Warehouse keeper. A person in charge of a WAREHOUSE. If it is a bonded warehouse, he will need to give SECURITY for the duty that may become due on the GOODS in his charge.

Warehouse keeper's order. ◊ WAREHOUSE.

Warehouse officer. Bonded WAREHOUSES are controlled by a warehouse officer employed by the Customs and Excise in addition to a WAREHOUSE KEEPER. He inspects many of the GOODS on receipt and on delivery – delivery is only allowed when proper documents (e.g. the ◊ WAREHOUSE KEEPER'S ORDER) are produced. The documents must have been passed at the collector's office.

Warrant. A receipt for GOODS deposited in a public WAREHOUSE. The receipt identifies the goods and may be transferred by ENDORSEMENT.

Warranty. A statement of fact in a CONTRACT, either express or implied. If it is unfulfilled the injured party cannot repudiate the contract but may be able to claim damages. The difference between a warranty and a CONDITION is that a condition is fundamental to a contract, whereas a warranty is not.

Warranty, floating. A WARRANTY which may be enforceable by a third party, i.e. by a person not a party to the CONTRACT when the warranty is given. If A asks B to contract with C, C may have an enforceable warranty against A. For instance, if A asks B to paint his house and obtain the paint from C (A having obtained C's advice as to suitability), if B buys the paint from C and it proves faulty, A may be able to sue C even though he was not party to the contract. For C has in fact warranted the paint to A. The principle is important in HIRE PURCHASE contracts when the VENDOR sells through a hire purchase company. The buyer buys from the company but may enforce warranties against the vendor.

Warranty of attorney. A type of POWER OF ATTORNEY given to a SOLICITOR, whereby the solicitor attends court and pleads on behalf of an accused person.

Warranty of authority. ◊ BREACH OF WARRANTY OF AUTHORITY.

Wasting assets. An accounting term for ASSETS which are used up gradually in producing goods. It is sometimes applied to FIXED ASSETS generally, but is perhaps better applied to assets which are exhausted after a certain period of time, such as quarries, mines, etc.

Watering stock. An accounting term for the issue of additional SHARES without any prospect of maintaining the old DIVIDEND on this new CAPITAL.

Ways and means advances. A short-term loan made to the government by the BANK OF ENGLAND, to supplement money raised on TREASURY BILLS.

Weather working days. Working days, particularly at a port, when the weather allows work to be done.

Wharfage. ◊ WHARFINGER RECEIPT.

Wharfinger receipt. A receipt given by a wharfinger for GOODS put into his charge before being shipped. Wharfage charges are payable when goods are put on a wharf either before or after being shipped (the wharf being the place where the ship ties up for loading or unloading). When goods are received off a ship for collection, the wharfinger will issue a WARRANT giving details of the goods and to whom they are to be delivered.

Wharfinger warrant. ◊ WHARFINGER RECEIPT.

Wholesaler. The middle man between manufacturer and RETAILER. He is able to buy in large quantities and then break these into smaller parcels for the benefit of the retailers. The wholesaler takes a profit either by adding to the manufacturer's price or by charging a COMMISSION to the retailer. Where SELLING PRICES are fixed by the manufacturer, the manufacturer in effect gives a share of his profit by way of discount to the wholesaler who passes on a share to the retailer. This is often referred to as a ◊ TRADE DISCOUNT. The wholesaler's justification is that without him it would be necessary for the manufacturer himself to set up depots in various parts of the country to facilitate distribution and keep careful track of local demand.

Whole-time service directors. ◊ CLOSE COMPANY.

Windfall profit. A profit not anticipated. One might arise perhaps from changes in legislation. An increase in tax, or duty, might result in the manufacturers' making additional profit on stock whereon the lower rate of duty has already been paid. Windfall profits being exceptional, they are normally shown separately in COMPANY accounts.

Winding-up. ⟡ LIQUIDATION.

Winding-up, commencement of. In voluntary LIQUIDATION the winding-up dates from the resolution. In a compulsory liquidation it dates from the presentation of the petition. For the purpose of preferential payments, it dates from the appointment of a provisional LIQUIDATOR.

Winding-up, compulsory: petition. A petition may be presented by a CONTRIBUTORY and/or a CREDITOR; it may also be presented by the COMPANY by SPECIAL RESOLUTION; the BOARD OF TRADE may petition as a result of an investigation; or the OFFICIAL RECEIVER may petition when a VOLUNTARY WINDING-UP is in process. A contributory must have held his SHARES for at least six months during the preceding eighteen months (this could include a person on the B list). The court will probably call meetings to discover the wishes of creditors and other contributories.

In the case of a creditor's petition, the court must make an order for winding-up, if the creditor has an undisputed debt and the company is INSOLVENT. The court may order the petition to stand over for a while – generally where the debt is disputed. The court may also consult the wishes of the other creditors before making an order.

The ASSIGNEE of a debt can petition, as can creditors, for CONTINGENT LIABILITIES, though they will have to show that there are good grounds for winding-up. In any event the debt must be a liquidated debt. DEBENTURE holders cannot normally petition, where there is a trust deed, neither may they petition where there is power to appoint a RECEIVER and they have not done so.

Winding-up, compulsory: procedure. Winding-up begins with a petition to a court, supported by an AFFIDAVIT. The proper court is the County Court if the CAPITAL of the COMPANY is not more than £10,000; the High Court if it is. The court may dismiss the petition, order it to stand over, make an order for winding-up with or without court supervision, or make any other order it thinks fit. If a compulsory winding-up order is made the court appoints a LIQUIDATOR. Winding-up commences either with the presentation of the petition, or, where the company was previously winding up voluntarily, from the date of the resolution to wind up. From the point of view of preferential debts, it dates from either the resolution to wind up voluntarily, or the date of the order, or the date a PROVISIONAL LIQUIDATOR was appointed.

Winding-up: conduct of. (1) The COMPANY ceases to carry on business except for purposes of winding-up. All the company's stationery must indicate that the company is being wound up.

(2) The LIQUIDATOR makes out a list of CONTRIBUTORIES and makes calls if necessary. The sanction of the court is needed in a COMPULSORY WINDING-UP. A shareholder cannot set off calls due against debts owing to the company.

(3) The order of payment of debts is similar to bankruptcy (◊ BANK-RUPTCY: PAYMENT OF DEBTS).

(4) A CREDITOR wishing to be paid must prove for his debt within a time to be fixed by the liquidator. If he does not prove in time it may still be paid if there are ASSETS remaining. The cost of proof may be added to the debt. Debts provable include 'debts payable on a contingency and all claims against the company, present or future, certain or contingent, ascertained or sound only in damages' (Companies Act 1948, Section 316). The liquidator should not pay STATUTE-BARRED DEBTS.

(5) The liquidator may disclaim leasehold property. If he occupies it, he must pay the RENT in full during the time of occupation. There may be a provision in the lease allowing for forfeiture on LIQUIDA-TION, but the liquidator may apply to the court. If the liquidator disclaims, he also needs court permission and the landlord may sue for any damage suffered.

(6) ◊ INTEREST ceases at the commencement of liquidation.

(7) Certain dispositions of the property of the company may be avoided by the liquidator, e.g. an ASSIGNMENT to a TRUSTEE of all property for the benefit of creditors will be void, and floating charges made within twelve months of the winding-up by insolvent companies are void though this does not apply to cash paid with interest at 4 per cent. The charge is void, not the loan.

(8) All servants of the company are automatically dismissed.

(9) Proceedings may if necessary be taken against DIRECTORS and OFFICERS OF THE COMPANY on the grounds of ◊ FRAUDULENT TRADING, etc. (◊ PUBLIC EXAMINATION: WINDING-UP ◊ MIS-FEASANCE SUMMONS).

(10) Proceedings against the company may be stayed (◊ CESSOR OF ACTION).

(11) The company is dissolved by (a) in a compulsory winding-up an application to the court by the liquidator. The court makes an order dissolving the company. The order goes to the Registrar of Com-

panies. (b) In a voluntary winding-up, by the liquidator's sending a return to the Registrar within a week of the final meeting. The company is then automatically dissolved three months afterwards. (c) In a reconstruction, by order of the court. (d) By striking off the Register. ⟡ REGISTER OF COMPANIES. Dissolution can be avoided within two years by application to the court.

⟡ LIQUIDATOR ⟡ LIQUIDATION: ADMISSION AND REJECTION OF PROOFS ⟡ LIQUIDATION: COMMITTEE OF INSPECTION.

Winding-up: public examination. In a compulsory WINDING-UP the LIQUIDATOR has power to call DIRECTORS or OFFICERS OF THE COMPANY to be publicly examined in court, on oath. This also applies to PROMOTERS. This power is only used where there is evidence of FRAUD.

Winding-up: supervision by a court. After a resolution to wind up voluntarily has been passed, a CREDITOR (or any other interested person) may petition a court that the winding-up should proceed with the supervision of the court. The winding-up is conducted as a normal VOLUNTARY WINDING-UP, except for any restrictions the court may order. There are many advantages in court supervision: one is that proceedings cannot be commenced or continued against the COMPANY without the leave of the court.

Winding-up, voluntary. A COMPANY may wind up voluntarily in the following ways: (1) by ORDINARY RESOLUTION (unless the ARTICLES OF ASSOCIATION specify otherwise) when the company has achieved what it intended, or has reached the end of its life through age, (2) by SPECIAL RESOLUTION – for any reason, (3) by EXTRAORDINARY RESOLUTION, when by reason of its liabilities it cannot continue in business and ought to be wound up. Voluntary winding-up commences on the date of the resolution. The resolution must be published in the LONDON GAZETTE. The results of the winding-up are: (1) that a company ceases to carry on business except for the purpose of winding-up, (2) that transfer of SHARES and alteration in the status of MEMBERS are prohibited. The LIQUIDATOR may allow a transfer of shares.

There are two kinds of voluntary winding-up – members' voluntary winding-up, and CREDITORS' voluntary winding-up. In members' voluntary winding-up, much will depend on whether the DIRECTORS have been able to make a successful declaration of SOLVENCY. This is a statutory declaration that the company will be able to pay its debts in full within twelve months. It must be made within five weeks before the resolution and must contain a statement of ASSETS and liabilities. A liquidator is appointed by the company. If he is not satisfied that the declaration was properly made, he must call meetings of creditors and the winding-up will then in effect become a creditors' voluntary winding-up. Where he is happy with the statement he takes over completely: the powers of the directors cease except where he states otherwise. He must call annual meetings of members and account to them, and also a final meeting where FINAL ACCOUNTS are presented. He then notifies the Registrar of Companies, sending him a copy of the accounts, and after three months the company is dissolved. (The final meeting has to be advertised in the *London Gazette*.) Where the voluntary winding-up is a creditors' voluntary winding-up, where no declaration of solvency is made, the company must call the meeting of creditors on the same day as, or on the day after, the resolution. The meeting must be gazetted and the creditors given a statement of affairs and a list of creditors. The creditors may appoint a liquidator as well as the members, but the creditors' appointment will take preference. The creditors may also appoint a COMMITTEE OF INSPECTION. The company can appoint members to the committee with the creditors' approval. Everything is then as in a members' voluntary winding-up except that final meetings of creditors must be held as well as final meetings of members. Additional matters applicable to both methods are (a) that the liquidator must pay the debts of the company and settle rights of CONTRIBUTORIES, (2) that he may carry on business for the purpose of winding-up but does not become personally liable, (3) that after payment of costs of liquidation, monies are applied first in payment of creditors (◊ PREFERENTIAL CREDITORS) and anything remaining is distributed to members, (4) that the liquidator settles the list of contributories – this list is *prima facie* evidence of liability, (5) that dissolution can be deferred where this is thought necessary, (6) that during the course of a voluntary winding-up, a creditor may petition for a COMPULSORY WINDING-UP; a contributory may also petition but the court will not grant it unless there are serious grounds for believing that the winding-up is being carried on fraudulently.

Window dressing. Strictly, showing GOODS in a shop window to maximum advantage, so that the public will be attracted either to buy the goods or at least to enter the shop.

The word is also used in COMPANY finance for the lawful manipulation of accounts to make the BALANCE SHEET show a company or business in the most favourable light, and so attract investments or increase the SHARES' MARKET VALUE.

Window shopping. Parading up and down a shopping street, to envy rather than purchase.

Without recourse. These words added to a BILL OF EXCHANGE indicate that the holder has no recourse to the person from whom he took the bill, should it not be paid. It is often written as 'sans recours'. It often appears after an ENDORSEMENT.

Woodlands, taxation of. Since the abolition of land tax as such, the occupation of woodlands does not give rise to a liability for tax unless they are managed on a commercial basis and with a view to profit.

Wool auctions. Auctions organized by a committee of London wool brokers. There are eight series of sales in one season: each series normally lasts a fortnight. Bidders come from many parts of the world, and there are no particular regulations. Where the AUCTIONEER does not know the buyer, a 25 per cent deposit may be necessary. Settlements are made a fortnight on the Friday of the week of the sale. Settling day is known as prompt day. The AUCTIONS are held at the London Fruit and Wool Exchange, Brushfield Street, London E1. Wool FUTURES are not dealt with at this market but at Plantation House.

Work and materials, contracts for. ♢ GOODS.

Work in progress. A term usually found attached to ♢ STOCKS in a BALANCE SHEET: i.e. 'stocks and work in progress'. It represents the VALUE of work commenced but not completed. In a manufacturing business this will be in partly finished GOODS. In a contracting business it will be in the form of uncompleted CONTRACTS. Difficulties arise in valuation, one problem, particularly on a long term contract, being whether to include part of the anticipated profit and how to deal with cash paid in advance. The traditional method is to take profit into account in the same proportion as the amount paid is to the work certified. This applies to contractors' accounts and profit is normally reduced by any anticipated losses. The valuation is important: often a large proportion of total assets is represented by 'stocks and work in progress'.

Work study. A study concerned with improving working methods and deciding how long particular jobs should take. Its aim is to reduce effort involved in various operations, to organize labour in the most economical manner and to provide data for planning, estimating, and financial incentive-schemes.

Working capital. A vague term for that part of the CAPITAL of the COMPANY which is continually circulating. The figure is calculated by deducting CURRENT LIABILITIES from CURRENT ASSETS. As a general rule, if this figure is negative the company is not in a very happy position as it has insufficient money or LIQUID ASSETS available to pay its current liabilities.

Working days. Days when work is normally done (particularly at a port).

Working director. Working DIRECTORS may be full-time or part-time. The distinction was important mainly for tax purposes. ◊ CLOSE COMPANY.

Workmen's wages in winding-up. ◊ LIQUIDATION: PREFERENTIAL DEBTS.

World bank. ◊ INTERNATIONAL BANK FOR RECONSTRUCTION AND DEVELOPMENT.

Writ. A legal document summoning a person to attend at a certain place or to perform a certain act. There are penalties for failure to comply.

Writer to the signet. A person acting in the Supreme Court of Scotland as a SOLICITOR does in England.

Written down value. An accounting term for the cost or valuation of an ASSET, less the written-off DEPRECIATION. It is no indication of the present selling price of that asset.

Y

Year's purchase. A term used in calculating the VALUE of a business or of land where the PRICE is related to the estimated average annual profits or RENT. The price is then stated to be X years' purchase of the profit or rent.

Yield. The return earned on an investment, taking into account the annual income and its present CAPITAL value. It also has other, more particular, meanings – perhaps as many as there are financial editors. ◊ EARNINGS YIELD ◊ DIVIDEND YIELD ◊ REDEMPTION YIELD.

York–Antwerp rules. Optional rules drawn up in 1877 to help those engaged in the carriage of GOODS by sea, with GENERAL AVERAGE CLAUSES in BILLS OF LADING, MARINE CHARTERING, and INSURANCE policies.